KENT HISTORY PROJECT

2

RELIGION AND SOCIETY IN KENT, 1640–1914

KENT HISTORY PROJECT

ISSN 1352–805X

Already published

Traffic and Politics: The Construction and Management of Rochester Bridge, AD 43–1993, ed. Nigel Yates and James M. Gibson

Volumes scheduled for publication in 1995

Faith and Fabric: Rochester Cathedral 604–1994, ed. Nigel Yates and Paul A. Welsby
The Economy of Kent 1640–1914, ed. Alan Armstrong

Volumes in progress

Kent to AD 800, ed. Alec P. Detsicas

Kent 800–1220, ed. Richard Eales

Kent 1220–1540, ed. Nigel Ramsay

Kent 1540–1640, ed. Michael Zell

The Government of Kent 1640–1914, ed. H. C. F. Lansberry

Kent since 1914, ed. Alan Armstrong and Nigel Yates

RELIGION AND SOCIETY IN KENT, 1640–1914

NIGEL YATES
ROBERT HUME
PAUL HASTINGS

THE BOYDELL PRESS

KENT COUNTY COUNCIL

First published 1994
The Boydell Press, Woodbridge, and
Kent County Council

ISBN 0 85115 556 1

The Boydell Press is an imprint of Boydell & Brewer Ltd
PO Box 9, Woodbridge, Suffolk IP12 3DF, UK
and of Boydell & Brewer Inc.
PO Box 41026, Rochester, NY 14604-4126, USA

British Library Cataloguing-in-Publication Data
Yates, Nigel
Religion and Society in Kent, 1640–1914. –
(Kent History Project, ISSN 1352–805X; Vol.2)
I. Title   II. Series
942.23
ISBN 0–85115–556–1

Library of Congress Cataloging-in-Publication Data
Yates, Nigel.
Religion and society in Kent, 1640–1914 / Nigel Yates, Robert
Hume, Paul Hastings.
      p.   cm. – (Kent history project, ISSN 1352–805X ; 2)
Includes bibliographical references and index.
ISBN 0–85115–556–1 (hardbk. : alk. paper)
1. Kent (England) – Church history.   2. Kent (England) – Social
conditions.   3. Church and state – England – Kent – History.   I. Hume,
Robert, 1955–   .   II. Hastings, Paul, 1933–   .   III. Title.   IV. Series.
BR763.K46Y38   1994
942.2'3–dc20   94–14000

This publication is printed on acid-free paper

Printed in Great Britain by
St Edmundsbury Press Ltd, Bury St Edmunds, Suffolk

Contents

Acknowledgements   vii
Notes on Contributors   viii
List of Tables   x
List of Figures   xi
List of Plates   xii

NIGEL YATES
Introduction   1
Papists and Puritans 1640–1714   3
The Anglican Establishment and its Critics 1714–1830   22
An Age of Religious Pluralism 1830–1914   53

ROBERT HUME
Education in Kent 1640–1914   91

PAUL HASTINGS
The Old Poor Law 1640–1834   112
The New Poor Law 1834–1914   154
Epidemics and Public Health 1640–1914   189

Guide to Further Reading   225
Index   227

Acknowledgements

Kent County Council acknowledges with gratitude all those who have permitted the reproduction of or reference to the following copyright material:

The University of Kent at Canterbury in respect of references to unpublished diploma and undergraduate extended essays;

Maidstone Museum and Art Gallery (Fig. 3);

The editors and publishers of the *Economic History Review* (Figs 4–7);

The Guildhall Museum, Rochester (Plates 16a and b).

All other material reproduced as illustrations in this volume is taken from the originals in the ownership of or deposited on permanent loan with Kent County Council.

Notes on Contributors

Nigel Yates was born in 1944. He read history at the University of Hull, from which he also holds a masters degree for a thesis on 'The Dean and Chapter of Hereford, 1240–1320' and a doctorate in recognition of his published work in modern religious history. He has taught at the Universities of Hull, Exeter and Southampton, and is currently Visiting Senior Research Fellow in Economic and Social History at the University of Kent. He was City Archivist of Portsmouth 1975–80 and County Archivist of Kent 1980–90. Since 1989 he has been the General Editor of the Kent History Project and is a consultant on historical and other matters to Kent County Council, the Museum of Kent Life, the Dioceses of Canterbury and Rochester and several other national and local bodies. He has published more than forty books and articles mostly, though not exclusively, on various aspects of religious history, including *The Oxford Movement and Anglican Ritualism* (Historical Association, London 1983) and *Buildings, Faith and Worship: The Liturgical Arrangement of Anglican Churches 1600–1900* (Clarendon Press, Oxford 1991).

Robert Hume was born in 1955. He read History and Psychology at the University of Keele before undertaking two separate research studies into the history of education in Kent and Shropshire. An experienced teacher, public examiner and moderator, he began his teaching career in the county in 1982, when he joined the staff of the Geoffrey Chaucer School in Canterbury. In 1985 he moved to Tonbridge to become Head of History at Hillview School for Girls. Since 1988 he has been Head of the History Department at Clarendon House Grammar School for Girls in Ramsgate where he was recently voted Radio Invicta FM/Woolworths '1992 Teacher of the Year'. Dr Hume has lectured before audiences of teachers in Kent (where he was Secretary of the Kent History Teachers' Association between 1984 and 1989), northern Italy and the USA. In December 1992, as part of the 500th anniversary commemorations, he was invited to give lectures on Christopher Columbus on board the QE2. In addition to a number of articles in history journals, Dr Hume has written *Early Child Immigrants to Virginia, 1618–1642* (Magna Carta, Baltimore 1986) and a GCSE textbook *Education Since 1700* (Heinemann 1989). His latest book is *Christopher Columbus and the European Discovery of America* (Gracewing 1992).

Paul Hastings was born in 1933. He read history at the University of Birmingham where he also secured his master's degree. A specialist in English local and regional social and political history he has lived and worked in Warwickshire,

Herefordshire, North Yorkshire, Cleveland, Durham and Kent. He was awarded his doctorate by the University of York for research into 'Poverty and the Treatment of Poverty in the North Riding of Yorkshire c.1780–1847'. He has been sometime schoolmaster, head teacher and Principal Lecturer in History at a college of education. From 1980–93 he was inspector for history for Kent Local Education Authority. He combined this post with that of Senior Inspector (Secondary Education) 1983–8. He has written 35 books and articles and three programmes for BBC television. Since 1960 he has also worked at intervals as a part-time lecturer in local history for the extra-mural departments of the Universities of Birmingham, Durham, Leeds and Kent and for the WEA. He is currently an independent educational consultant.

Tables

1. Anglican communicants, Protestant dissenters and Roman Catholics in Kent towns 1676. — 16
2. Patronage of Kent benefices 1790. — 23
3. Incidence of pluralism in Canterbury archdeaconry 1806. — 25
4. Sunday services in the churches of Canterbury archdeaconry 1716 and 1786. — 26
5. Weekday services in the churches of Canterbury archdeaconry 1716 and 1786. — 27
6. Holy Communion in the churches of Canterbury archdeaconry 1716 and 1786. — 27
7. Condition of fabric and fittings in the churches of Rochester archdeaconry 1732–4. — 33
8. Charitable bequests to Kent parishes 1786–8. — 36
9. Surviving churches and chapels built or rebuilt in Kent 1714–1830. — 44
10. ICBS grants towards church building and extension in Kent 1818–1927. — 49
11. Summary of religious census for the county of Kent 1851. — 61
12. Percentage share of denominational attendances in non-metropolitan Kent 1851. — 62
13. Attendances at Sunday services in Cranbrook 1851. — 63
14. Religious allegiances in Maidstone 1851 and 1880. — 66
15. Communion services and communicant numbers in selected Kent churches 1865–1905. — 73
16. Weekly early communion and daily services in Anglican churches in the main Kent towns 1882–1913. — 74
17. Places of worship built or rebuilt in Kent 1830–1901. — 77

Figures

1. Provision of schooling in Kent by parish 1662.   94
2. Provision of schooling in Kent by parish 1807.   96
3. Handbill advertising a sermon to raise funds for charity schools at Maidstone 1826.   100
4. Total spent on poor relief in three southern counties 1790–1834.   122
5. *Per capita* poor relief expenditure in three southern counties 1790–1834.   123
6. Real *per capita* poor relief expenditure in three southern counties 1790–1834.   124
7. Real *per capita* poor relief expenditure in agricultural parishes only 1790–1834.   125
8. Kent Workhouses by 1776.   138
9. Kent Gilbert Unions and Workhouses built under Local Act.   140
10. Rules and regulations for the poor house in St Margaret's parish, Rochester, c.1820.   142
11. Kent Poor Law Unions created after the 1834 Act.   156
12. General dietary of Hollingbourne Union Workhouse 1835.   170
13. Regulations relating to the visiting of inmates at Blean Union Workhouse 1914.   175
14. Regulations relating to the hours and places of work, and the hours of rising and going to bed, at Blean Union Workhouse 1914.   177

Plates

Plates appear between pages 52 and 53, 84 and 85, 116 and 117, 148 and 149

1. (a) Interior of Chiddingstone church 1792.
   (b) Interior of Brenchley church in the late nineteenth century showing the altar rails ordered to be installed by Archdeacon Warner in 1670.
2. (a) Francis Atterbury, bishop of Rochester 1713–23.
   (b) George Horne, dean of Canterbury 1781–90.
   (c) Samuel Horsley, bishop of Rochester 1793–1802.
   (d) Charles Manners-Sutton, archbishop of Canterbury 1805–28.
3. (a) Interior of St Clement's, Sandwich, showing the three-decker pulpit at the west end of the nave, c.1860.
   (b) 'Spy' cartoon from *Vanity Fair* of Benjamin Harrison, archdeacon of Maidstone 1845–87.
   (c) Enthronement of John Bird Sumner as archbishop of Canterbury 1848.
4. Plan and elevation of Hildenborough church 1843.
5. (a) Seating plan of Sellindge church 1847.
   (b) Seating plan of Snargate church 1870.
6. Seating plans of St Nicholas', Rochester (a) before and (b) after the restoration in 1861.
7. (a) Plan and (b) elevation of the galleries at St Nicholas', Rochester 1861.
8. (a) Dean Stanhope school, Deptford, showing the effigies of a boy and girl wearing charity clothes, 1871.
   (b) Advertisement in the *Post Office Directory* for Kent of a school for young ladies at Deal 1867.
9. Advertisement in the *Post Office Directory* for Kent of a school for young ladies at Margate 1867.
10. Plan of St John's National School, Sevenoaks, 1870.
11. Elevation of St John's National School, Sevenoaks, 1870.
12. Clarendon House Grammar School for Girls, Ramsgate, built in 1909.
13. (a) Pupils at Rolvenden National School c.1900.
    (b) Presentation of attendance certificates at Great Mongeham School c.1912.
14. Applications for poor relief at Sellindge 1822.
15. (a) The Kent and Canterbury Hospital 1810.
    (b) Proposed Union Workhouse at Canterbury 1846.
16. Slum property in Rochester demolished in c.1900: (a) cottages in Corporation Street and (b) houses in Ironmonger Lane.

Introduction

This is one of three planned volumes covering the major aspects of the history of Kent between 1640 and 1914. The other volumes are devoted to the economy and the government of the county in this period. This volume brings together three topics – religion, education and social welfare – that have always had some overlap and in which the links were particularly strong before the second half of the nineteenth century, when they were to some extent separated by the growing secularisation of both government and society.

The unifying factor of the themes explored in this volume is the parish, which until 1894, was, within identical boundaries, a unit of both civil and ecclesiastical government. The parish minister had some responsibilities, notably the conduct of the services, over which he had total control subject only to the authority of the bishop, archdeacon and ecclesiastical courts. For all other matters the sovereign body was the parish vestry, a meeting of all the parishioners who were ratepayers, which met at least once a year to appoint its officers and to levy a rate. Frequently vestries met more often than this, or they appointed select vestries – in effect a standing committee – to undertake the detailed business. Select vestries were frequently appointed to administer the poor law. The vestry elected churchwardens, overseers of the poor and surveyors of the highway. They might appoint other officials for both civil or ecclesiastical purposes, such as constables, organists, parish clerks or sextons. From time to time, on contentious matters, it might be necessary for the vestry or its officers to organise a poll of all the ratepayers. The vestry and its officers cared for the fabric of the church, apart from the chancel which was the rector's responsibility, for the maintenance of the poor, the upkeep of the roads, and were likely to take an interest in other matters such as the schooling of children and the prosecution of criminals.

This unity of church and state at a local level was maintained until well into the nineteenth century. It was strengthened by the large number of clergymen acting as justices of the peace, though this situation changed in the nineteenth century with the alteration in clerical attitudes that turned what had been a profession into a vocation. The role of the parish, and by definition therefore of the church, in social welfare was significantly reduced when responsibility for administering the poor law was transferred to the new Boards of Guardians set up by the Poor Law Amendment Act of 1834. The Education Act of 1870 still provided a role for the church and parish in the management of schools but it was significantly reduced. Yet throughout the eighteenth and early nineteenth centuries the parishes and individual churchmen had been at the forefront of educational provision whether it was through tutorial arrangements financed by the church rate, the establishment of charity schools, or the work of the National Society for Education founded in 1811.

Nonconformity, although technically outside the parochial system, was nevertheless constrained by it and, in a sense, almost a part of it, reacting to the payment of church rates or the restrictions on marriage and burial. Nonconformists made their own significant contributions to education and social welfare and these too were challenged by the growing secularisation of Victorian society and the legislation that transferred important undertakings from the voluntary to the public sector.

The final separation between the civil and ecclesiastical functions of parishes came with the legislation of 1894 which created separate civil parish councils in any village with more than 300 inhabitants. Civil parishes frequently had different boundaries from ecclesiastical parishes. Nevertheless there were a number of new parish councils of which the parish clergyman was an elected member, and sometimes the chairman. The parish vestries, described by the President of the Local Government Board, who introduced the legislation, as 'decrepit survivals of former days . . . useless and obstructive', which had existed since the Middle Ages, gradually withered away, their remaining ecclesiastical powers being taken over in 1920 by the new Parochial Church Councils. To the new civil parish councils went many of the former parochial charities and even some of the parish halls, if it could not be shown that they had been built for purely ecclesiastical purposes.

For most of the period covered by this volume the unifying bond between church and state, between the ecclesiastical and the secular, provided by the parish and its vestry, survived intact. Their separate areas of responsibility or influence – religious affairs, education, social welfare – are dealt with separately in this volume, though from time to time the overlap between them will be specifically commented upon. Even when this is not the case it is important to emphasise that this unity was a reality and that the influence, and indeed control, of the churches, and the established Church of England in particular, in the fields of education and social welfare, was a most significant factor in English life, and life in Kent, until the middle of the nineteenth century.

Papists and Puritans 1640–1714

(1) The Religious Situation in 1640

In 1640 it was assumed that everybody in England was a member of the Church of England by law established. The least that was expected was occasional conformity. Those who habitually absented themselves from the worship of the established church could be, and from time to time were, heavily fined. The few, mostly noble or gentry, families and their households who remained Roman Catholic were regarded as traitors at times of anti-papist hysteria and ran the risk of imprisonment, torture and execution. Though the Church of England had been finally claimed by the reformers after the accession of Elizabeth I in 1558, the religious settlement which she imposed was a compromise as dissatisfying to extreme Protestants as it was to the Roman Catholic recusants who placed loyalty to the papacy above loyalty to the monarchy. Alone of the major national reformed churches of Northern Europe, Calvinist or Lutheran, the Church of England had no official confession of faith, for the simple reason that it would have been impossible to produce one that could have commanded general support. The doctrines of the church were laid down in a series of different, sometimes inconsistent, documents: the Book of Common Prayer as revised in 1559, the Thirty-Nine Articles of 1563, the two Books of Homilies completed in 1571, and the Canons of 1604. During the latter part of Elizabeth's reign the bishops had a difficult task resisting pressure from those known as Puritans to move the church in a more Protestant direction by abolishing what they regarded as popish ceremonies and insisting on a stricter interpretation of the Calvinist doctrines to which the church generally subscribed.

By the second decade of the seventeenth century there had arisen a strong anti-Calvinist party within the church keen to emphasise those ceremonies and traditions of the Church of England that separated it from the much stricter Protestantism of the Dutch and Scottish churches with which it otherwise had much in common. These Anglican high churchmen began to be promoted by James I. Under his son Charles I they acquired a majority of the bishoprics and other senior positions in the church. By their emphasis on the divine nature of monarchy high churchmen bound church and state closer together. How far the changes that took place as a result were determined by theological innovation and how much as a result of royal initiative is a matter of current debate.[1] What is not in dispute is that

---

[1] There is a considerable recent literature on the religious history of England in the late sixteenth and early seventeenth centuries. See especially P. Collinson, *The Elizabethan Puritan Movement*, London 1967, and *The Religion of Protestants*, Oxford 1982; K. Fincham, *Prelate and Pastor: the Episcopate of James I*, Oxford 1990; N. Tyacke, *Anti-Calvinists*, Oxford 1987; and J. Davies,

the attempts of the high church bishops, under the leadership of Archbishop Laud, to move the church in a direction that their opponents regarded as popish, produced an outcry from the Puritan nobility and gentry who used the opportunity of Parliament being called in 1640, for the first time for eleven years, to demand that a stop be put to these developments. The opposition, however, was divided on how far it wanted to go in securing an altered religious establishment. The more extreme critics revealed their position in the Root and Branch Petition of December 1640:[2]

> The great conformity and likeness both continued and increased of our Church to the Church of Rome, in vestures, postures, ceremonies and administrations, namely as the bishops' rochets and the lawn-sleeves, the four-cornered cap, the cope and surplice, the tippet, the hood and the ceremonial coat; the pulpits, clothed, especially now of late, with the Jesuits' badge upon them every way.
> The standing up at *Gloria Patri* and at the reading of the Gospel, praying towards the East, the bowing at the name of Jesus, the bowing to the altar towards the East, cross in baptism, the kneeling at the Communion.
> The turning of the Communion-table altar-wise, setting images, crucifixes, and conceits over them, and tapers and books upon them, and bowing or adoring to or before them, the reading of the second service at the altar, and forcing people to come up either to receive, or also denying the sacrament to them, terming the altar to be the mercy-seat, or the place of God Almighty in the church, which is a plain device to usher in the Mass.

There is, however, plenty of evidence to show that there was little support for such religious extremists in Kent. The majority of Kent parishes were strongly anti-Puritan and there were several attacks on Puritan ministers. Puritan activity was largely confined to the towns. At Cranbrook the rector, Robert Abbot, offered his Puritan parishioners a daily lecture founded on scripture but this was rejected; they wanted Abbot to give up using the Book of Common Prayer, which he refused to do.[3]

The position of the Kent gentry was largely that of their principal spokesman, the distinguished parliamentarian and amateur theologian, Sir Edward Dering. Dering wanted the dioceses of England re-organised so that each county was a diocese with the bishop residing in its chief town and confining his activities to his diocese, ceasing thereby to act as an agent of royal authority which was the chief complaint against the Laudian bishops. Bishops were to be chosen from a list of three names to be determined as the result of an election by the clergy of that diocese. The revenues of cathedral chapters were to be regularly surveyed by local

The Caroline Captivity of the Church, Oxford 1992. Tyacke has added a foreword to the paperback edition (1990) of his book in which he deals with the criticisms raised by some reviewers.

2 Petition printed in *Constitutional Documents of the Puritan Revolution*, ed. S. R. Gardiner, 3rd edn, Oxford 1906, pp. 137–44. The passages quoted are clauses 14–16 inclusive of the 'particular of the manifold evils, pressures, and grievances caused, practised and outlined by the Prelates and their dependents'.

3 A. M. Everitt, *The Community of Kent and the Great Rebellion 1640–1660*, Leicester 1966, pp. 87, 127.

commissioners. The parish clergy were to have more power, operating through a hierarchical system of weekly vestries, quarterly ruri-decanal meetings and annual diocesan synods, with a national synod of the whole English church meeting once every three years. Dering's primary aim, and that of his supporters, was to restrict the power of both crown and bishops. Unlike the more extreme Puritans he did not want to make any major changes in the Book of Common Prayer.[4] If Parliament had been able to unite behind men like Dering an acceptable reform of the Church of England, and indeed the preservation of the monarchy, might have been possible. The real difficulty was that, although there was a majority in Parliament against the religious establishment as defined by Charles I and his bishops, there was no agreement about what to put in its place. Some favoured the moderate reforms and limited episcopacy advocated by Dering, some wanted the imposition of strict Presbyterianism on the Dutch or Scottish models, others wanted complete toleration for all but the most extreme sects and no religious establishment whatsoever.

(2) The Impact of the Civil War

Between 1642 and 1660 the religious situation in Kent, as in England as a whole, was one of total confusion. The Church of England was, in a sense, gradually dismantled through a series of parliamentary ordinances, but no new religious establishment was put in its place, and recent research has suggested that, despite these moves, a good deal of Anglican activity and practice survived through until the re-establishment of the Church of England in 1660. The Church of England was in effect, to borrow a phrase, 'in a state of suspended animation'.[5] This is certainly the case with the bishops. Parliament resolved to abolish them in 1642, and did so by ordinance in 1646 in order to lay hands on the income of their estates, but there is some evidence of continued episcopal activity even after this. As the bishops died their sees were not filled, but this was a gradual process. Sodor and Man was not filled after the death of Richard Parr in 1643, yet new bishops were consecrated for Bristol and Lichfield in 1644. Of the 27 bishoprics in England and Wales, only a third were vacant in 1650, a third fell vacant in the 1650s, and a third of the bishops survived to be restored to their sees or translated to more lucrative ones in 1660. An analysis of bishops' registers and act books suggests that several were still active until at least 1648–9.[6] As late as September 1652 an entry in his register shows that Bishop Warner of Rochester instituted Edward Archbold to the rectory of Trottiscliffe in his gift; the parish register records that baptisms and burials were performed without a break throughout the 1650s, though arrangements were made for complying with the parliamentary

---

4 *Ibid.*, pp. 53–4.
5 J. P. Kenyon, *Stuart England*, 2nd edn, Harmondsworth 1985, p. 162. For the best recent study of the church in this period see J. Spurr, *The Restoration Church of England 1646–1689*, New Haven and London 1991.
6 See D. M. Smith, *Guide to Bishops' Registers of England and Wales*, London 1981.

requirements in respect of civil marriage, Robert Hills being chosen as 'register' by the parishioners on 24 August 1653 and sworn before the justices on 5 October 1654.[7]

The principal Anglican casualty of the Civil War was the cathedrals. Dignities and prebends were not filled as their occupants died. By the restoration the deanery and six prebends at Rochester were all vacant and most had been so since 1647. At Canterbury the dean appointed in 1643 was not installed until 1660 and only two of the twelve prebendaries were still alive at the restoration. The cathedrals were seen as the outward manifestation of Laudianism at its most extreme and therefore the recipients of much criticism from extreme Puritans. According to one of their number at Canterbury:[8]

> The Pettie Canons, and Singing men there, sing their Cathedral Service in Prick-Song after the Romish fashion, chanting the Lord's Prayer, and other Prayers in an unfit manner, in the chancell, or Quire of that Cathedrall; at the East end whereof they have placed an Altar (as they call it) dressed after the Romish fashion, with candlesticks, and tapers, for which Altar they have lately provided a most Idolatrous costly Glory-cloth or Back-cloth; towards which Altar they crouch, and duck three times at their going up to it, and reade there part of their service apart from the Assembly.

The fate of the cathedrals depended largely on the strength of local feeling. Some were partitioned for use by different congregations. At Exeter the cathedral choir was used by the Presbyterians and the nave by the Independents.[9] At Rochester the damage was less than at some other cathedrals. The altar rails and velvet frontal of the altar were removed and the altar table placed in the nave. The dean was ordered not to preach in a surplice but refused. No Puritan ministry was established in place of the former chapter and the cathedral was simply allowed to decay with parts turned over to secular uses.[10] At Canterbury the situation was rather different. The cathedral was effectively taken over by the extreme Puritan minister, Richard Culmer, appointed one of the cathedral's Six Preachers in 1644.[11] Culmer was personally responsible for destroying much of the cathedral's stained glass. Many other fittings were destroyed including the font that had been presented by Bishop Warner of Rochester, though the pieces of this were rescued by the local antiquary, William Somner, and restored to the cathedral after 1660. It had been the practice from the early seventeenth century for the congregation to adjourn to the Chapter House for sermons on Sundays and festivals, though the rest of the service took place in the choir. An attempt by the Laudian chapter to have the sermon preached in the choir was fiercely resisted by the Puritans in Canterbury and had to be

[7] Centre for Kentish Studies, Maidstone (hereafter cited as CKS), DRb/Ar1/17, f. 98v; P373/1/1.

[8] R. Culmer, *Cathedral Newes from Canterbury*, London 1644, p. 2. Copy in CKS, U235 Z1.

[9] A. L. Drummond, *The Architecture of Protestantism*, Edinburgh 1934, p. 41.

[10] C. E. Knighton, 'The Reformed Chapter 1540–1660', *A History of Rochester Cathedral*, ed. P. A. Welsby and W. N. Yates, forthcoming.

[11] D. I. Hill, *The Six Preachers of Canterbury Cathedral*, Ramsgate 1982, pp. 52–4.

abandoned. No services took place in the cathedral after the late 1640s, but the chapter house was placed at the disposal of the Independents who used it for Sunday services.[12]

In the parish churches the situation was even more confused. In the dioceses of both Canterbury and Rochester steps had been taken to enforce the Anglican canons and to prevent the appointment of Puritans to benefices during the 1630s. After 1640 some parishes took advantage of the attack on the bishops to remove high church clergy and to abolish what they regarded as popish practices. At Chatham in June 1643 the parishioners washed out the 'antique painted works' and the sentences in the chancel relating to the sacrament of the Lord's Supper and replastered the walls. The images in the church porch, regarded as superstitious, were broken down, the medieval choir stalls demolished and eight new pews erected in the chancel, and the communion table removed from the chancel into the body of the church.[13] Such activity was largely confined to the towns. At Sandwich the Puritan lecturer burned all the prayer books in St Peter's Church. Technically the Book of Common Prayer was proscribed and replaced by a Calvinist Directory of Public Worship in 1645 but many clergy in Kent continued to use the prayer book and to maintain ceremonial where they could.[14] The ejection of orthodox Anglican clergy was gradual and in some places never took place. The Earl of Westmorland continued to present high churchmen to his livings in West Kent. The Puritans of Brenchley had to walk seven miles to East Peckham to have their children baptised by a minister with whom they were in sympathy. Thanet remained a bastion of orthodox Anglicanism, and Richard Culmer, the Canterbury Puritan intruded into Minster in 1644, never received any support from his parishioners. It has been calculated that at least 233 out of 450 Kentish benefices were sequestered or the incumbents forcibly removed from office in the 1640s and 1650s, and the figure may have been as high as 75%. Puritan clergy tended to move more frequently than their predecessors, this contributing to social instability in the parishes.[15] There were however some parishes where clergy occupying the living in the 1630s were still doing so in the 1660s. In the diocese of Rochester this was the case at Cowden, Footscray, Horton Kirby, Longfield and East Malling.[16] The pattern of appointments at Horsmonden, however, is not untypical: in 1643 the extreme Royalist, Jeffery Amherst, was sequestered and replaced by John Crouch, a moderate Puritan; he was in turn sequestered and replaced by a more extreme Puritan, Edward Rawson, in 1653; in 1662 Rawson, who refused to accept the Act of Uniformity, was deprived, and his predecessor, who was now prepared to use the Book of Common Prayer, was restored to the living.[17]

[12] C. E. Woodruff and W. Danks, *Memorials of the Cathedral and Priory of Christ in Canterbury*, London 1912, pp. 321–33.

[13] Rochester-upon-Medway Archives at Civic Centre, Strood, P85/8/1.

[14] Everitt, *op. cit.*, pp. 200–4, 231.

[15] *Ibid.*, pp. 225–6, 299–300.

[16] See C. H. Fielding, *Records of Rochester Diocese*, Dartford 1910.

[17] E. Hasted, *History and Topographical Survey of Kent*, 2nd edn, Canterbury 1798, v, p. 322.

In some places the failure to replace the Anglican establishment with an alternative model allowed religious extremists to form their own congregations and threaten the political stability of the local community to such an extent that eventually it became necessary for the government to take steps to control them. The more moderate Puritans, who formed the congregations of Presbyterians, Independents or the less radical groups of Baptists were not a concern to the civil authorities in the 1650s. The religious crises of the 1640s, however, produced several extremist sects that were: the Diggers who believed that Christian principles required the cultivation of crown property and common land with the spade; the Levellers with their extreme notions of democracy and religious freedom; the Muggletonians whose founders claimed to be the two witnesses referred to in the eleventh chapter of the Book of Revelation; the Ranters who denied all forms of religious and scriptural authority; and the Fifth Monarchy Men who based their beliefs on an obscure reference in the Book of Daniel. By the mid 1650s, however, the sect that was causing the most concern in Kent was the Quakers, later known as the Society of Friends. The main complaints against the Quakers, and the reasons for later prosecutions, were their disruption of church services with their own unauthorised preaching and their refusal to take oaths, to pay church rates and tithes, or to undertake military service.[18]

> George Rose in ye yeare 1655 going into ye steeplhous at Lidd after ye preist had ended his service; He began to speake to ye people to ye turning theire minds from darkness to ye light and was interrupted and by ye mayors command was violently halled by ye rude multitude and was kicked and beaten in ye mayors presence and at last (with much violence) was throwne downe a high place of stone stayres soe as his life was indangered thereby; one of his leggs being sorely wounded with ye fall and was under care many dayes after.

In the same year two London Quakers, William Caton and John Stubs, undertook a missionary visit to Kent. They began at Dover visiting both the parish churches and the meetings of Baptists and Independents there, but were ordered to leave by the mayor and corporation. They then visited Folkestone, where they were thrown out of the parish church; Hythe 'where at their publique place of worship they were violently dealt with by ye rude multitude'; the Baptist and Independent meetings at Lydd; then Ashford, Tenterden, Cranbrook and Staplehurst, 'where they found a very open People that were very ready to receive and embrace ye Everlasting Truth'; and finally Maidstone:

> They went into a Meeting of ye People called Baptists . . . and then John Stubs went to their publique Place of Worship, where ye people called Presbiterians mett . . . They were striped naked and their necks and arms put in ye stocks, and there cruelly whipped with coards in a bloudy manner, in the sight of many People . . . And when they had thus cruelly proceeded they fastened Irons upon them, with great Cloggs of Wood, and put them in amongst transgressors . . .

18 CKS, N/FQZ1, p. 4.

And their cruelty was so great, they would not let them have any victualls or drinke for their money, for some dayes, only a little water they had once a day . . . And when they came to bring their Bookes and other things, they had taken from them, they burnt their letters and papers before their faces.

Caton and Stubs were then conveyed back to London. On a later expedition to Kent they returned to Maidstone, with less dramatic consequences, visited the Baptist and Independent meetings at Canterbury, and continued on to Sandwich, where they 'had some service in particular among the Dutch people there, at their steeple-house; but at that time ye truth could get but little Entrance in that place'.[19]

(3) The Anglican Re-Establishment

The religious difficulties of the 1650s were a major contribution to the strong desire to overthrow England's only republican experiment and to restore the monarchy. This did not mean that either clergy or laity were any more united in their theological beliefs in 1660 than they had been in 1640, but the experience of the intervening decades had impressed upon them the need for a religious settlement that could command the support of most people. The events of 1660–2, which culminated in the Act of Uniformity and some minor alterations to the Book of Common Prayer, are, like the nature of early seventeenth century Anglicanism, being re-interpreted. The belief that the settlement of 1662 was the final triumph of Laudianism,[20] has given way to an acceptance that it was a genuine, if not entirely successful, attempt at compromise.[21] The surviving bishops had not been wholly inactive during the interregnum and speedily re-occupied their sees. Bishop Warner of Rochester was said to have spent not less than £8,000 in helping to relieve clergy ejected from their livings.[22] There was, however, a clear recognition that there had been abuses in the church before the Civil War and that these should not be repeated. A frequent one had been the failure of the clergy to preach regularly. This had been the case at Yalding, where the parishioners alleged that sermons had not been preached for more than thirty years; others, such as the rector of Stone-next-Dartford, had allowed his church to get out of repair, or, like the vicar of Dartford, had been 'excessively given to drinking of wine, insomuch that he many times reeleth in the street, and cannot go upright'.[23] Bishops were not to act as agents of the crown as they had done in Charles I's reign, and the ecclesiastical courts, though they were revived, were not used in the aggressive way that they had been in the 1620s and 1630s.

The liturgical ceremonial of the Laudian church, which had proved so irksome to many Puritans, was largely reimposed. The revised Book of Common Prayer made no significant concession to Puritan consciences. The reinstated bishops and

[19] CKS, N/FQZ 2, pp. 7–14.
[20] See R. S. Bosher, *The Making of the Restoration Settlement*, London 1951.
[21] See I. M. Green, *The Re-establishment of the Church of England*, Oxford 1978.
[22] A. J. Pearman, *Diocesan Histories: Rochester*, London 1897, pp. 280–1.
[23] *Ibid.*, pp. 285–9.

their senior clergy were assiduous in ensuring that churches should be properly repaired and ordered to meet the minimum requirements of the Anglican Canons. Archdeacon Warner of Rochester carried out a detailed visitation of all the churches in his archdeaconry noting repairs to be undertaken and articles to be purchased. At several churches, such as that at Brenchley, he ordered 'the seats at the upper end of the chancel to be removed and the communion table to be sett up ther and rayled in as formerly'.[24]

There was, however, a general desire for compromise and the majority of parish ministers, most of whom had Puritan sympathies, were able to accept the settlement of 1662. Those who could not do so and subscribe the Act of Uniformity were deprived of their livings. The settlement of 1662 went some way towards a recognition that the Church of England could not be totally comprehensive and that some limited toleration for nonconformists was inevitable. The number of parish clergy who refused to subscribe the Act of Uniformity and were therefore deprived of their livings was comparatively small. In Kent a total of 76 clergy were deprived.[25] Many of these went into quiet retirement as had those who lost livings in the 1640s and 1650s, but some set up dissenting congregations either in their own parishes or in another one. They included John Barton at Barham, Richard Gyles at Rolvenden, Peter Johnson at St Lawrence-in-Thanet and Daniel Poyntel at Staplehurst; Nathaniel Wilmot of Faversham ministered to a dissenting congregation in Dover and Edward Alexander of Wickhambreux to one in Canterbury; Nicholas Thoroughgood, the ejected minister of Monkton, ministered first at Canterbury, then at Sandwich, where he and two colleagues preached 'twice every Lord's Day . . . carried on a Friday lecture there' between 1668 and 1670, and finally at Rochester. Some ministers entered other professions; John Swan of Ickham became a physician and Thomas Shewell of Lenham kept a private school in Leeds. Some toleration was even allowed by the Anglican authorities with John Crump, ejected from Maidstone, being occasionally allowed to preach at Boxley.[26]

The period after 1660 was one of consolidation for the Church of England after the disruption of the interregnum. There seems to have been some improvement in the economic status of the clergy. However, about a quarter of the livings in the diocese of Canterbury were worth between £30 and £50, a sum generally regarded as inadequate, another quarter of the livings were worth between £50 and £80; less than a fifth of livings were worth more than £100 and less than one in twenty over £200. In order to make ends meet clergy had either to hold livings in plurality, though often these were neighbouring benefices which could be served without difficulty, or be permitted to supplement their incomes by establishing schools in their parishes. Part of an incumbent's income was derived from tithe, which he had

24 CKS, DRa/Vb 6, f. 43.
25 C. W. Chalklin, *Seventeenth Century Kent*, London 1965, p. 223.
26 T. Timpson, *Church History of Kent*, London 1859, pp. 178–207, 399–400; G. F. Nuttall, 'Dissenting Churches in Kent Before 1700'; *Journal of Ecclesiastical History*, xiv (1963), pp. 175–6.

to collect, part from farming his glebe and part from fees and Easter offerings. The questions of tithe and fees were a frequent source of dispute between an incumbent and his parishioners.[27] After 1660 the Church of England was to develop a standard of pastoral care and a liturgical outlook which was to remain largely unchallenged for the best part of two centuries. The pattern of church services was Morning Prayer, Litany and Ante-Communion on Sunday mornings, a service usually lasting about 105 minutes, and Evening Prayer in the afternoons, lasting about 85 minutes; in each case about 45 minutes would have been devoted to preaching or catechising. Holy Communion was generally celebrated as part of the morning service quarterly in most rural parishes and monthly in the urban ones. In small rural parishes, particularly where these were held in plurality, it was normal for only one service to be held each Sunday and certainly for only one sermon to be preached. The number of weekday services varied considerably from none at all, except at Christmas, in many rural parishes, to daily services in some town ones.[28]

There was relatively little need for major church building in the later seventeenth century. A new church was built at Plaxtol in the extensive parish of Wrotham and completed in 1654-5;[29] a separate parish was created in 1647 by Parliamentary ordinance and the new church, begun in 1648, paid for by 'a collection . . . directed to be made throughout this County', but the separate parish was suppressed and re-united with Wrotham in 1660.[30] The other important building project was the chapel of King Charles the Martyr erected at Tunbridge Wells between 1676 and 1696. The new chapel cost £2,278 1s 7d, raised almost entirely by subscription, including donations from many visitors to this fashionable spa. Heading the lists of subscribers were Princess Anne of Denmark (the future Queen Anne), the Duchess of York, the Duke of Monmouth, the Earl and Countess of Thanet, the Earl and Countess Clarendon, and the Bishop of Rochester. £128 was paid to Henry Dogood for his plastered ceiling, £24 for the altarpiece, £33 17s 0d for velvet coverings for the pulpit and desks, and £4 9s 0d for prayer books for the altar and desks.[31]

Much damage had been done to the cathedrals at both Canterbury and Rochester in the Civil War. At Rochester the cost of making good all this damage was £14,640.[32] In 1662-3 Prebendary Ralph Cooke presented the cathedral with new communion vessels to replace plate lost or destroyed in the 1640s; this consisted of two chalices and covers, two patens, two flagons, an almsdish and two

---

[27] Chalklin, *op. cit.*, pp. 219-22.

[28] See W. N. Yates, *Buildings, Faith and Worship: the Liturgical Arrangement of Anglican Churches 1600-1900*, Oxford 1991, pp. 47-65.

[29] CKS, P406C/1/1.

[30] Hasted, *op. cit.*, v, pp. 22-5.

[31] CKS, P371E/8/1.

[32] P. Mussett, 'The Reconstituted Chapter, 1660-1820', *History of Rochester Cathedral*, forthcoming.

candlesticks.[33] At Canterbury a similar process took place. A description of the interior of the cathedral in 1660 noted:[34]

> the Quire stripped of her faire and goodly hangings, her Organ and Organ-loft: the Communion table, of the best and chiefest of her furniture and ornaments, with the raile before it, and the skreen of Tabernacle-Worke, richly overlayd with gold, behind it . . . to carry on the work of perfecting the furniture of our Quire with an Organ, and our Communion table with plate and other necessary utensils and ornaments which partly by contract, partly by the estimate of judicious persons we find cannot cost us lesse than £1000 0s 0d.

In fact the total cost of repairing the cathedral and restoring its furniture and ornaments, though less than at Rochester, still came to £7921.[35] This included the purchase of new communion plate, including 'two greate silver flaggons double guilt', two chalices and covers, two patens and two offertory basons. Other purchases included an eagle lectern for reading the lessons and two prayer books for the altar 'bound in Turky leather with gilt leaves the one redd the other blew'. The strongly Royalist Dean Turner placed a portrait of Charles I, showing the King in an attitude of prayer, with a crown descending from the clouds, closely resembling the engraving in the popular *Eikon Basilike*, over the central arch of the choir screen between the stalls of the dean and vice-dean. He also presented 'a costly Folio Bible with covers of beaten silver gilt'. This was placed on the altar together with a pair of lighted candles and the communion plate during services of Holy Communion. This was celebrated weekly until 1790, when it became monthly. Morning Prayer was sung daily at 10.00 am until 1684, when it was put back to 9.00 am; Evening Prayer was sung daily at 3.00 pm in summer and 4.00 pm in winter. A new screen was erected behind the altar in 1664; this originally had behind it IHS in a glory until 1680 when Dean Tillotson replaced this by 'a faire frame with the commandements written in gold'.[36]

During the Civil War and interregnum cathedrals were largely at the mercy of the municipal authorities. The 1662 settlement re-established the independence of cathedral chapters as wholly self-governing bodies. At Canterbury this was clearly stated in the chapter's replies to Archbishop Sheldon's queries to them on this matter in 1671. Sheldon wanted to know whether the mayor and corporation claimed any jurisdiction inside the cathedral close; whether the King's writs were executed in the precincts by the corporation, the High Sheriff of Kent or the chapter; whether in the collection of taxes the close was regarded as part of the city or of the county; what accommodation was provided in the cathedral for the mayor and corporation; and whether the cathedral was fully exempt from the jurisdiction

---

33 W. N. Yates, 'Worship in the Cathedral 1540–1870', *History of Rochester Cathedral*, forthcoming.
34 *Inventories of Christchurch Canterbury*, ed. J. W. Legg and W. H. St J. Hope, London 1902, p. 270.
35 Woodruff and Danks, *op. cit.*, p. 341.
36 *Ibid.*, pp. 338, 342–4; *Inventories*, pp. 271–82.

of the city. On all points the dean and chapter where able to establish their complete independence. The corporation's sword and mace were lowered and veiled within the cathedral and surrounding liberties, whereas elsewhere in the city they were carried erect before the mayor and aldermen. No writ could run in the precincts without the consent of the chapter exercised through its steward. The precincts were part of the county for taxation purposes. The mayor and corporation were placed 'in the uppermost stalls and seates' of the choir or alternatively on the south side of the church 'among the gentlemen'. This arrangement was by invitation of the dean and chapter, the corporation having no statutory right to specific seats in the cathedral, nor any rights over those seats. This was in clear contrast to the arrangements for seating in the parish churches of corporate towns where it was normal for corporations to have a prescriptive right to pews.[37] Finally it was stated that the cathedral was fully exempt from the jurisdiction of the city. The whole reply amounted to 'an absolute denial of municipal authority over the Cathedral, its members, and precincts'.[38]

Some surviving correspondence of Archbishop Sancroft throws interesting light on the state of religion in Kent in the three decades following the restoration of the monarchy. An element of compromise on matters of ceremonial detail was clearly necessitated by the fact that many clergy were still Presbyterians at heart, but had conformed either to retain their livings or out of loyalty to their parishioners; some, such as the incumbents of St Mary Northgate at Canterbury and St Mary's, Sandwich, were foreign Protestants. A survey of religious conditions in the early 1660s noted that there was 'noe font, nor surplice' at Deal and that at Great Mongeham the 'church [was] much out of repayre [the incumbent] preaches in ye chancell, parish much infected with sectaryes. . . noe surplice'; and that at St Peter's, Sandwich 'Presbyterians and Sectaryes much infest the towne and parish, noe surplice, nor will be endured'. The surplice was not worn at Barfrestone.[39] Nearly two decades later there was not much improvement in some parishes. Thomas Paramore, who served the neighbouring churches and parishes of Guston with East and West Langdon, has left a vivid account of the state of affairs there in 1679:[40]

> As for Guston . . . the parishioners being all (within 2 or 3 families) dissenters from our church, as Anabaptists chiefly and some Quakers, there is noe pulpit cushion, noe pulpit cloth, noe surplice, noe common prayer book, the Bible out of the cover and imperfect, and I think noe table, neither have they any churchwardens or a clerk, so that my predecessor was, and I am, forced to carry our Public Liturgy in my pocket, and to give my own clerk his dinner to

[37] See W. N. Yates, 'The Mayoral and Corporation Seats in Faversham Parish Church', *Archaeologia Cantiana*, cvi (1989), pp. 37–43.

[38] R. Beddard, 'The Privileges of Christ Church, Canterbury: Archbishop Sheldon's Enquiries of 1671', *Archaeologia Cantiana*, lxxxvii (1972), pp. 81–100.

[39] C. E. Woodruff, 'Letters Relating to the Condition of the Church in Kent during the Primacy of Archbishop Sancroft', *Archaeologia Cantiana*, xxi (1895), pp. 176–8.

[40] *Ibid.*, pp. 194–5.

accompany me in the afternoon where though there be but 3 or 4 families that frequent the Church there is a good country congregation because my own parish doe unanimously follow me thither . . . As for West Langdon the other parish, the church of it is fallen down and noe use can be made of it, but the walls of it are standing both east and west, north and south, and may be serviceable again uppon occasion, the roof is quite down and the pews and whatever was within are broken and either laying under the rubbish or carried away.

It was in order to rectify such situations as this that, as archbishop, Sancroft attempted to revive the office of rural dean. Rural deans were appointed to the six historic deaneries of Canterbury, Charing, Ospringe, Sandwich, Sutton and Westbere in 1682, and were ordered to enquire into the condition of the churches in their deaneries and to report back to the archbishop. The report of Dr Henry Ullock, rector of Great Mongeham and rural dean of Sandwich, has survived. Ullock was a distinguished churchman, a Six Preacher of Canterbury Cathedral and prebendary of Rochester, becoming dean of the latter cathedral in 1689.[41] Ullock reported that though ten of the nineteen incumbents in his deanery were pluralists, only three were non-resident. The rector of Ham was usher at Merchant Taylors' School in London but employed a curate; the rector of Little Mongeham, which had no church, was a French Huguenot beneficed in the Channel Islands; the rector of Stonar was also non-resident but the parish only had two families. Most of the pluralists served neighbouring churches: St Mary's and St Peter's in Sandwich, East and West Langdon, Eythorne and Waldershare, Northbourne and Sholden, Eastry and Worth. The same incumbent served both Deal and Lydd, residing mostly at the former and employing a curate at the latter, but with an arrangement whereby these positions were reversed from time to time. Some incumbents also acted as curates of neighbouring churches with non-resident incumbents. The vicar of St Clement's, Sandwich, at Ash; the rector of Betteshanger at Sutton-next-Dover; the vicar of Tilmanstone at Whitfield. Ullock's account of his rural deanery clearly portrays a situation in which parishes were being adequately served by their clergy and with no serious cases of neglect.[42]

(4) The Growth of Nonconformity

What was more worrying to the Anglican authorities after 1660 than standards of pastoral care or the minutiae of public worship was their need to come to terms with the fact that some of their parishioners had been permanently alienated from the Church of England by the events of the previous twenty years and, for them, the unsatisfactory nature of the 1662 religious settlement. The rector of Biddenden had to cope with a substantial congregation of Brownists; at St Lawrence-in-Thanet the parish was full of Presbyterians led by the ejected minister; St Mary's Sandwich,

[41] Hill, op. cit., pp. 67–8.
[42] Woodruff, op. cit., pp. 173–4, 179–82.

had 'many sectaryes and enemies to ye late King, some subscribers to his death'; Northbourne was full of Anabaptists and Quakers, or so it was alleged.[43] For a brief while these groups of disaffected parishioners unwilling to worship in their parish churches had no official status. In 1672 it became possible for ministers and congregations to apply for licences to set up dissenting meetings, and a total of fifty licences were taken out for such meetings in Kent in the first year of the new dispensation. The majority of meetings were established in the towns. Deal and Tenterden had meetings licensed for Baptists, Independents and Presbyterians. There were Baptist and Presbyterian meetings at Cranbrook, Dover, Lenham, Rolvenden, Staplehurst and Wye; Independent and Presbyterian ones at Ash, Canterbury and Sandwich. Some of these newly licensed meetings were for congregations that had been in existence for many years. Independent meetings had been established before 1650 at Canterbury, Dover, Sandwich and Staplehurst. Some of the Baptist congregations in Kent had even earlier origins, in the case of Deptford and Eythorne back to the 1620s. There were fourteen Baptist meetings in Kent by the 1650s, of which five were represented at the general assembly of Arminian Baptists held in 1656.[44]

The strength of Protestant nonconformity in Kent, as well as the weakness of Roman Catholic recusancy, is shown in the Compton Census of 1676. The census listed by parish those who communicated in the Church of England, Protestant dissenters and Roman Catholics. It is not entirely accurate since it does not allow for occasional conformists: those who communicated in the Church of England, often as a means of holding office, restricted to Anglican communicants under the provisions of the Test Act of 1673, but who were also members of dissenting congregations. Nevertheless the census provides a reasonable guide to those parts of Kent in which Protestant nonconformity was a significant element in the local community. The returns were made by the Anglican clergy who were asked to number as dissenters all those 'who did obstinately refuse, or wholly absent themselves from the communion of the Church of England, at such times as by law they are required'. Of the towns in the county only Faversham and Rochester, as shown in Table 1, had relatively few nonconformists.

The number of nonconformists in Canterbury may suggest that the attacks on the Laudian cathedral clergy in the 1640s had a good deal of popular support. Outside the main towns there were three parishes (Ripple, Walmer and Willesborough) in which Protestant dissenters outnumbered Anglican communicants and a further twelve in which they formed at least a fifth of the population. These were with the exception of Woolwich, Snodland and West Malling, all parishes in East Kent or the Weald: St Lawrence-in-Thanet, Boughton Malherbe, Frittenden, Rolvenden, Smarden, Sandhurst, Staplehurst, Ash-next-Sandwich and Pembury. The dearth of Roman Catholics in the towns was repeated in the countryside, despite the fact that recusancy was largely confined to the country gentry and their tenants. Only at Benenden, Lamberhurst, Mereworth and East Peckham did the

[43] *Ibid.*, pp. 175–8.
[44] Nuttall, *op. cit.*, pp. 179–82.

Table 1

Anglican Communicants, Protestant Dissenters
and Roman Catholics in Kent Towns 1676

Town	Communicants	Dissenters	Papists
Canterbury	2831	2083	28
Sandwich	1100	315	1
Cranbrook	898	400	2
Tenterden	899	300	1
Faversham	1157	40	3
Dover	1628	301	21
Maidstone	2690	310	–
Chatham	1500	300	3
Rochester	1850	144	5

number of Roman Catholics reach double figures. There was a strange entry for Wrotham in which, out of a parish population of 532, 71 were described as 'Papish . . . or papishly effected obstinate refusing ye Holy Communion'.[45]

Although there were a significant number of dissenting congregations in Kent by the 1670s they were slow to build permanent chapels, most renting rooms for worship in secular buildings. At Staplehurst the congregation established by the ejected minister, David Poyntel, occupied hired premises until 1756.[46] At Tunbridge Wells Protestant dissenters 'hired a ballroom, in Mount Ephraim House, and having it licensed, they assembled there on the Lord's Day, the pulpit for the minister being affixed temporarily to the Wainscot by iron hooks'.[47] The earliest chapels in Kent appear to have been built at Ashford before 1689, Ramsgate in about 1690, Deal in 1692 and Canterbury in 1696. Zion Chapel at Dover, opened in 1703 on a site conveyed by the town's leading merchant, Philip Papillon, was a converted maltings and mill.[48] The privileges of a somewhat restricted religious freedom obtained by the more orthodox Protestant dissenters – Baptists, Independents and Presbyterians – was not extended to the more radical religious groups, such as the Quakers, that had become active in Kent in the 1650s. They continued to be prosecuted for refusing military service and for other demonstrations of their religious radicalism:[49]

John Edwards of Lidd one ye 19 of ye 8 month 1661 was taken from his house by a warrant from Richard Masters Depute Governor of Dover Castell and

[45] C. W. Chalklin, 'The Compton Census of 1676', *Kent Records*, xvii (1960), pp. 153–74. Chalklin does not include any returns for the Shoreham peculiar but these were published by M. J. Dobson, 'Original Compton Census Returns – the Shoreham Deanery', *Archaeologia Cantiana*, xciv (1978), pp. 61–73.

[46] Timpson, *op. cit.*, pp. 439–41.

[47] *Ibid.*, p. 464.

[48] *Ibid.*, pp. 306–8, 405–7, 414–15, 422–4, 508–9.

[49] CKS, N/FQZ 1, pp. 300, 391.

brought prisoner to ye Castle because for conscience sake he could not appear at the Generall Muster of the trained bands and hath beene kept prisoner above fower months allredy under the hands of ye cruell marshall John Slowman

. . . Henry Lownes of Ashford constable indited Thomas Kingham, William Roberts and Robert Puttin at ye sessions in Canterbury inhabitants of ye said towne for opening theire shopes windows one a fast day kept ye 22 day of ye 10 month 1680.

Despite their troubles the Kentish Quakers were able to establish a formal structure for themselves when four monthly meetings were set up in 1668. These were for East Kent with meetings at Dover, Canterbury, Wingham, Sandwich, Deal and Nonington; West Kent with meetings at Folkestone, Swingfield, Waltham, Ashford, Mersham and Lydd; Cranbrook with meetings there and at Tenterden; and Rochester with meetings there and at Maidstone. The burst of Quaker activity in Kent was short-lived. By the middle of the eighteenth century the society was in decline. The Rochester and East Kent monthly meetings were amalgamated in 1759, and this meeting amalgamated with Cranbrook in 1767. The West Kent monthly meeting which had divided into two, based in Ashford and Folkestone, in 1673 was reunited in 1761.[50]

(5) The Impact of the Glorious Revolution

For the Church of England the political events of 1688–9, following the abdication and flight of James II, were potentially traumatic. In the long run there was no change to the church, but that was not always clear to contemporaries. The religious settlement of 1662 was barely a generation old and not necessarily a lasting one. There was still pressure for religious change, and in Scotland this happened with the established church ceasing to be episcopal. The succession of a Dutch Calvinist to the English throne offered the possibility that, if there was sufficient support for it, what was to happen in Scotland might happen in England as well. The key to the survival of episcopacy and of the Anglican liturgy was that at the end of the day there was not sufficient support for change, or at least there was no agreement as to what the alternative structures ought to be. The enforced abdication of James II did pose serious problems for Anglican theologians for whom the doctrines of divine right and non-resistance to lawful authority were very powerful. Archbishop Sancroft, seven other bishops and about 400 clergy refused to take the oath to William III and were deprived. But the effects of the non-juring schism were very limited. Gradually the non-jurors made their way back into the Church of England during the course of the eighteenth century, and there was little appreciable difference between their theology and that of the many high churchmen who felt able to take the oath. The two positions were represented in Kent by, respectively, Thomas Brett and John Johnson. Brett (1667–1744) felt able to take the oath

[50] K. Showler, *The Society of Friends in Kent*, Canterbury 1970, pp. 9, 12.

originally but in 1715 he resigned the rectory of Ruckinge and in the following year became a non-juring bishop. He was an eminent liturgical scholar who took part in abortive negotiations for reunion between the non-jurors and the Greek Orthodox Church. Johnson (1662–1725) held successively the livings of Boughton-under-Blean, St John-in-Thanet and Cranbrook. He was a personal friend of many non-jurors but remained in the Church of England. His major work, *The Unbloody Sacrifice*, was a vigorous defence of the doctrine of the real presence in the Eucharist, yet he also installed a total immersion font in his church at Cranbrook in the vain hope of reclaiming Baptist dissenters for the established church. What Brett and Johnson were united in was their dislike for the low churchmen who they felt, one suspects quite unfairly, were gaining too much influence among the members of the higher clergy.[51]

In looking at the pattern of religious development over the whole period from 1640 it became clear that, whatever doubts may have been expressed about the Church of England as by law established, it was stronger in the 1690s than it had been in the 1630s. It may have failed in its attempts to enforce uniformity, yet with hindsight it is clear that the eventual, though grudging, recognition of limited nonconformity outside the confines of the established church, both allowed those uncomfortable within the Anglican straightjacket to escape from it, and at the same time permitted the Church of England to begin to develop a theology of its own, freed from the pressures imposed by the wider Protestant world on all those national churches given birth to by the Reformation in the earlier years of their existence. In this context the events of 1688–9 were a minor domestic distraction. The non-juring schism did not denude the Church of England, as some would have us believe,[52] of its major theologians. Most of them, and their high church disciples, remained. By the end of the 1690s, and in the first two decades of the eighteenth century, the Church of England experienced one of its many spiritual renaissances, a period marked by the establishment of religious societies and parochial libraries, by charitable bequests and by the gift of ornaments and plate to churches.[53]

The Society for Promoting Christian Knowledge was founded in 1698 and from its inception encouraged the establishment of parochial libraries. Although these were aimed primarily at the needs of the clergy it was expected that they might be made accessible to the laity as well and their management was regulated by the

---

[51] For a useful discussion on these matters, including some brief study of both Brett and Johnson, see E. G. Rupp, *Religion in England 1688–1791*, Oxford 1986, pp. 5–101. See also T. Brett, *Life of John Johnson*, London 1748.

[52] E.g. the statement 'the loss to the Church of the Non-Jurors, men of piety and learning, cannot be exaggerated', in S. Dark, *Seven Archbishops*, London 1944, p. 156 is typical of the popular Anglo-Catholic attitude to church history that has permeated much Anglican historical thought until quite recently.

[53] In much of what follows I am greatly influenced by the views of Dr W. M. Jacob whose promised study of the Church of England in this period is eagerly awaited. See his 'Church and Borough: Kings Lynn 1700–1750', in *Crown and Mitre: Religion and Society in Northern Europe Since the Reformation*, ed. W. M. Jacob and W. N. Yates, Woodbridge 1993, pp. 000–00.

Parochial Libraries Act of 1708. At least eight parochial libraries were established in Kent during the eighteenth century. Those at Detling and Preston-next-Wingham were two of the 62 libraries paid for by the SPCK itself and date from 1710. Four Kentish clergymen bequeathed their books to their successors in their respective livings to form parochial libraries: Henry Dering, vicar of Thurnham 1673–1720; Richard Forster, rector of Crundale 1698–1729; Daniel Somerscales, vicar of Doddington 1694–1737; and John Bowtell, vicar of Patrixbourne 1697–1753. At Westerham the parochial library was bequeathed by a layman, Charles West, in 1765. The most important of the eight known libraries was that of Maidstone, probably established in 1716 and substantially augmented in the 1730s; this library permitted the borrowing of books by the inhabitants of Maidstone and clearly operated as an embryo public library.[54]

One of the supporters of the parochial library movement in Kent was John Lewis, vicar of St John-in-Thanet from 1705 until his death in 1746. Lewis was both a distinguished antiquary, publishing *The Antiquities of Thanet* and *The History of Faversham*, and an energetic parish priest anxious to promote the highest standards of pastoral care, not just in his own parish, but in those of his neighbours as well. In his replies to Archbishop Wake's visitation queries in 1716, Lewis appended an extensive commentary on the canons of the Church of England which he felt should be revised to bring them more in line with what it was practical to enforce. He regarded it as unrealistic to expect the clergy, as they were officially required, 'to catechise every Sunday, which neither is done nor can be done in abundance of Churches, especially those where the Congregations are large, there is but one Minister, and preaching twice'. He complains about the inadequacy of arrangements for confirmation, and the practice, contrary to the Canons, of indiscriminately admitting non-parishioners to Holy Communion, 'by which means there is room left for very scandalous men to be admitted to the H Communion in order to qualify themselves for Offices'. He also added some even more pungent comments on the inadequacy of ecclesiastical provision in a number of Kent towns:

The City of Canterbury and Suburbs has fifteen parish Churches, but they are generally so small that if every one of them was to be open and officiated in at the same time there would be room enough for all the Inhabitants. But now by the Union of 12 of these churches they not being singly any tolerable mainten-ance for a Minister they are reduced to Nine, there being but so many of them, at most, open and officiated in at the same time. Nay in a Morning on Sundays, there is, generally, preaching in but Five of these Nine. It is true there is the Cathedral. Where there is preaching every Friday Morning. But the Quire is very ill contrived for any considerable Auditory, and that Venerable Body have thot fit for a long time to disuse the Sermon House commonly so called tho' a most commodious place for divine Worship, and where on Sundays, Morning

---

54 W. N. Yates, 'The Parochial Library of All Saints, Maidstone, and other Kentish Parochial Libraries', *Archaeologia Cantiana*, xcix (1983), pp. 159–73.

Prayer and preaching might be used without prejudice to the Cathedral Service.

Lewis notes that in Ramsgate people resorted to a Presbyterian meeting house 'not out of principle, but because they have not room in the Church'. At Sandwich not all the three parish churches were in use at the same time. In some towns the benefice income was too small to support an adequate ministry. Lewis proposed that this problem could be solved by annexing the incomes of other benefices, 'when a sine cure, or desolate Church or Six preachers place', to such meagre livings; he proposed the annexation of the rectory of Little Mongeham to the newly established chapel at Deal, the rectory of Ham to the church of St Peter in Sandwich, a Six Preachership to the other two churches in Sandwich, and the church of West Hythe, now desolate, to the chapel at Hythe. In the case of Canterbury, Lewis thought that 'it would be mightily for ye advantage of the people . . . if every prebend had a parish Church annexed to it'.[55]

The reforming zeal of John Lewis was a testimony to the vigorous condition of the Church of England in Kent in the early eighteenth century. Another was the substantial number of gifts, especially of plate, to churches. Between 1690 and 1720 no fewer than 108 churches in Kent, a quarter of the total, received gifts of plate. These totalled 90 patens, 37 flagons, 33 chalices, 28 almsdishes and a spoon. Some churches acquired completely new sets of communion plate: New Romney in 1698, Rolvenden in 1706, St Margaret's at Canterbury in 1708, Goodnestone-next-Wingham in 1710, Hunton in 1714–16 and Detling in 1715.[56] Major improvements were carried out to a number of churches. At Queenborough the roof was painted with clouds, angels and cherubs in about 1695. In 1704 Archbishop Tenison presented Canterbury cathedral with a new throne, probably designed by Nicholas Hawksmoor and certainly carved by Grinling Gibbons, of which only the canopy now survives. At Deal, St Leonard's Church was given a new west gallery by the town's pilots in 1705, and the corporation erected a new chapel in the central part of the town, dedicated to St George, between 1706 and 1716. Crundale acquired a new reredos and altar rails, at the same time as a new chalice and paten, in 1704.[57]

The religious situation in Kent in 1714 was somewhat different from what it had been in 1640. The Church of England, episcopal in government and conservative in doctrine and practice, had survived the major upheavals of the Civil War and interregnum, and the potential threat to its constitution created by the revolution of 1688–9. The Puritan lobby within the church had not been satisfied by the religious settlement of 1662 and a schism had taken place. England after that date was no longer a country in which the established church could cater for the spiritual requirements of the whole population. There had to be a limited toleration for

55 T. Shirley, 'John Lewis of Margate', *Archaeologia Cantiana*, lxiv (1951), pp. 39–56.

56 W. A. Scott Robertson, 'Church Plate in Kent', *Archaeologia Cantiana*, xvi (1886), pp. 404–17.

57 J. Newman, *Buildings of England: North-East and East Kent*, Harmondsworth 1969, pp. 203, 266, 269–70, 404–5.

nonconformity and the more orthodox groups – the Presbyterians, Independents and Baptists – were granted that. Equally however, there was a recognition, after the religious troubles of the 1650s, that complete toleration was not consistent with political stability and that the privileges extended to nonconformity had to be modest and not permitted to include the more radical sects. There was no change to the character of the Church of England as a result of the revolution of 1688–9. The effects of the non-juring schism were limited. In the years that followed some in the Church of England flirted with the non-jurors and the Jacobites, though more frequently for political than religious reasons. This was certainly so in the case of Francis Atterbury, bishop of Rochester from 1713. Atterbury was a high church-man and a Tory who increasingly found himself estranged from the Whigs on the episcopal bench and in government. His injudicious contacts with the agents of James Stuart led to his trial, deprivation and enforced exile in 1723. His biographer has commented:[58]

> Francis Atterbury may be justly described as a tragic figure: one who by defect of vision and a flawed personality hastened the events which he most feared. He came to exercise his undoubted powers of leadership and persuasion at a time when the clergy of the Church of England were faced with a critical choice, and he urged them to agitate for a return to the past.

In a very real way that was the essential difference between the 1660s and 1690s. Whilst it would be simplistic to see the religious settlement of 1662 as a return to the past there was a sense in which during the reign of Charles II the Church of England was marking time. By the 1690s there was a recognition that the church had to move on and even though this did not mean any change of government, doctrine or liturgical practice, a subtle change began to occur in the relationship between church and state at both the national and the local level. Later critics saw the attitude of those they labelled 'Church Whigs' as compromising the independ-ence of the church, and it was partly as a reaction to what they regarded as a unduly cosy relationship with the state that movements arose within the Church of England aimed at re-asserting its missionary and pastoral role. Recent research on the eighteenth century Church of England has, however, questioned the attitudes of such critics and found evidence which clearly contradicts it.[59] That for Kent will be considered in the next chapter.

---

[58] G. V. Bennett, *The Tory Crisis in Church and State 1688–1730*, Oxford 1975, p. 309.

[59] See especially J. Gregory, 'The Eighteenth Century Reformation: The Pastoral Task of Anglican Clergy after 1689', *The Church of England c.1689–c.1833: From Toleration to Tractarianism*, ed. J. Walsh, C. Haydon and S. Taylor, Cambridge 1993, pp. 67–85.

The Anglican Establishment and its Critics 1714–1830

(1) Georgian Churchmanship Reconsidered

The Georgian Church has yet to find its authoritative historians in the way that its Victorian successor has done. Nevertheless enough work has been done to indicate that the traditional view of the Georgian church as corrupt and lethargic requires radical revision.[1] The view that at a senior level the established Church of England was simply an instrument of government, dominated by latitudinarians and rationalists, in which the flame of traditional Anglican high churchmanship was barely a flicker until the revival of the 1830s, and in which Evangelical enthusiasm was vigorously crushed by an unsympathetic episcopate, is at best simplistic and at worst positively misleading. It has been shown in the preceding chapter that Anglican high churchmanship was still very much alive in the first quarter of the eighteenth century, and this remained true throughout the rest of the succeeding century. It is now becoming clear that in the last quarter of the eighteenth century there was a major reform movement in the Church of England which had both a liturgical and a pastoral impact. It also has to be remembered that in the eighteenth century England was part of a wider Protestant community including Calvinist Holland and Scotland and Lutheran Germany and Scandinavia. To a greater or lesser extent these churches were also affected by both rationalism and Evangelicalism; in the latter case the Pietist movement within the Lutheran churches was an important influence on the Methodist movement within the Church of England. Whilst it is true that there was a view that the government could use episcopal appointments as a means of strengthening its majority in the House of Lords, this political use of ecclesiastical preferment was hardly new and parallels could be found throughout Europe. The aristocratic antecedents of many English bishops was parallelled to an even greater extent in France where the majority of the Roman Catholic bishops were members of landed families.[2] The dramatic effect on

---

[1] The title of this section is borrowed from F. C. Mather, 'Georgian Churchmanship Reconsidered', *Journal of Ecclesiastical History*, xxxvi (1985), pp. 255–83. The theological issues affecting the eighteenth century are considered in depth in E. G. Rupp, *Religion in England 1688–791*, Oxford 1986; the political ones in J. C. D. Clark, *English Society 1688–1832*, Cambridge 1985; and the social ones in A. D. Gilbert, *Religion and Society in Industrial England*, London 1976; P. Virgin, *The Church in an Age of Negligence*, Cambridge 1989; and W. R. Ward, *Religion and Society in England 1790–1850*, London 1972. The pioneering work of N. Sykes, *Church and State in England in the Eighteenth Century*, Cambridge 1934, though now outdated, should not be overlooked.

[2] J. McManners, 'Aristocratic Vocations: the Bishops of France in the Eighteenth Century',

the French church of the revolution of 1789 had some impact on the churches in England. There were emigré clergy in Kent at Canterbury, Dover, Lenham and Tunbridge Wells and the Dean and Chapter of Canterbury had given fifty pounds in 1793 towards their support.[3]

The administrative structure of the Church of England remained much as it had been since the Middle Ages. In Kent the two dioceses of Canterbury and Rochester were very unequal in size and that of the latter was reduced by the parishes in the Shoreham peculiar which were under the jurisdiction of the archbishop of Canterbury. This arrangement remained intact until 1845. Episcopal jurisdiction was itself severely constrained by the complicated network of patronage which had grown up haphazardly since the Middle Ages, and been further complicated by the lay acquisition of the rectories appropriated to monasteries before the Dissolution. In Kent, however, rather more patronage was in ecclesiastical hands than in most other parts of the country as is shown in Table 2.[4] The patronage of the archbishop of Canterbury was unique; no other diocesan bishop had as many livings in his own diocese to which he could appoint his own nominees without seeking to influence other patrons.

Table 2

Patronage of Kent Benefices in 1790

Patrons	Canterbury	Rochester	Total	%
Private Patrons	81	65	146	34.8
Archbishop of Canterbury	122	16	138	32.9
Rochester Chapter	12	17	29	6.9
Lord Chancellor	17	10	27	6.4
Canterbury Chapter	20	1	21	5.0
Bishop of Rochester	2	14	16	3.8
Colleges and Schools	9	5	14	3.3
Archdeacon of Canterbury	11	0	11	2.7
Other Chapters	4	2	6	1.5
Miscellaneous	6	5	11	2.7
TOTAL	284	135	419	100.0

Of the patronage vested in colleges and schools, All Souls College at Oxford presented to six livings in Kent, and St John's College at Cambridge to three. The

Studies in Church History, xv (1978), pp. 305–25. See also N. Ravitch, *Sword and Mitre: Government and Episcopacy in France and England in the Age of Aristocracy*, The Hague 1966.
[3] D. A. Bellenger, *The French Exiled Clergy*, Bath 1986, pp. 4, 31.
[4] These statistics are based on the lists of Kent churches, their patrons and incumbents included in the diary of 1790 of the Revd J. E. Gambier, Rector of Langley: CKS, U194 F8/1. These figures differ somewhat from those in Virgin, *op. cit.*, p. 173 who calculates that the archbishop of Canterbury and the bishop of Rochester together presented to 36.0% of the benefices in Kent whilst lay patrons presented to 27.7%.

other chapters presenting to Kent livings were Chichester, St Paul's (2), Westminster (2) and Christ Church, Oxford. It is notable that the dean and chapter of Rochester presented to almost as many livings in Canterbury diocese as they did in that of Rochester. In the miscellaneous category it is significant how few livings were in the gift of the crown, municipal corporations or parish clergy. The crown presented only to Burmarsh, Greenwich and Northfleet; the living of Queenborough was in the gift of the corporation, the rector of Hollingbourne appointed to Bredhurst, the rector of Orpington to Downe and Hayes, and the rector of Wrotham to his own chapelry of Plaxtol. Two livings were in the gift of the inhabitants or parishioners and one in that of the Master of Eastbridge Hospital.

All patrons could be expected to appoint those connected with them. Both Archbishops Moore (1783–1805) and Manners-Sutton (1805–28) appointed friends and relations to valuable livings in their gift.[5] No private patron in Kent held the advowson of more than three livings,[6] but many used their patronage to provide for their relations. Some were clergymen who as owners of the advowson could present themselves. Of the 146 benefices in Kent in the gift of private patrons no fewer than 36 had incumbents in 1790 who were either members of the patron's family or the clergyman patron himself. The clergyman patron of Boughton Aluph and Kenardington had appointed himself to the latter and a relative to the former. David Papillon, who shared the advowson of Bonnington with the Earl of Lauderdale and that of Eythorne with the Earl of Guilford, was able to secure both livings for Philip Papillon in 1784–5.[7]

Pluralism was endemic in the Georgian church but this did not necessarily mean that livings were poorly served. Many pluralists held two or more neighbouring small parishes, residing in one of them and serving the others personally. This was particularly so in East Kent where the majority of country parishes were small. In cases where pluralist incumbents held more than one benefice at such a distance from each other that they could not be served personally they would employ a curate to carry out their duties in one or more of them. Some clergymen who were curates to non-resident incumbents were also themselves incumbents of neighbouring parishes. Some of the prebendaries and minor canons of Canterbury and Rochester cathedrals held parochial preferment in the vicinity or patronage of their respective cathedrals.

The extent of pluralism in the archdeaconry of Canterbury is revealed in the replies to one of Archbishop Manners-Sutton's visitation queries in 1806 where he asks whether clergy held more than one benefice. Not all clergy answered the question but of those 155 that did, just over half served only one benefice and the remainder were pluralists. The details are summarised in Table 3.[8]

5   Virgin, *op. cit.*, p. 91.
6   *Ibid.*, pp. 178–9.
7   CKS, U194 F8/1.
8   Lambeth Palace Library, Archiepiscopal Visitation Queries and Replies, 1806. There are micro-film copies of these and other visitation queries and replies beginning in 1716 at the Centre for

Table 3

Incidence of Pluralism in Canterbury Archdeaconry 1806

Incumbents with one benefice and one church	66 (42.%)
Incumbents with consolidated benefices (includes churches with dependent chapelries)	17 (11.0%)
Incumbents with two neighbouring benefices	14 (9.0%)
Incumbents with two separated benefices in Canterbury archdeaconry	25 (16.1%)
Incumbents with one benefice in Canterbury archdeaconry and one in another diocese	23 (14.8%)
Incumbents with three benefices in Canterbury archdeaconry	5 (3.2%)
Incumbents with three benefices in more than one diocese	5 (3.2%)
TOTAL	155

The difference between incumbents in the second and third categories was largely a technical one, though the latter counted as pluralists, since both personally served two churches within a short distance of each other without any difficulty. It was those in the last four categories, nearly 40% of the total, who were obliged to make arrangements for at least one of their livings to be served by a curate. The incumbent of Boxley was also dean of Rochester; the incumbent of Harrietsham held the fashionable London church of St Mary-le-Strand and the living of Ashow in Warwickshire. A number of incumbents, whilst not technically enjoying another benefice, had other responsibilities; the incumbent of Newenden and Rolvenden was also chaplain of Smallhythe, and the incumbent of Eastry and Worth was both a Six Preacher of Canterbury cathedral and the chaplain of a proprietary chapel at Ramsgate. Some incumbents acted as curates in the parishes of neighbouring incumbents who were non-resident: the incumbents of Denton at Wootton, of Dymchurch at St Mary-in-the-Marsh, of Leysdown at Eastchurch, of Lynsted at Luddenham, and of Ripple at St Margaret's-at-Cliffe. It must not be assumed that it was only relatively small benefices that were held in plurality. The incumbents of some town churches also held other livings: the incumbent of Ashford also held Bilsington, the incumbent of Cranbrook held Appledore and Ebony, and the incumbent of Faversham held Badlesmere and Leaveland.

Although the question was not always framed so precisely as it was in 1806, it is clear that by the early nineteenth century there were fewer livings held in plurality in the archdeaconry of Canterbury than there had been throughout most of the eighteenth century. Non-residence was even more difficult to quantify. Some of it was unavoidable since not all benefices had parsonage houses and incumbents were obliged to find their own accommodation which might have to be in a

Kentish Studies. The incidence of pluralism and non-residence in two other dioceses, Llandaff and Norwich, has been examined by J. R. Guy and W. M. Jacob in two complementary papers in *Studies in Church History*, xvi (1979), pp. 315–33.

neighbouring parish. Out of 94 livings in the archdeaconry of Rochester in the 1730s no fewer than fourteen had no parsonage house.[9]

There is no evidence to suggest that the incidence of pluralism and non-residence had much impact on the frequency of divine worship. Parishes in which divine service might only have been held once each Sunday in the early eighteenth century on account of neighbouring parishes having been held in plurality still only had one Sunday service in the early nineteenth century, even when their incumbent served no other cure, on the grounds that one Sunday service had become the custom over many years. Similarly many clergy blamed the lack of weekday services on the unwillingness of parishioners to attend them. Tables 4–6 summarise the variations of frequency in divine service and the celebration of Holy Communion between the first and last quarters of the eighteenth century in the archdeaconry of Canterbury.[10]

Table 4

Sunday Services in the Churches of
Canterbury Archaeaconry in 1716 and 1786

Churches with:	1716	1786	Both Years
Monthly Services	5	5	1
Fortnightly Services	18	8	3
Once each Sunday	163	156	150
Twice each Sunday	63	82	57
Defective/Missing	4	2	0
TOTAL	253	253	211

As in other parts of the country not all those churches with two Sunday services had preaching at both services, though in the more important town churches two sermons each Sunday was the norm. The overall increase in the number of churches with two Sunday services in the period between 1716 and 1786 is modest but notable, as is the increased provision of services in some of the smallest rural parishes where it had been either monthly or fortnightly in 1716.

Of the ten churches with regular weekday services in both years all were in towns or large villages: four consolidated benefices in Canterbury, Ashford, Cranbrook, Folkestone, Goudhurst, Lenham, Maidstone, New Romney, Staple-hurst and Tenterden. There had been daily services at three of these – Ashford, Cranbrook and Maidstone – in 1716, as well as at Charing, but these had been reduced to the more customary practice of Wednesdays, Fridays and Holy Days by 1786. The churches that had abandoned regular weekday services between 1716

---

[9] CKS, DRa/Ve 1–3.

[10] Lambeth Palace Library, Archiepiscopal Visitation Queries and Replies, 1716 and 1786. For comparative statistics for other dioceses see Mather, *loc. cit.*, and W. N. Yates, *Buildings, Faith and Worship*, Oxford 1991, pp. 55–64.

Table 5

Weekday Services in the Churches of
Canterbury Archdeaconry in 1716 and 1786

Churches with:	1716	1786	Both Years
No Weekday Services	210	206	184
Occasional Weekday Services	22	29	7
Regularly Weekday Services	13	16	10
Daily Services	4	0	0
Defective/Missing	4	2	0
TOTAL	253	253	201

and 1786, in addition to Charing, were Loose, St John-in-Thanet and Sitting-bourne. In 1786 there were regular weekday services at St Lawrence-in-Thanet and at two churches for which no return for 1716 survives, St George's Chapel at Deal and Faversham. Where weekday services were occasional this usually meant the observance of some holy days and the penitential seasons, especially Lent. Much depended on the ability to attract a congregation and this may explain why so few churches appear in this category in both 1716 and 1786: these were the churches of two small towns – Lydd and Queenborough – and four large villages – Borden, Boxley, Ospringe and Sutton Valence; there was an arrangement at Sandwich whereby the incumbents of the town's three parish churches took it in turn to take the occasional weekday services in St Peter's church, the most centrally located of the three.

Table 6

Holy Communion in the Churches of
Canterbury Archdeaconry in 1716 and 1786

Churches with:	1716	1786	Both Years
HC at Major Festivals	61	4	2
Quarterly Communion	168	220	155
Monthly Communion	19	21	14
No Communion Services	1	2	0
Defective/Missing	4	6	0
TOTAL	253	253	171

It would seem that there had been a concerted campaign between 1716 and 1786 to ensure that incumbents provided an additional communion service between Whitsun and Christmas and this was usually celebrated on the Sunday nearest to Michaelmas. Although still counting as quarterly communion, a number of the larger parishes had more than one communion service at the major festivals, usually on Good Friday or Low Sunday, Trinity Sunday and the Sunday after Christmas. Some parishes with monthly communion had additional celebrations at the major festivals as well. At Cranbrook in 1716 there were celebrations on the first Sunday of each month and on Christmas Day, Good Friday, Easter Day, Ascension Day and Whit Sunday. At Dover in 1786 there were celebrations in St Mary's church on the first Sunday of each month and on Christmas Day, the Sunday after Christmas, Good Friday, Easter Day, Low Sunday, Whit Sunday and Trinity Sunday. The best provision of all was at Deal in 1806 where the sacrament was celebrated on the first Sunday of each month in the parish church, on the third Sunday of each month at St George's Chapel, and at both on the three major festivals. Of the fourteen churches with monthly celebrations in both 1716 and 1786 all apart from Boxley were in towns or large villages: three consolidated benefices in Canterbury, Ashford, Cranbrook, St Leonard's in Deal, Goudhurst, Maidstone, St John-in-Thanet, St Peter-in-Thanet, Tenterden and Wye; at Sandwich the sacrament was celebrated at one of the town's three parish churches at least once a month on a similar co-operative basis as that in the case of the weekday services. Churches with monthly communion in 1716, which later abandoned the practice, were one additional consolidated benefice in Canterbury, Folkestone, Hothfield, Linton and Loose. Churches which had introduced monthly communion by 1786 were the small rural parish of Bicknor, St Mary's at Dover, the combined benefice of Leeds and Broomfield, Minster-in-Thanet and St Lawrence-in-Thanet; to these can be added St George's Chapel at Deal and Faversham for both of which there is no surviving 1716 return.

Rural parishes with monthly communion or weekday services do not generally seem to have maintained them for long periods. By 1806 only Bicknor and Goudhurst still had monthly communion. The churches with both monthly communion and regular weekday services were all to be found in the towns: Ashford, Cranbrook, St George's at Deal, St Mary's at Dover, Maidstone, Margate, Ramsgate and Sandwich. What emerges from all this evidence is, with the exception of the additional celebration at Michaelmas, that of a remarkably constant picture of religious worship in the Canterbury archdeaconry over a long period. In more than 80% of the churches both Sunday or weekday services remained the same and in nearly 70% there was no change in the frequency of communion services. The prevailing patterns in what was a predominantly rural archdeaconry was one Sunday service, quarterly communion and no other public religious observances. It was a pattern not inconsistent with the national one and that went also for the character of the services: long and solemn with morning service probably averaging about 105 minutes, and the afternoon one about 85 minutes, if a sermon was included. The sermon was usually omitted when the sacrament was celebrated as part of the morning service. Most churches had some form of musical accompaniment for the singing of the psalms and canticles, and sometimes more ambitious settings of scripture sentences, either an organ or a small orchestra. The surviving music books for Kemsing and Trottiscliffe show that the standard of music in at least two country churches was quite high.[11] At Kenardington in 1773 a

11 CKS, P 205/1/8 and P 373/28/1–2. For a more detailed analysis see Yates, op. cit., pp. 64–5.

group of nine men, later increased to sixteen, contracted to provide singing for church services:[12]

> As it is the Duty of all Christens to joyne in that Great and Christen part of our Duty to Sing our Lord and Makers Praise in that Glorious part of Psalm Singing we whoes names are heere set do agree to meet every Sunday in the Even at five of the clock and whosoever is not there to answer to their name by seven that same even shall be farfet the sum of 2d for the benfet of the Company.

Later that year 'ann agreement made for the company of Psalm singers in Kennard-ington' stated:[13]

> We do agree to forfitt two pence on all Sundays for not being at Church in Divine Sarvis time to joyne to sing the praise an glory of God and to meet on Sunday Evening at Six O'Clock or forfitt one penny and to meet on all Thursday Evenings at Six O'Clock or forfitt one penny for each neglect of not being there at the time the Money to be gathered by one whom the Company apoint for that purpus and ye furfitt money to be spent on Jan ye 1st 1774 at a place apointed by the Company.

By the beginning of the nineteenth century, under the influence of the Evangelicals, some attempt was made to introduce a greater variation in the musical part of the service by the singing of hymns. This was resisted by some clergy on the grounds that it lacked authority. The curate of Wateringbury noted that at Christmas 1826 'the singers sang one Hymn for the Day, but not the one attached to the New Version of the Psalms. I am determined from this time to refuse the singing any Hymns or Psalms which are not in the authorized versions, the Old and New Versions. I conceive I might as well read a Psalm not in the Prayer Book, as they sing one not authorized by the Head of our Church.'[14]

For the average country clergyman of the eighteenth and early nineteenth centuries the sacramental and ministerial functions of his office were far less demanding than they later became as the expectations of the church in general, clergy and laity, rose after 1850. However, another factor in the very different perception of the role of the clergymen lay in the nature of his income. The clergyman was not, unless he was an unbeneficed curate, paid a fixed stipend. His income was likely to be made up from a number of different sources the most important of which were the profits of his glebe and the receipt of tithes. Other sources of income such as surplice fees, pew rents or special endowments usually formed a very small part of the income of a rural incumbent. In the towns income from sources less dependent on agriculture were much greater and frequently more reliable. The rural incumbent probably depended for his livelihood on his skill as a farmer. At Langley the

---

[12] CKS, P 206/7/2.
[13] CKS, P 206/7/3.
[14] CKS, P 385/1/3.

glebe comprised two pieces of land of about ten acres each on either side of the
turnpike road from Maidstone to Tenterden, one of which contained the rectory
house, barn, outhouse and stables.[15] The rectory house itself was a modest building, built in 1767, on two levels at the front and three at the back. A plan of the
interior in 1793 shows on the ground floor a parlour, study, kitchen, back kitchen
with oven and a water closet; on the upper floor were two principal bedrooms
separated by a dressing room, one further bedroom and the nursery; at the back of
the house the middle floor had a room labelled 'old study' and one room each for a
manservant and maidservant.[16] Mark Noble, who became rector of Barming in
1786, has left a valuable description of how he was able to increase the income
from his glebe:[17]

> The church land, so valuable as part of the rectory, I allotted partly for my own
> use, and the rest I let . . . What I keep is about 65 acres of land. It was quite as
> much as my capital could cultivate to the best advantage. It was the best
> ground and nearest the house. The improvements I have made have been
> obvious even to envy, especially in planting hops, fruit and wood for hop poles.

Not all clergy were able to turn their glebe to their best financial advantage by their
ability to invest properly at the outset. Nevertheless, in general, clerical incomes
seem to have risen during the eighteenth and early nineteenth centuries. Kent was a
prosperous county and the average value of its ecclesiastical benefices reflected
this; the median value of Kent benefices, as reported to Parliament in 1835, was
£257 per annum, compared with £102 in Cumberland and Westmorland.[18]
     It was the question of tithes that was likely to produce the greatest potential
conflict between an incumbent and his parishioners. Tithe, or a tenth part, was
payable on corn and other grain, hay, pasturage, wood, hops, roots and garden
vegetables, fruit, cattle, pigs, lambs and wool, milk and cheese, deer, poultry, bees,
mills and fisheries. To some extent the practical implications were regulated by
custom, but the law was enormously complicated[19] and disputes frequent. In order
to free themselves from both disputes and from the difficulties of collection many
clergy attempted to convert payment in kind to a monetary composition. Kent,
however, was one of the counties in which such change was resisted and even at the
end of the eighteenth century five out of every eight parishes still tithed in kind.[20]
Mark Noble, rector of Barming from 1786 until 1827, 'began to think of having
something like a compensation for tythe . . . taken in kind' but could make no
progress. One of the objectors 'struck me in my canonicals one Sunday as I was
going to church, because I complained of his sheep trespassing in the churchyard. . . The blow was so unexpected that one of my hands was still in my cassock

15 CKS, U194 Q5.
16 CKS, U194 Q8.
17 CKS, TR 1884/1, p. 102.
18 Virgin, op. cit., p. 145.
19 See R. Burn, Ecclesiastical Law, 4th edn, London 1781, pp. 373–521.
20 E. J. Evans, The Contentious Tithe, London 1976, p. 21.

pocket. I would not return the violence, but my whole conduct shewed him he could not make me fear him.'[21] Objections to paying tithes led farmers to under-cultivate. At Marden 'they prefer letting their lands be ill cultivated to the permitting the tithe owner to profit by a better mode of culture'. At Hawkhurst farmers were accused of 'laying down to pasture land well adapted to the growth of hops and corn'.[22] At Sevenoaks the rector, Thomas Sackville Curteis, had to compromise in his attempts to obtain what he regarded was due to him in tithes from the Duchess of Dorset, who declined to pay for the deer in her park.[23]

The clergy were sometimes obliged either to abandon what they regarded as legitimate income due to them by law and to settle for what they could get either in kind or in an unfavourable cash conversion or to face years of struggle and violence. Some clergy encouraged their brethren to stand firm. J. E. Gambier, rector of Langley, argued in 1790 that composition must be fair:[24]

Farmers are frequently desirous of substituting the tenth part of their *profits* instead of the tenth part of their *produce*. But by what right such a substitution is made is hard to discover. . . If therefore the farmers desire that the clergyman should not take them in kind, they are bound in equity to give him all the information which may be necessary to enable him to form a just idea of their worth. For no man can fairly be required to make a contract about a thing of which he does not know the value, and it is inconsistent with justice to take advantage of the ignorance of the persons with whom we deal, especially if, as in the present case, information can be obtained from nobody but ourselves.

Opponents of tithes, however, were keen to point out that their opposition was not an attack on the clergy, and that if tithes were to be abolished, alternative means of supporting them had to be found. Lena Tadman, a Kentish farmer stated:[25]

My opinion is, that unless we keep in view the support of religion, church and clergy, we shall do harm instead of good, by making any alteration in the tithe laws. . . Our established church, religion and ministry must be liberally supported, or England herself must fall which God forbid.

By the second quarter of the nineteenth century the pressure for the abolition of tithes had become unstoppable. It was a major element in the Swing Riots of 1830–1 when alliances were formed between farmers and labourers to bring pressure on the clergy to reduce their tithe demands. At Goudhurst the farmers told their labourers they could only expect increased wages if tithes were abolished. A petition of landowners in the Rochester diocese to the House of Commons in 1830 demanded 'an early abolition of the Tithe Tax, a measure which would give more

---

[21] CKS, TR 1884/1, pp. 103–5.
[22] Evans, *op. cit.*, p. 71.
[23] W. N. Yates, 'A Kentish Clerical Dynasty: Curteis of Sevenoaks', *Archaeologia Cantiana*, cviii (1990), p. 6.
[24] CKS, U194 F12/1.
[25] Evans, *op. cit.*, p. 78.

satisfaction to the Country and reflect greater credit on the Legislature than any enactment that has been carried for centuries past'. George Gunning of Frindsbury expressed the view that the tithe system 'checks improvement, paralyses industry, promotes pauperism and tends to destroy the virtuous spirit and meritorious exertion of the labouring poor. The petitioner is firmly persuaded that by fixing a percentage on real rents in lieu of tithes, that it will soon decrease vagrancy, lessen crime and promote the happiness of all classes of society'. Well attended meetings at Rochester and Penenden Heath passed resolutions calling for the abolition of tithes.[26] The matter was finally resolved to the general satisfaction of both clergy and farmers by the Tithe Commutation Act of 1836 which imposed a money payment fixed on the average price over seven years of wheat, barley and oats to equate to not more than 75% nor less than 60% of the gross value of tithe, and exempted from any future payment subsequent improvements in the cultivation of the land.[27]

Victorian critics of the Georgian church were scathing in their comments on the conditions in which churches had been kept, but there is little contemporary evidence to support their views, and even when there is action was usually taken to remedy it at the time.[28] At Barming, Mark Noble, who became rector in 1786, noted:[29]

> When I came into possession nothing could be more out of repair, all was in seeming ruin and dirtiness. Having entirely repaired the chancel giving an altar piece, table, rails, press for the surplice as well as a pulpit cloth, cushion and painted the pulpit and reading desk as well as all within the chancel . . . yet still the body of the church remained in great disorder until 1800 when the belfry was parted off from the church, the seats entirely repaired, lined and painted and now few country churches can vie with Barming for elegance and neatness. I gave a new communion table being a marble slab in a mahogany frame. I mean to place some painted glass given me from several churches, but chiefly Otham, in the slip windows at the east end of the chancel. The pleasure I have had in making the sacred edifice a fit house of prayer and procuring the parish to second my efforts is more than a little. When I came to Barming the church was indecently neglected, the walls and other fences of the cemetery were equally ruinous.

In 1732–4 Archdeacon Denne of Rochester carried out a visitation of the churches in his archdeaconry. The replies to his queries bound in three volumes covering the three rural deaneries of Dartford, Malling and Rochester, provide a detailed record of the condition of 94 churches in West Kent.[30] Denne's charge and the queries attached to it cover the fabric, furniture, books, vestments, utensils, ornaments, churchyard and parsonage house. He wanted to know whether the fabric was in

26 *Ibid.*, pp. 81–2, 120.
27 W. O. Chadwick, *The Victorian Church*, London 1966–70, i, p. 142.
28 See Yates, *Buildings, Faith and Worship*, pp. 48–55.
29 CKS, TR 1884/1, pp. 33–4.
30 CKS, DRa/Ve 1–3.

good repair, whether the churchyard was well maintained, and whether there were any defects in the parsonage house or its outbuildings. The standard requirements that a church was expected to possess were laid down for the other items. In the case of furniture this meant seats in repair, pulpit, reading desk, a stone font and cover, communion table and rails, bier, and separate chests for alms and for the parish registers and records. Books required were prayer books for the reading desk and communion table, a bible, Book of Homilies, parchment register, strange preachers' book and a table of prohibited degrees within which marriage could not be solemnised. Specified vestments were a surplice, hood, pulpit cushion, hearse cloth, altar carpet, linen cloth and napkin to cover the sacred elements at Holy Communion. Parishes were expected to provide, in the way of utensils a chalice, paten, flagon and alms dish. Books, vestments and utensils were expected to be listed in an inventory which is in most cases incorporated with the returns. The ornaments required were the Ten Commandments, Creed and Lord's Prayer and other suitable sentences from scripture, to be placed on walls that were otherwise plastered and whitewashed.

The replies to the queries revealed that, though there were few churches in the archdeaconry that were in a serious state of neglect, even fewer could meet the stringent requirements of the archdeacon and were obliged to make good defects within a specified time. The evidence is summarised in Table 7.

Table 7

Condition of Fabric and Fittings in the
Churches of Rochester Archdeaconry 1732–4

Deanery of	Dartford	Malling	Rochester	Total	%
Defects in fabric	23	33	32	88	93.6
Defects in furniture	24	32	33	89	94.7
Defects in books	26	33	34	93	98.9
Defects in vestments	21	33	34	88	93.6
Defects in utensils	6	14	15	35	37.2
Defects in ornaments	18	29	31	78	83.0
Defects in churchyards	25	30	33	88	93.6
Defects in parsonages	9	18	21	48	60.0*
Defects in all categories	3	6	12	21	22.3
Total number of churches	26	34	34	94	100.0
Without parsonages	4	3	7	14	14.9

* This figure is expressed as a percentage of the total number (80) of parsonages.

Some of these defects were comparatively minor. The main defects in the provision of books was the absence of strange preachers' books and tables of the prohibited degrees. Many churches did not possess a hearse cloth and were thus defective in the provision of vestments. The surviving inventories, however, record that some parishes made provision for their churches in excess of those required by law. At Beckenham there were 'benches to kneel at the Communion table scarlet plush, purchased by the Rector with £17 10s given by late Lady Elwil to that use'. At Bromley there were both green and black carpets for the altar. At Greenwich there was 'a very good organ', pictures of Elizabeth I and Charles I, the latter in an attitude of prayer, a silver server for the communion bread and a gilt spoon for the wine. At Woolwich the inventory lists a spoon or strainer for the communion wine and two brass candlesticks for the altar complete with snuffers. There were two altar carpets at West Peckham and at Shorne the inventory notes one old altar carpet and 'one new ditto made of superfine purple cloth with gold fringe bought in the year 1735 . . . one new gilt folio Church Prayer Book given by the vicar for the communion table in 1735', a silver salver bought in 1735 and copies of Bishop Jewel's *Apologia Ecclesiae Anglicanae* and Erasmus' *Paraphrase on the Gospels and Acts of the Apostles*. At the other extreme, order was given at Cooling to keep the church 'free from ye defilement of birds'. At Tudeley the seats were 'in bad condition'. At Plumstead there was a requirement to repair the painting in the chancel 'where it is soyled'. There was no parsonage house at All Hallows, Hoo, since it had been burned down many years ago.

The role of the clergy in the life of the community in the eighteenth and early nineteenth centuries is well documented. Very much less is known about the involvement of the laity in the life of the church. An exception is at Barming, where the rector, Mark Noble, provided interesting details about his parishioners in registering their burials between 1788 and 1812.[31] There were clearly a high number of parishioners who absented themselves from worship. Henry Smith 'was an industrious, civil man but I never saw him at church except once at a baptism'. William Bridgland was 'blasphemous, lewd, drunken, dishonest, a cruel husband and a severe parent. I never saw him at church more than once or twice'. William Brook 'had used to very regularly come to church on Sundays but latterly giving himself up entirely to drunkeness he omitted this and all others his duties'. James Brook 'never came to church for a great number of years; the only excuse he could urge was deafness'. Mary Tanner 'since I have had the rectory . . . has never been at church till she was taken for interment'. Thomas Matthew, the horse doctor and cow leech, 'for 16 years or perhaps more' had not been seen 'attending divine service'. Others were more faithful. Ann Streeter 'was constant at church'. Rebecca Barns, who died in childbirth, 'regularly attended divine service on the Sundays'. Thomas Latter was 'a constant church attendant, honest, sober, industrious and civil'. Catherine Marshall 'came to church as often as lameness permitted'. John Soman was 'constant in his duty in the church and in the chancel. Happy if there were many such'. John Marshall 'was one of the very few of the poor who not only came regularly to church on Sundays but staid to receive the Holy Sacrament of the Lord's Supper'. Perhaps the most interesting entry is that for John Selby:

---

[31] CKS, P 16/1/4.

He was always kind to the poore, took great pains to have his children instructed in the principles of the Christian religion, brought them regularly to church, and the older ones to the Altar, yet so inconsistent is the human character, that this man was an habitual drunk and, addicted to swearing, nor did he pay any regard to truth in speaking of every person whom he knew, and was constantly formenting quarrels between neighbours.

If Noble is to be believed, and if his parish was typical, the levels of drunkenness among all classes, and sexual incontinence among the younger members of the poorer classes, was considerable, and the majority of these absented themselves from worship.

The tone of much preaching was highly moralistic. For a church that officially adhered in its doctrinal formularies to belief in justification by faith alone there was an enormous emphasis in eighteenth century sermons and practical handbooks on the value of good works.[32] In the view of George Carr (1705–76), minister at the Episcopal Chapel in Edinburgh, 'if we look up to the Supreme Being, we shall find, that nothing can be more acceptable to him, or make us approach nearer his nature, or render us more the objects of favour, than works of beneficence and mercy'.[33] In another sermon he expands on this theme:[34]

Moral duties seem to be held in small estimation by some persons, who consider them as of the lowest importance in religion, and as fitter subjects of instruction from a heathen philosopher, than from a disciple of the gospel of Christ. But such opinions have no foundation in reason or scripture; for we have seen, that they both agree in representing the moral duties, as what God chiefly values and requires, and what therefore ought principally to be taught and inculcated.

The results of such teaching and understanding are to be seen in the works of piety carried out between the late seventeenth and early nineteenth centuries, frequently commemorated in churches in the boards containing lists of benefactions. The extent of parochial charities is impressive. In Kent, excluding the hundred of Blackheath which was rapidly becoming a suburb of London, towards the end of the eighteenth century only 127 out of 405 parishes, and these mostly very small, had no parochial charities. The remaining 278 parishes had a total of 980 charities, a detailed breakdown of which is given in Table 8.[35]

[32] See F. Deconinck-Brossard, 'Eighteenth Century Sermons and the Age', *Crown and Mitre: Religion and Society in Northern Europe since the Reformation*, ed. W. M. Jacob and W. N. Yates, Woodbridge 1993, pp. 105–21.

[33] G. Carr, *Sermons*, Edinburgh 1778, i, p. 382.

[34] *Ibid.*, ii, pp. 80–1.

[35] *Abstract of the Returns of Charitable Donations in 1786–1788*, London 1816, pp. 519–66. See also D. Valenze, 'Charity, Custom and Humanity: Changing Attitudes towards the Poor in Eighteenth Century England', *Revival and Religion since 1700*, ed. J. Garnett and C. Matthew, London 1993, pp. 59–78.

Table 8

Charitable Bequests to Kent Parishes 1786–8

Type of Charity	No. of Parishes	% of Parishes with Charities	% of Total No. of Parishes
Monetary relief of poverty	237	85.3	58.5
Provision of food	80	28.8	19.8
Educational provision	75	27.0	18.5
Provision of clothing	50	18.0	12.3
Provision of accommodation	43	15.5	10.6
Provision of apprenticeships	31	11.2	7.7
Provision of fuel	9	3.2	2.2
Sermon endowments	6	2.2	1.5
Provision for church repair	3	1.1	0.7
Other charities	7	2.5	1.7

There were a total of 41 separate charities in Dover, 32 in Canterbury, 23 in Faversham, 21 in Dartford and 20 in Bexley. Among the more unusual charities were ones for the relief of prisoners, soldiers and sailors, and plague victims; for the support of the workhouse; for the support of a curate or a parish clerk; and for the purchase of prayer books. Although a few charities were of medieval origin, the bulk had been established in the seventeenth and eighteenth centuries.

Recent research has indicated that in the last quarter of the eighteenth century there seems to have been a period of intense episcopal and pastoral activity in the Church of England, which in turn stimulated in the first three decades of the nineteenth century a period of liturgical renewal which had a considerable impact on the re-ordering of church buildings.[36] Some concern was expressed about the impact of the French revolution on both political and religious stability. William Jones, appointed to the rectory of Pluckley in 1765, and letter beneficed at Nayland in Suffolk, and indeed known as Jones of Nayland, preached in Canterbury cathedral on Friday 20 September 1789 a sermon, later published,[37] in which his congregation was invited to 'behold the sad condition of that kingdom [of France] which was once the haughty rival of our greatness'. Jones later helped to found a Society for the Reformation of Principles, designed to counteract the influence of the French Revolution. The revolution was a distraction, despite the fears it induced in high churchman like Jones of Nayland, from the reform movement within the Church of England, the chief protagonists of which in Kent were

[36] Yates, *Buildings, Faith and Worship*, pp. 108–23.
[37] W. Jones, *Popular Commotions Considered as Signs of the Approaching End of the World*, London 1789.

the dean of Canterbury and later bishop of Norwich, George Horne, and the bishop of Rochester, Samuel Horsley.

George Horne was born at Otham, near Maidstone, in 1730. Elected to a fellowship of Magdalen College, Oxford, in 1750, he became President of the college in 1768 and vice-chancellor of the university in 1776. In 1781 he was appointed to the deanery of Canterbury, resigning it on his consecration as bishop of Norwich in 1790. His tenure of that see, however, was shortlived as he died in 1792. Horne had a considerable reputation as a preacher and his published sermons give a clear insight into the priorities of the Anglican reform movement of the late eighteenth century. In 1784, at the opening of the new cathedral organ in Canterbury, he defended the choral services of the Church of England,[38] and he was also a strong supporter of the role of the clergy, and of the cathedrals in particular, in the provision of education:[39]

> The pleasures of wisdom exceed all others, in kind, degree, and duration, far as heaven is higher than earth. . . A studious disposition makes those who are blessed with it valuable, good and happy. It enables them to find a paradise in solitude, and profitably, as well as agreeably, to fill up the intervals of business. It renders them little sensible to the allurements of external objects, to those trifles and improprieties which disgrace other men, and degrade the Christian. The ill instructed and unemployed are the persons whose imagination is always wandering and afloat. For want of solid nourishment, their curiosity and their appetites turn to objects either vain, or dangerous; and hence proceed on those inventions for squandering away thought and time, which generally end in a forgetfulness of God and ourselves.

Horne's major initiative as dean of Canterbury was his encouragement of Sunday schools as an extension of the practice of catechizing which bishops had encouraged and clergy had implemented since the late seventeenth century. He preached in support of them at St Alphege's, Canterbury on Sunday 18 December 1785:[40]

> By a Sunday school a number of children are kept out of harm's way; they are collected together, and inured to early and regular habits of attendance on God's worship; they are instructed in what is right; they are enabled to employ well their leisure hours, when they grow up; and teach others after them to do

---

[38] G. Horne, *The Antiquity, Use and Excellence of Church Music*, Oxford 1784.

[39] *Id., The Character of True Wisdom, and the Means of Attaining It*, Oxford 1784.

[40] *Id., Sunday Schools Recommended*, Oxford 1786. For the general development of Sunday schools see T. W. Laqueur, *Religion and Respectability*, New Haven and London 1976. Although Lacqueur (pp. 5, 31) recognises the importance of Horne as an early advocate of Sunday schools he wrongly classifies him as an Evangelical in the mistaken belief that only Evangelicals supported Sunday schools. See also J. Gregory, 'The Eighteenth Century Reformation: The Pastoral Task of Anglican Clergy after 1689', *The Church of England c.1689–c.1833: From Toleration to Tractarianism*, ed. J. Walsh, C. Haydon and S. Taylor, Cambridge 1993, pp. 71–5, 77–9.

the same. . . . It is hard to conceive a scheme which promises more benefits to the community. And wherever it has been tried, the expectation has been answered.

In the published version of his sermon, Horne gave examples of a number of Kent parishes that had experimented with Sunday schools. They included two of the united benefices in Canterbury, Boughton-under-Blean and Wye. At Boughton 'a number of children from 7 to 14 years of age, attend regularly at church and school, many of whom (it was to be feared) from the ignorance and ill example of their parents, would never have been seen within the walls of the former perhaps their life through'. At Wye the Sunday school started on 4 September 1785 with 104 children. As at Boughton children were admitted between the ages of seven and fourteen. School began an hour before the morning service, an hour before the afternoon service and continued for two hours after the latter. The incumbent of Boughton noted that 'many parents of poor children, who themselves were never in the habit of going to church (nor can be persuaded to it) and who set evil examples in every shape to their children, are yet very desirous of having those children partake of the advantages of these schools'.

Samuel Horsley was successively bishop of St Davids 1788–93, of Rochester 1793–1802, and of St Asaph 1802–6. He was an energetic and reforming bishop in all three dioceses. He was keen to discourage non-residence as a means of enabling the parish clergyman 'to exhibit in his own deportment, and in the good order of his family, the example of a godly and religious life . . . and by the means of reconciliation offered in the sacraments of the church – to assist the penitent in making his peace with God'.[41] As bishop of Rochester, which was apart from Bristol by far the poorest of the English bishoprics, Horsley was, like his immediate predecessors and successors, obliged to combine the see with another preferment, in Horsley's case, as with most, the deanery of Westminster. Horsley's bishopric was worth only £600 *per annum*, his deanery £900. Like other bishops Horsley was obliged to spend the winter in London in order to participate in the business of the House of Lords, which he could combine with deanery business without undue difficulty. The deanery also gave Horsley the benefit of a house in London, which he would otherwise have had to maintain out of the income of his see. Diocesan business had to be crammed into the summer months and this could be very difficult when dioceses were extensive. Fortunately Rochester was the smallest diocese in the provinces of Canterbury and York, apart from Sodor and Man, and had the added advantage of not being too far distant from London. The livings of the diocese were well above average value for England and Wales as a whole with only two benefices having a population of more than 500 being worth less than £150. In his 1796 charge Horsley dwelt primarily on the neglect of parochial duty which ought to have been minimal in a diocese with such comparatively wealthy livings. He was prepared to exempt from residence clergy who were scholars or who held distinguished office in the church provided there was a

---

[41] F. C. Mather, *High Church Prophet*, Oxford 1992, p. 149.

resident curate. At his second visitation in 1800 Horsley concentrated his efforts on attempting to procure a more decent observance of confirmation, then administered to large numbers of people at convenient area centres, and frequently accompanied by riotous behaviour. He adopted the practice of other bishops in issuing a printed circular to the clergy instructing them on how to prepare candidates for confirmation. They were to be at least fourteen years old; must have been taught to say the Lord's Prayer, Apostles Creed and Ten Commandments; were expected to be familiar with the catechism and to have been instructed on the significance of the rite they were about to undergo 'in private conferences as well as in public discourses from the pulpit'. Only those who attended confirmation services with a ticket of recommendation from their clergyman would be confirmed. His biographer has noted that, although Horsley is known to have had reservations about the value of Sunday schools, he was clearly encouraging his clergy to introduce confirmation classes.[42] The effect of Horsley's reforms were to be seen in later years, for example in the curate of Wateringbury's description of a confirmation by Horsley's successor but one, Walker King:[43]

On Saturday the 13th of May 1826, the day before Whitsunday, the Bp. of Rochester himself confirmed at Malling. It was only a confirmation. There was no sermon after but an address before conf: which the Bp's chaplain read out of a pew in which the Bishop was. Prayers were first read by Mr Bates. The Bp. laid his hands upon four at a time by joining two heads together, and laying one of his hands upon two heads. There were ninety and seven confirmed out of this parish. We were ordered to be at Malling by 10. When the church was filled, the Bp. came in about 11 and service began. The girls filled the church 1st and were confirmed 1st. The church was filled twice. The question therefore was put from the Altar twice and 'I do' twice repeated. We had three weeks notice of the Confirmation. I distributed here, the 'Order of Confirmation', 'Nelson's Instructions for Confirmation' and Abp. Secker's Sermon on Confirmation, and gave them each a ticket with 'Examined for Confirmation and approved' written on it with my signature. All of which tickets were required in the church. The Bps Chaplain, viz. one of his sons, officiated within the Altar rails in a surplice and hood.

Samuel Horsley represented a distinct variety of Anglican high churchmanship, manifesting 'a stiffness with regard to rubrics, articles of belief, canons, and statutes, and even an adherence to ancient ceremonies like bowing to the altar'[44] which was as strong in the 1820s as it had been a century before, deeply conservative but at the same time recognising the need for the reform of abuses and anxious to promote the highest standards of pastoral care by the clergy for the laity.

[42] *Ibid.*, pp. 177–82.
[43] CKS, P 385/1/3.
[44] Mather, *op. cit.*, pp. 304–5.

(2) Challenges to the Establishment

The pattern of nonconformity in Kent that had emerged by the latter quarter of the seventeenth century changed little if at all over the next hundred years. Most of the chapels of Baptists, Independents and Presbyterians were in the towns:[45]

> In the rural parts of Kent, only the traditional Puritan areas around Tenterden, Cranbrook and Maidstone showed any very marked propensity to Dissent. . . Elsewhere in the shire Dissenters were thinner on the ground than in almost any other part of England. . . There can be little doubt in fact that the weakness of rural Nonconformity in much of Kent was due to the remarkable strength of the old squirearchy of the county in these downland and chartland areas. Honywoods and Derings, Tokes and Twysdens, Oxindens and Knatchbulls, Streatfeilds and Robertses, Austens, Gibbons and Polhills: these and many similar Kentish dynasties still extended in the first half of the nineteenth century the same aristocratic influence as in the days of Charles I. . . Wherever they predominated Nonconformists rarely numbered more than a quarter of the village population, and in most parishes where were few or none.

As in other parts of England a distinction can be drawn in Kent between parishes with a single major landowner and those in which landownership was divided into a number of smaller estates. The Church of England was comparatively weaker in the latter than the former and nonconformity comparatively stronger. In 86% of the parishes in Kent with a single major landowner there was no dissenting place of worship of any kind, whereas in parishes with more than one landowner 70% had at least one dissenting chapel, and 17% more than one.[46] The total number of members of the historic dissenting sects in Kent was very small. An estimate of their numbers in 1715–18 suggests that the Presbyterians were the most numerous with between 2% and 3% of the population; the General Baptists had between 1% and 2%, the Particular Baptists between 0.5% and 1%, and the Independents and Quakers less than 0.5%.[47]

Despite the smallness of their numbers there is some evidence to suggest that what came in due time to be known as 'Old Dissent' was already in decline by the early eighteenth century. By 1720 the Kent and Sussex General Baptist Association found itself unable to support the Baptist mission to Virginia either financially or with new recruits. A further threat to nonconformist numbers later in the eighteenth century came from the election of chapel members to municipal office. In order to achieve this they were obliged to take the sacrament in the Church of England, and some seceded permanently. The Presbyterian congregation at Dover was considerably weakened by the secession of those elected to the municipality to the Church of England.[48] The main threat, however, to nonconformist

---

[45] A. M. Everitt, *The Pattern of Rural Dissent*, Leicester 1972, pp. 57–61.

[46] *Ibid.*, p. 21. See the useful comparable evidence in J. Obelkevitch, *Religion and Rural Society: South Lindsey 1825–1875*, Oxford 1976, especially pp. 8–14.

[47] M. R. Watts, *The Dissenters*, Oxford 1978, pp. 272–6.

[48] *Ibid.*, pp. 385, 389, 485.

congregations came from rationalist theological opinions, which had an impact on all the Protestant churches of Northern Europe, and were widely propagated in Britain.[49] Chief among them were two forms of anti-Trinitarianism, Arianism and Socinianism. Those who subscribed to Arianism 'acknowledged the pre-existence of Christ, looked upon him as in some sense divine, and retained the concept of the atonement, the more radical Socinians denied both the divinity and the pre-existence of Christ and rejected the doctrine of vicarious atonement'.[50] From the first quarter of the eighteenth century an increasing number of Presbyterian ministers adopted Unitarian views and were able to carry the majority of their congregations with them. The minority who seceded usually either joined the Independents, who were less influenced by Unitarianism, or, where this was not possible, set up their own Independent congregations. This happened at Maidstone in 1745 and Sandwich in 1798.[51] The schism amongst the Presbyterians caused alarm bells to ring in the Church of England, fearful that some of its more liberal divines were veering in the same direction. George Horne, dean of Canterbury, preached a strongly anti-Socinian sermon at the primary visitation of Archbishop Moore in 1786, repeating much of the substance of an earlier sermon delivered on the previous Trinity Sunday entitled 'the Trinity in Unity':[52]

> Our opponents are shrewd, active, busy, bustling, and indefatigable. They regard toleration not as leave only to exercise their own religion unmolested, but as a door opened to unlimited free enquiry, or, in other words, a free permission to attack the church in every possible way... They inform us, that the nation abounds with Socinians, at present concealed, but ready, on a proper occasion, to declare... The Church of England, from the time of the Reformation, has gloried in a learned clergy, who stood prepared to repel, with skill and vigour, the advances of her various adversaries... Say no more, then, that the doctrine of the Trinity is a matter of curiosity and amusement only. Our religion is founded upon it.

Another clergyman beneficed in Kent who was a severe critic of Unitarianism was Richard Laurence, rector of Mersham and later archbishop of Cashel.[53] Unlike their Presbyterian and, to a lesser extent, their Independent contemporaries, the Baptists managed to steer fairly clear of the more speculative theology of the eighteenth century by imposing stringent discipline on their members and ministers. The General Baptist meeting at Speldhurst admonished a member who dared to attend a Presbyterian service and suspended from communion a woman who accepted a gift of a chicken, which she then ate, although she knew it had died by drowning, this being in contravention of the scriptural prohibition on the eating of

[49] Rupp, *op. cit.*, pp. 243–77.
[50] Watts, *op. cit.*, p. 371.
[51] *Ibid.*, p. 468.
[52] G. Horne, *The Duty of Contending for the Faith*, Oxford 1786.
[53] R. Laurence, *Critical Reflections upon Some Important Misrepresentations Contained in the Unitarian Version of the New Testament*, Oxford 1811.

beasts which had died from natural causes. At the same time, however, the Speldhurst meeting looked after those of its members in need, paying for one to stay at Tunbridge Wells for six weeks to take the waters and collecting thirty shillings towards the repair of another's house damaged 'in the late dreadful and amazing high wind'.[54]

Towards the end of the eighteenth century further nonconformist schisms were created as a result of independent preachers proclaiming extreme Calvinist, and frequently also millenarianist, views. One of these was William Huntington (1745–1813), the illegitimate son of a Kentish farmer by the wife of one of his labourers. After a chequered youth, including a period as a coal-heaver, he was converted as a result of a casual meeting with a strict Calvinist and took up preaching. Despite his lack of education he became minister of an independent Calvinist chapel in London, which attracted a fashionable congregation including the future prime minister, Lord Liverpool, and members of the royal household, and published no fewer than 81 religious works. From the date of his conversion Huntington put the letters 'S.S.', standing for 'Sinner Saved', after his name. His followers were numerous in the Weald of Kent, and in much of Sussex, where two of the chapels established by him – Jireh at Lewes, where he is buried, and Providence at Chichester – are still in use and preserve their original fittings.[55] The principal Huntingtonian chapel in Kent was at Cranbrook, long a centre of nonconformist activity which also had Baptist, Independent, Unitarian and Wesleyan Methodist places of worship by the early nineteenth century. Another, more extreme and short-lived, religious sect in Kent was founded at Dunkirk by John Nichols Tom, who styled himself Sir William Courtenay, and claimed to be the Messiah. This sect was dispersed when Tom was killed by the Kent militia at the battle of Bossenden Wood in 1838.[56] Associations for promoting itinerant evangelism on an undenominational basis were set up for Greenwich, East Kent and West Kent in 1797–8.[57]

The challenge to the Anglican establishment from 'Old Dissent' and the new sects that emerged from it was, in Kent at least, very limited. A greater potential challenge came from Evangelical clergy and laity within the church itself; some of these eventually separated themselves from the Church of England to form the groups known collectively as 'New Dissent'. The roots of the Evangelical movement were similar to those of the Pietist movement within the Lutheran churches of Germany and, to a more limited extent, Scandinavia, and English Evangelicals acknowledged the influence that Pietism had had on them. Both movements laid great stress on the personal conversion experience. Evangelicalism, however, was not strong in Kent. Its only early adherents of any note were Vincent Perronet, vicar of Shoreham 1728–85, Henry Piers, vicar of Bexley 1739–69, and James Ramsay, rector of Teston 1781–9. Ramsay was one of the earliest advocates of the abolition

[54] Watts, *op. cit.*, pp. 326, 334, 339.
[55] *Dictionary of National Biography*, xxviii, pp. 309–11. See also J. S. Reynolds, *Providence Chapel*, Chichester 1961.
[56] Everitt, *op. cit.*, pp. 25, 29.
[57] Ward, *op. cit.*, p. 49.

of the slave trade, a cause very closely associated with the Evangelicals in Parliament.[58] Whilst many Evangelicals remained within the Church of England, two groups were eventually to leave it. These were the Methodists whose leaders were Charles and John Wesley, and the group of Anglican Calvinists under the patronage of Selina, Countess of Huntingdon. Until his death in 1791 Wesley remained a clergyman of the Church of England and managed to restrain his more enthusiastic disciples from seceding from it. The Methodists saw themselves as a society within the established church and were careful not to hold their own services at times when they took place in parish churches. Wesley told the Methodist Society at Deptford in 1787 that if they did not cease to arrange their services to take place at the same time as those in the two Anglican churches he would never visit Deptford again.[59] Wesley's chief supporters among the Anglican clergy in Kent were Perronet and Piers. He was invited to preach in both their churches and Perronet opened a room for Methodist meetings at Shoreham. Wesley also preached at Brompton in 1753.[60] The attitude of many Anglican clergy to what they regarded as the misplaced enthusiasm of the Methodists, together with the support for that view offered by some bishops, meant that Methodists could not rely on the hospitality of Anglican pulpits and were obliged to hold their own field-preachings and eventually to build their own chapels, which had to be licensed as dissenting places of worship. Methodist chapels were organised into circuits under the charge of a superintendent minister and a circuit for Kent was established in 1766. Chapels were opened at Canterbury in 1764 and Chatham in 1770. By 1773–4 there were also Methodist societies at Ashford, Dover, Faversham, Margate, Sandwich, Sheerness and Sittingbourne. Further chapels were opened at Sevenoaks in 1774, Tonbridge in 1780, Maidstone in 1788 and Brompton, in a ceremony at which John Wesley himself presided, in 1789. At Chatham the society grew so quickly that the first chapel had to be replaced by a much larger one in 1810.[61]

It was not long after Wesley's death that the tensions among his disciples, which only he had been able to hold together, led to them gradually breaking away from the Church of England, and for the movement to be divided by schism. From the original body, later known as the Wesleyan Methodists, there seceded the Methodist New Connexion in 1797, the Independent Methodists in 1805, the Primitive Methodists in 1810, the Bible Christians in 1815, the Leeds Protestant Methodists in 1827, the Wesleyan Methodist Association in 1835, and the Wesleyan Reformers in 1849. Thereafter, from the union of the last three bodies by 1857, a gradual process of reversing the schisms took place until in 1932 most of the Methodist sects were reunited. Only three of the Methodist sects were active in Kent – the Wesleyans, the Primitives and the Bible Christians – and even these were largely

[58] G. R. Balleine, *History of the Evangelical Party*, London 1909, p. 134; I. C. Bradley, *The Call to Seriousness*, London 1976, p. 86.

[59] Watts, *op. cit.*, p. 447.

[60] A. J. Pearman, *Diocesan Histories: Rochester*, London 1897, pp. 305–6. See also J. Wesley, *A Plain Account of the People called Methodists in a Letter to the Revd Mr Perronet, Vicar of Shoreham in Kent*, London 1755.

[61] R. C. Jenkins, *Diocesan Histories: Canterbury*, London 1880, pp. 399–402.

confined to the urban areas. New dissent was no stronger in Kent than old dissent had been. The process by which Methodists gradually moved from being a society within the Church of England to several sects outside it was repeated by the Countess of Huntingdon's Connexion. The Countess, like the Wesleys, had her Anglican supporters and she was originally able to get around the requirement to license her chapels as dissenting places of worship by building houses which she owned to which the chapels were attached, the ministers being regarded as her own private chaplains. Such was the chapel erected at Tunbridge Wells in 1769. However, her claim that she could, as a peeress, appoint as many clergy of the Church of England as she wished as her chaplains was challenged and disallowed by the consistory court of the diocese of London in 1779 and she was, like the Wesley's, obliged to register future chapels as dissenting places of worship. In 1790, the year before her death, she formed her chapels into a Connexion. They then numbered 64, of which seven were her own private property and were vested by her in the custody of four trustees.[62]

(3) Church Building and Extension

The eighteenth century saw, for the first time in nearly two hundred years, a modest programme of church building and rebuilding, partly brought about by the need of the nonconformist sects to build themselves churches and partly by the desire of the Anglican establishment to provide better accommodation for all the inhabitants for which, as an established church, it was theoretically responsible. Many of these buildings still survive, and the details are given in Table 9. All have been altered internally.

Table 9

Surviving Churches and Chapels Built or Rebuilt in Kent 1714–1830

Denomination	1714–80	1780–1818	1818–30	Total
Church of England	6	4	10	20
Presbyterian/Unitarian	3	–	–	3
Baptist	1	1	2	4
Independent	–	–	3	3
Methodist	–	1	1	2
TOTAL	10	6	16	32

A number of other Anglican churches retain virtually unaltered liturgical arrangements of the eighteenth century with two or three-decker pulpits, box pews and galleries: Badlesmere, Brookland, Fairfield, Old Romney and Stelling. There are important eighteenth century fittings at Lullingstone, remodelled by the Jacobite

---

[62] Watts, *op. cit.*, p. 400.

and non-juror Percivall Hart, who died in 1738, and at Trottiscliffe, which acquired the pulpit of 1775 formerly in Westminster Abbey in 1824.[63]

Of the buildings erected in the middle of the eighteenth century the most ambitious architecturally was the church at Mereworth, rebuilt in 1744–6. The rebuilt churches at Otterden, Teston and Tudeley were homely and modest, as were the Presbyterian, later Unitarian, chapels at Bessels Green, Maidstone and Tenterden, and the Baptist chapel at Bessels Green. St George's church at Gravesend was rebuilt in 1731–3, following its destruction by fire, with money provided by an Act of 1711, under which fifty new churches were to be built in the London suburbs from the proceeds of a tax on coal. It was designed by a local architect, Charles Sloane, cost £3,824 and was provided with a marble altar.[64] A major overhaul of the interior was carried out in 1818–19 but all this work was destroyed when the church was enlarged in 1892–7. The vestry had resolved in 1818 to provide a new pulpit, reading and clerk's desks, north and south galleries, and additional seating on the south side of the nave at a cost of £418. A committee was set up to superintend the work and to solicit subscriptions by placing books for contributions in the local banks.[65] The plan attached to the contract shows a typical town church of the period with the pulpit, reading and clerk's desks placed directly in front of the altar, and with an organ in the west gallery.[66] The rebuilding work at Faversham resulted from an agreement between the municipal and parochial authorities to repew parts of the church, relocate the gallery containing the seats for the mayor and corporation and erect a new organ. However, the architect appointed to supervise the work, the elder George Dance, found that the central tower was on the point of collapse and advised both its demolition and the rebuilding of the nave. In 1754 the incumbent and churchwardens petitioned for a faculty to demolish the central tower and rebuild the nave, stating in their petition that 'in order to make the charge of such alteration easy to the parishioners' the corporation had agreed to contribute the sum of £500 'toward the charge thereof'.[67]

Relatively few churches and chapels were built in Kent in the last two decades of the eighteenth century and the first two of the nineteenth century. Chart Sutton was rebuilt in 1779–82 after its predecessor had been struck by lightning, and at Strood the main body of the church was rebuilt in 1812 to the designs of Sir Robert Smirke, rather better known for his public buildings, such as the Sessions House of 1824 at Maidstone.

The Wesleyan Methodists at Canterbury built themselves a handsome new chapel in 1811–12. There had been Methodists at Canterbury since 1750 when the Wesleys first visited the city:[68]

---

[63] For details of church buildings in Kent see J. Newman, *Buildings of England: North-East and East Kent* and *West Kent and the Weald*, Harmondsworth 1969.

[64] CKS, DRa/Ve3/12.

[65] CKS, Gr/ZPGv2/1.

[66] Rochester-upon-Medway Archives, P 159/6/33.

[67] W. N. Yates, 'The Mayoral and Corporation Seats in Faversham Parish Church', *Archaeologia Cantiana*, cvi (1988), pp. 39–40.

[68] J. A. Vickers, *The Story of Canterbury Methodism*, Canterbury 1961, p. 3.

They preached in a Farmhouse near the City, and the new doctrines (for tho' old, they were new to the hearers) taught by them, and the uneasiness that was excited in the minds of awakened sinners, began to make no small stir. The general opinion was that they were false prophets. Opposition and persecution now became pretty general. Some little time after, a gentleman residing in the precincts of the Cathedral, for greater convenience, opened his house, and had preaching in his large Hall. This much incensed the Clergy. A mob was raised, and a company of 40 soldiers was collected to assist. The house was broken open, and the desk got out and burnt in the market place.

After a number of temporary meeting houses a permanent chapel was opened in 1764 and Canterbury became the chief town of the Kent circuit. As Methodism increased separate circuits were established for Chatham in 1790, Rochester in 1791, Dover in 1799, Margate in 1808 and Ashford in 1811. Methodists at Canterbury were slow to establish themselves as independent from the Church of England and an attempt by some members to have communion services in their own chapel in 1796 was resisted by the trustees.[69] In 1808 a meeting of trustees and others resolved 'that seeing the present chapel is too small to contain the people who wish to attend the same, it is exceedingly desirable, that a new, large, and commodious Chapel be built, on ground that may hereafter be fixed upon'. A site was, however, not acquired until 1810, and then only at the considerable cost of £1,800. A contract was drawn up with a builder in 1811 and William Jenkins, a minister and the architect of several other Methodist chapels, including that at Rochester opened in 1810, was appointed to supervise the work. The new chapel was completed in time for it to be opened on 1 January 1812. It had three services each Sunday at 10.30 am, 2.30 pm and 6.30 pm. The total cost was £8,287, which was well beyond the means of the congregation to raise, and could only be met through substantial loans. The debt was to cripple the trustees for years to come. It still stood at £6,721 in 1830 and was not finally cleared until 1880. Internally the new Methodist chapel was arranged much like an Anglican town church of the same period. There was a central pulpit with the communion table and rail in the apse behind the pulpit. An oval gallery ran around the whole of the interior, the area in it behind the pulpit and over the communion table being occupied by the organ.[70]

As well as new buildings a number of Anglican churches were repaired and substantially re-ordered internally, frequently at considerable expense. In March 1810 a meeting of the Sevenoaks vestry expressed concern that the roof of the parish church was 'in a very ruinous state' and appointed a special committee to consider the 'best mode of putting the same into compleat repair'. The committee recommended a general restoration of the church and appointed a London architect, James Carr, to prepare estimates for such a restoration. Carr put forward a range of options varying in cost between £5,949 and £10,582. In February 1811

---

[69] *Ibid.*, pp. 13–14.
[70] *Ibid.*, pp. 15–18.

the vestry resolved to adopt the cheapest option and to petition for an Act of Parliament to raise the necessary funds and to levy a church rate of two shillings in the pound. The Act for Repairing the Parish Church of Sevenoaks permitted the trustees appointed under it to order repairs, make contracts, borrow money, assign the church rates as security subject to a maximum loan of £10,000, levy rates over several years, sell old materials and replace the organ.[71] The first meeting of the trustees was held in June 1811.[72] In March 1812 the trustees agreed to advertise their intention of raising a sum not exceeding £2,000 'by way of sale or granting annuities for lives, or by way of loan or mortgage upon the credit of the rates or assessments'. By the end of the year loans totalling £2,950 had been secured. Carr completed the first stage of the work on the church tower but then resigned, to be replaced as architect by Henry Rose, who was allowed by the trustees to complete work on the tower. Clearly the trustees were disappointed with both Carr and Rose and resolved to consult a more distinguished architect, S. P. Cockerell. Cockerell recommended unroofing the church which meant it had to be closed for worship; during the closure services were held in a building known as the Coffee House, which was fitted up for worship and licensed by the archbishop of Canterbury. The cost of repairing the chancel roof was met by the rector, T. S. Curteis, though he declined to contribute to any other part of the restoration. The work had proceeded far enough by December 1813 for the trustees to consider the future liturgical arrangements:

> Resolved that the pulpit and desk shall be fixed against the pillar adjoining His Grace the Duke of Dorset's pews on the north side of the middle aisle, His Grace to have pews in the middle aisle in lieu thereof, and the pews immediately adjoining the pulpit to be occupied by the Revd Mr Curteis and family.

The pews were to be 'painted of a wainscot colour' and the occupiers of pews in the nave were to pay for the frontage of their pews at one guinea per foot. The new pews were then apportioned by the trustees. In March 1814 Cockerell was asked to design 'a screne with tablets for the Commandments, Lord's Prayer and Creed' together with a new communion table and rails, and in April the trustees agreed to install benches for children in the north and south aisles. A contemporary plan[73] shows the pulpit and reading desk located in the middle of the north side of the nave in a position where it was clearly visible from all parts of the church. The cost of restoration was considerable. Including the cost of promoting the Act of Parliament the bills totalled more than £7,800. Although £9,200 had been raised in annuities and loans, the trustees were responsible for paying the annuitants and for meeting the interest on the loans. Between 1814 and 1822 the cost of this and maintaining the trust, including annual payments of £75 to its clerk, was nearly £4,800.[74] The trustees had great difficulty in raising the necessary funds. Many

71 CKS, P 330/6/1.
72 CKS, P 330/8/2.
73 CKS, P 330/6/5.
74 CKS, P 330/5/3.

parishioners refused to pay the additional church rates and had to be proceeded against for the recovery of debt, again at further expense. The trust was not finally wound up until May 1870 when 'the churchwardens reported that they had raised a sufficient sum by voluntary contributions to make up the necessary amount . . . to pay off the principal and interest due'.[75] Difficulties of a similar sort were faced by many other parishes embarking on ambitious restoration schemes.

One piece of ecclesiastical initiative which has received the universal condemnation of subsequent historians for its antiquarian insensitivity was the action of the vicar of Reculver, C. B. Nailor, in demolishing most of what had been one of the major surviving Anglo-Saxon churches in England. The events are recorded by the parish clerk:[76]

> 1805 Reculver church and willage stood in saftey. 1806 The sea began to Make a Little incroach on the willage. 1807 the farmers be gun take the sea side stone work and sold it to the Margate pieor Compney for a foundation for the new pier and the timber by action as It was good oak fit for their hoane use and than the village became a total Rack to the Mercy of the Sea.

> Oct 13 1802 The chappel house fell down. This been all dun and spred a broad the peopel Come from all parts to see the ruines of village and the church. Mr C b nailor been vicar of the parish his Mother fanced that the Church wos keep for a poppet show and she persuade har son to take it down so he took it in consideration and named it to the farmers in the parash a bout taking it down. Sum wos for it and sum against it then Mr nailor wrote to the Bishop to know If he Might have the Church took down and is answer wos it Must be dun by a Majority of the peopel in the parish so hafter a long time he got the Majority of one so down Come the Church.

This took place in 1809 and a new church, itself replaced by another building in 1876, was built further inland at Hillborough.

In 1818 two events took place which were to give a major impetus to new church building and the enlargement of existing buildings within the established Church of England. They were the foundation of the Incorporated Church Building Society and the setting up of the commission appointed under the first Church Building Act for the erection of new churches in populous places.[77] Although Kent had few large towns, and did not suffer from the same lack of church accommodation as some places in the Midlands and the North of England, five towns benefited from the first series of parliamentary grants with new churches erected at Chatham (St John's 1821–2), Maidstone (Holy Trinity 1826–8), Margate (Holy Trinity 1825–9), Ramsgate (St George's 1824–7) and Tunbridge Wells (Holy Trinity 1827–9). The impact of the Incorporated Church Building Society on church extension was

[75] CKS, P 330/6/50–2.
[76] H. Gough, 'A Fresh Look at the Reculver Parish Clerk's Story', *Archaeologia Cantiana*, xcix (1983), p. 135. I have slightly altered Mr Gough's transcript of the original manuscript by inserting minimal punctuation aimed at making the sense of the text more obvious.
[77] See M. H. Port, *Six Hundred New Churches*, London 1961.

enormous. One of its principal aims was to increase the amount of free accommodation available in churches and its grants were only made available on the strict understanding that at least half the additional accommodation, and preferably more, would be free. Before this date the bulk of the sittings in town churches had to be paid for, either through annual pew rents or through outright purchase of the sittings. Although pew rents were not common in village churches, pews were normally assigned to particular properties in the parish and the amount of accommodation in the churches for the poor or for strangers was very limited. The church at Westcliffe preserves a common arrangement whereby the principal families sat in appropriated box pews lining the walls of the nave whereas the poor, children and others sat on benches filling the central part of the nave. The extent of the Incorporated Church Building Society's contribution to the erection of new church buildings in Kent and the enlargement of existing ones is shown in Table 10, the statistics for the diocese of Canterbury excluding those for the detached archdeaconry of Croydon.

Table 10
ICBS Grants towards Church Building and Extension in Kent 1818–1927

Diocese of	Canterbury	Rochester	Total
Number of grants	248	155	403
Additional sittings	37,262	34,899	72,161
Additional free sittings	32,301	29,826	62,127
Amount of grants	£20,074	£17,144	£37,218

The number of free seats represented 86.1% of the additional accommodation funded by the Society.[78]

From the end of the eighteenth century a movement was taking place within the Church of England aimed at creating a better liturgical focus in Anglican churches. This resulted in breaking up the two and three-decker pulpits and placing the pulpit and reading desk, as separate pieces of furniture, on either side of the chancel arch or of the sanctuary where churches had no proper chancel. An attempt was also made to give greater prominence to the altar, by raising it on steps and by clearing away furniture that might obscure it.[79] At Holy Trinity, Tunbridge Wells, the architect, Decimus Burton, submitted two alternative plans for the arrangement of the interior. The first showed a town church of the traditional late eighteenth century type with the pulpit, reading and clerk's desks in front of the altar, a wide central aisle with open benches in the middle of the nave, and with the seats facing inwards in the aisles. In the second plan all the seats, except for those in the galleries, were made to face east; the pulpit now stood with the churchwardens'

[78] *Annual Report of the Incorporated Church Building Society*, London 1927, pp. 79–80, 133–4.
[79] Yates, *Buildings, Faith and Worship*, pp. 108–23.

pew at the east end of the nave on the south side; the reading and clerk's desks stood with the minister's pew at the east end on the north side; the place occupied by the pulpit and desks on the first plan was now occupied by the font.[80] At Broadstairs no fewer than three internal arrangements were proposed for the new Holy Trinity chapel, eventually built in 1828–30 with a grant of £400 from the Incorporated Church Building Society.[81] The two submitted by Richard Collard, and not adopted, both had the pulpit and reading desk as separate pieces of furniture permitting a clear view of the altar. In one there were two blocks of pews in the nave with pulpit and reading desk at the eastern end of the two blocks. In the other there were three pew blocks, shallow ones against the north and south walls, and a wide central one in the middle of the nave; pulpit and reading desk were shown at the northern and southern ends of this central block, both being entered by staircases from the altar space. In the plan eventually adopted, by David Barnes, a much more old-fashioned arrangement is shown, a three-decker pulpit being placed at the east end of the nave on the south side, effectively blocking any view of the altar from a substantial proportion of the sittings.

The building of the new church of Holy Trinity, Margate, now demolished, was an ambitious undertaking. The population of the town was returned at 7843 in 1821, and there was accommodation for less than a quarter of that number in the parish church of St John-in-Thanet. The situation was made worse by the fact that the population was considerably increased in the summer months by visitors anxious to sample the attractions of one of England's major seaside resorts. Plans for a new church to accommodate two thousand people – 800 in rented sittings and 1,200 free – at a cost of £16,000 were first laid in 1825. This cost soon rose to a new estimate of £24,000 but by the end of the year £18,000 had already been raised in voluntary subscriptions. Among those contributing to the new church, no doubt in the hope that it would attract even more visitors to Margate, were the directors of the Pier and Harbour Company, several of whom were also members of the new church committee; they promised £2,000. In 1826 the Church Building Commission included the new church in the list of buildings they were prepared to support with grants. It was completed and consecrated in 1829 at a total cost of somewhere between £25,000 and £28,000, a sum greatly in excess of the cost of most new church buildings at this time. Of this £10,000 was provided by the commission and the bulk of the remainder provided by voluntary subscriptions. Several items in the church, such as the organ, the coverings and hangings for the pulpit, reading desk and communion table, the communion plate, and the stained glass in the east window, were donated by individuals. Very little of the cost of the new church was met from church rates, the proceeds from the two special rates levied in 1828 amounting to just over £1,900. The new church had galleries over the north and south aisles, and at the west end of the nave a lower gallery and an upper one containing the organ. There were box pews in the nave and aisles but a wide central passageway in which 'were placed benches that reached as far as the

---

[80] CKS, P 371L/6/5.
[81] Two plans in Ramsgate Library, the third in Lambeth Palace Library, ICBS 912.

font' at its west end. Pulpit and reading desk, of equal height, were placed on the north and south sides of the altar space.[82]

Two churches rebuilt or enlarged with grants from the Incorporated Church Building Society were St Margaret's at Rochester and Sutton Valence. At St Margaret's the vestry resolved in 1823 to enlarge the church by 260 sittings to compensate for the deficiency of free seats in the existing building and to levy a rate for this purpose of four pence in the pound for one year, the remaining cost to be raised by voluntary contributions and an application for grant aid to the Incorporated Church Building Society. The churchwardens were instructed to convene a meeting to solicit subscribers. It was to be advertised in the Rochester and Chatham newspapers and not confined to parishioners but extended to any others 'disposed to assist in this charitable work'. The building committee consisted of the dean and chapter of Rochester as patrons of the living, the vicar and churchwardens, and twelve inhabitants. The application to the Incorporated Church Building Society resulted in the offer of an initial grant of £200 and further grants if required. By that time just over £500 had been raised in subscriptions. The Society was applied to for a further grant of £500 towards an estimated cost of £1,900 and the remaining £700 was to be 'borrowed on annuity'. When the estimated cost rose to £2,670 it was agreed to levy a rate of sixpence in the pound annually to repay the interest on and principal of a loan which now needed to be £1,400. When the work of enlargement was finally completed in 1825 the cost had risen to £3,230, of which £600 was met by the Incorporated Church Building Society, £790 from subscriptions, £310 from the proceeds of a church rate over three years, and the remaining £1,530 from a loan repayable over twenty years.[83] Sutton Valence church was rebuilt in 1823–8 with a grant of £100 from the Incorporated Church Building Society. It provided the parishioners with an additional 300 sittings of which 280 were free and unappropriated. A plan of the interior shows a building with a wide nave and shallow apsidal chancel. The tall pulpit, which has survived, was free-standing on the north side with reading and clerk's desks placed in front of it, an interesting variant of the traditional three-decker. Unusually the font was placed in a pew at the east end of the nave on the south side rather than at the west end.[84] When the church was internally remodelled in 1874 arcades were inserted to create an aisled nave but the original plastered ceilings were retained in the aisles.

Not all applications to the Incorporated Church Building Society were successful. The society applied a number of tests, in addition to the stipulations on free sittings, before agreeing to make grants. It would not contribute to 'ornamental architecture beyond what shall . . . be deemed essential to give to the Buildings to be erected and enlarged . . . the character of Churches and Chapels of the Church of England'. Applications would only be supported if the society was satisfied that the applicant parish was making a sufficient contribution to the cost, having stated

---

[82] H. M. Walton, *A Short History of Holy Trinity Church*, Margate 1932, pp. 6–33.

[83] Rochester-upon-Medway Archives, P 305/8/2.

[84] Lambeth Palace Library, ICBS 598.

'the extent of their population, their pecuniary means, and the efforts they have made, or are willing to make, towards accomplishing the object'. In particular all applications had to have the support of the incumbent, patron and diocesan bishop. In 1819 the parishioners of Dymchurch petitioned the archbishop of Canterbury to be allowed to enlarge their church by erecting a north aisle. They stated that the existing building could only accommodate 200 of the 548 parishioners, a figure later revised to 578, and that several neighbouring churches were so dilapidated that their parishioners also worshipped at Dymchurch. They expressed concern about a dissenting meeting held in the parish and 'we do hereby feel a most earnest disposition to encourage the principles of the established church'. The archbishop advised them to apply for a grant to the Incorporated Church Building Society and they accordingly sent off for and completed the necessary forms. The enlarged church was to have 400 sittings, all the additional ones to be free, and the total cost was estimated at just over £670 of which £450 had been raised locally. The archbishop, however, had clearly had second thoughts since he now told the parishioners he would not sign the papers; he was concerned about the number of applications being made for grant aid, many of which had greater merits than that from Dymchurch, and stated that he thought the parishioners should modify their requirements so as to bring down the cost of the proposed extension to a sum that was within their means to raise themselves.[85] This was clearly done since the extension was completed in 1821.

The work of church building, extension and restoration, a steady trickle before 1830, snowballed thereafter. It is important to emphasise, however, that many of the hallmarks of this movement – the emphasis on free seating, the desire for liturgical innovation, the concern about lack of accommodation and the resulting competition from dissenting chapels – were all present some time before 1830. A revolution did not burst upon the Church of England after that date. A process of change, already well established, simply gathered greater momentum.

85 CKS, P 125/6/1–2.

Plate 1a. Interior of Chiddingstone church 1792.

Plate 1b. Interior of Brenchley church in the late nineteenth century showing the altar rails ordered to be installed by Archdeacon Warner in 1670.

Plate 2a. Francis Atterbury, bishop of Rochester 1713–23.

Plate 2b. George Horne, dean of Canterbury 1781–90.

Plate 2c. Samuel Horsley, bishop of Rochester 1793–1802.

Plate 2d. Charles Manners-Sutton, archbishop of Canterbury 1805–28.

Plate 3a. Interior of St Clement's, Sandwich, showing the three-decker pulpit at the west end of the nave, c.1860.

Plate 3b. 'Spy' cartoon from Vanity Fair of Benjamin Harrison, archdeacon of Maidstone 1845–87.

Plate 3c. Enthronement of John Bird Sumner as archbishop of Canterbury 1848.

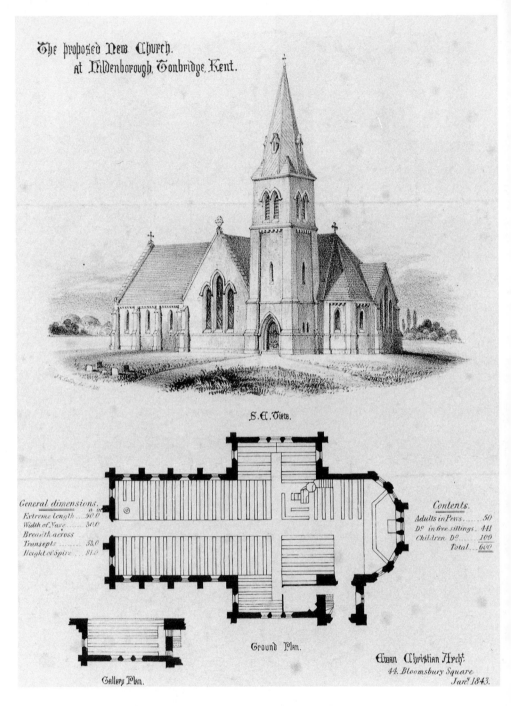

The proposed New Church.
at Hildenborough, Tonbridge, Kent.

S.E. View.

General dimensions.
Extreme length ... 90.0
Width of Nave ... 30.0
Breadth across
Transepts ... 52.0
Height of Spire ... 81.3

Contents.
Adults in Pews ... 50
Do. in free sittings ... 441
Children Do. ... 109
Total ... 600

Ground Plan.

Gallery Plan.

Ewan Christian Archt.
44, Bloomsbury Square
Jany 1843.

Plate 4. Plan and elevation of Hildenborough church 1843.

An Age of Religious Pluralism 1830–1914

(1) Ecclesiastical Reform

The Victorian Church has received much attention in recent years.[1] The emphasis has been, almost overwhelmingly, on the impact of reform on the religious establishment. The reform of the church was just one aspect of a reform movement that encompassed virtually every aspect of contemporary life: economic, political and social. Part of the argument of this chapter will be that the process of reform was perhaps not as dramatic as has been painted. That reform took place will not be challenged but the impact and the pace of that reform will be the subject of some discussion. This is particularly important in the case of Kent since even at the end of the nineteenth century the majority of those who were regular churchgoers worshipped in the established Church of England. Nonconformity made no greater impact on Kent in the nineteenth century than it had in the eighteenth. Roman Catholicism, rapidly expanding in many other parts of Britain, largely as the result of Irish immigration, remained very weak in Kent until comparatively recent times.

The reform of the established church was already part of the political agenda by 1830. In 1828 the Test and Corporation Acts, which technically disbarred dissenters from office, though they had been got round for years, were repealed. In the following year, after several earlier failed attempts, Catholic Emancipation was carried, though not without massive opposition in the country from those who feared it was the first step towards reversing the clause in the Thirty Nine Articles that stated that 'the Bishop of Rome hath no jurisdiction in this realm of England'.[2] In Kent a county meeting was requested by 38 freeholders and held on Penenden Heath, outside Maidstone, 'for the purpose of petitioning Parliament to adopt such measures as may be best calculated to support the Protestant Establishment of the United Kingdom in Church and State'.[3] The majority of those who spoke, including Lords Camden, Teynham and Winchelsea, and Sir Edward Knatchbull, MP,

---

1   The authoritative study is W. O. Chadwick, *The Victorian Church*, 2 vols, London 1966–70. Other particularly valuable studies are D. Bowen, *The Idea of the Victorian Church*, Montreal 1968; A. D. Gilbert, *Religion and Society in Industrial England*, London 1963; J. H. S. Kent, *Holding the Fort*, London 1978; G. I. T. Machin, *Politics and the Churches in Great Britain*, 2 vols, Oxford 1977–87; P. T. Marsh, *The Victorian Church in Decline*, London 1969; and E. R. Norman, *Church and Society in England 1770–1970*, Oxford 1976.

2   There is much useful material on Protestant attitudes to Roman Catholicism in nineteenth century Britain in E. R. Norman, *Anti-Catholicism in Victorian England*, London 1968, and *The English Catholic Church in the Nineteenth Century*, Oxford 1984. See also J. Wolffe, *The Protestant Crusade in Great Britain*, Oxford 1991.

3   *Report of Speeches delivered at the Kent County Meeting*, London and Chatham 1828; *Correct Account of the Proceedings of the Kent Meeting*, Faversham 1828.

who described Kent as 'decidedly Protestant', vigorously condemned proposals for Catholic Emancipation. The minority, including Lords Darnley and Radnor, were shouted down. It was estimated that about thirty thousand people attended the meeting and the petition to Parliament was carried by an overwhelming majority, estimated at 'four fifths of the Meeting' on a show of hands. Thereafter Kent continued to support extreme Protestant organisations. There were branches of the Reformation Society in Canterbury, Dover, Maidstone, Margate, Ramsgate and Tunbridge Wells, those in Dover and Maidstone being particularly active, and of the Protestant Association in Maidstone and Margate; Protestant Association meetings were also held in Dover.[4] In 1850, at the height of the furore over the re-establishment of a Roman Catholic hierarchy for England and Wales, the bishop of Rochester, Lord George Murray, wrote to his cathedral chapter:[5]

> I fully concur in the sentiments of just indignation which you entertain towards the Roman Pontiff and his emissaries, for the insults they have offered to our Sovereign, our National Church, and to the Protestant Faith, and I hope that the general burst of indignation, which has proceeded from all parts of the Kingdom, will have a salutary effect in urging upon the Ministers of the Crown the adoption of such measures as shall vindicate the supremacy of the Queen, and at the same time counteract the present, and any future attempts of the Church of Rome to extend its baneful system of Religion in this Kingdom.

Similar sentiments were expressed by John Woodruff, vicar of Upchurch, who noted in his journal on 7 March 1851: 'although the divisions which exist among Protestants are greatly to be lamented, yet no encouragement beyond mere tolerance ought to be given to the Roman Catholic Religion.'[6]

After 1830 the internal reform of the Church of England proceeded apace, but it was mainly concentrated on those areas that had been sources of criticism from Protestant nonconformists and those who professed no Christian belief, most of whom were also political radicals. The bishops had made themselves particularly unpopular in these quarters when a majority of them had voted against the reform of parliamentary constituencies and other aspects of the electoral system in 1831-2. When Archbishop Howley arrived at Canterbury, to begin his primary visitation of the diocese, on 7 August 1832, he 'was met by a hissing crowd. Hats, caps, brickbats, cabbage stalks were flung at the carriage, breaking one of the windows, but not harming the archbishop'. At Crayford the crowds at the annual Guy Fawkes procession changed the words of the traditional song:[7]

> Remember, remember
> That God is the sender
> Of every good gift unto man;

4   Wolffe, *op. cit.*, pp. 51, 151, 153.
5   Rochester-upon-Medway Archives, DRc/AZz2/2.
6   CKS, P 377/28/34.
7   Chadwick, *op. cit.*, i pp. 29, 32.

> But the devil, to spite us
> Sent fellows with mitres
> Who rob us of all that they can.

For some years there had appeared what purported to be reliable publications listing the incomes and pluralities of the clergy. The techniques employed were fairly crude. The *Clerical Guide*, first published in 1817 and re-issued in 1822 and 1829, lumped clergymen with common Christian and surnames together, claiming for instance that a mythical John Jones held no fewer than 34 livings in Wales, London, Liverpool and Oxfordshire. The *Black Book* of 1820, the *Supplement to the Black Book* of 1823, and the *Extraordinary Black Book* of 1831, covered similar ground.[8] Their allegations, which churchmen preferred to ignore than refute, were widely believed and even those who dismissed the detail as inaccurate were left with an overall impression of clerical indolence and widespread corruption. The first priority, therefore, of the ecclesiastical reformers in parliament was to deal with the questions of clerical incomes, patronage, pluralities, and non-residence. In the process however changes were made to diocesan boundaries and the constitutions of the cathedrals thoroughly overhauled. In 1835 the Municipal Corporations Act removed all town churches so affected from municipal patronage, which effectively meant municipal control. An Ecclesiastical Commission was set up to oversee the rest of the reforms, building on the work of augmentation of poor livings that had been carried on for many years by the administrators of Queen Anne's Bounty.[9] Most of the bishops, including Archbishop Howley, who is sometimes portrayed as more deeply conservative than he was in reality, recognised that reform was inevitable and actively co-operated with government ministers as members of the commission, though the bulk of the clergy were deeply hostile. The recommendations of the commission were implemented in three Acts of Parliament between 1836 and 1840.

New bishoprics were created at Manchester and Ripon. Of the proposals to amalgamate smaller sees only the union of Bristol with Gloucester was implemented, the unions of Bangor with St Asaph, and of Carlisle with Sodor and Man being abandoned in the face of local hostility. The boundaries of several dioceses were, however, altered and this particularly affected Kent when most of the diocese of Rochester was in 1845 transferred to that of Canterbury so that the former could embrace the counties of Essex and Hertfordshire formerly in the diocese of London. This very unsatisfactory arrangement, with the bulk of the diocese and the residence of its bishop being separated from its cathedral and a few parishes in North Kent by the river Thames, survived until 1877, when the diocese of St Alban's was created. Thereafter the diocese of Rochester was reorganised to embrace a little more of Kent and large areas of London south of the Thames until 1905, when the diocese of Southwark was created, and the boundary between the

---

8 P. Virgin, *The Church in an Age of Negligence*, Cambridge 1989, pp. 203–5.
9 See G. F. A. Best, *Temporal Pillars: Queen Anne's Bounty, the Ecclesiastical Commissioners and the Church of England*, Cambridge 1964.

dioceses of Canterbury and Rochester was altered to something very similar to what it had been prior to 1845. Ecclesiastical peculiars, such as those of Cliffe and Shoreham in the Rochester diocese, were also abolished as part of the general reorganisation of dioceses. Measures were taken to equalise the annual incomes of bishoprics, reducing that of Canterbury to £15,000, and increasing those of poor bishoprics, such as Rochester, to a minimum of £4,000. It was therefore possible to abolish the holding of livings *in commendam* with sees, as had invariably been the case at Rochester; Richard Bagot, dean of Canterbury 1827–45, was also bishop of Oxford from 1829, only resigning the deanery on his translation to the bishopric of Bath and Wells.[10] The number of benefices to be held by other clerics was limited to two, which had to be within ten statute miles of each other, with a joint value of not more than £1,000, and with the population of neither living exceeding 3,000. The powers of the bishops to enforce residence were strengthened and they were empowered to require in every parish church two full services each Sunday to include a sermon or lecture. There was a major reform of the cathedrals. All non-residentiary prebends were suppressed and the number of resident canons restricted to between four and six at each cathedral. The separate estates of deans and canons, as opposed to the corporate estates of the chapter, were to be vested in the Ecclesiastical Commission, which was constituted a permanent body, on the expiry of the existing life-interests. Similarly, the patronage of the chapters was retained but that of their individual members was transferred to the bishops.

The effect of all these reforms was slow and their impact on some parishes barely noticeable for many years. Changes had to await the death or resignation of those in office. The majority of the clergy were neither Evangelical nor Whig reformers, but old-fashioned Tory high churchmen, whose view of the relationship between church and state, and of the way in which the church should conduct its own business, had been formed in the years before the setting up of the Ecclesiastical Commission. In Kent both dioceses were controlled by clerics of this type until well into the second half of the nineteenth century. Archbishop Howley remained at Canterbury until his death in 1848, when he was succeeded by the Evangelical J. B. Sumner. His protégés, however, W. R. Lyall and Benjamin Harrison, remained respectively dean of Canterbury until 1857 and archdeacon of Maidstone until 1887.[11] At Rochester, Lord George Murray, bishop from 1827 until his death in 1860, and before that bishop of Sodor and Man, was even more reactionary. He refused to accept men with Durham degrees for ordination since he 'disapproved of encouraging the lower classes to aspire to stations for which there were already too many candidates from the classes immediately above them', and was the last surviving bishop to wear his episcopal wig outside church.[12] Murray's archdeacon

---

[10] J. M. Cooper, *Lives of the Deans of Canterbury*, Canterbury 1900, pp. 215–19.

[11] See C. Dewey, *The Passing of Barchester*, London 1991. Harrison is described on pp. 140–1 as 'the last surviving member of the Hackney Phalanx', a loose-knit group of high churchmen including both Howley and Lyall, Howley's predecessor (Archbishop Manners-Sutton) as well as bishops Van Mildert of Durham and Lonsdale of Lichfield.

[12] Chadwick, *op. cit.*, i pp. 40, 134.

for virtually the whole of his episcopate at Rochester was the son of one of his predecessors in the see, Walker King, another high churchman of the traditional type. It is important to emphasise that high churchmen of this type were not ineffective. They had been among the most enthusiastic supporters of the National Society for Education and the Incorporated Church Building Society. Archdeacon Harrison was praised by contemporaries for 'his intimate knowledge of the clergy, his regularity at the cathedral services, his activity in the business of various church societies . . . his geniality, wit and tolerance . . . his readiness to take part . . . in the gatherings like County Cricket Week or the meetings of the agricultural . . . societies'.[13]

The one issue not addressed by the reforming legislation of 1836–40 was that of church rates. It was the responsibility of all parishes and their ratepaying parishioners to raise and contribute to a church rate for the maintenance of the church building and its services, in the same way that rates were levied for the relief of the poor or for municipal purposes. In parts of the country in which dissenters were numerous, especially the Midlands and the North of England, it had become virtually impossible to raise such a rate by the 1830s. Dissenters were elected as churchwardens to prevent rates being levied, or they were refused by the annual meetings of the vestry, or there were so many parishioners who refused to pay that prosecution became impractical. Some clergy abandoned trying to collect a rate and relied on other means of voluntary support to maintain buildings and services, but they were severely criticised by the majority who took the view that the law should be enforced.[14] In Kent the campaign against the payment of church rates was fairly limited. The rate was opposed in only eighteen parishes.[15] Archdeacon Walker King commented:[16]

I am happy to believe that opposition to Church Rates has been confined to a few large Towns in the Archdeaconry, where, considerable bodies of Dissenters being congregated, and possessing numerical strength, it might be expected that such a feeling would be exhibited. I cannot admit the validity of the plea of Dissenters to be exempt from the payment of Church Rates. I think it founded neither on justice nor reason. The established religion of a Country is entitled by law to certain Rights and Privileges. . . When therefore the church demands

[13] Dewey, op. cit., p. 104.
[14] See Chadwick, op. cit., i pp. 81–9, 146–58; W. R. Ward, Religion and Society in England 1790–1850, London 1972, pp. 178–89.
[15] Gilbert, op. cit., p. 118.
[16] W. King, Instructions to Churchwardens, Rochester 1841. These instructions formed a printed preface to the visitation books, several of which survive, presented by King to all the churches in his archdeaconry, with the instruction that the incumbents were to 'hand over to your Successors in Office, this Book, in which it is my intention to enter whatever directions, I may think it to be my duty to leave with you, from time to time, upon the occasion of my parochial visitation'. These books survive for Hadlow (CKS, P 163/6/1), Wateringbury (CKS, P 385/6/3) and a number of other parishes in West Kent, and were used to record not just Walker King's comments, but also those of his successor, Benjamin Harrison, after the reorganisation of diocesan boundaries in 1845.

a rate, she is calling for what is her own; and withholding it appears to be depriving her of her just right and property.

In Scandinavia, where such arguments were accepted by most of the population, the equivalent of church rates has survived to the present day. In England and Wales, where acceptance was far from universal, church rates were officially abolished by Act of Parliament in 1868, but many rural parishes with predominantly Anglican populations continued to levy what was referred to as a 'voluntary' church rate rather than relying on collections at the services.[17]

Before 1840 one of the main targets of the ecclesiastical reformers had been the cathedral chapters but, despite the legislation aimed at reforming them, they remained deeply conservative for many years. Canterbury before 1860 has been described as 'a bastion of the old high churchmen. The clergy who set the tone of the precincts were high and dry when they arrived, or the cathedral soon dried them out'.[18] The slow impact of reform was clear from the evidence presented to the Cathedrals Commission in the early 1850s. At Canterbury there were a dean and six residentiary canons, all of whom were required to reside at least ninety days in each year. Two of the canonries were annexed to the archdeaconries of Canterbury and Maidstone. The cathedral also had six minor canons, four of whom held other preferment, and the six preachers appointed by Henry VIII, who shared with the residentiary canons the duty of preaching in the cathedral. The chapter also employed an auditor, surveyor, two vesturers, two virgers, two porters and four bell-ringers. The chapter held the patronage of 33 benefices, four being united benefices in the city of Canterbury, 15 being parishes elsewhere in Kent and 14 being parishes in other counties, including seven in the City of London. The services in the cathedral were much as they had been since 1660. There was daily choral service morning and afternoon, and sermons were preached in the choir on the mornings of all Sundays, the lesser festivals and fasts, Rogation Days, and the Wednesdays and Fridays in Lent; two sermons, morning and afternoon, were only preached at Christmas, Easter and Whitsun. The weekly celebration of Holy Communion, after the morning service on Sundays, which had been temporarily abandoned in 1790, had been reintroduced, and the sacrament was also celebrated at Christmas and on Ascension Day. The cathedral made modest contributions to education and social welfare. The chapter maintained a grammar school with two masters and 89 scholars varying in age from nine to nineteen. Provision was also made for the education of ten choristers, aged between eight and fifteen, who, with the organist and twelve lay clerks, provided the music for the cathedral services. The cathedral library, having about 5,000 volumes, was open to 'the clergy and gentry of the neighbourhood' every Tuesday and Saturday between 11.00 am and 2.00 pm, and one of the minor canons was paid £20 *per annum* to act as sub-librarian. The chapter had not, however, unlike those at Chichester and Wells, established a postgraduate theological college for the training of ordination

17 Chadwick, *op. cit.*, ii pp. 195–6.
18 Dewey, *op. cit.*, p. 61.

candidates: 'no such endeavour has been made. A proposition was made by a member of the chapter to the late Archbishop [Howley]; but not meeting with his approval, it was never submitted to the chapter'. There were twelve beadsmen attached to the cathedral, who attended services on Sundays and State Days,[19] being paid an annual stipend of £6 13s 4d plus one shilling for every service attended. The cathedral made virtually no contribution to the diocese as a whole. It was only very rarely used for ordinations. Over a period of fourteen years the chapter had contributed £5,783 12s towards building, enlarging and improving churches and schools, and other charitable purposes.[20]

The situation at Rochester was much the same. The dean was required to reside for at least four months each year, and the four residentiary canons at least two; one of the canonries was annexed to the archdeaconry and another to the provostship of Oriel College, Oxford. Two of the four minor canons held other preferment. There was a grammar school with two masters and twenty King's scholars aged between eleven and eighteen. The choir consisted of the organist, six lay clerks, eight choristers and four probationary scholars. There was choral service twice daily, except on Wednesdays and Fridays in Lent when it was plain. Sermons were preached in the choir at both services on Sundays, Christmas Day and Good Friday, but in the mornings only on Ascension Day and the three State Days. Holy Communion was celebrated on the first Sunday of each month and at the major festivals. The seating arrangements in the cathedral were not designed for large attendances. Seats were assigned to the bishop, archdeacon, canons, chapter clerk, schoolmaster, minor canons, under-master, organist and their families, together with 'some of the occupiers of houses in the precincts' and the corporation of Rochester which had 'also pews assigned for the use of the mayor, aldermen and common councillors, recorder, town clerk, and clerk of the peace: none of the seats or pews are let'. The library had 1,100 volumes available to the clergy of the diocese who were allowed to borrow up to three volumes at a time. The dean was expected to present books to the value of £10, and each canon books to the value of £5, to the library when taking up their respective appointments. The chapter held the patronage of 31 benefices, ten in the diocese of Rochester, eighteen in that of Canterbury, and three in other dioceses.[21]

The cathedrals were slow to reform. At Rochester the energies of the chapter were exhausted by a long-running dispute with their schoolmaster over the funding and management of the cathedral school.[22] Weekly communion was not introduced

---

[19] The anniversaries of the execution of King Charles I on 30 January, the restoration of King Charles II on 29 May, and of the Gunpowder Plot on 5 November, for which special services were printed in the Book of Common Prayer until 1859 when the observance of these days was repealed by Act of Parliament. See W. K. L. Clarke, *Liturgy and Worship*, London 1932, pp. 216–17.

[20] *First Report of Her Majesty's Commissioners appointed to inquire into the State and Condition of the Cathedral and Collegiate Churches in England and Wales*, London 1854, pp. 1–15.

[21] *Ibid.*, pp. 343–62.

[22] See R. Arnold, *The Whiston Matter*, London 1961, and the chapter by P. A. Welsby in the forthcoming *History of Rochester Cathedral*.

1 1868. At Canterbury there was no sermon at the afternoon service until it was oduced by Dean Alford (1857–71) and no evening service until its inauguration by Dean Smith (1871–95). The box pews were not removed from the cathedral choir until 1879 when new choir stalls were designed by Sir G. G. Scott. Archbishop Howley had, however, presented a new throne to the cathedral in 1844, to replace that given by Archbishop Tenison in 1704, and a new choir pulpit was designed by William Butterfield in 1846.[23] Progress towards reform was also slow in many parishes. In an analysis of three English dioceses in 1848 only 74% of the clergy in the two southern ones, Chichester and Oxford, were resident or non-resident but doing duty. By 1888 this figure had increased to 96% in the diocese of Oxford and to 99% in that of Chichester.[24]

(2) The Religious Census of 1851

On Sunday 30 March 1851, as part of its general census of the population, the government attempted for the first and last time to estimate the number of people attending religious services in England and Wales. The controversy that this caused at the time meant that the experiment was never repeated, though some local censuses were attempted in later years, including one in Kent at Maidstone in 1880. The simple fact that only one such census took place has led to considerable debate in interpreting the evidence.[25] That for Kent is summarised in Tables 11 and 12.[26] The total population of the whole county, including the metropolitan areas in 1851, was 615,766. The returns showed therefore that there was sitting accommodation in places of worship for just under half the population. Allowing for people who went to church more than once on the census Sunday, perhaps as much as a

---

[23] C. E. Woodruff and W. Danks, *Memorials of the Cathedral and Priory of Christ in Canterbury*, London 1912, pp. 363, 366, 368.

[24] A. Haig, *The Victorian Clergy*, London and Sydney 1984, p. 179.

[25] On the general background to the census see K. S. Inglis, 'Patterns of Religious Worship in 1851', *Journal of Ecclesiastical History*, xi (1960), pp. 74–86; W. S. F. Pickering, 'The 1851 Religious Census: A Useless Experiment?', *British Journal of Sociology*, xviii (1967), pp. 382–407; D. M. Thompson, 'The 1851 Religious Census: Problems and Possibilities', *Victorian Studies*, xi (1967), pp. 87–97, and 'The Religious Census of 1851', *The Census and Social Structure*, ed. R. Lawton, London 1978, pp. 241–86. See also W. N. Yates, 'Urban Church Attendance and the Use of Statistical Evidence', *Studies in Church History*, xvi (1979), pp. 389–400. The edited returns for several areas have been published, e.g. for Leicestershire by D. M. Thompson, for Oxfordshire by K. Tiller, for Hampshire and for Sussex by J. A. Vickers and for Wales by I. G. Jones. The evidence for the south of England is summarised in B. I. Coleman, 'Southern England in the Census of Religious Worship, 1851', *Southern History*, v (1983), pp. 154–88. The original returns for Kent are in the Public Record Office, HO 129/49–74, and there are copies of these on microfilm at the Centre for Kentish Studies in Maidstone. There are printed summaries by registration district in *Parliamentary Papers 1852–3*, lxxxix: Census 1851. It is possible to compare these with the original returns in the case of Sussex as both pieces of evidence are published in *The Religious Census of Sussex 1851*, ed. J. A. Vickers, *Sussex Record Society*, lxxv (1989), which also has an excellent introduction. Only the returns for the larger towns in Kent have been published, in W. N. Yates, 'The Major Kentish Towns in the Religious Census of 1851', *Archaeologia Cantiana*, c (1984), pp. 399–423.

[26] Table 11 is based on the figures published in the *Post Office Directory for Kent* (1855) pp. 255–6, and Table 12 on the information in Coleman, *op. cit.*, p. 401.

Table 11

Summary of Religious Census for the County of Kent 1851

Denomination	Places of Worship	Sittings	Attendances	Sunday Schools	Scholars	Teachers
Church of England	479	194,443	219,880	301	24,613	1,735
Old Dissent						
Presbyterians	3	776	1,738	1	187	–
Independents	86	27,091	32,054	77	9,685	1,212
Baptists	107	25,668	33,063	60	5,881	809
Society of Friends	10	1,753	342	–	–	–
Unitarians	2	662	456	2	153	35
New Dissent						
Wesleyan Methodists	184	33,759	41,701	138	11,893	1,948
Primitive Methodists	26	2,877	3,027	6	420	72
Bible Christians	27	3,298	3,286	18	847	132
Other Methodists	13	1,690	1,763	10	1,020	92
Lady Huntingdon's	5	2,297	3,202	5	809	117
Other Groups						
Roman Catholics	13	3,337	4,636	–	–	–
Latter Day Saints	7	592	1,277	1	22	–
Jews	5	315	345	–	–	–
Irvingites	2	288	197	–	–	–
Brethren	2	105	90	–	–	–
Swedenborgians	1	70	60	–	–	–
French Protestants	1	30	21	–	–	–
Isolated Congregations	24	2,897	3,589	19	2,457	–
TOTAL	997	302,948	350,526	638	57,987	6,416

third of the total number of attendances, it would appear that fewer than 40% of the population were regular churchgoers. Very few churches were full at every service and some were comparatively empty. On the other hand the progress of the Sunday school movement over a period of little more than fifty years had been remarkable, with two thirds of all churches in Kent, and even more than 60% of Anglican ones, making such provision. The continued strength of the Anglican establishment in Kent is very clear from the evidence of the religious census: it was still attracting two thirds or more of regular churchgoers in large parts of the county; in only one registration district (Sheppey) and three of the county's ten largest towns (Chatham, Margate and Sheerness) were Anglicans outnumbered by the main branches of Protestant dissent. There was also a clear pattern of strength and weakness in the case of dissent. Methodism was strongest in the area of its beginnings in Kent: the Medway towns, the Hoo peninsula, Faversham and the Isle of Sheppey. The older branches of dissent – the Baptists and Independents – were generally weakest in the predominantly rural areas (Hoo, East Ashford, Bridge, Romney Marsh) and comparatively strong in the towns. However, in those parts of

Table 12

Percentage Share of Denominational Attendances in Non-Metropolitan Kent 1851

Registration Districts	Church of England	Old Dissent	New Dissent	Others
Bromley	66.2	22.1	11.7	–
Dartford	55.4	33.0	8.6	3.0
North Aylesford	61.2	28.0	10.8	–
Hoo	61.9	3.2	31.8	3.1
Medway	52.5	17.1	25.3	5.1
Malling	75.5	15.0	9.5	–
Sevenoaks	68.8	19.8	9.8	1.6
Tonbridge	62.8	22.9	13.2	1.1
Maidstone	66.1	22.0	11.2	0.7
Hollingbourne	68.2	17.5	24.3	–
Cranbrook	57.9	23.1	11.8	7.2
Tenterden	66.1	13.6	20.3	–
West Ashford	70.3	14.2	14.4	1.1
East Ashford	70.8	3.4	17.0	8.8
Bridge	81.5	2.1	16.4	–
Blean	78.4	10.0	11.6	–
Faversham	59.9	12.3	26.5	1.3
Milton	66.5	12.5	21.0	–
Sheppey	41.8	21.5	27.6	9.1
Thanet	52.2	21.7	20.5	5.6
Eastry	66.4	21.3	8.7	3.6
Dover	70.8	12.8	14.2	2.2
Elham	66.1	11.7	22.2	–
Romney Marsh	69.0	4.7	26.3	–
Main Towns				
Canterbury	60.5	19.1	18.8	1.6
Chatham	46.5	25.7	23.1	4.7
Dover	64.5	17.5	11.8	6.2
Gravesend	54.6	27.9	15.6	1.9
Maidstone	65.4	18.6	15.6	0.4
Margate	46.7	23.2	29.1	1.0
Ramsgate	52.7	23.7	11.6	12.0
Rochester	69.2	14.0	15.8	1.0
Sheerness	37.6	22.2	26.8	13.4
Tunbridge Wells	55.9	23.1	18.4	2.6

Note: The boundaries of the urban areas and the registration districts were coterminous in respect of Canterbury and Gravesend and they have therefore been excluded from the list of registration districts.

Table 13

Attendances at Sunday Services in Cranbrook on 30 March 1851

Denomination	Morning	Afternoon	Evening
Church of England	800	800	–
Particular Baptist	34	33	–
Independent Calvinist	180	300	–
Huntingtonian	70	100	–
Independents (2 chapels)	174	246	130
Unitarian Baptist	26	40	–
Wesleyan Methodist	–	55	24
TOTAL	1,284	1,574	154

the Kentish countryside where 'old dissent' had been comparatively strong in the seventeenth and eighteenth centuries, notably in the Weald, the attendance figures were still significant, registering more than a fifth of the total number of worshippers in the Cranbrook, Maidstone and Tonbridge registration districts.

Cranbrook had retained its reputation as a centre of religious radicalism right through the eighteenth and early nineteenth centuries. The town itself, with a population of under 2,000, had places of worship for Anglicans, Baptists, Calvinists, Huntingtonians, Independents, Unitarians and Wesleyan Methodists, the attendances on 30 March 1851 being given in Table 13.[27] These attendances include Sunday scholars. The Huntingtonian chapel at Cranbrook had been established by a local draper, Isaac Beeman, in the first decade of the nineteenth century. Beeman had been born at Boughton Malherbe on 24 November 1764. He was brought up in the Church of England but, after being apprenticed to a draper in Cranbrook in 1778, he started to attend a Baptist meeting there, being received into membership in 1782 and becoming one of the deacons in 1785. By 1787 he was able to set up in business on his own account. After a conversion experience, emulating that of St Paul on the road to Damascus – in Beeman's case on a journey from Cranbrook to Maidstone – he severed his fellowship with the Baptists in 1800 and was formally excluded, with two close friends, for non-attendance in 1803. He then came under the influence of the popular Evangelical preacher, William Huntington, who occasionally occupied the pulpit of a local Independent chapel, later providing one of his own workshops as a chapel in which Huntington could preach. On Huntington's death, Beeman himself was invited to take over the ministry and, according to his own account of events, accepted very reluctantly in 1814. He soon developed a reputation himself as a preacher of no mean ability:[28]

> Some who were poor in this world's goods but rich in faith walked every Lord's Day distances of eight and ten miles, each way, to attend his ministry. While

27 Public Record Office, HO 129/60.
28 CKS, U 1583 Z 76.

others in better circumstances rode or drove twenty miles and more to hear him. It is believed that his hearers often numbered 700 or 800 souls. Provision was made whereby those of small means, who had brought their midday meal with them, could eat it in comfort in a room under the chapel.

Beeman suffered a stroke in 1837 and died the following year. He was succeeded in the ministry by his son, Thomas Oyler Beeman, who, on the evidence of the census returns, clearly did not have the drawing power as a preacher attributed to his father.

The popularity of the preacher was a major factor in the success or otherwise of many nonconformist chapels. Disputes between congregations and ministers who were seen not to have fulfilled the potential which had led to their original call to accept the ministry of a particular chapel were not infrequent. At Sandwich the congregation of the Independent chapel invited D. R. Thomason to become the minister in 1827. They undertook to raise £100 for his support during the first year of his ministry, to find supplies for five Sundays, to have an annual collection for him and to let him use the chapel house rent free. The congregation, however, quickly became dissatisfied with Thomason and asked him to resign. He refused and managed to retain possession of the chapel even though the majority of the members seceded. When he eventually left Sandwich in 1830, he handed over the chapel to the minister of Zion Baptist Chapel, and the congregation were obliged to pay the Baptist minister £60 to vacate the building and permit them to repossess it.[29]

Some nonconformist bodies, notably the Bible Christians and Primitive Methodists, and later in the nineteenth century the Salvation Army, made a particular impact on the working classes, many of whom were unattracted by the Church of England or the more traditional nonconformist churches. The Bible Christians, founded in the West Country by William O'Bryan, had been approached by William Clark, a Wesleyan Methodist in Brompton, asking for two preachers to be sent to Kent. Chapels were established at Sheerness and Hartlip in 1821. By 1825 there were nearly a thousand Bible Christians in Kent and nearly sixty local preachers. The Kent Mission became the base for forays into London and Sussex. One of the innovations of the Bible Christians was their use of women as local preachers at a time when many religious groups confined such activities to men.[30]

One of the most significant pieces of evidence in the Kent returns of the religious census is the continued weakness of Roman Catholicism in the county, at a time when in other parts of the country it was expanding rapidly. There was no Roman Catholic church in Maidstone until 1880, though a congregation had worshipped in temporary premises from 1858, and a school was established 1863.[31] However, at Ramsgate, the new Roman Catholic church of St Augustine

[29] R. W. Young, *History of the Sandwich Congregational Church*, Sandwich 1925, pp. 19–20.

[30] M. J. L. Wickes, *The West Country Preachers: a History of the Bible Christians 1815–1907*, Hartland 1987, pp. 40–3.

[31] K. M. Topping, *The Church of St Francis, Maidstone: A Narrative History*, Maidstone 1980, pp. 10–18.

was described in 1851 as 'a true Catholic Church with a chancel and rood screen, stalls for the singing clerks, a Lady Chapel and a Chapel of St Lawrence',[32] and at Gravesend a former Church of England proprietary chapel was re-opened as a Roman Catholic church in October 1851 to serve a mission established in 1841:[33]

> The Church having been slightly altered, was opened by His Eminence Cardinal Wiseman, who preached at the Pontifical High Mass. . . The Right Rev Dr Grant, first Bishop of Southwark, being the celebrant. Handel's majestic Hallelujah Chorus, pealed forth in sonorous tones from the choir, whilst the white-robed array of acolyths and priests, the Bishop - and the Lord Cardinal – wended their measured pace up the spacious aisle to the sanctuary, where the altar was ablaze with wax lights, amidst a profusion of choice flowers and plants. The Church was well filled, the choir and organist being from the Oratory, King William Street, Strand, and with the assistance of a few Anglicans, rendered a satisfactory musical service.

At a time when there was much public agitation over the restoration of the Roman Catholic hierarchy, the ceremony did not pass without incident. There were demonstrations after the service and 'the Cardinal was beset by a crowd, but he quietly repelled them, some of the zealots offered him scurrilous tracts'. On 5 November following the opening ceremony the church was attacked by a mob who broke most of its windows. Some of the later services in the church attracted large congregations 'but the behaviour of some of the strangers was most unseemly'.

The changes in religious allegiances during the second half of the nineteenth century can be illustrated in Maidstone by comparing the returns of the religious census of 1851 with a local census taken in January 1880, as summarised in Table 14.[34] What is most remarkable about these two sets of figures is the general collapse in religious observance, assuming that the returns for 1851, which were made by the ministers whereas in 1880 people were counted as they entered the church building, had not been greatly exaggerated. In proportionate terms the differences were not very great, the Church of England accounting for 65% of adult attendances in 1880 compared with 67% in 1851.[35] The large collapse in Baptist support is largely accounted for by the fact that the King Street Chapel, Baptist in 1851, had become undenominational by 1880. Nevertheless it is clear that of the religious bodies in Maidstone the ones that had fared best in the intervening years had been the Independents and the Methodists.

The other remarkable aspect of the two sets of statistics for Maidstone is that,

---

[32] Yates, *op. cit.*, p. 407.

[33] CKS, Gr/Z9: *St John the Evangelist: The Rise and Progress of Catholicism in the Borough of Gravesend 1842–1884.*

[34] 1880 figures published in J. M. Russell, *History of Maidstone*, Maidstone 1881, pp. 145, 161; those for 1851 in Yates, *op. cit.*, pp. 416–18.

[35] The slight discrepancies between these figures and those for Maidstone in Table 12 are accounted for by the fact that the figures in the earlier table include Sunday scholars as well as the general congregation.

Table 14

Religious Allegiances in Maidstone 1851 and 1880

Denomination	1851			1880		
	Churches	Sittings	Attendances	Churches	Sittings	Attendances
Church of England	5	5,236	7,974	7	6,197	4,376
Independents	1	700	564	2	1,110	477
Baptists	3	1,297	1,456	2	556	520
Unitarians	1	400	140	1	303	137
Society of Friends	1	250	57	–	–	–
Wesleyan Methodists	1	1,046	798	1	866	577
Primitive Methodists	1	192	59	1	179	77
Lady Huntingdon's	1	600	800	–	–	–
Undenominational	2	130	62	1	591	451
Presbyterians	–	–	–	1	388	133
TOTAL	16	9,851	11,910	16	10,190	6,748

despite the growth in the population of the town, from 20,901 in 1851 to 29,632 in 1881, the number of churches in the town including mission buildings,[36] had not increased at all, and there had been only a marginal increase in the number of sittings available. All religious bodies had been shocked by the evidence from the 1851 religious census that showed that in many parts of the country the level of church accommodation was not sufficient to enable the whole population, should it wish to do so, to attend church. There was an assumption that lack of accommodation contributed to poor attendances. Horace Mann, who analysed the 1851 returns, concluded that 'the sittings provided for public worship, in order to be sufficient, ought not to fall short of 58 per cent [of the population] in each separate locality'.[37] In Kent in 1851 there were sufficient sittings overall to accommodate 53.1% of the population; by 1877 it was calculated that there were only sittings for 47.1% of the population. The main deficiencies were in Bromley (1799 sittings), Beckenham (1380), Erith (1460), Gillingham (1853), Tunbridge Wells (2189) and Margate (1351). This was despite the fact that the total number of churches in Kent had increased from 997 in 1851 to 1390 in 1877. Contemporaries took the view that 'the deficiency in the accommodation for public worship in Kent is very serious. It amounts to 123,500 sittings. So that if all who are able to attend public worship wished to do so, that number of persons would be excluded'.[38] This, however, begged the question of whether the majority, or indeed any, of those who were absent really wanted to be present at public worship. Religious sociologists

---

[36] The figures for 1851 comprised 12 churches and four missions, two undenominational and the predecessors of St Faith's (1871) and St Philip's (1857); the other new Anglican churches were St Paul's (1861) and St Michael's (1876).

[37] Quoted in *Provision for Public Worship in the County of Kent*, London 1878, p. 11.

[38] *Ibid.*, p. 41.

have effectively challenged the view prevalent within the churches until the present day that most churches were full before 1914, that new churches were built because they were needed, and that competitive church building raised the general level of churchgoing.[39] An analysis of churchgoing in Cumbria has shown that there was a steady decrease in the number of full Anglican churches from 1821, and of nonconformist ones from 1851,[40] confirming in the process that the religious census of that year seems to have been taken at a time when Protestant nonconformity reached the highest point of its numerical strength in many parts of England. Whilst some of the arguments about numbers and sittings may have been of doubtful validity, it was undoubtedly the case that if churches were inconveniently located this would have a detrimental effect on church attendance:[41]

> Evidence collected by a Parliamentary Commission on church building, which reported in 1853, indicated that – given good roads and weather – people would travel a mile to church, but probably no further; and it may be doubted whether churches have ever recruited more than a very small fraction of their membership from persons living as much as two miles distant from the nearest church building. The desire to increase proximity stimulated both the eighteenth century Methodist system of itinerancy, whereby preachers made circuits or rounds throughout the country to conduct services in remote areas, and the large-scale church building and clergy training programme which the Church of England initiated in the 1830s.

Those who argued for more churches were meeting a genuine need in some parts of the country where the population was thinly spread over a large area. But in the more populous parts of the country it would appear with hindsight that many new buildings were potentially redundant before they had even been opened.

(3) The Impact of the Oxford Movement

On 14 July 1833 John Keble preached the Assize Sermon at Oxford. What was in itself a fairly unremarkable event, an attack on the government for reducing the number of Irish bishoprics, was later seen by Newman and his disciples as a

---

[39] R. Gill, *The Myth of the Empty Church*, London 1993, pp. 2–12. Professor Gill puts the contrary view that religious decline had set in well before 1914, that in rural areas there was generally an excess of church seating over population, that churches were built 'to counter churchgoing decline rather than because existing churches were full', and that this was therefore largely counter-productive as it simply led to a larger number of empty churches.

[40] *Ibid.*, pp. 296–7. The statistics are as follows:

Full Churches		Rural Area %	Small Towns %	Large Towns %
Church of England	1821	55.7	64.6	62.3
	1851	13.4	34.4	36.1
	1902	8.3	14.8	13.6
Nonconformists	1851	30.1	29.2	27.6
	1902	3.9	15.8	20.7

[41] R. Currie, A. Gilbert and L. Horsley, *Churches and Churchgoers*, Oxford 1977, pp. 59–60.

watershed in the doctrinal standpoint and pastoral practice of the Church of England. Whilst the Oxford Movement clearly had a considerable impact, not just on the Church of England, but on all religious bodies in Britain, this impact can be exaggerated. The fact that much of what the movement stood for eventually came to represent the position of the Church of England throughout much of the twentieth century has led to extravagant claims that virtually every radical ecclesiastical initiative in the nineteenth century came from those connected with it. The history of the Church of England in the period 1830–1914 has been seen as a battleground between the supporters and opponents of the Tractarians, as those involved in the movement were termed from the *Tracts for the Times*, published between 1833 and 1841. In fact there were many respects in which Evangelicals, early Tractarians and even some traditional high churchmen had a common agenda in the 1830s, the most important element of which was the defence of the interests of the Church of England against dissenters, the irreligious and parliamentarians demanding ecclesiastical reforms that sought to weaken the Anglican establishment. Keble saw the suppression of Irish bishoprics by parliament as the precursor of disestablishment and, in the case of the Irish church, and that of Wales, he was correct, as they were disestablished in 1869 and 1920 respectively.[42] But in other respects his attitudes were widely alarmist. The Irish and Welsh churches were supported by only a small minority of the populations of Ireland and Wales and the clamour for them to be treated as such was widely seen as only just in the circumstances. The religious census of 1851 may have shown that the Church of England had competition from other religious bodies, but it was not a small minority among those professing religious belief, and there was never any more threat to it than there was to the presbyterian establishment in Scotland.

Although the Oxford Movement had begun as a defence of the Anglican establishment it was soon to move in a direction that was to cause the most serious divisions within the Church of England since the early seventeenth century. In a number of the Oxford tracts, and more particularly in Froude's *Remains*, published in 1838–9, a debate was promulgated which, for the first time, challenged the consensus in Protestant England about the Reformation. Whatever their theological differences in the past, everybody in the Church of England – Evangelicals, high churchmen, liberals – had accepted that it was a church of the Reformation, catholic in its recognition of the creeds and early councils and its retention of the historic three-fold ministry of bishops, priests and deacons, but fundamentally purified from Roman error, and a part of the international Protestant community that encompassed Calvinists and Lutherans in mainland Europe. When Tractarian writers began to challenge that view of the church, and sought to go back behind the Reformation, to recover aspects of medieval Christianity, alarm bells began to ring. And when the more advanced Tractarians, or ritualists as they were soon to be termed, began to advocate the revival of ceremonial abandoned by the Church of

---

[42] See P. M. H. Bell, *Disestablishment in Ireland and Wales*, London 1969.

England for more than two centuries, to encourage the foundation of religious orders of monks and nuns, and to stress the value of personal disciplines such as confession to a priest, they were vigorously condemned as Romanisers.[43]

The impact of the Oxford Movement, irrespective of its impact on church building and restoration, which will be dealt with later in this chapter, has to be seen on two levels. Despite the heat they generated, which was far from being confined to just ecclesiastical circles, the number of extreme Tractarians or ritualists remained very small throughout the nineteenth century. On the wider front, however, Tractarians managed to make campaigns which they had not always even inaugurated, such as the abolition of appropriated or rented seating in churches, or the increase in both weekday services and celebrations of Holy Communion, very much their own, and in these areas they were much more successful, to the extent that by the 1920s the agenda of the Anglican establishment was an updated version of the Tractarian agenda of the 1840s. The situation in Kent very much mirrored the nation as a whole. In the 1840s a small number of Kent parishes had incumbents who identified with the more advanced Tractarians: Henry Wilberforce at East Farleigh, William Hodge Mill at Brasted, Francis Murray at Chislehurst.[44] Wilberforce and Mill were both the subject of petitions against them from aggrieved parishioners and the former, following the example of some of the leading Tractarians, such as Newman and Manning, who was a close friend, resigned his living and became a Roman Catholic. These secessions to Rome only fuelled the attacks on Tractarians and ritualists and confirmed their critics in their worst fears that the Tractarians' hidden agenda was the reunion of the Church of England with the Holy See on any terms available. This was not fair. Many Tractarians and ritualists, however much they aped Roman Catholic liturgical practices or accepted Roman Catholic doctrines, were strong critics of Rome itself and those aspects of Roman Catholicism which had developed since the Reformation. Within the Church of England most of the liberals or broad churchmen had been hostile to the Oxford Movement from its earliest manifestations. The Evangelicals did not really begin to attack the movement until the late 1830s. Traditional high churchmen were in a difficult position. Initially they welcomed much Tractarian teaching but they were nervous of the accusations of Romanising; some publicly attacked the Tractarians whilst privately supporting them. The difference in attitude can be seen in the fairly supportive stance that Archbishop

---

[43] For modern general studies of the Oxford Movement see Chadwick, *op. cit.*, i pp. 167–231; G. Rowell, *The Vision Glorious*, Oxford 1983; W. N. Yates, *The Oxford Movement and Anglican Ritualism*, London 1983. The impact of the movement in Kent is considered, with a useful selection of contemporary documents, in W. N. Yates, *Kent and the Oxford Movement*, Maidstone 1983. The opposition to the Oxford Movement is well covered in P. Toon, *Evangelical Theology 1833–1856: A Response to Tractarianism*, London 1979.

[44] For contemporary material see Yates, *loc. cit.*, and W. H. Mill, *Dr Mill's Reply to an Address by J. W. Faulkner, Esq.*, Brasted 1850. See also W. N. Yates, 'Francis Henry Murray, Rector of Chislehurst', *Archaeologia Cantiana*, xcviii (1982), pp. 1–18.

Howley and Archdeacon Harrison, both traditional high churchmen, took towards Henry Wilberforce at East Farleigh, compared with the strong condemnation of William Hodge Mill at Brasted by the Evangelical Archbishop Sumner. There was a short-lived Tractarian experiment at Gravesend. In 1833 a company had been set up to build a new proprietary chapel in the town and the shareholders appointed the first minister in 1834, when the chapel was licensed for worship by the bishop of Rochester. The chapel was never financially viable. In desperation the directors eventually sold the chapel, which had cost over £7,000 to build, for £4,000 in 1842 to the Revd W. J. Blew. Blew was a Tractarian who introduced daily services. In 1844 Blew tried to regularise the chapel's position by offering to build a parsonage house at his own cost and to present the patronage to the bishop of Rochester, if the bishop would consent to assign the chapel an ecclesiastical district. The bishop, however, did not respond favourably to this suggestion as plans were already in hand to build a new district church and assign it a parish, this being done in 1845. In 1851 Blew was inhibited by the bishop for subscribing, with a majority of his congregation, a memorial to Cardinal Wiseman regretting the manner of his reception in England after the restoration of the Roman Catholic hierarchy. Blew responded by selling the chapel to the Roman Catholics in Gravesend. Although the majority of his congregation transferred their allegiance to Rome whilst continuing to worship in the same chapel, Blew himself, although he attended the re-opening ceremony, remained a member of the Church of England, though never beneficed, until he died in 1894.[45]

Enormous pressure was put on the bishops of the Church of England to suppress the more extreme ritualist practices, such as the introduction of lighted candles, vestments and incense, or clergy celebrating the Holy Communion eastwards with their backs to the people, mixing water with wine in the chalice and using wafer bread. A typical expression of such views were the comments made by Viscount Sydney at the annual dinner of the West Kent Agricultural Association in 1866:[46]

> He adverted to what was now going on in the Church of England. All thinking men, members of that church, looked with great concern and alarm at the proceedings of a great part of the clergy. (Hear, hear). By degrees they were alienating the friends of the church from the Church of England, and he was quite convinced if things went on in their present state, before long there would be a secession from the church. They heard of movements for the abolition of church rates, and of the efforts of Liberation Societies, but the danger to the Church of England was not from without, but from within. He trusted that before many months were passed strong action would be taken on the part of the Church, of the English Episcopacy and the laity to prevent those proceedings which so alarmed all the true friends of the Church of England.

[45] R. H. Hiscock, 'The Proprietary Chapel of St John, Gravesend', *Archaeologia Cantiana*, xciii (1978), pp. 1–24.

[46] *Maidstone Journal*, 29 October 1866. I am grateful to Geoffrey Copus for drawing this reference to my attention.

Many bishops were reluctant to take extreme measures, partly because as high churchmen they had some sympathy with ritualism, partly because the ritualist clergy had a number of powerful patrons and supporters among the aristocracy and leading parliamentarians such as Gladstone and the Kent MP, Alexander Beresford-Hope. The main stronghold of ritualism in later Victorian Kent was Folkestone following the appointment of Matthew Woodward to the vicarage of the parish church in 1851. As well as introducing ritualist practices to the parish church, Woodward was able, as patron of the new district churches being erected in this expanding seaside resort, to offer preferment to ritualist protégés. Episcopal efforts to control ritualism having been perceived as inadequate, an alliance between Archbishop Tait, a liberal who had always been hostile to the Tractarians, and the incoming Conservative government in 1874 resulted in the Public Worship Regulation Act, which was designed to assist in the suppression of ritualism. The first clergyman to be prosecuted under the act was one of Woodward's protégés, C. J. Ridsdale, incumbent of St Peter's, Folkestone. Unlike some of those prosecuted after him, who almost pleaded to be imprisoned for contempt of court, Ridsdale came to a compromise with Tait, by stating that, though he felt himself obliged to carry out certain ritual observances, he would accept a dispensation from this obligation. Tait decided that an element of discretion was justified:[47]

> I gather that while you consider yourself as being under a sacred obligation to act upon what you conceive to be the literal meaning of the ornaments rubric in the Prayer Book, you yet acknowledge a general dispensing power in this matter to reside in me as your bishop; and you are ready under such dispensation to abstain from the use of the alb and chasuble, and lighted candles at the time of the Holy Communion, and the mixed chalice. I am quite ready to satisfy your conscience in this matter, and do hereby grant you a complete dispensation from the obligation under which you believe yourself to lie.

Ridsdale was true to his word and never wore vestments again at St Peter's, Folkestone, though he remained there until 1923. Most ritualist clergy were nothing like so co-operative. When clergy were imprisoned for refusing to obey the decisions of secular courts they declined to recognise, they elicited so much public sympathy that bishops used their power under the Act to veto further prosecutions and the legislation became unenforceable. The ritualists had won and their right to operate within the Church of England without undue restraint was reluctantly conceded.[48]

It is, however, important to stress that, although some aspects of Tractarian teaching and practice had been widely accepted within the Church of England by the last quarter of the nineteenth century, full-blown ritualism was not widespread

---

[47] Yates, *Kent and the Oxford Movement*, pp. 95–6.
[48] See Marsh, *op. cit.*, pp. 158–92, 218–41; also J. Bentley, *Ritualism and Politics in Victorian Britain*, Oxford 1978.

even as late as the years immediately before the outbreak of the First World War. In the diocese of Canterbury the eastward position at Holy Communion was taken in 72% of the churches in 1903, lighted candles were used in 47%, the mixed chalice in 38%, but vestments in only 12%. In the diocese of Rochester the comparable figures were eastward position 40%, lighted candles 30%, mixed chalice 27%, vestments 14%. Both dioceses were, however, above the national average at that time. In the Kent part of the two dioceses there were 33 churches in which vestments were worn, and only three (St Saviour's at Folkestone, St Mary's at Strood, and Egerton) in which incense was used. There were major towns such as Canterbury and Maidstone, with fifteen and ten Anglican churches respectively, in which vestments were not worn in a single church.[49] There were even some parts of the county in which even the most modest liturgical innovations, such as more frequent communion, had made little impact. On the Isle of Sheppey most churches still had only monthly communion in 1884; there was a weekly communion service in the united benefice of Leysdown and Harty. By 1889 there were weekly communion services at both Anglican churches in Sheerness, but only a monthly celebration at Elmley and Minster and fortnightly ones at Eastchurch and Queenborough. Not a single church had what was considered the minimum high church requirement of the 1880s, a weekly communion service at an early hour so that the sacrament could be received fasting. Evening communion services, by this date always an indication of Evangelical sympathies, were introduced in Sheerness at Holy Trinity in 1886 and St Paul's in 1888.[50]

The growth in more frequent communion services, which together with more weekday services, were the most visible legacies of the Oxford Movement, though the Tractarians themselves had built on earlier Evangelical initiatives, can be charted both for individual churches with continuous surviving runs of service registers, and for churches in the larger towns. This is shown for Kent in Tables 15 and 16.[51] As well as the increase in the frequency of communion services, there was generally a growth in the number of communicants during the latter part of the nineteenth century. The increase in the number of communicants is also shown in Table 15. This did not indicate any general increase in churchgoing, but simply a greater willingness to receive the sacrament, rather than just attending the services of Morning and Evening Prayer. The point is well made in the case of Rolvenden where some of the service registers, unusually, show not just the number of communicants, but also the number of those attending the other services. Between 1865 and 1885 there was a substantial reduction in the number of those attending the other services at all the major festivals, despite the significant increase in the

[49] W. N. Yates, 'Bells and Smells: London, Brighton and South Coast Religion Reconsidered', *Southern History*, v (1983), pp. 146–51.

[50] CKS, P 227/28/1: *Sheppey Church Magazine*, 1884–9.

[51] Table 15 based on service registers in CKS for Aldington (P 4/1/15A, 16), Chiddingstone (P 89/1/18–21), Holy Trinity at Maidstone (P 241A/1/23–4, 27), Riverhead (P 330C/1/23, 25, 27A) and Rolvenden (P 308/1/21–2, 31, 34).

Table 15

Communion Services and Communicant Numbers in
Selected Kent Churches 1865–1905

Parish	1865	1885	1905
Aldington	HC monthly No figures	HC monthly Easter 25 No celebration at Whitsun Christmas 12 (population 675)	HC weekly Easter 54 Whitsun 14 Christmas 23 (population 540)
Chiddingstone	HC monthly Easter 65 Whitsun 25 Christmas 25–30* (population 1200)	No register	HC weekly Easter 69 Whitsun 41 Christmas 61 (population 1051)
Maidstone, Holy Trinity	HC fortnightly Easter 235 Whitsun 131 Christmas 43 (population c.4900)	HC weekly Easter 143 Whitsun 105 Christmas 59 (population 4938)	HC weekly* Easter 358 Whitsun 185 Christmas 261 (population 4923)
Riverhead	HC monthly Easter 86 Whitsun 41 Christmas 52 (population c.700)	HC weekly Easter 75 Whitsun 28–38* Christmas 57 (population 917)	HC weekly Easter 109 Whitsun 55 Christmas 129 (population 868)
Rolvenden	HC fortnightly Easter 48 Whitsun 33 Christmas 25 (population 1483)	HC weekly Easter 66 Whitsun 56 Christmas 45 (population 1286)	HC weekly Easter 112 Whitsun 55 Christmas 61 (population 1065)

* 1865: No Christmas figures for Chiddingstone; information from 1864 and 1866.
　1885: No Whitsun figures for Riverhead; information from 1884 and 1886.
　1905: At Holy Trinity, Maidstone, there were two or three celebrations of Holy Communion on
　some Sundays.

Table 16

Weekly Early Communion and Daily Services in Anglican Churches
in the Main Kent Towns 1882–1913

Town	Churches	Early Communion				Daily Services			
		1882	1891	1903	1913	1882	1891	1903	1913
Beckenham	6	1	1	6	6	2	2	4	4
Canterbury	15	2	4	9	11	2	2	4	5
Chatham	3	0	2	2	2	0	2	2	3
Dartford	3	0	0	1	3	0	0	1	1
Deal	3	2	2	2	3	2	2	2	3
Dover	9	3	4	4	6	2	5	5	6
Faversham	3	0	0	2	3	0	1	2	2
Folkestone	7	5	5	6	7	4	5	4	4
Gravesend	5	1	3	3	5	1	1	1	2
Maidstone	10	1	2	4	8	1	2	4	6
Margate	4	0	0	1	4	0	0	0	2
Ramsgate	6	0	2	4	5	0	2	3	2
Rochester	5	0	1	4	5	1	1	2	4
Sevenoaks	3	0	2	2	3	0	2	2	2
Tunbridge Wells	10	1	2	4	6	2	2	2	3
TOTALS	92	16	30	54	77	17	29	38	51
(%)	(100)	(17.4)	(32.6)	(58.7)	(83.7)	(18.5)	(31.5)	(41.3)	(55.4)

number of communicants. However even in 1885 the number of communicants
only represented about a quarter of those attending the other services.[52]

By the beginning of the twentieth century the lack of early communion and daily
services no longer indicated the survival of liturgical conservatism but a positive
resistance on the part of Anglican Evangelicals to the type and frequency of
services favoured by those clergy who had been influenced by the Oxford Movement but would not have regarded themselves as Anglo-Catholics. In some towns
there was a polarisation, and hardly any communication, between churches that
were either extreme Anglo-Catholic or extreme Evangelical, despite the fact that
they were all part of the Church of England. This was the case in Dover where, out
of nine Anglican churches, three were Anglo-Catholic with daily communion and a

[52] The figures are as follows:

1865	Easter:	morning 255, afternoon 257, evening 239
	Whitsun:	morning 207, afternoon 249, evening 267
	Christmas:	morning 285, afternoon 126
1885	Easter:	morning 180, evening 250
	Whitsun:	morning 200, evening 180
	Christmas:	morning 120, evening 100

Sung Eucharist on Sundays, and three were Evangelical. By 1913 the towns with the highest number of Evangelical churches were Canterbury (4 out of 15), Dover, Maidstone (2 out of 10) and Tunbridge Wells (4 out of 10). At Tunbridge Wells the Evangelicals were led by Edward Hoare, the incumbent of Holy Trinity from 1853 until 1894. Hoare's opposition to ritualism led him to oppose the establishment of the new district church of St Barnabas in 1881 on the grounds that it was likely to become, as it did, a centre of ritualist practice and teaching.[53] At Folkestone a 'free' Church of England was established in 1882 to offer services of absolute Evangelical purity, though conducted by an Anglican clergyman using the Book of Common Prayer:[54]

> That such a witness is urgently needed in Folkestone is clearly shewn by the fact, that out of the seven Church of England places of worship in the town, no less than five are Ritualistic, and only two Evangelical, and in both of these that old Protestant landmark, the black gown, has been discarded, and the surplice substituted as the garb of the Preacher.

The divisions in the Church of England were also taken advantage of by Protestant nonconformists, though many of them had their own divisions to worry about. In 1844 there had been a major schism within the West Kent and Sussex Baptist Association over whether only baptised believers should be admitted to communion. Seven churches withdrew to form a new Association of Strict and Particular Baptists and refused to hold fellowship with Baptist churches permitting open communion. Four of these churches were in Kent: Borough Green, Hadlow, Meopham and Tunbridge Wells. A similar pattern of secession could be observed among individual congregations. At Maidstone secessions from the King Street chapel, founded in 1797, resulted in the setting up of the new Providence and Zion chapels in 1820 and 1831 respectively; within two years of its foundation, in 1833, the minister and 73 members of the Zion chapel had withdrawn to set up the new Bethel Chapel.[55]

(4) Church Building and Restoration

Between 1830 and 1901 no fewer than 839 churches and chapels were built or rebuilt in Kent, excluding those areas transferred to London in 1889, and many more were restored and re-ordered. This was part of a widespread programme of church building and restoration by all the major denominations in the belief, largely mistaken, that increased accommodation for worship would lead to

---

[53] Yates, *Kent and The Oxford Movement*, pp. 97–8.

[54] *Ibid.*, p. 102.

[55] F. Buffard, *Kent and Sussex Baptist Associations*, Faversham 1963, pp. 83–4, 103. For an excellent general introduction to the whole range of Evangelical belief and practice as it affected all religious bodies in the nineteenth century see D. W. Bebbington, *Evangelicalism in Modern Britain*, London 1989. The earlier European and American background is explored in W. R. Ward, *Protestant Evangelical Awakening*, Cambridge 1992.

increased churchgoing. The breakdown for Kent is given in Table 17;[56] as well as the totals for the county as a whole, separate figures are given for two of the main areas of population growth, Thanet and the Medway Towns. Although the Church of England and the main branches of Protestant dissent still accounted for almost 90% of this building activity, there was a significant growth in the number of churches built by other religious groups. As well as Roman Catholics, there were a number of millenarianist or extreme groups, of which one sect of Kentish origin was the Jezreelites. They were founded by a private in the army, built a tower in Gillingham which remained unfinished for lack of funds until its demolition in 1960, and were accused of a variety of sexual deviations.[57] From about 1840 the programme of church building and restoration was influenced by another factor in addition to the desire to provide accommodation for a growing population. Before 1840 church buildings aimed at being decent but practical. Influenced by the writings of the architect A. W. N. Pugin, a movement grew up which urged that churches should be designed to imitate in style, detail and internal arrangement, the churches of the Middle Ages, even if this meant sacrificing practicality. This movement was known as the ecclesiological movement and its disciples known as ecclesiologists. Societies to spread their aims and ideas were established at both Oxford and Cambridge. Initially these ideas found their strongest response among Roman Catholics and Anglican high churchmen but eventually they spread to influence all the mainstream Christian bodies in Britain.[58] What has been termed the ecclesiological revolution, however, requires modification. Until the last quarter of the nineteenth century even many Anglican churches were built with a complete disregard for ecclesiological principles, maintaining ideas about worship which had been inherited from the late eighteenth and early nineteenth centuries.[59] The fact that the main promoters of ecclesiology in the Church of England were also Tractarians, or even ritualists, created hostility to ecclesiological views within many sections of the established church, and among Protestant nonconformists. The Evangelical Francis Close summed up this opposition in a nutshell:[60]

> Romanism is taught analytically at Oxford, it is taught artistically at Cambridge . . . it is inculcated theoretically, in tracts, at one University, and it is sculptured, painted and graven at the other.

Thus churches built at East Peckham in 1840–2, Platt in 1842, Hildenborough in 1843, Pembury in 1846–7, Collier Street and Fordcombe in 1848, Walmer in 1849 and Deal in 1850, were wholly traditional in their liturgical arrangements. Platt and

[56] Based on the lists of churches published in R. Homan, *Victorian Churches of Kent*, Chichester 1984, pp. 33–103.

[57] *Ibid.*, pp. 21–2. See also R. A. Baldwin, *The Jezreelites*, Orpington 1962, and P. G. Rogers, *The Sixth Trumpeter*, London 1963. On the general background to millenarianism see J. F. C. Harrison, *The Second Coming*, London 1979.

[58] See P. Stanton, *Pugin*, London 1971, and J. F. White, *The Cambridge Movement*, Cambridge 1962.

[59] See W. N. Yates, *Buildings, Faith and Worship*, Oxford 1991, pp. 150–74.

[60] F. Close, *The Restoration of Churches is the Restoration of Popery*, London 1844, p. 4.

Table 17

Places of Worship Built or Rebuilt in Kent 1830–1901

Denomination	Kent	%	Medway Towns	%	Thanet Towns	%
Church of England	248	29.6	12	21.1	11	26.2
Old Dissent						
Independents/Congregationalists	101	12.0	6	10.5	4	9.5
General Baptists	75	8.9	5	8.7	3	7.1
Particular/Strict Baptists	33	3.9	4	7.0	2	4.8
Other Baptists	5	0.6		–		–
Calvinists	5	0.6	–		1	2.4
Presbyterians	8	1.0	2	3.5	–	
Unitarians	1	0.1	1	1.8	–	
Society of Friends	1	0.1	–		–	
Total	229	27.2	18	31.5	10	23.8
New Dissent						
Wesleyan Methodists	171	20.4	8	14.0	4	9.5
Primitive Methodists	48	5.7	3	5.2	4	9.5
Bible Christians	28	3.3	2	3.5	–	
Other Methodists	5	0.6	2	3.5	–	
Countess of Huntingdon	5	0.6	–		1	2.4
Total	257	30.6	15	26.2	9	21.4
Other Groups						
Roman Catholics	38	4.5	2	3.5	3	7.1
Brethren	12	1.5	1	1.8	1	2.4
Salvation Army	7	0.8	2	3.5	1	2.4
Catholic Apostolic	3	0.4	2	3.5	–	
Free Church of England	3	0.4	–		–	
Disciples of Christ	2	0.2	–		1	2.4
Swedenborgians	2	0.2	–		–	
Undenominational	32	3.8	2	3.5	5	11.9
Total	99	11.8	9	15.8	11	26.2
Extreme Sects						
Jezreelites	2	0.2	1	1.8	–	
Peculiar People	1	0.1	1	1.8	–	
Latter Day Saints	1	0.1	–		–	
Total	4	0.4	2	3.6	–	
Jews	4	0.4	1	1.8	1	2.4
Total	839	100.0	57	100.0	42	100.0

Hildenborough (Plate 4) both had three-decker pulpits.[61] At East Peckham, Pembury, St Saviour's at Walmer and St Andrew's at Deal, the pulpit and reading desk were placed on opposite sides of the entrance to a shallow chancel, an arrangement much favoured by the Incorporated Church Building Society which grant-aided so many church buildings and restorations.[62] Collier Street had a long chancel but it was not stalled for a surpliced choir, as the ecclesiologists would have wished, being empty apart from the altar.[63] The building of the new church at Fordcombe was promoted by the rector of Penshurst to serve the outlying hamlets of Fordcombe and Walters Green which were some three miles distant from the parish church and contained a combined population of 400. By January 1845 £920 had been promised to build the new church and £375 as an endowment for the minister.[64] The plans of the completed church, consecrated in January 1849, showed a building containing 236 sittings, of which 212 were free and unappropriated. There was tiered seating for children at the west end of the nave, and the pulpit and reading desk, though separate pieces of furniture, were placed adjacent to each other on the north side of the entrance to a shallow chancel. The Incorporated Church Building Society contributed £100.[65]

The first Anglican churches in Kent to incorporate, to a greater or lesser extent, ecclesiological principles of design were those of Kilndown, Rusthall and St Gregory's at Canterbury. Kilndown, completed in 1845, owed its embellishment to Alexander Beresford-Hope, the most distinguished of the young Tractarians in Parliament, and has been well documented.[66] The church at Rusthall was built in 1849–50. It was an unaisled cruciform building, but the chancel was stalled and the reading desk faced inwards (not westwards), as favoured by the ecclesiologists.[67] St Gregory's at Canterbury, built as a memorial to the late Archbishop Howley, and consecrated in 1852, was a completely ecclesiological design. All the seats were free and faced east in the nave and north aisle. The font was placed next to the entrance from the south porch. The pulpit was modestly tucked into the south-east corner of the nave, the chancel was stalled and raised two steps above the level of the nave, the reading desk was replaced by a stall in the chancel for the officiating minister, and the altar was raised four steps above the level of the chancel.[68] However, non-ecclesiological churches continued to be built for a few

[61] Plans in CKS, U 840 Q 421 and P 371C/6/4.
[62] Plans in Lambeth Palace Library, ICBS 2790, 3696, 3837–8; for the building of the new church at East Peckham see M. Lawrence, *The New Church*, East Peckham 1988.
[63] CKS, P 408B/6/1.
[64] CKS, U 1950 Q 1.
[65] Lambeth Palace Library, ICBS 3973.
[66] See White, *op. cit.*, pp. 157–8; Yates, *op. cit.*, p. 155 and *Kent and the Oxford Movement*, pp. 52–6; J. Newman, *Buildings of England: West Kent and the Weald*, Harmondsworth 1969, pp. 338–9. The interior remains largely intact. Beresford-Hope was also involved in the building of St Augustine's College at Canterbury, built for the training of missionaries, in 1844–8. The most thoroughly early ecclesiological church was Pugin's Roman Catholic church of St Augustine at Ramsgate, though most of the fittings have been either destroyed or re-ordered.
[67] Lambeth Palace Library, ICBS 4118.
[68] Lambeth Palace Library, ICBS 4205.

years after that and the re-ordering of St Nicholas, Rochester, in 1860–2 was an essay in liturgical conservatism (Plates 6 and 7). The aim was to increase the number of sittings from 714 to 954 and the total cost of the work was £1,930. The west gallery was extended along the north and south walls, and the three-decker pulpit was retained; although the pews, described as 'unequal in width and cumbrous in height', were re-ordered, the chancel remained full of seats, most of which faced west towards the pulpit.[69]

Two early Victorian restorations which showed the difference between ecclesiological and traditionalist attitudes took place at All Saints, Maidstone, and Stockbury. Indeed the initial impetus for the Maidstone restoration came from an antiquarian study of the fabric by a local architect.[70] Before 1823 the pulpit and reading desk were at the west end of the nave, the chancel, which had retained its medieval stalls, being used only for the monthly communion services; this was not a unique arrangement, two other Kent churches, St Clement's at Sandwich and King Charles the Martyr at Tunbridge Wells, having pulpits and desks at the west end of the nave until well into the nineteenth century. There were galleries across the north and south aisles, erected in 1714 and 1667 respectively, and at the west end of the nave, which housed the organ purchased by public subscription in 1747. The church had provided a total accommodation of 1682 sittings 'of which 387 were declared to be free for the use of the poor'. In 1823 the pulpit and reading desk were moved from the west to the east end of the nave and placed directly in front of the chancel arch in the middle of the central passageway, which was filled with loose benches to provide more accommodation for the poor. In 1840 the west gallery was demolished and the organ moved to the east end of the north aisle. On 7 December 1848 the vestry resolved to petition for a faculty to remove the other galleries and to completely re-seat the church. They were obliged to come to an accommodation with Lord Romney who, as owner of Mote House, the College and the former Archbishop's Palace, had the use of 67 seats in the north gallery and the body of the church for himself, his family, guests and servants. They also had to come to an agreement with the corporation over the relocation of the seats appropriated for the use of the mayor and corporation and of the grammar school.[71] The scheme cost £1,700 to which Lord Romney contributed £500 and the Incorporated Church Building Society £160. The church was re-opened on 7 September 1849. The new seating arrangements increased the existing accommodation by 340 sittings, despite the demolition of the galleries, and provided a total of 770 free sittings. It had been supervised by the architect R. C. Carpenter, an early advocate of ecclesiological principles, though what he achieved was something of a compromise. There were still loose benches between the blocks of pews. Seating for

---

[69] Rochester-upon-Medway Archives, P 306/6/4–5.

[70] J. Whichcord, *History and Antiquities of the Collegiate Church of All Saints*, Maidstone 1845. Whichcord's lithograph showing an idealistic reconstruction of the interior of the church in the late fourteenth century is reproduced in Yates, *op. cit.*, p. 123.

[71] Cf. the similar negotiations at Faversham in 1873–4: W. N. Yates, 'The Mayoral and Corporation Seats in Faversham Parish Church', *Archaeologia Cantiana*, cvi (1988), pp. 42–3.

children was placed in front of the medieval stalls in the chancel and behind them in the choir aisles. The pulpit and reading desk were broken up and placed one on each side of the entrance to the chancel.[72]

Although the restoration at Stockbury was carried out by an antiquarian incumbent, David Twopeny, it paid far less regard to ecclesiological principles. The church had been patched up after a fire in 1836, and in 1845 Twopeny laid before the vestry proposals for a proper restoration. He reported that he had access to subscriptions totalling nearly £255, to which he would add a personal donation of £105 if the vestry would approve a church rate of 1s 6d in the pound. Although the vestry initially agreed to levy a rate it subsequently changed its mind and resolved unanimously that 'no rate should be granted towards the alterations in the church at present, owing to the very unsettled state of the parish'. This was a reference to the disputes in the parish that had resulted from Twopeny's initiative. In 1846 the vestry permitted Twopeny to install an organ in the church, provided no expense should fall on the parishioners. The question of restoration was not re-opened until 1851. Even then Twopeny was obliged to meet most of the cost himself, partly from his own pocket and partly from the subscriptions he had raised and placed in a fund outside the control of the vestry. The work was completed in 1853, and the new arrangements illustrated by a coloured plan in the vestry minute book. They were very conservative. Pulpit and reading desk were placed in the middle of the seating which filled most of the church including the western part of the chancel. Separate accommodation was provided for single men, single women and for families. There was also tiered seating for children, which still survives, at the west end of the church. All sittings were technically allocated, but the vestry resolved that any which remained unoccupied after the first lesson at either morning or evening prayer could be allocated to any persons without seats, and that the parish clerk be authorised to show such people to any vacant seats.[73]

The restorations at Maidstone and Stockbury came up against all the features involved in the restoration of churches: ecclesiological pressure for the removal of unsightly galleries and large box pews; the campaign, by no means confined to the ecclesiologists, to abolish rented or appropriated seats; the problem of vested interests, especially in relation to pews; the reluctance of some parishes or congregations to raise money for church restoration. Nevertheless church restoration proceeded apace. The condition of churches in Kent, both restored and unrestored, in the middle of the nineteenth century has been recorded by Sir Stephen Glynne[74] and a local ecclesiologist, W. P. Griffiths.[75] An attack on appropriated pews was

---

[72] Russell, *op. cit.*, pp. 128–31; contemporary plans in the library of the Society of Antiquaries; contemporary illustrations and vestry minutes for 1842–59 at All Saints, Maidstone.

[73] CKS, P 348/8/1.

[74] *Notes on the Churches of Kent*, ed. W. H. Gladstone, London 1877; see also W. N. Yates, 'Sir Stephen Glynne and Kentish Ecclesiology', *Studies in Modern Kentish History*, ed. A. P. Detsicas and W. N. Yates, Maidstone 1983, pp. 187–202.

[75] W. N. Yates, 'The Condition of Kentish Churches before Victorian Restoration', *Archaeologia Cantiana*, ciii (1986), pp. 119–25.

launched by an old-fashioned high churchman, Walker King, archdeacon of Rochester, in 1841:[76]

> Sometimes a few of the principal Inhabitants, to the exclusion or inconvenience of others equally respectable, are allowed to appropriate to themselves all the most conveniently situated seats in a Church. Again allotments of Pews are made, totally disproportionate in size to the Wants of those demanding them... The Parishioners indeed have a claim, recognised by law, to be seated according to their rank and station. But the higher classes must not be accommodated beyond their real wants, to the exclusion of their poorer neighbours, who are equally entitled to accommodation, though not to the same degree of accommodation, supposing the seats to be not all equally convenient.

Whilst the amount of free seating in churches which operated a system of pew rents undoubtedly increased after 1820, pew rents survived in some churches until well into the twentieth century. In most nonconformist chapels, and some Anglican churches, pew rents provided the major part of the income and were used both to pay the minister and maintain the fabric. Nevertheless by 1851, in seven out of the ten largest towns in Kent, the Church of England had more free sittings than rented ones; by contrast only in Ramsgate did the nonconformist chapels have a majority of free sittings, and in Maidstone the number of free sittings in nonconformist chapels were less than a quarter of the total number of sittings available.[77] Pew rents were often a vital ingredient in the clearing of building debts where buildings, especially those of nonconformists, had been financed by loans. In Kent the debts of all the Independent chapels in the county totalled £19,410 in 1869; the chapels at Ashford, Gravesend, Hythe, Maidstone and Sevenoaks each had debts ranging between £885 and £1,500.[78]

Between 1840 and 1870 restoration schemes were as likely to produce a non-ecclesiological re-ordering plan as an ecclesiological one, or parishes compromised by presenting schemes that did not fall clearly into either category. In Kent this was the case in the plans of reseating schemes at Westerham in 1852 and Linton in 1860.[79] On the other hand, G. F. Bodley's drawings for his proposed restoration of Bicknor in 1858 show a fully ecclesiological re-ordering,[80] whereas the plans for a re-ordering at Sellindge in 1847 (Plate 5a) show the pulpit still placed in the middle of the nave, the eastern part of the chancel empty apart from the altar and seats for children under the west tower.[81] There were still pews in the chancel at Seal in 1856,[82] and a completely non-ecclesiological arrangement at Snargate in 1870 (Plate 5b).[83] In some churches restoration did not take place until almost the

[76] King, loc. cit.
[77] Yates, 'Kentish Towns in the Religious Census', p. 403.
[78] Kent Congregational Magazine, September 1869, p. 114.
[79] CKS, P 389/6/12 and U 24 P 21.
[80] CKS, U 449 P 6; reproduced in Yates, Kent and the Oxford Movement, pp. 126-7.
[81] CKS, P 329/6/3.
[82] CKS, U 840 Q 16.
[83] CKS, P 340/28/5.

end of the nineteenth century, and a few escaped it altogether, surviving long enough for their interiors to be appreciated by a generation for whom non-ecclesiological arrangements were not something that demanded immediate destruction.

The progress of church restoration can be minutely observed at Hadlow and Wateringbury in the record of archidiaconal visitation begun by Walker King and continued by Benjamin Harrison. At Hadlow King commented in 1844: 'I would observe that the Pews in the chancel are of an inconvenient height and to a degree shut out the Communion Table and the chancel from the body of the Church'. Nothing, however, was done and Harrison referred in 1849 'to the great desirability of their being lowered to allow a better view of the Chancel from the body of the Church, and of the reading desk from the seats in the Chancel'. By 1853 Harrison was able to record that 'I have much satisfaction in seeing the manner in which the enlargement and restoration of the Church have been carried into effect, to the great improvement of the building, as well as the better accommodation of the parishioners for Divine Worship'. This, however, had not included the seats in the chancel, where presumably the lay rector had resisted any pressure for change. In 1858 Harrison pressed the point again:

I have only to suggest that a great improvement would be made to this church – completing what has already been done with excellent effect in the body of the church – if, whenever opportunity offers, the chancel was re-arranged, the high pews being lowered, the seats placed longitudinally, and new Communion rails substituted for the present, the space within the rails being at the same time increased.

Not until 1873 was Harrison able to record 'I have great satisfaction in seeing how great an improvement has been made in the Church, by the rearrangement, long desired and recommended, of the seats in the chancel, completing the work which had already so well been done in the body of the Church'.[84] At Wateringbury in 1841 Walker King was clearly very dissatisfied with arrangements in the church:

It is very inconvenient to erect a pew adjoining the rails, at the Communion Table, and can scarcely be justified by the additional sittings afforded to the congregation. The churchwardens should not allow Parties to hang up curtains round their Pews. By such a practice the general view of the congregation is interrupted and great offence would be given by granting an allowance to one Person and not to another and a general practice of this kind would be highly inconvenient and improper.

In 1849 Benjamin Harrison 'ordered . . . that the pew be removed adjoining the rails of the Communion Table. It is strongly recommended that the Church be repewed and the seats lowered, whenever a general re-arrangement of the interior can be effected'. He was still pressing this point, though fairly gently, in 1853: 'I find everything in good order, and have only to commend to the consideration of

84 CKS, P 163/6/1.

the parishioners the desirability of adopting some plan by which increased accommodation may be provided in the Church, with re-arrangement of seats and lowering of pews'. Reseating took place in 1856 and Harrison recorded in 1858 that 'I have to express my complete satisfaction at the manner in which the enlargement and rearrangement of the Church, with the lowering of the old pews, has been carried into effect'. But the restoration of 1856 had been a modest affair which had fallen well short of what the dedicated ecclesiologist would have required. By 1879 this point of view was expressed by the rural dean, J. R. Hall, deputising for, the by now elderly, Archdeacon Harrison: 'I find . . . the internal arrangement of the seats and galleries is very unsightly and inconvenient, and I am glad to hear that there is a plan in contemplation for an entire rearrangement of the seats in the interior of the Church'.[85]

(5) The Churches and the Local Community

For those actively involved in the management of churches and chapels, whether as ministers or as lay officers, matters relating to accommodation, services and restoration were of great importance. But the changes that took place in the nineteenth century did not just affect the internal life of the churches, but also their role in the local community and their relationship to society as a whole. There was a significant change in the role of the clergy themselves, particularly within the Church of England.[86] This was not just the result of Evangelical and Tractarian influence. Indeed the role of both in the changes that took place has almost certainly been exaggerated. Change came because it was adopted by the mainstream of Anglican clergy, those inheritors of the high church tradition that stretched back to 1660 and beyond:[87]

> The differences between the generations [of high churchmen] was mainly differences of emphasis and style. The old high churchmen were dignified and emollient; the young militants were exhibitionist and provocative, so they made a bigger splash in the media.

Nonconformity became more outward looking as well, influenced one suspects by the arrival of the Methodists, who in the eighteenth century had been very much the counterparts of the high church 'militants' in the nineteenth. All the churches adopted a missionary zeal. The fact that they were in competition with one another, and that the results of the 1851 religious census clearly demonstrated to those who had not realised it already that Britain had entered into a period of religious pluralism, enhanced such developments. At a local level churches developed societies, some quasi-political, others missionary or devotional; they inaugurated

---

[85] CKS, P 385/6/3; plans of 1856 restoration also in CKS, P 385/6/5.
[86] See G. K. Clark, *Churchmen and the Condition of England*, London 1973, and W. D. B. Heeney, *A Different Kind of Gentleman*, London 1976.
[87] Dewey, *op. cit.*, p. 138.

coal and clothing clubs; they ran soup kitchens and other welfare schemes; they produced magazines; they provided wholesome entertainment and social functions for their members and potential members. By the end of the nineteenth century most churches, even in the rural areas, were supporting a wide range of activities over and above the usual round of Sunday and weekday services. A typical example of such varied activity is provided by the Sandwich Congregational Church. This was an Independent congregation that dated back to the mid-seventeenth century. By 1870 it was in decline and there was a strong likelihood that the chapel might have to close. It was saved through the intervention of the Kent Congregational Association who organised the appointment of a new minister after a three year vacancy. By 1875 the congregation had revived to such an extent that they were able to establish a Sunday school.[88] The archives of the chapel contain programmes for fund-raising bazaars and musical entertainments; a Christian Home for Youths and Temperance Society, a Young Men's Mutual Improvement Society and a Social and Literary Society were established.[89] The rules of the Congregational Church at Ash-next-Sandwich, published in 1865, stated that it was the duty of the minister to 'visit those members who are in affliction and trouble',[90] and a large proportion of the week for most clergy was spent in visiting their flocks; some were able to involve their laity in this visiting programme. Visiting was used not just as a means of showing the concern of the church with sickness and suffering but as a way of encouraging greater church attendance.

Why did the churches develop this new role in the second half of the nineteenth century? The recognition, resulting from the evidence of the 1851 religious census, on the part of both the Church of England and the other, non-established, churches that their relationship had changed was probably a major factor. Until the first half of the nineteenth century the Church of England had relied heavily on its role as an established church. Whilst it encouraged elements of what might be regarded as missionary activity, whether through private devotion, or education, or social welfare, it relied on this to be provided through individual initiative, through societies, through charitable bequests. For the Church of England there was a growing recognition, given firm evidence by the 1851 religious census, that this was no longer enough. Those who dissented from the Church of England had, largely as a result of sporadic persecution and only limited toleration, seen themselves as gathered communities making provision for their own members but nervous of aggressive proselytisation for fear of establishment reaction. For them their growing numbers led to increased confidence and a willingness to further expand their activities and to react positively to occasional setbacks. The growing toleration of the early nineteenth century and the legislation that helped to promote it was another major factor in shifting attitudes. By the middle of the nineteenth century, whatever complaints dissenters might still level against the privileges of the Anglican establishment, they recognised that these were very limited, and that for most

88 Young, *op. cit.*, p. 21.
89 CKS, N/C 323 Z 3–8.
90 CKS, N/C 323 A 22.

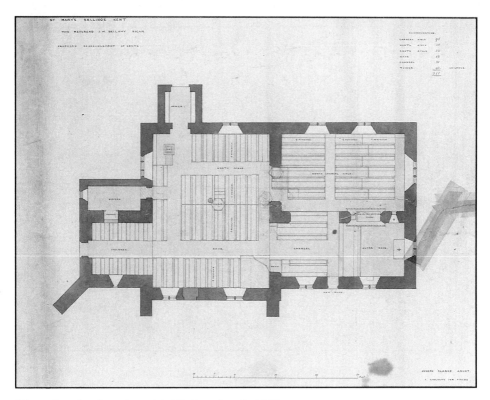

Plate 5a. Seating plan of Sellindge church 1847.

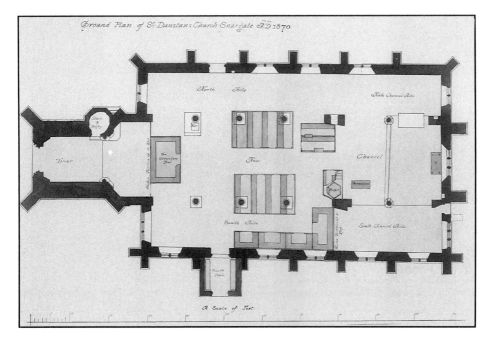

Plate 5b. Seating plan of Snargate church 1870.

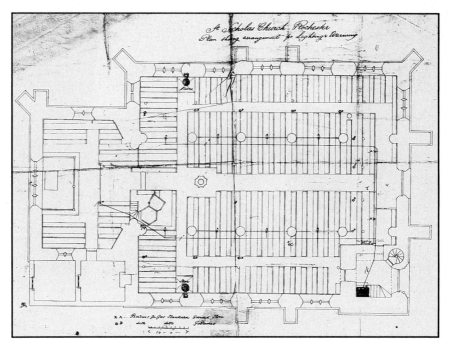

Plate 6. Seating plans of St Nicholas', Rochester (a) before and (b) after the restoration in 1861.

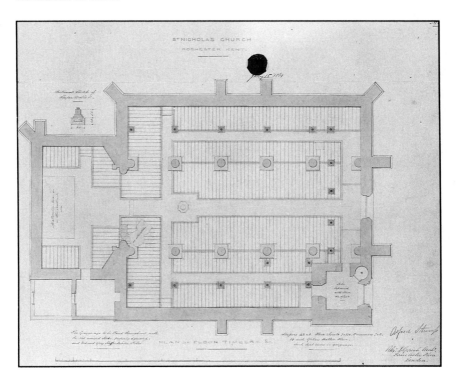

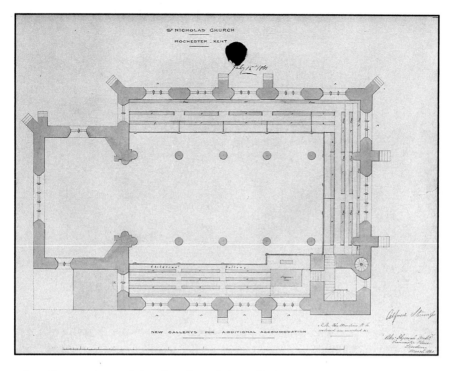

Plate 7. (a) Plan and (b) elevation of the galleries at St Nicholas',
Rochester 1861.

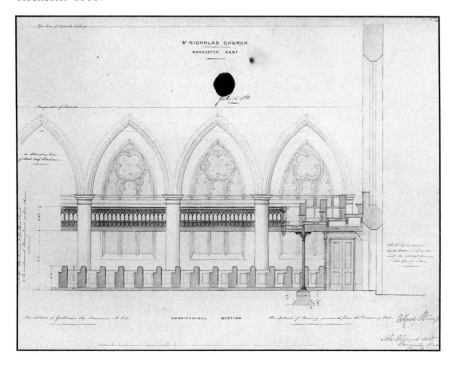

Plate 8a. Dean Stanhope school, Deptford, showing the effigies of a boy and girl wearing charity clothes, 1871.

SELECT ESTABLISHMENT

FOR

YOUNG LADIES,

2, ALBERT TERRACE,

UPPER QUEEN STREET,

DEAL,

(NEAR THE SOUTH EASTERN RAILWAY TERMINUS.)

MRS. EASTES

Continues to receive Six Young Ladies to board and educate with her own daughters.   Every attention paid to their Education, Morals and Comfort.   References to Parents of Pupils.

Prospectuses may be had on Application.

Terms Moderate.   Good Sea Bathing.

Plate 8b. Advertisement in the *Post Office Directory* for Kent of a school for young ladies at Deal 1867.

practical purposes all the churches were competing on the same level playing field. Whereas the nonconformists adopted the concept of the gathered church, developed in the eighteenth century, to meet the needs of their extended numbers, the lesson was not lost on the Church of England. It borrowed from nonconformity the concept of the gathered church, recognising, however reluctantly, that it too had become sectarian in character, and developed its own model. From the middle of the nineteenth century to the middle of the twentieth century, when it began to break down as local communities changed, the Anglican concept of the gathered church in the local community was a church building with its own resident clergyman, and assistant clergy in parishes with significant populations, its own dedicated parsonage house, its church day school and its parish hall or institute as the meeting place for a whole host of quasi-religious and social activities that would have been regarded as sectarian, and by definition therefore not part of the pastoral role of the parish church, by churchmen of a previous generation. As the Church of England developed its own concept of the gathered church to promote an ever-growing range of pastoral activities, so the nonconformist churches emulated them, both to retain their existing members and to attract new ones, in virtually every respect. By the end of the nineteenth century all large centres of population, most small towns and even some of the larger villages could boast a wide selection of different places of worship offering some elements of individuality, but a great many more that it was difficult to tell apart. In the large centres of population the Church of England itself offered places of worship of different kinds of churchmanship: Anglo-Catholic, Central, Evangelical or some gradation between them. The churches offered as much choice to the potential worshipper as the vast expansion in the number and variety of shops offered to the potential customer.

In 1861 the Kent Congregational Association set up a system of lay evangelists. By 1866 evangelists were working in 61 towns and villages in Kent; 7,595 families were regularly visited, 4,481 services had been held in chapels or private houses and 215 in the open air, 218 visits had been made to the bedsides of the dying and a total of 134,000 tracts distributed; 'the agents have rejoiced over 79 precious souls hopefully converted unto God, many of whom are now living in church fellowship'.[91] It was reported that at Ashford 'there is an evangelist employed in this district who has a large number of families under visitation and the prospects of usefulness are generally encouraging'. At Newnham the visits of the evangelist 'among the poor are well received, the attendance of the chapel has largely increased, and much interest is excited in the movement'.[92] This increased level of nonconformist activity was not welcomed by the Anglican clergy. One lay evangelist reported that he had[93]

> . . . called on the Rector. We had about five minutes' conversation in his hall.
> He was civil but cold and formal; wished to know upon what authority I acted,

---

[91] *Kent Congregational Magazine*, August 1866, p. 228.
[92] *Ibid.*, May 1866, pp. 147, 148.
[93] *Ibid.*, March 1869, p. 85.

&c. I told him, upon the authority of our Saviour; that the field was the world, and that the Lord of the harvest had ever used a variety of labourers to reap those fields. But he could see no farther than his own church and parish; and thought that all Dissenters were intruders and without authority. He said, moreover, that, as such, he could not recognise me.

This attitude was not untypical, certainly among high churchmen, whether of the old or the new school. Anglican Evangelicals, however, were prepared to co-operate with dissenters, and dissenters were prepared to co-operate with each other, particularly in those areas that crossed doctrinal divisions, such as the promotion of the temperance movement or opposition to ritualism and Roman Catholicism. There was also a recognition among many nonconformist sects that they ought to target those areas in which there was no active Evangelical ministry of any type, such as Romney Marsh:[94]

The spiritual destitution of the Marsh may be firstly inferred from the fact that there is not, as we learned, one evangelical, earnest and laborious clergyman of the Established Church in the whole district. . . . and what are Dissenters doing: There is not one congregation of Independents. An aged Baptist minister preaches to a few people at Dymchurch. The Wesleyans are the only denomination who are putting forth efforts for the salvation of souls.

Even the Wesleyans had no resident minister and were dependent on circuit preachers from Rye. The author concluded 'that Romney Marsh offers a fine field for the labours of a lay evangelist'.

In their missionary efforts all churches recognised the special needs of certain types of people. One of the Congregational lay evangelists pointed out that 'the hop gardens in September furnish an excellent field of labour. . . . gave away 152 tracts and 100 books and magazines. An old person was very willing to take the tract offered.'[95] The workers were, on the whole, not local people but temporary immigrants, mostly from London, who came each year at harvest time. In 1877 a Church of England Missionary Association for Hop-pickers was formed at Maidstone, with an inaugural meeting chaired by Archdeacon Harrison. The Association aimed to provide the parish clergy with the assistance of lay or clerical missionaries during the hop-picking season, as well as tents in which special services could be held. In 1878 tents for hoppers' services were erected in the parishes of Barming, East Malling, Nettlestead and Wateringbury. The mission employed 29 helpers and provided services for 28,000 hoppers. At East Malling over 200 hoppers attended a special service in the parish church at the end of the hop-picking season. The tent services were usually held on Sunday afternoons or evenings, the missionaries using Sunday mornings to encourage the hoppers to attend. During the week the missionaries visited people at work and read to them from religious books during the dinner hour. They also encouraged the hoppers to

[94] *Ibid.*, January 1869, pp. 367–8.
[95] *Ibid.*, March 1869, p. 86.

have their children baptised. The failure of the hops in 1882 meant that the mission had to be scaled down. Only thirteen helpers were employed to minister to 8,400 hoppers. Although the primary aim of the mission was to promote religious education among the hoppers and to make them regular churchgoers, those involved in the mission, such as J. Y. Stratton, rector of Ditton, were also concerned to secure improvements in the living conditions of these seasonal workers.[96] Another organisation set up in 1890, that aimed to make provision for seasonal visitors to Kent was the West Kent Church Fruit Pickers' Mission. The missionaries were supplied by the Church Army and the costs met by collections and subscriptions in the participating parishes. In 1892 missionaries were sent to Crockenhill, Farnborough, Halstead, Orpington, St Mary Cray, St Paul's Cray, Shoreham and Swanley. In 1914, on the outbreak of the First World War, it was decided that the mission could no longer be centrally organised and 'that each parish should undertake its own individual work among the fruit pickers'. In that year the Church Army supplied nine missionaries and two nurses at a cost of £104 4s 1d.[97]

Harvests were not used simply as an opportunity for missionary work among seasonal workers. They were also seen by the rural clergy as one of the events of the year that could be used to integrate the church with the whole community. From the 1840s the clergy endeavoured to transform the traditional celebration of the harvest 'with beer and drunkenness' to 'a special service in church followed by a dinner of beef and plum pudding and beer'.[98] At Frittenden in 1866 there was a service in church at 12 noon, followed by the men's dinner at 1.30 pm, the farmers' dinner at 3.00 pm, tea at 5.00 pm and community singing at 6.30 pm. The celebration also included a cricket match and athletic events. Admission to the grounds cost 4d and to the grounds and tent 6d, but the occasion was heavily subsidised from parish funds as the budget provision for the dinner itself was 2s 2d per head.[99] Every effort was made by the Victorian clergy to give churches and chapels a social as well as religious dimension, though frequently the one led to the other. Within the Church of England the most important of these organisations was the Mothers' Union, which began in a Hampshire parish in 1876, became a diocesan organisation in 1887 and a national one in 1893. By 1912, when it had a membership of 278,500, it had a branch in virtually every parish.[100]

The development of a new attitude on the part of the clergy can be seen in three Kent parishes in the survival of records from the vicariates of John Woodruff at Upchurch (1834–69), John Rumsey at Rolvenden (1855–84) and Cleave Warne at

---

[96] See J. Y. Stratton, *Hops and Hop-pickers*, London 1883, which also (pp. 171–84) gives an account of the missionary activities. Another association, established in Hampshire in 1874, which placed greater emphasis on supplying tracts to hoppers, was also active in the parishes of East Farleigh and Nettlestead. On the distribution of tracts in the nineteenth century see Chadwick, *op. cit.*, i pp. 443–4.

[97] CKS, P 145/28/3–4.

[98] Chadwick, *op. cit.*, i p. 517. See also J. Obelkevitch, *Religion and Rural Society: South Lindsey 1825–1875*, Oxford 1976, pp. 58–60.

[99] CKS, P 152/28/9.

[100] Chadwick, *op. cit.*, ii pp. 192–3.

Stoke (1893–1907). Woodruff was an old-fashioned high churchman moderately sympathetic to the Tractarians and a severe critic of the Evangelical Archbishop Sumner. Rumsey was a Tractarian though not a ritualist. Warne represented what had become the 'central plus' school of Anglican churchmanship by the end of the nineteenth century. Woodruff took an interest in ecclesiastical architecture, reseating his church, 'the Pews in the Centre Aisle . . . being altered from the large square wooden box to low open seats, so that the Congregation face the Minister'. In 1854 he paved the sanctuary with encaustic tiles, 'black and white in alternate squares with red and blue pattern tiles intermixed'. At the harvest festival he held a collection for the Kent Ophthalmic Institution and he ran a clothing club for the benefit of his poor parishioners.[101] At Rolvenden Rumsey introduced more music into the services, abolished the practice of receiving fees at baptisms, 'opened a Bible class for all ages', introduced collections at all services and started daily services in church in 1859. In 1863–4 he experimented with the issue of Erskine Clark's *Parochial Magazine*: 'I added a local cover containing much interesting matter, parish records, monthly service calendar, &c. The working classes liked it much but the gentry and farmers would not support it, and after losing about 5 or 6 £ annually I was obliged to give it up'.[102] Many other churches and chapels in Kent also introduced some sort of magazine at this time; the mixture was usually some sort of local cover or outer section, running perhaps to several pages, and a middle section comprising that month's edition of one of the many popular national religious publications. The local section would not only advertise church activities and record church events, but often also contain secular information, whereas the national magazine insert tended to be filled largely with fiction of a moral or uplifting nature.[103]

Cleave Warne, a curate in Essex whose parents lived in Rochester, had long hoped that he might be offered the living of Stoke. On 6 May 1892 he recorded in his diary: 'drove . . . to Stoke. Looked at Church. Both parish and church a disgrace'.[104] He achieved his ambition the following year. In his inaugural sermon he declared his intention of visiting the sick, introducing an evening service, and replacing the afternoon service with a Sunday school.[105] Warne inherited a fairly run down parish by the standards of the 1890s. Out of a parish of 648 people, the Sunday morning congregation was only thirty, but he was able to attract 130 people to his new evening services. Holy Communion was celebrated on the first Sunday of each month and on Christmas and Ascension Days at noon; there were only ten regular communicants. This was despite the fact that the Church of England had little competition from dissent. There were Bible Christian and Roman Catholic chapels in the parish. The Bible Christians had no resident minister and the

---

[101] CKS, P 377/28/34.
[102] CKS, P 308/1/2/1–12.
[103] On religious periodicals in the nineteenth century see P. Scott, 'Victorian Religious Periodicals: Fragments that Remain', *Studies in Church History*, xi (1975), pp. 325–39.
[104] CKS, U 1390 F 6, p. 43.
[105] CKS, U 1390 Q 3.

congregation was declining. The Roman Catholic chapel was served by a visiting priest twice a month; it was attended by twelve people, all of Irish extraction, but their numbers were also gradually reducing. The main moral problem in the parish was drunkenness. Warne told the bishop 'the Restoration of the Ch: is absolutely imperative. The existing high pews and general uncared for appearance obviously hinder that reverence befitting God's house'.[106] In 1894 he bought a cross and vases for the altar, cassocks and surplices for the choir, and introduced an early celebration of the Holy Communion at Easter, Ascension Day and Whitsun. In 1895 he contacted an architect about the restoration of the church, beginning with the chancel; the Malmayne's Hall pew was demolished in November 1895 and in October 1896 the rest of the chancel fittings were removed. Between 28 December 1896 and 1 January 1897 'the old "three-decker" was demolished and the seats given us by St Mark's Reigate substituted. The pulpit was erected against the north pier of the chancel arch . . . a clear sweep having been made of the "three-decker" and box pews which flanked it, and the pews against the west tower being cut down'. Finally, in June 1898 the restoration of the church was completed 'by "gutting" the nave. It was a grand sight to witness the demolition of the box pews and partition in north aisle'. The church was re-opened in October 1898, 'a red letter day in the history of the parish'. Warne used the opportunity of the re-opening to hold a mission in the parish. Holy Communion was celebrated daily at 8.00 am during the week of the mission. Thereafter Holy Communion was celebrated every Sunday (first Sunday of each month at noon, others at 8.00 am) and on all the principal Saints' days. Morning Prayer was said daily in church at 9.00 am.[107] Further embellishments were made to the chancel in 1899 when Warne 'went to London. Gave orders for Easter altar frontal at Ponting's. Bought candle stocks, shields etc at Wippell's and banners for chancel arch at Golding and Plummer's'. Later that year he 'ordered green altar frontal at Ponting's' and used the occasion of an episcopal visit for a confirmation service to have the chancel arch decorated.[108]

The relationship of the churches to the local community was vastly different in 1914 from what it had been in 1830. Yet that change had occurred quite gradually and, for some people, imperceptibly. Although the Church of England remained the established church it was widely recognised that it was on a much more even footing with dissent than had been the case before 1830. This indeed had been the cause of so much of the controversy within the Church of England in the 1830s, 1840s and 1850s, as it saw its privileges threatened. By the end of the nineteenth century the Church of England had come to terms with its new role and some clergy welcomed the greater freedom that they believed had resulted from the changed situation. Internally too the churches had changed. The buildings were different. The role of the clergy was different. The services had changed. The churches were no longer there to provide just worship and preaching, but a wide

[106] CKS, U 1390 Q 4.
[107] CKS, U 1390 F 9, p. 108; F 12, pp. 55, 98; Q 5–6.
[108] CKS, U 1390 Q 7.

range of social activities. In short the nineteenth century had seen, in terms of ecclesiastical plant, an enormous explosion in religious activity. This activity had, however, been bought at a price. All this religious expansion was taking place at a time when, generally speaking, churchgoing was already in decline. Congregations built up debts they found hard to clear. They erected buildings which had become redundant within a few generations. Already, in the larger cities, churches and chapels were beginning to close well before 1914. In Kent, where the problem of inner-urban decay was not really apparent before 1914, this trend was delayed until somewhat later. It is difficult to know how it could have been avoided. The religious expansion programme of the nineteenth century was based on a false premise: that availability and variety would find a response that would enable the churches to recover their investment. It did not materialise. All the new buildings and initiatives, the division of ecclesiastical areas into units that were ideal for the development of a social ministry, were expensive to maintain and labour intensive. If the congregations did not materialise and if, later on, candidates could not be attracted to the ministry, rationalisation and contraction became inevitable. The twentieth century has seen the reversal of much that the Victorian churches aimed to achieve; that, however, does not invalidate their vision or what looked to them like successes at the time.

Education in Kent 1640–1914

(1) The Situation in 1640

It is generally agreed that England as a whole in the late sixteenth century saw something of a 'revolution' in the huge growth of educational opportunity at all levels of society.[1] An increasingly wealthy gentry aspired to make their sons literate, educate them in manners, and gain places for them at University and the Inns of Court. Meanwhile, ambitious smallholders and craftsmen were attracted by openings available for literate boys in the clergy, law, medicine and in clerical work, where it was a great advantage to be able to sign a bond and check a bill.

Kent responded to this demand, witnessing a great deal of educational activity after the Reformation. By 1640 its five public boys' grammar schools which pre-dated the Reformation – at Canterbury (A.D.731), Sevenoaks (1432), Wye (1448), Tenterden (1510) and Faversham (1527) – had been supplemented with new foundations at Rochester (1542), Tonbridge (1553), Sandwich (1566), Biddenden (1566), Cranbrook (1573), Maidstone (1574), Sutton Valence (1575), Dartford (1576), Milton (1594) and Ashford (1638). This brought the grand total of endowed grammar schools to fifteen, three-quarters of which were to be found in the increasingly prosperous mid and west Kent.

Petty schools acted as feeder schools for these grammar schools. Dr Clark has contended that by 1640 most towns with more than a thousand people in Kent had three or more petty schools; and Canterbury most probably had ten. Several petty schools were endowed and provided education free of charge, as at Jesus Hospital, Canterbury (c.1600), where poor children, 'by nature prone to idleness and stealing', were taught 'to know God and be trained up in labour and made apt members of the commonwealth'.[2] These schools often had a rather precarious existence. Possessing an endowment too slender to provide for a special schoolhouse, teaching was often conducted in a corner of the church, or in the teacher's own house. Here the children – who may have numbered only three or four – were taught to read the catechism and the primer, to write and (sometimes) to do arithmetic. Boys might be trained in the basics of a craft, whereas girls (who were usually educated separately) might be taught how to sew. At best, the children were in the hands of conscientious teachers, struggling to do a good job in what were frequently poor conditions, and remunerated with only a meagre salary. At worst, petty schools were run by those least qualified to do the job well – the negligent, ignorant and

---

[1] L. Stone, 'The educational revolution in England, 1560–1640', *Past and Present*, xxviii (1964), pp. 41–80.

[2] Canterbury Cathedral Archives U32 (Orders of Jesus Hospital), ff. 21–2.

drunk – who taught merely as a side-line to occupations as diverse as gunnery, weaving and surgery.

Alongside the grammar and petty schools, a variety of select private schools catered for children from genteel families who in medieval times would probably have been taught at home by a private tutor. There are several recorded instances of pupils using these schools to very good advantage in preparing for university. Of particular distinction seems to have been Thomas Walter's school at Westerham. Between 1623 and 1640 he sent up at least eleven boys from Westerham to Christ's College, Cambridge.[3] Many other such schools were also to be found in the countryside, close to where the gentry lived. Great emphasis was laid on being taught the social graces – dancing, deportment, fencing and the 'polite' language of French.

Beneath all this, there was by 1640 a whole variety of much less-institutionalized, more *ad hoc* and discontinuous provision in the towns and countryside alike. These arrangements are only drawn to our attention from a survey of church visitation presentments:

> that Mr Johnson teacheth children and keepeth school . . . having no licence in that behalf   [St John's, Thanet, 1594][4]

> Lewis Rogers, schoolmaster . . . a common ale-house haunter and gamester [St Lawrence, Thanet, 1613][5]

> a schoolmaster called Robynson . . . is not licensed . . . and saith there is noe hell   [Goudhurst, 1603][6]

> . . . Thomas March, teaching schole without license being once already by the judge of this Court inhibited and monished to desist   [Ashford, 1622][7]

The survival of such visitation presentments is haphazard; they only provide pin-point evidence for specific years; and the questions were certainly answered much more conscientiously in some places than others. Nevertheless, the evidence that does exist indicates a substantial infrastructure of schools beneath the great endowed foundations with their feeder petty schools and the more reputable private schools.

(2) Education During the Puritan Revolution, 1640–1660

Continued interest was shown during the Civil War and Interregnum towards education. The Puritans were convinced of the importance of education as a means of improving society and the individual. It was the great ambition of John

---

3   P. Clark, *English Provincial Society from the Reformation to the Revolution*, Hassocks 1977, p. 445 n. 58.
4   A. Hussey, 'Visitations of the Archdeacon of Canterbury', *Archaeologia Cantiana*, xxvi (1904), p. 21.
5   *Ibid.*, p. 34.
6   Canterbury Cathedral Archives X.9.3, f. 52v.
7   Canterbury Cathedral Archives Z.4.3, f. 174.

Comenius – the leading educationalist of the day – who visited England in 1641, that education should be extended to everybody through a compulsory state system of free schools. It was a great waste, wrote the economist William Petty, how many men capable of high office were merely ploughing the fields.

In practice, activity lagged well behind the grandiose plans of the reformers. The political and economic insecurity brought about by the upheavals of the Civil War discouraged philanthropic investment in education, and schemes to establish schools were sometimes thwarted, as at Dover; or, at best, delayed, as at Greenwich in the same year. Nevertheless, four local efforts did materialize in the 1650s. Staplehurst, a major centre of Puritan activity, managed to establish an endowed school in 1651, where children were taught reading, writing and religion. Shortly afterwards, a local subscription was raised to pay the schoolmaster there. The following year, Abraham Colfe endowed a grammar school (complete with library and scholarships) and a reading and writing school at Lewisham under the management of the Leathersellers' Company. In East Kent, John Smith of Wickhambreux built a school for the poor with accommodation for the master in 1656. Finally, in the Weald, writing schools were founded by the Calvinist Freegift Tilden in 1657 at Smarden and at neighbouring High Halden.

(3) From the Restoration to the Church Societies, 1660–1811

By the Restoration, schools were well-scattered and hardly anywhere was more than nine miles from a grammar school or a writing school.[8] Not merely did all the large market towns have a school but sparsely-populated rural areas were also well-provided for. The only notable areas of neglect were Romney Marsh and the north Kent coast.

Immediately after the Restoration, the Clarendon Code (named after Charles II's leading minister) imposed stricter ecclesiastical control over schoolteachers. Under the Act of Uniformity (1662) schoolteachers had to swear to 'conform to the liturgy of the Church of England'; and the Five Mile Act (1665) effectively prevented Protestant Dissenters from teaching at all. Schoolteachers also now had to subscribe to the Thirty-nine Articles of the Church of England and take out a licence to teach. This licence they were required not merely to purchase but to pay for the privilege of exhibiting at visitations. This applied to *all* schools until 1700, and continued to apply to grammar schools after this date.

Using schoolteachers' testimonials, oaths, subscriptions and licences, schools are well-documented in a total of thirty-nine Kent parishes in 1662 [see fig. 1]. This estimate is clearly a very conservative one, seeing as no women are included; and it makes the unwarranted assumption that all teachers bothered to obtain a licence. The most ancient of these schools was at Canterbury, being first recorded in Bede's *Ecclesiastical History* (A.D.731). By Henry VIII's time the school was endowed, had a fixed constitution and was known as the King's School. Drawing

---

[8]   W. K. Jordan, 'Social Institutions in Kent, 1480–1660', *Archaeologia Cantiana*, lxxv (1961), p. 90.

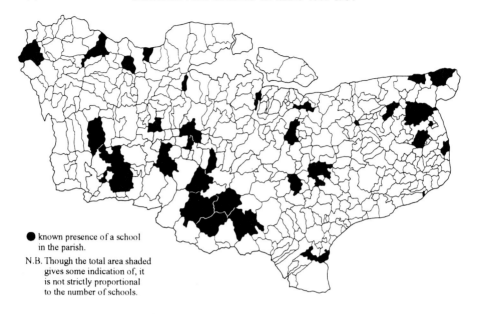

● known presence of a school
  in the parish.

N.B. Though the total area shaded
     gives some indication of, it
     is not strictly proportional
     to the number of schools.

Figure 1. Provision of schooling in Kent by parish 1662.

their finances from extensive cathedral revenues, the Dean and Chapter were empowered to admit to the school fifty poor boys 'destitute of the help of friends, and endowed with minds apt for learning'. Although a number of local gentry at this time and since demanded that the school be filled exclusively with the sons of gentlemen, they were not successful, for by the mid seventeenth century many boys came from much more modest backgrounds and were only too ready to be bound apprentices to tradesmen or to go into farming.

Treating these ecclesiastical sources with caution, they do nevertheless suggest that the spread of schools by the 1660s was somewhat haphazard. In an otherwise fairly disparate scatter, there seems to have been a concentration of parishes with some provision in the densely populated Weald, another in the north-east and yet another in the north-west of the county. They included the important port-towns of Gravesend, Dartford, Dover and Deal. Most of the remaining parishes in which schools were recorded included a substantial town – Ashford, Faversham, Maidstone and Rochester. On the other hand, in the more sparsely populated areas – the infertile Isles of Grain and Sheppey, together with Romney Marsh – only one school is *known* to have existed.

The situation was to change radically over the next century and a half. On the basis of much more wide ranging sources covering the first decade of the nine-teenth century,[9] we can be certain that there was a school of some description in very nearly one half (172) of the parishes in Kent. The pattern of provision,

---

[9] Based on the *Abstract of Returns Relative to the Expence and Maintenance of the Poor* (1803–4) [British Library 433, i, 112 (2)]; trade directories; the incomplete visitation returns for the

however, still revealed some very well endowed as well as some very poorly provided for parts. The most densely-schooled regions were still those of a century and a half earlier. In the Weald, where the population remained rather static during the period on account of the decay of its cloth and iron industry, the number of schools had perhaps doubled over these years. This was indeed a modest increase when set against the rapid rates of expansion which had taken place in Thanet and, even more conspicuously, in the north-west where the number of parishes with provision may have more than quadrupled as both areas grew in importance as centres of market gardening and light manufactures. The more sparsely-provided areas, much as before, comprised the waste lands south-east of Canterbury; those parishes radiating from Faversham on the edge of the North Downs; and the Romney Marsh district – all with a relatively low number of inhabitants.

The presence, though more especially the absence, of a school in any given parish in about 1800 continued to correlate closely with its population. In fact, almost nowhere with one thousand or more inhabitants was without a recorded school. There were, in addition, and particularly in the more thinly populated east of the county, several parishes such as Kingsnorth near Ashford and Preston near Wingham, with far fewer inhabitants which nevertheless now had some provision [see fig. 2].

In the thirty-nine documented parishes with schools shortly after the Restoration, there was a total of some forty-five schools. Slightly over a quarter of these schools were maintained as private enterprises. The overwhelming majority *for which we have records* were, however, in receipt of a perpetual endowment. At least half of these schools are known to have taught a classical curriculum and were to be found in urban parishes. Endowed schools teaching reading and writing, on the other hand, tended more often to be located in rural communities where the study of Latin and Greek was irrelevant to the needs of children who would end up working in the fields.

Some of the more wealthy schools at the Restoration had special buildings but maybe almost half of all schools were to be found in non-specialist accommodation: churches, coffee houses, boatbuilders' shops and, of course, in teachers' own premises. Such make-shift buildings certainly reflect the voluntary mentality of contemporaries towards education. This lasted until the late eighteenth century when a rapid population increase and new ideas about rights and justice resulted in education becoming a real public issue.

By the early nineteenth century, the educational picture in Kent was very much more complex, with numerous different types of schools suited to all levels of society. There were an increasing number of academies and private boarding schools training young ladies and gentlemen in the social graces; day, boarding and evening schools for the various 'middling classes'; other schools with a small endowed foundation for the poor, where the teacher had to admit fee payers to make ends meet; and finally, several schools (including those in workhouses) intended for instructing poor children alone.

diocese of Canterbury, 1806, and the deanery of Shoreham, 1807 [Lambeth Palace Library VG 3/2a–d; VPII/2/2a–b]; and *C(harity) C(ommissioners') R(eports)* I and II (1819).

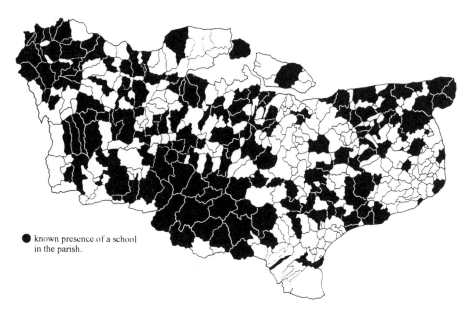

Figure 2. Provision of schooling in Kent by parish 1807.

An important change had taken place in relation to the endowed schools during this interval. Those teaching a classical and those offering an English curriculum had been fairly equal in number in about 1660; but by about 1800 the latter were outstripping the former by a factor of three to one. Geographically, the north-west, the Weald, Thanet and the principal towns were now especially well provided for, with new English schools at Greenwich and St Mary Cray; Goudhurst and Rolvenden; St Peter's and Birchington; and Rochester and Maidstone, respectively.

Significantly, the number of endowed classical schools had hardly increased at all during the period (a mere two having been established at Goudhurst and, nominally, at Leybourne). On the other hand, more than forty endowed English schools had been founded, bringing the total of such schools to over five times the 1660 figure. Many of them now offered places to girls as well as to boys. More generally, through a plethora of common day schools, subscription schools, new 'Schools of Industry'[10] and hundreds of little 'dame schools' throughout the county, education by the beginning of the nineteenth century was increasingly being matched to the aspirations of those lower down the social order.

This extensive growth was made possible by a massive outpouring of largely private philanthropy. The overall sum made available to education in Kent between 1660 and 1786,[11] either in the form of uninvested legacies, annual returns on invested stock and rents on land, can be estimated at £128,000. This was, even

---

[10] Some 1,016 children were on roll in these schools at the opening of the nineteenth century [*Abstract of Returns Relative to the Expence and Maintenance of the Poor* (1804)].

[11] *Charitable Donations – Abstract of Returns* (1786–1788).

allowing for inflation, more than twice the total given to education in the period 1480–1660. When looking at charitable endowments generally, the share allotted to education in Kent rose quite spectacularly, from twenty-three per cent to thirty-nine per cent between these periods.

As far as the pattern of educational endowments is concerned, the years 1660 to about 1700 can be viewed as a relatively calm, though far from sluggish, period. It was followed by a shorter burst of activity, with a peak to be found *circa* 1710–25, marking the 'hey-day' of the charity schools.[12] A very successful example of a charity school built in this period would be the subscription school in Deptford (1715). Annual subscriptions of a guinea or half a guinea from local tradesmen were soon supplemented by donations and in 1723 the school was able to move to specially built premises in Butt Lane.

No new schools at all were endowed between 1736 and 1752, even though some fifteen educational bequests were made. The period between then and 1780 also witnessed for the most part augmentary endowments to established schools. In the last decades of the century, heightened interest in education resulted in a fresh wave of school building, with occasionally, as at Leybourne and at Benenden, the available finance serving to set up more than one school.

In 1660 educational opportunity for the poor in Kent had been very patchy, and in rural areas it was especially restricted. By the beginning of the nineteenth century, on the other hand, there was a modest proportion (about 8.5%) of new, subscription-based, schools designed wholly for the poor, some of which were connected with the recently established British or National Societies. These existed alongside other schools with legacies attached to them expressly for the education of a few poor children.

Those Kent parishes which still had no facility for educating their poor in 1800 were almost invariably to be found in the countryside. Having said this, many rural parishes which were able to offer no school places to their poor in 1660 had very good provision by the early nineteenth century, with sometimes, as at Keston and Milsted, almost certainly in excess of fifty per cent of poor children being educated. In strict contrast, the towns had generally coped much less well in providing for the vast increase in children of an educable age, occasioned by the huge increase in the population as a whole. Although the percentage of poor children schooled never seems actually to have deteriorated during the period, only if the town possessed a substantial 'School of Industry', as did Sevenoaks, is educational provision likely to have touched as many as half those eligible. Normally, urban facilities appear to have been *very* much less adequate than this, with many towns only managing to cater for perhaps one in twenty poor children.[13]

Who was behind this very mixed achievement? Support from the government towards education was unrealistic after the Restoration because grammar schools

---

[12] This correlates to similar bursts of activity nationally, in the establishment of parochial libraries, and in gifts of plate to churches.

[13] See R. Hume, 'The Schooling of the Kentish Poor from the Restoration until the establishment of the National Society, 1660–1811' (unpub. M.A. thesis, University of Keele, 1979), pp. 32–8.

in its eyes had been the very breeding grounds for seditious puritanism during the previous two decades. Education was now left to the church and to the patronage of individuals throughout the eighteenth and well into the nineteenth century.

It is frequently argued, however, that in place of government initiative, the (High Church) Society for Promoting Christian Knowledge (SPCK), assumed a pioneering role by creating a nationwide system of 'charity schools' for poor children. 'Nothing was too small for the Society's attention, and no task too great for it to undertake', wrote the late W. E. Tate.[14]

In spite of the proximity to its London headquarters, all the evidence suggests that the SPCK had a much more modest role in Kent. Although it published impressive lists of schools in its annual *Accounts*, in a material sense, the involvement of this small voluntary association was almost negligible. 'The Society raised hardly any money with which to back its advice', a recent secretary has written.[15] Certainly, there is no reference in its archives to the SPCK helping to fund any Kent school, and a great deal of evidence in its correspondence files to suggest that it was quite out of touch with the state of education in the county.[16] Such schools as do appear, based on whosoever's initiative, almost invariably failed to live up to the SPCK's ideal of teaching the 'three Rs', the Church of England catechism and also providing an apprenticeship.

In the absence of a central body with both sufficient interest *and* means to fund education for the poor, support needed to be enlisted at a local level. Here, those who could afford it, were encouraged to support the 'good work'; and their contributions, made, no doubt, from a mixture of philanthropic and more selfish motives, were quickly forthcoming. The strength of paternalism in this connection is very evident. Of the total of some 145 benefactors who provided for the education of poor children in Kent in the century and a half after the Restoration, perhaps some two-thirds bestowed endowments on their native parish. It has been noted elsewhere how the gentry were very much orientated towards their own estates, where they were expected to take the poorer classes under their protective wing and help alleviate their condition.[17] This is why many of their bequests would go beyond simply providing schooling for poor children, and extend to the welfare of the parish poor as a whole.

There was a change in the status of these benefactors to Kent education during the eighteenth century. Before 1700 the larger landowners and wealthy London merchants were predominant amongst their ranks. After this date, the clergy, encouraged by the SPCK, appeared for the first time in strength, and made a marked impression between 1702 and 1729. Their relative absence after this date was accompanied by a significant withdrawal by the nobility from the educational

14 'S.P.C.K. Archives', *Archives*, iii (1957), p. 106.

15 W. K. Lowther Clarke, *The History of the S.P.C.K.*, London 1959, p. 22.

16 R. Hume, 'Interest with impotence: the influence of the S.P.C.K. as a directive force for the development of education in eighteenth century Kent', *History of Education* (1982), vol. 11, No. 3, pp. 165–72.

17 C. W. Chalklin, *Seventeenth Century Kent*, London 1965.

scene. In contrast, the squirearchy, together with men and women of a comparatively modest social status, including the increasingly prosperous yeomanry already remarked upon, continued or even redoubled their number of contributions towards providing the poor with schooling; so that by 1800 there was a far greater degree of community involvement in education.

Local subscription presented an alternative means of raising and maintaining a school. The subscribers, in common with those leaving bequests, were usually resident in the parish their contributions were supporting. Their number might range from a single family and the vicar, as at Pluckley in 1806, to as many as the 120 subscribers supporting the Margate Charity School in 1792. Subscription was, however, a potentially precarious source of finance, with sums collected varying according to the climate of opinion, and, more mundanely, the depth of purses. When funds were high, it was possible to admit more children into the school, or perhaps provide equipment and items of clothing for the pupils. When they were low, on the other hand, teachers' salaries might be reduced and such 'services' as clothing the children curtailed. A charity sermon or a concert might be necessary to keep a school solvent during a financial crisis. Such a concert was held at the theatre in Deal in July 1795 when a comedy, 'The Beaux Stratagem', was performed to support the town's charity school.[18]

At some point between 1722 and 1731 there was a general tail off in subscriptions right across the county. By this date, the schools had lost a lot of their earlier popularity and were allegedly seed-beds of Jacobitism. The low church and frequently dissenting tradesmen of towns such as Deptford and Greenwich, on whose support the enterprises depended, had evidently become disaffected, and many subscription schools were to remain in decline until the church reawakened interest in education at the end of the century. Problems experienced in sustaining subscriptions into the second quarter of the eighteenth century were particularly severe at Ashford, where the SPCK correspondent tells us in 1725 'that the Charity School . . . is unhappily sunk by the total withdrawing of the subscriptions which supported it'.[19] Similarly, at St Mary Cray 'the late violent opposition to charity schools and collections . . . and the covetous discouragement of the rich, [had] ruined the school'.[20] Exceptional in this respect was the school at Tunbridge Wells (founded about 1680), which continued to attract contributions from the nobility and gentry who visited the spa. In more rural parishes, where there were few tradesmen, the subscription venture might barely even be able to get off the ground. Such was the situation at Orpington where the SPCK correspondent reported 'a strange want of religious zeal and publick spiritedness'.[21] When subscriptions did materialize in the rural areas, the existence of the schools they supported seems to have been fleeting, as at Boughton under Blean and Hollingbourne.

---

[18] *The Kentish Gazette* 30 June 1795.
[19] A(bstract) L(etter) B(ook) XIII 8482, 23 Sept. 1725, SPCK Archives, 25 Marylebone Road, London.
[20] SPCK ALB IX 5965.
[21] SPCK. Original Letter File IV 5622, 30 May 1718.

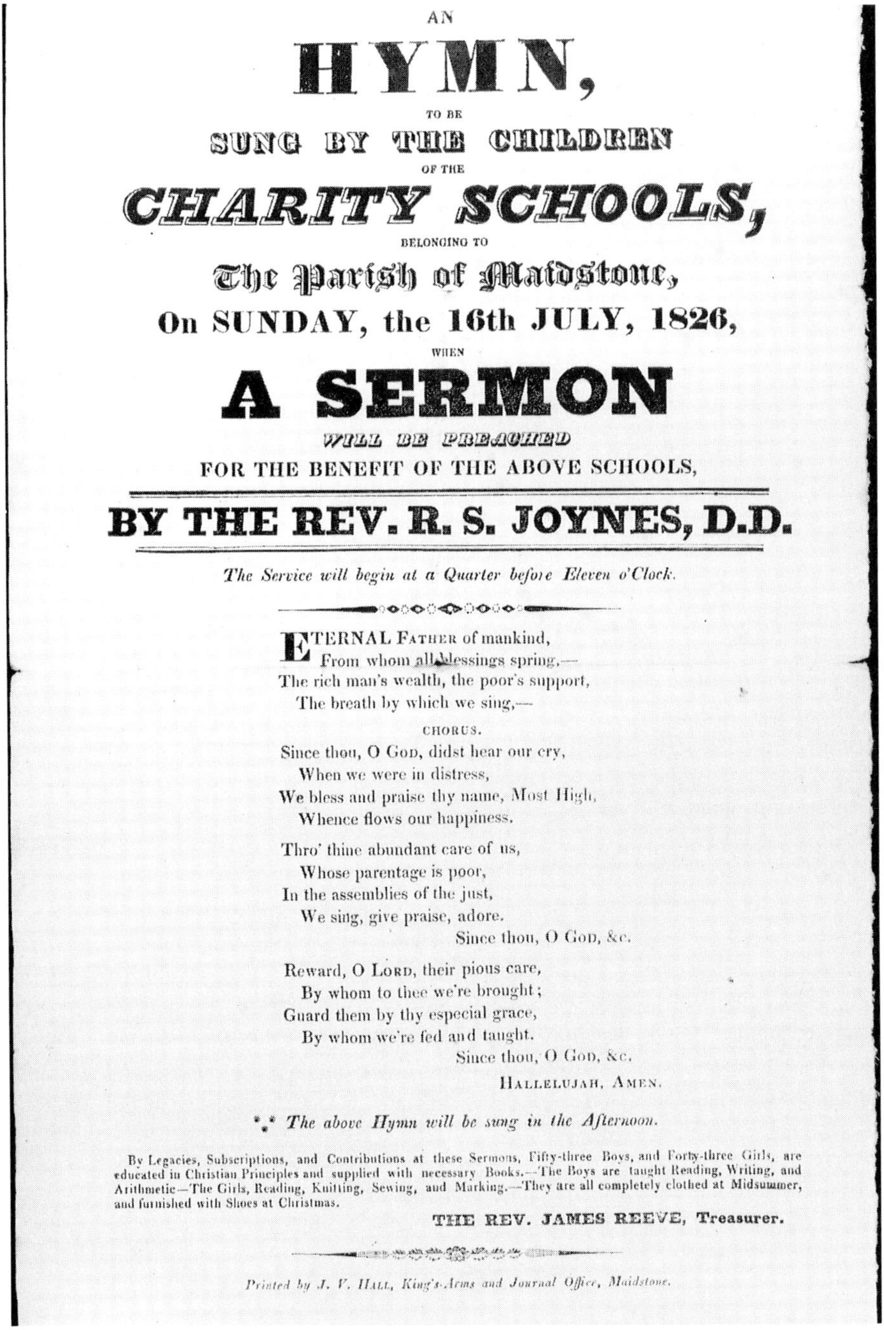

AN

HYMN,

TO BE

SUNG BY THE CHILDREN

OF THE

CHARITY SCHOOLS,

BELONGING TO

The Parish of Maidstone,

On SUNDAY, the 16th JULY, 1826,

WHEN

A SERMON

WILL BE PREACHED

FOR THE BENEFIT OF THE ABOVE SCHOOLS,

BY THE REV. R. S. JOYNES, D.D.

The Service will begin at a Quarter before Eleven o'Clock.

ETERNAL FATHER of mankind,
  From whom all blessings spring,—
The rich man's wealth, the poor's support,
  The breath by which we sing,—

CHORUS.

Since thou, O GOD, didst hear our cry,
  When we were in distress,
We bless and praise thy name, Most High,
  Whence flows our happiness.

Thro' thine abundant care of us,
  Whose parentage is poor,
In the assemblies of the just,
  We sing, give praise, adore.
                    Since thou, O GOD, &c.

Reward, O LORD, their pious care,
  By whom to thee we're brought;
Guard them by thy especial grace,
  By whom we're fed and taught.
                    Since thou, O GOD, &c.

HALLELUJAH, AMEN.

** *The above Hymn will be sung in the Afternoon.*

By Legacies, Subscriptions, and Contributions at these Sermons, Fifty-three Boys, and Forty-three Girls, are educated in Christian Principles and supplied with necessary Books.—The Boys are taught Reading, Writing, and Arithmetic—The Girls, Reading, Knitting, Sewing, and Marking.—They are all completely clothed at Midsummer, and furnished with Shoes at Christmas.

THE REV. JAMES REEVE, Treasurer.

Printed by J. V. Hall, King's-Arms and Journal Office, Maidstone.

Figure 3. Handbill advertising a sermon to raise funds for charity schools at Maidstone 1826.

The curriculum offered during this period by these and other schools was given shape by the demands arising from the unique economy and society of *individual* parishes or regions in the county. The tendency was for schools teaching reading alone to be much more rarely found in the towns than in the countryside; this was in direct contrast to schools teaching children to cast accounts (a skill in high demand by tradesmen and merchants) which were predominantly an urban phenomenon.

Special subjects, designed to fulfil local needs, made their appearance in some schools. At the Green Coat School in Greenwich the master was required not only to teach the children to read, write and cast merchants' accounts, but to 'make them capable of the art of navigation'.[22] Similarly, at the town's Royal Hospital School the children studied 'the Elements of Navigation'.[23] A school for boys at Dover also offered this subject;[24] and it was available to the most proficient senior boys at the town's subscription charity school by the end of the eighteenth century. In the same period, Folkestone's Harvey School rejected Latin, its trustees reasoning that 'for the boys of this place we consider the art of navigation more useful'.[25] Meanwhile, the developing importance of the trade in local hops with London, and of market gardening in the county, was reflected in the unashamedly vocational subject-matter studied by Canterbury's Grey Coat Scholars who spun hop-bagging 'at proper seasons' in the new workhouse, and who may also have learnt 'something of Gardning'.[26]

Regional differences made themselves felt in other ways in the curriculum. In nearly all the Wealden parishes around Cranbrook where religious radicalism remained strong after the Restoration (Goudhurst, Hawkhurst, High Halden, Rolvenden and Smarden), catechetical instruction seems to have been omitted in the schools and bible-reading emphasized in its place. In Cranbrook, John Hassell, master at Dence's School, was presented by the churchwardens in 1716 for failing even to take his scholars to church. Only in the great nonconformist centre of Maidstone, however, do distinct subscription schools, built and maintained by dissenters, seem to have taken root during the period.[27]

A change began to take place in the composition of the curriculum taught in Kent schools as the eighteenth century progressed and the economy developed. Whereas bequests made during the late seventeenth and early eighteenth century tended to lay down that reading alone be taught, those made after 1760 usually provided for the teaching of writing and arithmetic, in response to the call for more

---

[22] 'Rules, Orders and Constitutions', in J. Kimbell, *Account of Legacies, Gifts etc. to the Poor of St Alphege, Greenwich* (Greenwich, 1816), p. 112.

[23] SPCK ALB XIII 8713, 14 Mar. 1726.

[24] SPCK, *Account* 1721.

[25] *CCR* I (1819), Appx p. 161.

[26] SPCK ALB XV 10294, 11 Aug. 1729.

[27] Visitation enquiry, Archbishop Manners Sutton (1806) [Lambeth Palace Library, VG 3/2c] where one school was managed by Protestant Dissenters, and another by Independents and Baptists. Each taught and clothed twelve boys and twelve girls.

clerks and better-educated fine craftsmen. Unique was Sir Joseph Williamson's mathematical school founded at Rochester in 1701 to equip boys for service at sea.

Another important transformation was occurring in relation to the curriculum of the grammar schools of Kent, where classical teaching was being undermined by an ever more vociferous demand for learning which would be of real benefit to the parish. Such was its effect that at Sutton Valence only one boy was being taught classics when the Charity Commissioners made their visit;[28] and at Benenden, where the inhabitants consisted of farmers and labourers, Latin had been dispensed with altogether.[29] At Sandwich and at Tenterden there were specific complaints made that the curriculum was not suited to the needs of the poor.[30] So insistent had they been at the latter that some of the Free Grammar School's funds had been diverted to its National School, for 'as a grammar school, it was no longer of any use in the parish'.[31] At Colfe's School, Lewisham, the number of free scholars plummeted from thirty-one to a mere three in 1819 when the trustees attempted to raise the reputation of the school by restoring its purely classical curriculum.[32] Contemporary newspaper advertisements highlight the changes which the grammar schools needed to make so as to survive; the most usual being to extend the curriculum beyond classical Greek and Latin (which they were bound by their foundation deeds to teach without charge), to include more 'modern' and practical subjects – such as English and mathematics – for which parents would have to pay.

The teaching of religion in Kent schools also underwent a change in emphasis between the Restoration and the early nineteenth century. Before 1750, concern to use the schools primarily to inculcate Anglican doctrine was reflected in 41% of schools founded in Kent between 1701 and 1750 requiring that the catechism be taught. In contrast, at only 22% of those founded in the county between 1751 and 1800 was it prescribed.[33]

By the late eighteenth century numerous Sunday schools were being reported in episcopal and archidiaconal visitations. Their clear advantage over day schools was that children could work and still receive an education:

> The first view in establishing these Schools was to inure the Children to early habits of attending Divine Service, and of spending the leisure hours of Sunday in a decent & virtuous manner; and then to inculcate as much instruction of reading, as one day's attendance will permit.[34]

We are told that the forty children at the Langley Sunday school had their dinner

[28] *CCR* I (1819), Appx, p. 228.

[29] *Ibid.*, Appx, p. 131.

[30] *Ibid.*, Appx, p. 218.

[31] *Ibid.*, Appx, p. 232.

[32] L. L. Duncan, *The History of Colfe's Grammar School, 1652–1952*, London 1952, pp. 95–7.

[33] Hume, thesis, pp. 256–9.

[34] Charles Moore, vicar of Boughton under Blean [Lambeth Palace Library, Archbishop Moore's 1786 Visitation Presentments, VG 3/1c].

provided and that the school 'has had the happiest Effects'.[35] Less obviously, Sunday schools also served to educate adults who had been untouched by the more meagre educational opportunities of their own day.

The economy and society of individual parishes further affected the exact scheduling of school holidays, and brought a markedly seasonal toll on absenteeism which was to continue up to (and very often beyond) the era of compulsory education. The trustees of the Dover subscription school, for instance, would regularly grant at least a fortnight's vacation during the wheat harvest, 'that the children may be enabled to glean';[36] whilst lessons at Sandwich would be discontinued during the hop season.[37] Typical of the more liberal attitude towards absenteeism prevalent among school managers in a rural parish (where the demand for school places would have been much less great) is the candid reply of the Pluckley incumbent to Archbishop Secker's visitation enquiries of 1758:

> The Boys work at proper times, always in Harvest & Hopping time, & whenever their Parents particularly want them.[38]

For children in Pluckley, as for most of those in the rest of the county at this time, any schooling was fitted in as best it could between the more serious needs of work.

(4) From Voluntary Effort to Government Intervention, 1811–1914

During the eighteenth century, the government's policy had been one of non-intervention in education. It had been satisfied with whatever facilities the charity schools, the cheap 'dame', common day and Sunday schools could provide between them. Not surprisingly, therefore, the provision of schools in the county by 1800 was haphazard, and so often depended on local enthusiasm and charity. By what can only be described as a geographical accident, a boy might be able to take advantage of a grammar school education, although the reputation of many of these schools was now seriously being brought into question.

Changes in the methods of production, which quickened from about 1780, began to alter the structure of society, and called for a better educated workforce. This made it essential that the scope of education be broadened to include children from far less privileged backgrounds. By this time, there was also an increasing number of philanthropists, economists and social reformers who were drawing attention to the injustice of applying the *laissez-faire* principle to the poor, and who were calling for a system of national education.

What made the efforts of all these groups more difficult was the still widely held belief among the ruling élite that the poor should only receive a very basic

---

35 *Ibid.*, VG 3/1d.
36 'Rules (1805)' [Dover C.E. Primary School].
37 'Charity School Minutes', 15 July 1771 [Centre for Kentish Studies, Sa/QEc 1;4].
38 Lambeth Palace Library, MS 1134/1–6.

education – religion, social obedience and a few necessary occupational skills. They feared that if the poor were educated above their humble, labouring position in society they would become discontented with their lot and rebel. The bishops also disliked the flavour of any scheme which would remove schools from the control of the Established Church. Rivalry between the nondenominational British and Foreign School Society (established 1807) and the Church of England's National Society for Education (established 1811) delayed the progress of education in Kent, as it did in the rest of the country.

The first tentative step towards intervention by the government in education was made in 1833 when the Treasury granted £20,000 to be shared between the two church societies for building schools to educate the poorer classes throughout the country. A survey published in that same year, the *Abstract of Education Returns*, reveals the magnitude of the task before the supporters of a national system of education. It might be estimated that somewhat less than one third of all Kent children had places at day schools, and less than one quarter of children attended Sunday schools. Such restricted opportunities were provided by a miscellany of institutions.

The British and Foreign School Society had eighteen nondenominational and nonconformist schools in Kent by the middle of the century. Most of its schools were confined to towns. In the west of the county these included schools at Chatham, Maidstone and Tunbridge Wells; while in the east there were establishments at Ashford, Canterbury and Margate. There were also Wesleyan Methodist schools during the first half of the century at Boughton, Buckland, Ramsgate and Sittingbourne; and a school for Particular Baptists at Smarden. These schools arose out of earlier Sunday schools and catered largely for the poorer classes.

From its inception, the National Society aimed to establish an Anglican school in every parish in the country. The schools were to be closely linked with the parish churches, and laid great emphasis on the teaching of the prayer book and the catechism of the Church of England. The society depended upon voluntary subscriptions as its sole source of revenue. Spurred on by the prospect of financial help, many 'Applications for Aid' were received by the National Society from schools in Kent, and some two dozen National Schools were founded in the county during the first two decades of the society's existence. Although the society offered grants to schools, these were too small to pay for all the building costs. The remainder, together with the schools' day-to-day running expenses, had to be raised by local effort. In common with the British Schools, the typical arrangement provided by this combination of funds was a single large schoolroom where the master could keep the whole school under close scrutiny. The teaching – reading, writing and arithmetic in the boys' schools, with needlework in the girls' schools – was the responsibility of ten or eleven year old monitors.

Keen to implement the National Society's plans to extend religious education, the Canterbury Diocesan Board of Education (founded in 1838) promoted *commercial* or *middle class schools*. It also encouraged the teaching of a whole range of subjects from book-keeping, mensuration and mapping, to practical mechanics, singing and sacred music. There were schemes to set up schools in the larger towns. The Canterbury Commercial School opened in Ivy Lane in 1841 with twelve pupils. Its aim was to attract sons of 'respectable tradesmen, mechanics and others' living in Canterbury and the surrounding villages. Similar schools were attempted in Tenterden and Maidstone but all three ventures were short-lived. Their biggest problem was competition from the private schools. Another disadvantage was their unpopular Anglican connection. Nevertheless, three schools – at Hawkhurst, Ramsgate and Tunbridge Wells – did unite with the board in the 1850s and were granted money in return for continuing Anglican sympathies.

Other schools, known as *proprietary schools*, might be Anglican or nonconformist. These were essentially joint stock enterprises, and the share-holders retained the power of nominating the children. Several such schools existed in west Kent, for example at Chatham, Maidstone, Blackheath and Lee; but none, it seems, in the economically poorer east.

Rivals to both the commercial and the proprietary schools were an ever-growing number of *private schools*, the majority of which were run by women who offered a very refined education to young ladies. Pigot's 1839 *Directory* records a total of 213 in east Kent alone, with Canterbury and Margate being especially well endowed. Bagshaw's 1847 *Gazeteer* notes two dozen private schools each at Ramsgate and Dover, the majority of which were run by women. Shortly after this, the *Post Office Directory* of 1855 classified some three-quarters of the 1,930 schools in Kent as private schools.

Finally, educational provision for paupers was provided by workhouse schools where the teachers were often inmates themselves. The Thanet Union Workhouse at Minster in 1835 supplies a well-documented example. Children here were to be given a 'sound and sufficient education in the duties of religion and habits of industry and usefulness'. They were to rise at 6 a.m. and their day was to be made up of formal teaching, interspersed with practical instruction. For the boys, this involved stabling, gardening, tailoring and carpentry; whereas the girls were taught to make and mend their own clothes, knit stockings, wash clothes, help dress and wash the little ones, scrub rooms, make beds, clean knives, light fires and prepare vegetables.[39]

Nationally, from 1839 a committee of the Privy Council came to administer the education grant to the British and National Societies. Two inspectors – one for Church of England schools and one for schools run by the British and Foreign School Society – had the responsibility of checking that the grant was being properly spent and that discipline was good in the country at large. The committee minutes for Kent reveal an extremely mixed picture of standards in the elementary schools, but with much neglect. The situation appeared little or no better in 1868 when the Taunton Commission reported poorly-qualified teachers and low standards of learning in these schools. Dr Breton's Grammar School at Deptford was one of the worst, the commissioner concluding that from the examination of the

---

[39] J. C. Gilham, *The Isle of Thanet Union Workhouse at Minster in Thanet* (1991).

children the school was 'doing more harm than good to the education of the locality'. The report urged that more widespread elementary education be provided, and that girls in particular receive a more rigorous and less superficial curriculum.

In an effort to help provide more and better-qualified teachers, a 'pupil-teacher system' had been introduced in 1846. A lot was expected of the pupil-teachers, who were often only thirteen years old but had to be capable of teaching a junior class and be proficient in the 'three Rs', elementary geography, religious education and (if a girl) sewing and knitting. At Erith the strain had been so great that the health of several pupil-teachers had broken down over the years.[40]

By 1849 fifteen mechanics institutes, and literary and scientific institutions, had been founded for adults in the main towns – from Deptford in the west of the county, to Margate in the east. They mainly attracted tradesmen who were taught useful information and the scientific principles underlying their trades. The largest was at Greenwich with 1,200 members, while the smallest was at Bexley Heath with fifty members. Regardless of their size they nearly always had their own library attached with from 100 to 8,000 volumes.[41]

A further attempt to improve the quality of education came with the Newcastle Commission of 1858. Under the 'Revised Code', or 'Payment by Results' which it recommended in 1862, grants to schools were dependent upon pupils reaching a sufficiently high standard under examination. To meet these demands, teaching was done by rote, with little or no real understanding. There was no time to experiment with anything which was not directly relevant to getting the class through the 'Standards':

> Do you like the system of payment by results, as it is at present worked? – No.
> What is your objection to it? – The great objection is, that it hampers the teacher very much in his work.
> Because he has always to be working for examination, and not considering the intellectual teaching of the children? – Yes, it prevents his using the most intelligent methods, and confines his teaching within narrow limits.
>
> [part of an interview with Mr Edmund Stevens,
> headmaster of Hartlip Endowed School][42]

Apart from examination results, teachers were also worried about absenteeism.

---

[40] *Reports from Commissioners etc.*, xxix (1887), p. 828.

[41] *Report from the Select Committee on Public Libraries* (1849), Appx, No. 3, pp. 310–16. A good indication of the growing extent of adult literacy in Kent is shown by the great range of newspapers being printed. In mid-century there were already some twenty-one newspapers available in the county and by 1870 this figure had more than doubled. In addition to ten newspapers covering Kent as a whole or regions within it, seven Kent towns (including Chatham, Folkestone and Maidstone) had two or more newspapers, Dover had five in circulation and Tonbridge with Tunbridge Wells could boast seven newspapers [*British Parliamentary Papers. Newspapers 2* (1814–1888)].

[42] *Reports from Commissioners etc.*, xxix (1887), p. 21.

This was because attendance was an item of considerable interest to the inspectors and would affect the school's entitlement to a grant.

In spite of this, the influence of agriculture had a very serious effect on school attendance in the county. The Royal Commission reported in 1869 that 'many boys, especially in hop-growing districts, are employed by their parents at occasional work from the age of infancy'.[43] At Wateringbury, they were told how 'boys and girls leave school earlier than they used, as there is a greater demand for them'. If the boys were made to stay at school after they were eleven years old it 'would be a serious inconvenience in farm work, and still more to poor families'.[44] Girls were needed to manage the home while both parents were at work. A common practice in Wingham was to keep away the eldest girl from school so she could look after the children while the mother worked in the fields.[45]

Elsewhere, the commissioners heard of children being involved up to seven months a year in a wide range of jobs which included shaving hop-poles, bird-minding, hay-making, pig-keeping, minding horses, and sowing potatoes. To try to alleviate this problem and provide an education for children from farming families, thirteen of the forty-three parishes surveyed had set up night schools. For the most part, however, these seem to have been unsuccessful as children and teachers were simply too exhausted to attend regularly.

Innumerable absences were also reported in the new log books required by the Education Act of 1870:

Littlebourne, 15 May 1878
School falling off. Girls are needed hop-tying, Boys in weeding etc. Several of the little ones taken with their mothers to work – to 'mind baby' etc. The bad attendance at this time of year is greatly against their preparation for inspection.[46]

Brenchley, 19 October 1891
School reassembles today. Owing to the hop picking not being finished in parts of the parish only 44 Children present from our roll of 116.[47]

Under this Act, a census was made of elementary school places in each parish. Where a voluntary school already existed, nothing more was required to be done; but if there was no school, the parish was given six months to provide one. Should it fail to do so, the gaps in the system would be filled by a School Board, invested with the power of raising a compulsory rate, purchasing land and building a school. There was much opposition to the Act. The mayor of Canterbury was petitioned by city gentlemen to convene a great public meeting at the Guildhall in Canterbury. The purpose of the meeting was to discuss the Elementary Education

---

[43] Reports from Commissioners: Agriculture (Employment of Women and Children 2), vol. xiii (1868–9), p. 7.
[44] Ibid., Appx, p. 47.
[45] Ibid., Appx, p. 110.
[46] Littlebourne National School Log Book [Centre for Kentish Studies, C/ES 230 1/1].
[47] Brenchley Infants' School Log Book [Centre for Kentish Studies, C/ES 45].

Act and 'to show that the formation of a School Board and the imposition of an education rate in Canterbury were two things at present unnecessary and uncalled for'.[48]

One correspondent to *The Kentish Gazette* the following week, who wrote under the name of 'A. CITIZEN', summed up much of the opposition:

> Supposing, at some considerable expense to us all, they build and open a rate-school. In what way, I would ask, would the poor man, in whose interest they are now so earnest and who will have to pay his share of the rate, be advantaged by this new school?
>
> If he is a non-conformist and would not let his children go to his parish school on any account, has he not already the British school at his service?
>
> Or if he is short of work and cannot really pay for his children's schooling, has he not already the Ragged School open to him?
>
> What possible advantage, then, would a new rate-school offer which is not *already* freely within his reach?[49]

Meanwhile, the vicar of Maidstone was advising Anglican churchmen that they should try to prevent the formation of a school board in the town but that if they were unsuccessful they should do all they could to obtain a majority on the board and see that the Church of England scriptures were taught in the new schools.[50]

However, over half the Kent parishes of any considerable size already had an elementary school of some description; the 1870s saw the remaining gaps in the voluntary system being filled, so that by 1880 nearly everywhere (apart from the smallest rural parishes) had at least one school and the towns had several. Amongst these new schools were two industrial schools at opposite ends of the county. These schools offered vagrants, especially orphans, a basic and practical education. The Kent County Industrial School for Girls aged nine and above was opened at Greenwich in 1874. It was intended 'only for really destitute and unprotected children' without parents to look after them. Girls spent three hours each day in reading, spelling, writing, ciphering and the elements of history and geography; and a further six hours each day in needlework, washing and housework. The following year an industrial school for boys was opened at Kingsnorth near Ashford. The same basic subjects were taught as at Greenwich, though the industrial education here consisted of handicraft and farm and garden work.[51]

Although Mundella's Act (1880) attempted to enforce the compulsory attendance at school of children between the ages of five and ten years, many Kent children continued to be employed on the land. One commentator has observed that there was 'no other county where so many types of farming are followed'.[52] Between March and October children were needed to watch over grazing animals

---

48 *The Kentish Gazette*, 6 Dec. 1870, p. 2.
49 *Ibid.*, 13 Dec. 1870, p. 5.
50 *The Maidstone Telegraph*, 17 Dec. 1870, p. 5.
51 *Kent Industrial Schools Reports from 1874 to 1880* (Maidstone, 1880).
52 G. H. Garrad, *A Survey of Agriculture in Kent*, London 1954, p. 2.

and to scare birds with clappers and rattles. In June they were employed in shearing sheep, weeding cornfields and picking up stones to surface the roads. The following month saw them pea-cutting, haymaking and cutting fruit for the London market. In September, children helped their mothers and fathers pick hops. The headmistress of Ditton National School outside Maidstone highlighted not only the child employment problem but the ineffectiveness of the authorities to deal with it:

> What do you say about the regular attendance of the children; do they attend regularly? – Not so regularly as they ought to do.
> What are their parents? – Agricultural labourers.
> It is an entirely agricultural parish, is it not? – Yes, entirely agricultural.
> Have you a school attendance committee? – Yes, under the Board of Guardians.
> Do not they do their duty? – The school attendance officer does his duty, but I think the fault lies with the magistrates; the people have too many warnings . . . perhaps four or five. I think if they had less warnings and a small fine they would mind it more.[53]

The magistrates here were condoning half attendance, and would doubtless have approved when the laws were relaxed at the end of the century to allow farming children to work part time. But circumstances varied from place to place. At Hartlip, for instance, attendance was far better. This was largely due, it seems, to the sterling efforts of the Milton Union Attendance Committee, viewed by some to be 'one of the best in the country'.[54]

Excluding all the numerous private schools, there were by 1888 some 846 voluntary schools in Kent. Of these, the overwhelming majority (746) were Church of England, 50 were British and Foreign, 27 were Methodist and 23 were Roman Catholic. In all, 188,468 children were on the rolls of these schools, and the average attendance was about 70%. Alongside the voluntary schools there were now 191 board schools, operated by 118 new school boards. These schools tended to educate more children and have better attendance rates than their rivals.[55] They also had the reputation of being particularly well run and cost-effective.[56]

Spurred on by the requirements of the 1870 Education Act, Kent had a good coverage of elementary schools by 1900. Considerable advances had also been made in technical and higher education. Between 1889 and 1903 the Kent Technical Education Committee awarded over £72,000 to thirty-two institutions across the county from the Beckenham Technical Institute and School of Art, to the Dover School of Art, Science and Technology.[57] The grants went towards the cost of buildings, teachers' salaries, apparatus and equipment. Many of the awards went to well-established schools such as Ashford Grammar School and Cranbrook

---

[53] *British Parliamentary Papers. Education 35* (1887), p. 171.

[54] *Ibid.*, p. 215.

[55] *Ibid., 38* (1888), *Statistical Report*, p. 90.

[56] *Ibid.*, 35 (1887), p. 220.

[57] *Some Account of the Work of Education under the Kent Technical Education Committee up to the 6th April, 1903* (Kent County Council, 1903).

Grammar School but three new institutions were founded. The first of these, a horticultural college, was established at Swanley in 1889. It was intended for women who grew fruit for market, gardeners and future landowners. In the east of the county, an agricultural college was built at Wye in 1894 by the joint action of Kent and Surrey County Councils. Four years later, it was made a school of the University of London and could award a B.Sc. in agriculture. Originally there had been thirteen students but this number had soared to 114 by 1906. As well as attending lectures, students had practical experience on the college farm. The third institution, a school of domestic economy, was set up in Maidstone in 1898 but two years later moved to Bromley. Admitting pupils through an open examination, the school taught cookery, laundry work, dressmaking, hygiene and household man-agement.[58]

The position of secondary schooling, however, was much less satisfactory, and for girls it was particularly poor, with only eight girls' grammar schools in the county. In fact, across the country as a whole, it was becoming increasingly recognized that secondary education needed better management.

The Kent Education Committee came into being as a result of the Education Act of 1902. Excluding London, Kent was the fourth largest education authority in the country. Within three years, teachers in its employment had the opportunity of applying for one of the ninety-two reserved places at the newly-founded Goldsmith's College at New Cross in South London. Here, a two-year, university style, nondenominational course of general education and training was offered to them. In January 1907 Kent took the initiative amongst the authorities around London by funding the college's first hostel in Granville Park, Lewisham, accom-modating thirty-four women students.[59]

When it came to elementary education, the Kent Education Committee was responsible for only about half of the county area, as sixteen of the larger towns remained independent. Furthermore, about two-thirds of Kent elementary schools were controlled by denominational bodies which retained statutory powers, not least the appointment and dismissal of teachers. The Kent Education Committee was given full responsibility, however, for secondary education throughout the county, with just one exception – Canterbury – where it remained in the hands of the City Council. An estimated 2,348 boys but only 1,726 girls were attending public secondary schools in Kent at this time.[60] Redressing the balance between the provision of secondary schools for boys and girls was a top priority. Girls' gram-mar schools were very quickly established at Ashford, Bromley, Chatham, Dartford, Dover, Folkestone, Gravesend, Ramsgate, Sittingbourne, Tonbridge and Tunbridge Wells. With the help of a government grant from 1907 these schools were able to offer free places provided they admitted at least a quarter of their

[58] *Special Report on Higher Education in the County of Kent, 1906* (Kent County Council, London, 1906).

[59] D. Dymond (ed.), *The Forge. The History of Goldsmith's College, 1905–1955*, London 1955, pp. 6, 10.

[60] *Special Report on Higher Education in the County of Kent, 1906*, p. 7.

children from elementary schools. This was a great relief to the schools, and also introduced a socially less divisive intake. With free school meals and medical inspections also now in place, good progress was being achieved when the outbreak of war stalled further educational improvement.

All these great changes meant that the pattern of education in Kent was in many respects now vastly different from that at the beginning of the period under review. Schools then had very often been intermittent arrangements between teachers and pupils; now they were likely to be institutions with a more certain existence and employing properly qualified staff. Successive governments from the Restoration of Charles II until the mid nineteenth century had been reluctant to get involved in promoting education; this had very much placed the initiative on the various churches and individual philanthropists across the county. By 1914, in contrast, the provision of education was clearly recognised as the responsibility of the county council. In 1640, the available evidence suggests that nearly all schools taught boys only; whereas by the early twentieth century much progress had been made in the county towards evening up this provision in favour of girls. The curriculum had also changed from one which primarily catered for the sons of tradesmen and gentlemen, to become more in keeping with the demands of an expanding economy and the new skills required of the county's rapidly growing workforce.

Nevertheless, there were several respects in which the character of education remained unchanged throughout the period. Schools continued to reflect and respond to the social and economic needs of their immediate localities. In rural parishes, in particular, the competing demands of child employment on farms took a high toll on school attendance even after the era of compulsory education. Difficulties in raising and sustaining an adequate level of funding, however, seem to have presented schools with their most serious problems throughout this period, placing clear restraints on the extent and quality of education they could provide for the county's children.

The Old Poor Law 1640–1834

(1) The Nature of Poverty

In 1801 Kent was predominantly rural with 54,124 persons chiefly employed in agriculture as opposed to 43,253 in trade and industry. Thirty years later 31,667 (32.6%) of all Kent families were principally occupied in farming as compared to 29,419 (30.3%) in trade and manufacture. The former included 36,113 farm labourers as opposed to 15,245 labourers employed in non-agricultural work.[1] Beyond metropolitan Kent whole areas relied almost solely on farming and the only industries were the manufacture of paper and gunpowder. Wealden iron making had collapsed at the end of the seventeenth century. Maidstone's linen thread industry and Wealden cloth manufacture followed in the eighteenth century and at the turn of the century Canterbury's more enterprising silk weavers moved to Spitalfields.[2] Only 72 weavers remained in the county by 1831 when the census reported that 'the manufactures of . . . Kent employ very few males of twenty years of age'.[3]

Of Kent's other towns Sandwich had lost its overseas trading position by 1700 because of the silting of its haven and its 'inferior' location.[4] Defoe, in 1724, described it as 'an old, decayed, poor, miserable town'[5] while in 1832 assistant poor law commissioner Ashurst Majendie found 'the shipyard . . . broken up, the malting business abandoned' and such was the general poverty that 'they were not able to do even what they wish for the poor'.[6] Neighbouring Deal suffered even more severely after 1815. The dispersal of the fleet in the Downs and suppression of smuggling brought 'a total suspension of trade once so flourishing . . .' Deal became 'a place deserted' where 500 pauper children were fed daily with the 400–500 inmates of its two poorhouses.[7] The seasonal hazards of the 'maritime

---

[1] (P)arliamentary (P)apers 1801–02. Abstract of Answers and Returns, Census Enumeration, England and Wales, 1801. PP 1833. Abstract of Answers and Returns, Census Enumeration, England and Wales, 1831.

[2] Frank W. Jessup, *Kent History Illustrated*, Maidstone 1973, pp. 42–4. A. E. Newman, 'The Old Poor Law in Kent 1606–1834', Kent Ph.D. 1979, pp. 61–2. C. W. Chalkin, *Seventeenth Century Kent*, London 1965, pp. 122–8. James P. Huzel, 'Aspects of the Old Poor Law, population and agrarian protest in early 19th century England with particular reference to the county of Kent', Kent Ph.D. 1975, p. 31. Samuel Bagshaw, *History, Gazeteer and Directory of Kent*, vol. I, Sheffield 1847, pp. 31–2.

[3] PP 1833, pp. 282–3.

[4] Chalkin, *op. cit.*, p. 170.

[5] Daniel Defoe, *A Tour through England and Wales*, 1724, p. 136.

[6] PP 1834 (44), XXVIII, Appendix A, Part 1. Appendix to the First Report from the Commissioners on the Poor Laws.

[7] Stephen Pritchard, *History of Deal*, Deal 1864, pp. 242, 246.

class' were omnipresent at Folkestone, Ramsgate, Whitstable, Faversham and other coastal communities.[8] Dover was more fortunate with wider employment opportunities although the development of steam driven packet ships was blamed for acute poverty and in 1820 there was a drastic reduction of harbour expenditure.[9] The town, moreover, was often burdened with wives and families left by the regiments and by foreigners 'passed' down the country to return to the continent.[10] Chatham suffered from periodic government 'reductions' at its dockyard while Gravesend and Milton were vulnerable to their watermen 'whose improvidence created a heavy burden for Thames-side parishes'.[11] Of the inland towns Maidstone suffered from periodic unemployment in its paper mills and, like Canterbury, from fluctuations in the building trades.[12] While Kent towns were not at the mercy of any particular industry, as market towns they were vulnerable to the fortunes of agriculture and after 1817 the general post-war depression and a reduction in demand from the countryside brought increased poverty.[13]

In the countryside evidence points to a gradual deterioration in the position of the agricultural labourer throughout the eighteenth century. Enclosure played no part in this since, with the exception of some commons, Kent was already enclosed. Anthea Newman has shown, however, that in East Kent parishes, such as Ash and Chislet, consolidation of holdings was gradually depressing small farmers into the ranks of day labourers and leaving labourers, who had often owned some land, dependent solely on their wages.[14] At Ash there was a noticeable reduction in holdings of under £100 from mid-century and a further reduction in small farmers in the early nineteenth century.[15] Correspondingly there was an increase in holdings worth over £100. By 1841, the presence of two new farms of over 500 acres indicated the movement towards the larger unit. Land occupiers had fallen since 1705 by nearly 50% and represented less than 20% of the 1841 population.[16] At St Nicholas only a fifth of houses were rated in 1801 and a quarter in 1831. A small minority of ratepayers were, therefore, maintaining a majority of the poor.[17] John Boys in 1796 noted 'the putting together of small farms' while Cobbett in 1822 also remarked upon the division of the corn country of Thanet into 'great farms' emphasising 'the more purely a corn country the more miserable the labourers'.[18] In 1828 almost 2,000 acres of Otford's 2,771 acres were occupied by seven farmers, the tenants of some half dozen absentee landlords.[19] Nevertheless, as

[8] PP XXXVI, Appendix B2, pp. 59–60h.
[9] Newman, op. cit., p. 136.
[10] PRO MH 12, Dover Union, 4955. St Mary's Vestry to PLC, 18.9.1834.
[11] PP 1834, XXVIII, Appendix A, Part I, p. 219.
[12] PP XXXVI, Appendix B2, pp. 56h, 62h.
[13] Newman, op. cit., pp. 372–3.
[14] Ibid., pp. 223–30, 364.
[15] Ibid., pp. 223–4.
[16] Ibid., pp. 224, 229–30.
[17] Ibid., p. 239.
[18] William Cobbett, Rural Rides, first published 1830, reprint, Middlesex 1977, p. 206. John Boys, A General View of the Agriculture of the County of Kent, 1796, p. 35.
[19] D. Clarke and Anthony Stoyel, Otford in Kent, Battle 1975, p. 192.

James Huzel has demonstrated, the parishes of North-West Kent, especially those within a ten-mile radius of London, enjoyed lower poverty levels because of their proximity to the capital. The demands of the city developed market gardening and produced higher wages and employment opportunities outside agriculture. There was also a larger number of resident gentry bringing a more paternalistic approach to social problems.[20] Increased pauperisation of the landless labourer was compounded by the relentless growth of population from the late seventeenth century created by a fall in mortality. Population rose from an estimated 155,000 in 1701 to 259,000 in 1801 and 448,000 in 1841. In Ash, in 1705, the household size of the day labourer was under four. By 1841 it was over five producing a surplus rural labour market, unemployment and underemployment.[21]

G. R. Gleig, vicar of Ash, who described East Kent, and particularly Ash, in his fictitious *Chronicles of Waltham* (1835) portrayed the French Wars 1793–1815 as a golden age. 'During the good times of war, when the demand for labour was great, working men received . . . half a crown a day . . . wheat sold for ninety or a hundred shillings a quarter . . . working people throve and were contented.'[22] Landlords received high rents. Farmers made large profits and substantial capital investment to boost production. Labourers, however, reaped little benefit from agricultural profits. Instead galloping inflation between 1794 and 1812 had devastating effects on their real incomes and they had, moreover, to weather the great dearths of 1795–6 and 1799–1801.[23] Nevertheless there was full employment. As late as 1833 a Kent farmer could recall those years when 'it was scarcely possible to bestow too much labour for every shilling expended brought back 2 shillings'.[24]

By the Corn Law of 1815 the landed classes hoped to maintain high wheat prices and their increased arable acreage. The peace, however, after 1814 brought overproduction, deflation and demobilisation and a deep post-war depression with widespread unemployment as farmers sought to minimise their losses. A Board of Agriculture Inquiry in 1816 revealed the full extent of the distress. In the Maidstone area farmers were 'obliged to part with perhaps a third of their labourers'. In South-West Kent a similar number were unemployed and 'a portion of the remainder working at a price . . . insufficient to maintain their families'. In Tenterden neighbourhood the poor were reported 'in a very depressed state . . . the farmers not being able to have any more work done than is absolutely necessary'. For John Boys the condition of the poor was 'worse than ever known'.[25] Despite widespread

[20] Huzel, *op. cit.*, pp. 168–70, 189, 193. Newman, *op. cit.*, p. 66.

[21] Newman, *op. cit.*, p. 362. B. R. Mitchell and P. Deane, *Abstract of British Historical Statistics*, Cambridge 1962, pp. 20, 103.

[22] G. R. Gleig, *Chronicles of Waltham*, vol. 1 (1835), pp. 219–20.

[23] T. L. Richardson, 'The Agricultural Labourer's Standard of Living in Kent 1790–1840', in P. Oddy and D. Miller, *The Making of the Modern British Diet*, London 1976, p. 106. See also Roger Wells, *Wretched Faces: Famine in Wartime England 1763–1803*, Gloucester 1988.

[24] PP 1833, V. Report of Select Committee on Agriculture.

[25] Board of Agriculture, *The Agricultural State of the Kingdom in 1816*, pp. 123, 133–4, 136.

rent abatements distress continued into the 1820s.[26] In 1821 John Lake, a Bapchild farmer, told a select committee 'that agriculture was declining beyond anything I recollect'.[27] Kent Agricultural Associations petitioned Parliament over the distress in 1820, 1821 and 1822. By 1822 Kent farmers, who had lost confidence in both parliamentary committees and agricultural associations, were pressing county members. 450 Kent landowners attended the county meeting in 1822 to discuss agricultural distress and the need for reduced taxation.[28] At the close of 1822, however, corn prices increased and continued to rise throughout the middle twenties. There were renewed complaints of distress in 1828, a year in which Sir Edward Knatchbull, the Kent MP, informed Lord Colchester that 'all farmers in Kent were insolvent'.[29] Next year the Kent Grand Jury wrote to the Duke of Wellington describing 'the deep and unprecedented distress which . . . prevails among all classes throughout this county'.[30] This was followed in 1830 by a memorial to the Treasury from 23 Kent parishes to make known 'the overwhelming difficulties which the agriculturalists are now suffering . . .'.[31] Both the Whig Earl of Darnley, who lived in North-West Kent, and Lord Camden felt the distress 'was somewhat magnified' although accepting that 'wages were rather low'.[32]

In 1826, of 21,719 persons living in sixteen Wealden parishes, 8263 were paupers and a further 682 were unable to get work at any time of the year.[33] Even in the mid 1820s, when agricultural prices improved, real gains for the Kent labourer in work remained small.[34] In 1824, when the labourer in the high wage north of England earned 12s 0d to 15s 0d a week, in the Wingham division of Kent '. . . the lowest wages paid were in one parish 6d.; in four 8d.; in eleven 1s.6d.; and in four 2s.0d. and in the great number 1s.0d. a day'.[35] Moreover, until 1825, the index of real wages was 'almost continually depressed below its 1790 position' and even for the labourer in regular work real wages fell catastrophically for almost the entire period 1790–1840. If this was the situation in full employment the position of the substantial part of the labour force, who were unable to find winter work, must have been desperate.[36]

> For several years past the state of the poorer classes has been gradually becoming worse [wrote the *Maidstone Journal* in November 1829]. The want of prosperity amongst the farmers has necessarily produced a great diminution in the demand for labour and a considerable reduction in wages . . . while the

---

[26] *Ibid.*, p. 123. J. H. Andrews, 'Political Issues in the County of Kent 1820–1846', London M.Phil. 1967, pp. 191ff.

[27] PP 1821, IX. Report of Select Committee on the Distressed State of Agriculture.

[28] Andrews, *loc. cit.*

[29] *Loc. cit.*

[30] *Kent Chronicle*, 22.12.1829.

[31] *(M)aidstone (J)ournal*, 18.5.1830.

[32] Andrews, *op. cit.*, pp. 206–7.

[33] PP 1826, IV. I. Report from Select Committee on Emigration, pp. 135–8.

[34] Richardson, *op. cit.*, p. 108.

[35] PP 1824, VI. Report from Select Committee on Labourers' Wages.

[36] Richardson, *op. cit.*, p. 111.

increase in population has not ceased. The . . . poor who depend upon daily labour . . . are reduced to a condition lamentable to behold.[37]

It is small wonder that the bad harvest of 1829, the severe winter of 1829–30 and the failure of the hop crop precipitated open revolt in the Swing Riots of 1830–1. Two further parliamentary enquiries in 1833 and 1836 brought little extra comfort. While Thanet was said to have avoided the worst of the depression the Weald, Dover and North Kent were still in serious difficulty and there remained 'a super-abundance of unemployed' in a large part of East Kent.[38] The New Poor Law of 1834 was, therefore, accepted by many Kent farmers as a measure of relief for agriculturalists.[39]

Statistics concerning the nature and extent of Kent poverty are imprecise. In 1802–3 41,632 adults and children, excluding non-parishioners and vagrants, were receiving permanent or occasional relief. This suggests that 13.4% of the county population in 1801 was obtaining help as opposed to 11% nationally and 8.8% in a northern agricultural county like the North Riding.[40] Unfortunately these returns contain some duplication. Similarly the return for 1812–15 excludes children on outdoor relief thus producing an average total of only 41,926 persons or 11.23% of the 1811 population in receipt of permanent or occasional help.[41] This, however, is remarkably close to the 43,004 poor or 11.6% of the 1811 population listed in 1815.[42]

Many more were living close to subsistence. In winter, in depression or in dearth these were also driven below the poverty line. Of the 168 persons living in Fawk-ham in 1821 approximately one half figure in a list of parish poor.[43] Otford's assessment list for April 1819 lists 36 resident ratepayers and 43 'cottagers not assessed'.[44] Appledore's 120 paupers in 1819 meant that one person in five was a pauper which had increased to one in three by 1833.[45]

By the 1830s population growth and agricultural depression had combined to produce a labour surplus in which a substantial number of labourers were perma-nently or partially unemployed. In 1832 assistant commissioner Rev. Henry Bishop reported widespread winter unemployment at Sevenoaks, Brenchley and Horsmonden. Ashurst Majendie found 'evident surplus population' at Sundridge.

---

[37] Quoted by T. L. Richardson, 'The Agricultural Labourers in Kent in 1830', *Cantium* (Winter 1974), p. 74.

[38] PP 1833, V. Report from Select Committee on Agriculture, pp. 244–68, 291–302. PP 1836, VIII. II. Third Report from Select Committee on Agriculture, pp. 1–15.

[39] Andrews, *op. cit.*, p. 214.

[40] PP 1801–02. Abstract of Answers and Returns. Census Enumeration. PP 1803–04, XIII. Abstract of Answers and Returns relative to the maintenance of the poor 1802–1803. R. P. Hastings, *Poverty and the Poor Law in the North Riding of Yorkshire c.1780–1837*, York 1982, p. 2.

[41] PP 1818, XIX. Abstract of returns relating to the Poor 1812–15.

[42] PP 1819, IX. 2. Digest of Parochial Returns to Select Committee on the Education of the Lower Orders.

[43] F. Frank Proudfoot, *Fawkham: the story of a Kentish Village*, London 1951, p. 93.

[44] Clarke and Stoyel, *op. cit.*, p. 193.

[45] John Winnifrith, *A History of Appledore*, Chichester 1973, p. 59.

MISS HENDREY'S

Establishment for Young Ladies,

HAWLEY HOUSE,

HAWLEY SQUARE, MARGATE.

Terms :

BOARD and Instruction in the English and French Languages, including Writing and Arithmetic, History, Geography, with the Use of the Globes and Ornamental and Plain Needlework,

THIRTY-FIVE GUINEAS PER ANNUM.

Pupils under Ten Years of Age . . . . 30 Guineas per Annum
Weekly Boarders . . . . . 28 ,, ,,
Day ,, ... 16 ,, ,,

BY PROFESSORS :—

Harp . . . . 8 Guineas
Piano . . . . 6 ,,
Drawing . . . . 6 ,,
German . . . . 6 ,,
Italian . . . . 6 ,,
Dancing . . . . 4 ,,
Calisthenic Exercises . . . . . . 2 ,,

Laundress, 4 Guineas.

Each Young Lady to be provided with a Silver Spoon, Fork, and Six Towels, which will be returned on the Pupil leaving.

Young Ladies remaining during the Vacation, £5 5s.

A Quarter's Notice is required previously to the removal of a Pupil.

Ladies are received as PARLOUR BOARDERS, also MORNING PUPILS.

Plate 9. Advertisement in the *Post Office Directory* for Kent of a school for young ladies at Margate 1867.

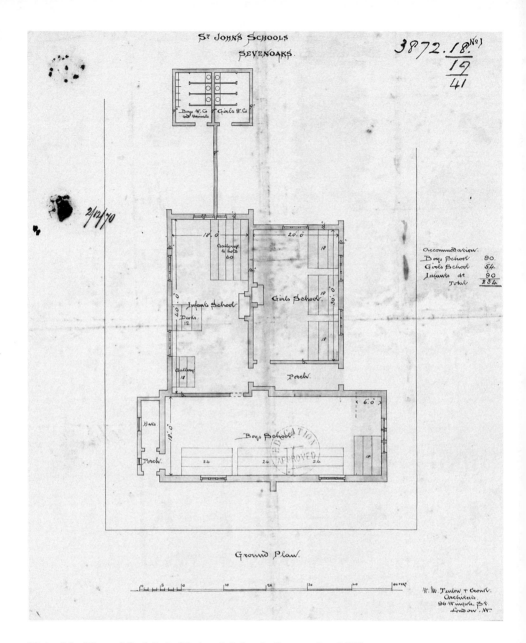

Plate 10. Plan of St John's National School, Sevenoaks, 1870.

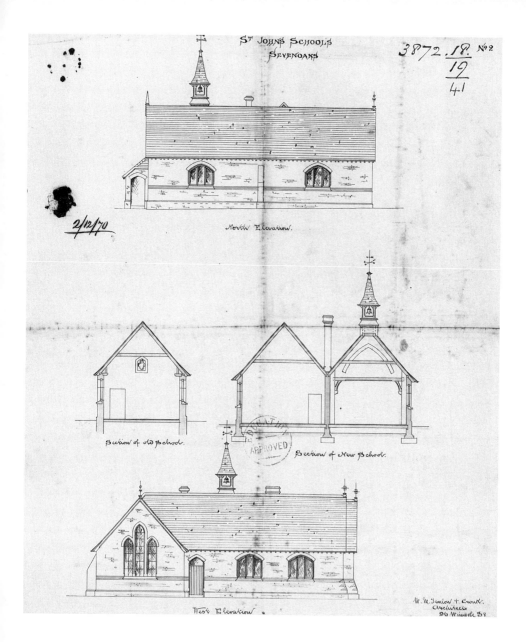

Plate 11. Elevation of St John's National School, Sevenoaks, 1870.

Plate 12. Clarendon House Grammar School for Girls, Ramsgate, built in 1909.

At Marden 1,230 (58.3%) of 2,109 persons were receiving relief; at Lenham 1,200 (54.5%) of 2,200 persons and at Sundridge 630 (49.6%) of a population of 1,268. These represented labourers and their families. At Wrotham in January 1834 the *Maidstone Journal* claimed that over half the population were paupers.[46] Of 36 respondent parishes to the Commissioners' Rural Queries, 20 acknowledged the existence of summer unemployment and 31 winter unemployment in their parishes which involved from 12.5% to 20% of day labourers.[47]

Nor were Kent labourers cushioned against economic difficulty. Only 4% of the 1801 population were members of the 198 friendly societies listed in 1803–4.[48] The northern labourer enjoyed a diet which was cheaper and more nutritious than his southern counterpart's bread, cheese and tea.[49] In 1833 only between 16% and 30% of Kent parishes had allotments since farmers feared they made labourers independent. This was one of the lowest percentages in the Midlands, South and East.[50]

While Kent's principal poverty problem, centred upon the day labourer, did not really exist in the northern counties it also had its share of 'impotent' poor in the form of the aged, sick, one-parent families, deserted wives, unmarried mothers and servicemen's wives. Seventy per cent of males worked beyond 65 years but of the 41,632 paupers in 1802–3 4,567 (10.9%) were over sixty or permanently disabled. A further 10,939 (26.2%) were children receiving outrelief. This was not the full total since children in workhouses were not enumerated.[51] In 1836 Maidstone was relieving '200 aged and infirm widows and 100 middle aged widows having 300 children'.[52]

Since employment opportunities in a rural county were limited there were attempts to solve the overpopulation problem by encouraging emigration overseas and internal migration to the northern industrial districts. Kentish emigration overseas quickened during the post-war depression. Many parishes were eager to offer assistance to rid themselves of unwanted paupers. Headcorn from 1823–6 sent some twenty emigrants a year to America at a cost of £8 0s 0d a head.[53] Thomas Law Hodges, MP for West Kent and a strong supporter of emigration, told the Select Committee on Emigration in 1826 that his parish of Benenden had financed 27 men, women and children to travel to New York. He personally lent £1,150 to Benenden to despatch a further 145 emigrants to America in 1827 and 1828.[54] In

46 PP 1834 (44), XXVIII, pp. 207, 209, 213–14, 220–1, 875–6. PRO MH 12. Sevenoaks Union, 5315. Head to PLC 26.11.1834. MJ 28.1.1834.
47 PP 1834 (44), XXX. Appendix B1, Part 1. Answers to Rural Query, 6.
48 PP 1803–04, XIII. Abstract of Answers and Returns . . .
49 R. P. Hastings, 'Poverty and the Treatment of Poverty in the North Riding of Yorkshire, c.1789–1847', York D.Phil., pp. 98–100.
50 Newman, *op. cit.*, p. 249.
51 PP 1803–4, XIII. Abstract of Answers and Returns . . . Patricia Knowlden and Joyce Walker, *West Wickham; Past into Present*, West Wickham 1986, p. 127.
52 PRO MH 12. Maidstone Union, 5195. C. T. Smythe to PLC, n.d.
53 H. J. M. Johnson, *British Emigration Policy, 1815–1830*, Oxford 1972, p. 100.
54 *Ibid.*, pp. 100–1.

the 1820s and 1830s Appledore vestry provided money for some 30 persons to leave for the United States, Canada and Australia. East Malling vestry set aside £200 for emigration in 1832, a year in which over 200 emigrants left Rochester and district. By 1830 130 emigrants had left Tenterden in eleven years. While some parishes claimed emigration brought a saving on the rates, and it is estimated Kent lost some 15,000 persons by migration in 1801–31, its population continued to climb.[55] Evidence of migration to the industrial districts is slight except for an attempt by Chatham vestry in 1792 to send pauper apprentices to 'the cotton manufactories at Manchester' though the outcome is unknown.[56]

(2) The Administration of the Poor Law

For those who could not emigrate there remained the system of poor relief which had evolved from the Acts of 1597 and 1601. These provided for the levy of a poor rate and the selection of overseers to care for the 'settled' impotent poor of each parish while the able bodied poor were to be set to work. Outside the towns most Kent overseers were farmers untrained for the posts they filled. Many parish vestries held annual elections but in some of Kent's 409 poor law authorities the principal householders served this time-consuming, unpaid office in a pre-determined order. Inevitably the nature of the office produced some incompetence and dishonesty. 'The office . . . is too often filled by incompetent persons', stated Henry Boyce of Waldershare. 'The intelligent occupier, rather than be annoyed with its duties will perform them by deputy'.[57]

At Sutton Valence one overseer was illiterate and the second 'quite ignorant of business'.[58] A Pembury overseer embezzled parish funds and left a debt of £350.[59] Ashurst Majendie reported that 'the accounts of many parishes were in so confused a state as to require being put in order by an accountant'. The duties, he felt, were so demanding that they could not 'be effectually discharged by persons engaged in business who often had only started to learn the job when their period of office expired'. When the office fell on small tradesmen it often became 'an abundant source of jobbing and peculation'.[60]

When the Sturges Bourne Act of 1819 authorised parishes to employ full-time, paid assistant overseers in a bid to increase efficiency, Kent took full advantage. By 1824–5 138 (33.7% of all parishes) had them. By 1834 they had grown to 188

---

[55] Winnifrith, *op. cit.*, p. 62. Michael McNay, *Portrait of a Kentish Village: East Malling*, London 1980, p. 96. B. R. Mitchell and P. Deane, *Abstract of British Historical Statistics*, Cambridge 1962, Table 25. PP 1834, XXVIII. Appendix to First Report from Commissioners on the Poor Laws, pp. 209–11. *(M)aidstone (G)azette*, 24.4.1832.

[56] (C)entre for (M)edway (S)tudies, St Mary's, Chatham Vestry Minutes, P85/8/3. Cit. E. Melling, *The Poor*, Kentish Sources IV, Maidstone 1964, pp. 131, 135.

[57] PP 1828, IV. HC 494. Report from Select Committee on that part of the Poor Laws relating to employment or relief of able bodied persons from the poor rates.

[58] PRO MH 12. Hollingbourne Union, 5134. George Bailey to PLC, 6.11.1834.

[59] PP 1834, XXVIII. Appendix A, Part I, p. 877.

[60] *Ibid.*, pp. 167–8.

(45.9%), a proportion second only to Lancashire.[61] Majendie felt that the best assistant overseers were occupiers of large farms with 'an interest in keeping rates low' and not millers or shopkeepers 'who spend the parish money in articles furnished by themselves'. While he hailed their appointment as 'one of the greatest improvements in the Poor Laws . . . introduced in modern times', not all assistant overseers were blameless. Marden's assistant overseer financed his farm from the 'parish purse' and left the parish £2,600 in debt. Faversham's assistant overseer defrauded the parish for many years. Nevertheless, while some were incompetent or corrupt, the majority seem to have performed their duties conscientiously and honestly. An over-zealous Sundridge assistant overseer was, however, burned in effigy and subsequently removed by a terrified vestry.[62]

Clashes between overseers and magistrates were frequent since paupers had a final right of appeal to the Bench. Here it was not unknown for vestry decisions to be overturned or allowances increased. Majendie believed 'the overliberality of magistrates' was a principal cause of high rates and the dependence of labourers on the parish.[63] This was echoed in the *Answers to Rural Queries* where some parishes felt magistrates had a role to play but others felt it best to exclude them. 'The most fertile source of the evils of the Poor Law', stated Thomas Bentley of Higham, is 'the injudicious decisions of the magistrates . . .'.[64] 'While the Justices can order relief without any control,' complained the parish officer of Birling, 'the poor find that either from fear or benevolence relief is always ordered'. This severe source of friction remained until magistrates lost this authority in 1834.[65]

As pauperism increased many parishes found it necessary to meet more often, or appointed committees to consider relief applications.[66] When the Sturges Bourne Act formalised creation of such standing committees some Kent parishes appointed select vestries but by no means as many as employed assistant overseers. Select vestries reached a peak of 61 (14.9% of all parishes) in 1825–6. By 1834 the total had dropped to 41 (10%).[67] The creation of select vestries was not always successful. Sevenoaks tried the expedient several times and failed leaving 'the jobbing of the parish vestry' to 'promote an expenditure beneficial to a few shopkeepers'.[68] Chartham select vestry, consisting of the parish's major employers, was ill-attended. So, too, was that at Lenham where there was 'a great division' among the parishioners and because of many overcharges the parish was forced to

---

[61] PP 1826, III. Appendix to Report of Select Committee on Poor Rate returns. PP 1835, XLVII. Abstract of Returns showing amount levied in expenditure in each county, 1833–34.

[62] PP 1834 (44), XXVIII. Appendix A, Part 1, pp. 168, 208–9, 216.

[63] *Ibid.*, pp. 168–9.

[64] PP 1834 (44), XXXIII. Appendix B1, Part IV, p. 250d. See also responses from Bapchild, Bexley, Chalk, Chiddingstone, Farningham, Goudhurst.

[65] PP 1824, VI. Appendix to Report from Select Committee on Poor Rates, 1824.

[66] (C)entre for (K)entish (S)tudies. See for example P329/8/3 Sellindge Vestry Committee, 1816–44.

[67] PP 1826–27, XX. Abstract of Returns showing select vestries. PP 1835, XLVII. Abstract of returns showing amounts levied and expended on the poor in each county.

[68] PP 1834 (44), XXVIII. Report from the Rev. Henry Bishop, p. 880.

borrow £100 from the Maidstone Bank in order to pay the paupers.[69] The rector of Great Chart, however, spoke out favourably for his select vestry while the parish officers of Holy Cross, Westgate felt that 'the care of the select vestry in the distribution of relief has materially contributed to the decrease in expenditure'.[70] Majendie felt that select vestries were generally beneficial but 'moreso in large towns than in purely agricultural parishes'. They were, perhaps, less popular in Kent because the Gilbert unions already had boards of guardians which in general 'gave satisfaction to employers and employed'.[71] Towns like Maidstone, Faversham and Canterbury, where managers of the poor had been established by local act, also already had their boards and sub committees.[72] At Greenwich a system whereby each overseer in alternate months 'exposed his door to . . . crowds . . . daily relieving them to the best of his judgement without having any check against fraud and imposition', had given way by 1830 to a system whereby detailed preliminary enquiries were made and relief paid weekly with a corresponding reduction in rates.[73] Kent's select vestry par excellence was at Ashford where poor law matters had been dealt with from at least 1770 by vestry committee. Under the influence of Henry Creed, a linen draper and newcomer to the town, the rules for relief were revised and made much harsher in 1786. A committee of the 1790s was a non-statutory predecessor of the select vestry of 1821 which halved expenditure. So impressed was assistant commissioner Sir Francis Head with Ashford's management of the poor that when forming the East and West Ashford unions in 1835 he omitted Ashford from both arguing that its select vestry should remain undisturbed. Ashford was only admitted to West Ashford union after petition by its vestry in 1837.[74] Since a considerable number of Kent poor law authorities had already taken what they believed to be suitable steps towards their own administrative reform by 1834 some of the resentment created by the New Poor Law is not hard to understand.

(3) Cost of Relief

The Hearth Tax returns of 1664 suggest that nearly a third of the population of seventeenth century Kent was living at subsistence level although there were considerable regional differences. The least poverty existed in North-West Kent where London and the growing dockyard towns offered alternative work. In

---

[69] *Ibid.*, pp. 214, 875. See also Michael J. D. Weller, 'Keeping the Poor Alive – The Old Poor Law in Chartham 1800–1835', Kent BA Dissertation 1982, pp. 1, 5–6.
[70] PRO MH 12. West Ashford Union, 4798. Rector to PLC, 29.8.1834. PP 1824, VI. Appendix to Report from Select Committee on the Poor Rates, 1824.
[71] PP 1834 (44), XXVIII, p. 168.
[72] *Ibid.*, pp. 215, 216, 217.
[73] PRO MH 12. Greenwich Union, 5091. Remarks and statement respectfully addressed to the parishioners of Greenwich by William Stacey and William Griffiths, overseers for 1830.
[74] A. W. Ruderman, 'Local Administration by Vestry 1750–1800', Kent Diploma in Local History, 1579, 1982, p. 9. Robert Furley, *History of the Weald of Kent*, Vol. 2. Part 2, Ashford 1874, pp. 667–8. PP 1834 (44), XXVIII, p. 168. Sir Francis Head, 'English Charity', in *Quarterly Review*, liii (Feb. and April 1835), No. CVI, pp. 512–17.

contrast East Kent and the Weald were particularly poverty stricken, the former because of engrossment and the latter because of the decaying cloth industry. In normal times, however, most of those living at subsistence level were able to maintain themselves without poor relief. In 1598 under one in fifteen people were aided at Shorne. In 1705 only one in nine were aided at Ash. Most recipients were the aged, disabled, widowed or children. Able bodied pauperism was insignificant.[75] During the first half of the eighteenth century poor rates held relatively steady except during the bad harvests of 1710, 1711 and 1739–40 which affected some parishes but not others. From about 1740, however, poor law expenditure began slowly to rise gathering pace after 1760 and moving in the same direction as population and prices.[76] At Shorne, until the mid-eighteenth century, the number of villagers regularly relieved each year was between four and six. By 1760 seventeen paupers were relieved to a greater or lesser extent and annual costs increased from about £60 to £245.[77] In 1740 Folkestone overseers disbursed £306. By 1786 their expenditure was £1,049.[78] There were still local variations as John Boys of Betteshanger emphasised.[79] West Wickham in 1763 still had only four permanent paupers, two pauper children, one casual pauper and paid allowances to five poorhouse inmates and several sums for relief in kind.[80] Nevertheless, county expenditure, which averaged £41,997 in 1748–50, had reached £80,150 by 1775–6. This was second only to Middlesex whose expenditure of £80,237 was for a much more populous county, a situation which still appertained in 1833–4. By 1783–5 Kent expenditure had risen to £106,606.[81]

Professor Daniel Baugh has used all available expenditure data 1790–1834, including the parish returns of 1801–17, to analyse poor relief costs in three southern counties including Kent.[82] In Kent a general pattern emerges of gradually increasing gross relief spending with sharp peaks during the 'great dearths' of 1795–6, 1799–1801 and 1812–13. A record outlay of £399,000 occurred in 1817–18 at the height of the crisis of 1817–21 when two bad harvests coincided with the post-war depression and were followed by a rapid fall in agricultural prices. There was a fall and levelling off in the mid 1820s before expenditure began to climb again in the 1830s which may have influenced ratepayers' thinking in 1834. This county pattern is reflected in the East Kent parishes studied by Anthea Newman; and also at Chartham, Appledore and Milton.[83]

[75] Chalkin, *op. cit.*, pp. 255–6. Newman, *op. cit.*, pp. 98, 100.

[76] Newman, *op. cit.*, pp. 100, 102–3.

[77] A. F. Allen, *Shorne*, Rainham 1987, p. 101.

[78] C. H. Bishop, *Folkestone*, London 1973, p. 71.

[79] John Boys, *A General View of the Agriculture of the County of Kent*, 1796, p. 39.

[80] Knowlden and Walker, *op. cit.*, p. 127.

[81] PP 1821, IV. Report of Select Committee on Poor Rate Returns.

[82] D. A. Baugh, 'The Cost of Poor Relief in South-East England 1790–1834', in *Economic History Review*, Second Series, xxviii, No. 1, February 1975, pp. 50–68.

[83] See Fig. 4. See also Newman, *op. cit.*, pp. 100–1. Weller, *op. cit.*, p. 20. Winnifrith, *op. cit.*, p. 59. Joan Margaret Miller, 'Poor Relief in the Parish of Milton Regis 1782–1833', Sittingbourne College of Education Dissertation 1975, pp. 14–15.

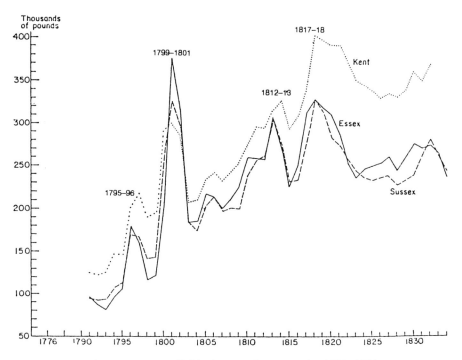

Figure 4. Total spent on poor relief in three southern counties 1790–1834.
Source: D. A. Baugh, 'The Cost of Poor Relief in South-East England 1790–1834' in
Economic History Review, 2nd series, xxviii, no. 1 (February 1975) p. 55.

It is impossible to know the spending levels per recipient but when expenditure
is expressed in relation to the total population on a per capita basis it is clear that
the Kent level of 1801 was equalled, but not surpassed, in 1818. The earlier peaks
are confirmed and Kent is shown to have spent less per capita than neighbouring
Essex and Sussex which had smaller populations.[84] In 1824–5 it also spent less per
capita than the agricultural counties of Buckinghamshire, Suffolk, Bedfordshire
and Huntingdon although nevertheless always high up the per capita table for
English and Welsh counties.[85] Kent poor law authorities were thus either less
generous or more circumspect than their neighbours.

Since the rural labourer in southern England spent some half of his income on
wheaten bread, Baugh also calculated the real value of per capita expenditure in
terms of the wheat it would buy. With the exception of upward movements in the
dearth years 1795–6 and 1801–4, when Kent parishes subsidised food prices for
the poor on a massive scale, real spending maintained a fairly steady level from
just before the outbreak of war in 1793 to the first year of demobilisation and

[84] See Fig. 5.
[85] PP 1826, III. Report of Select Committee on Poor Rate returns. PP 1823, V. Report of Select
Committee on Poor Rate returns.

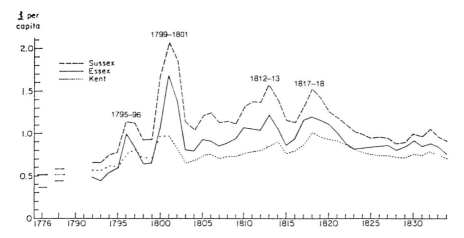

Figure 5. *Per capita* poor relief expenditure in three southern counties 1790–1834.
Source: Baugh, *op. cit.*, p. 56.

falling prices in 1814 (Stage 1). There was then an upward movement in the real
cost of relief until 1823 coinciding with the post-war depression, unemployment
and underemployment. The average level of real expenditure was higher after 1820
than before 1814.[86] After 1823 the real cost of per capita relief fell and levelled off
in the 1830s (Stage 3) perhaps under the influence of assistant overseers and to a
lesser degree select vestries. In purely agricultural areas the upward movement of
real expenditure was more pronounced in the 1830s since, as a reaction to the
Swing Riots, parish pay in rural areas was temporarily increased.[87] The contemporary concept of violently escalating, extravagant relief costs encouraged by gross
expenditure figures was, therefore, not wholly correct but expenditure in monetary
terms and in terms of wheat was generally higher after 1813 for ratepayers than
before.

(4) Outdoor Relief in Cash
As in other English counties monetary relief in the form of a regular weekly or
monthly 'cess' was the most characteristic method of help. Convenient for both
pensioner and overseer it could be increased or reduced to meet changing prices
and personal circumstances. Lists of recipients feature in overseers' accounts for
the seventeenth century. Cowden was paying weekly pensions by 1627. Some
twenty names were listed at Ash in the seventeenth century and this number had

[86] Richardson, *op. cit.*, pp. 105–6. Baugh, *op. cit.*, pp. 56–7. J. P. Barrett, *History of the Ville of
Birchington*, Margate 1893, pp. 154, 167. Robert Borrowman, *Beckenham Past and Present*,
Beckenham 1910, p. 44. C. H. Golding-Bird, *The History of Meopham*, London 1934, p. 185.
See also Fig. 5.
[87] See Figs 6 and 7. Also PP 1834 (44), XXVIII. Sundridge, Benenden, Tenterden, pp. 207,
210–11. Baugh, *op. cit.*, pp. 56–7.

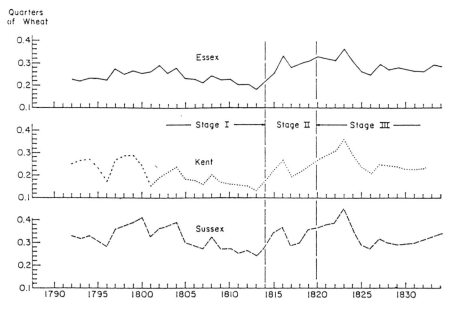

Figure 6. Real *per capita* poor relief expenditure in three southern counties 1790–1834. Source: Baugh, *op. cit.*, p. 57.

doubled by the eighteenth century. In the early nineteenth century 31 widows and 68 others got weekly pay. At Chislet there were seven weekly pensioners rising at mid century to seventeen and later 27.[88] In economic difficulties most parishes increased their number of pensions as rising prices forced those hitherto self-supporting onto relief. Regular pension lists normally contained largely impotent poor but increased numbers of able bodied appeared in crises. Parish policies varied. While Chislet in the early nineteenth century distributed only some 20% of its relief in weekly pay, Sellindge in 1801–2 gave out 52%.[89] The increasing number of 'worn out old men and women' assisted at Chartham and elsewhere suggests that more people were surviving into old age.[90] Without the flexibility provided by monetary relief the poor law system would have collapsed.

Payment of temporary pensions and occasional doles to the seasonal and other unemployed also feature in most overseers' accounts after 1800. There is little evidence, however, of the allowances in-aid-of-wages around which so much poor law debate has centred. Mark Blaug did not place Kent among the 'Speenhamland counties' in which earned incomes were supplemented from the poor rates in proportion to the price of bread and family size in broad imitation of the decision made by Berkshire magistrates in 1795 and earlier decisions elsewhere.[91] West

[88] Guy Ewing, *The History of Cowden*, Tunbridge Wells 1926, pp. 151–2. Newman, *op. cit.*, p. 151.
[89] Newman, *op. cit.*, pp. 151–2. CKS P329/12/3 Sellindge Overseers' Accounts 1801–2.
[90] Weller, *op. cit.*, p. 22.
[91] See Mark Blaug, 'The Myth of the Old Poor Law and the Making of the New', *Journal of*

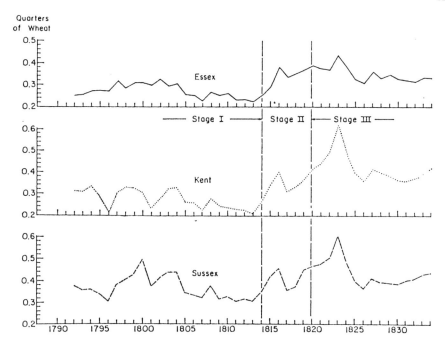

Figure 7. Real *per capita* poor relief expenditure in agricultural parishes only 1790–1834. Source: Baugh, *op. cit.*, p. 60.

Malling justices laid down a scale of maintenance in 1800. A magistrates' scale was in use on Wingham bench in 1819 but was discontinued. In 1822 Ash vestry produced a scale relating relief to family size and bread requirements but the Speenhamland system was not widely adopted in Kent.[92] Certainly by 1824 it did not operate in seven of the fifteen county divisions and was found only in a few parishes of the remaining divisions.[93] In 1834 only nine of forty-four respondents admitted that able bodied labourers received allowances or regular relief. Lenham stated that of 180 able bodied workmen the wages of about sixty were paid on a relief scale whether they worked or not. West Wickham's rector conceded that 'much of the farmers' work was paid for out of the Poor's Rate in the shape of relief on account of insufficient wages'.[94] In any event Baugh has demonstrated that in Kent and south-east England the existence or otherwise of Speenhamland did not influence poor law costs either during or after the war. During the war poverty was influenced by harvest failure and shortage. In the period 1814–20 the harvest crisis of 1816–18 and post-war unemployment kept real relief expenditure high while

Economic History, xxiii (1963), No. 2, and 'The Poor Law Report Re-examined', *Journal of Economic History*, xxiv (1963), No. 2.

92 Elizabeth Melling, *The Poor*, Maidstone 1964, pp. 149–50, 158. Newman, *op. cit.*, p. 162. PP 1834, XXVIII, p. 218.
93 PP 1825, XIX. Abstract of returns respecting labourers' wages, pp. 24–5.
94 PP 1834 (44), XXXI, pp. 252b, 266b. PP 1834, XXVIII, p. 214.

rural depression in 1820–32 brought distress from widespread unemployment, underemployment and low wages.[95]

In this context the widespread payment of child allowances to labourers in work, be it normal or parish employment, introduced to meet the post-war crisis was, however, all important. Outdoor relief from 1814 became an income rather than a wage subsidy. Relief given depended on need rather than the quantity of labour supplied.[96] Before c.1796 child allowances were unknown. In the crisis of 1800 it was feared that if wages were allowed to increase with food prices it would be hard to reduce them when prices fell. Consequently magistrates recommended that a sufficient wage should be calculated to maintain a man, his wife and two children and a regular weekly allowance made for children above that number.[97] Great Chart was paying allowances for the fourth child by 1797. After 1810 the practice spread rapidly. Rolvenden in 1816 allowed a gallon of flour per week for each child beyond three but most child allowances were in cash and accompanied by a scale of wages which were also made up regularly for single men.[98] Critics maintained that the making up of wages out of the poor rate demoralised the labourer and depressed the pay of single men. Barham's guardian of the poor reported in 1832 that the parish had never 'considered it right to pay any part of a man's labour out of the Poors' Rate'. There were no recipients of regular relief and only two or three persons were relieved on account of their families and then by occasional payments of rent.[99] Ash claimed 'the system of allowance to those in farmers' employ, though so fully established in many parts of Kent, was unknown'.[100] These were exceptions. In most rural parishes the situation was as at Goudhurst:

> The word 'scale' is unknown but the thing exists as effectually as if it were published . . . at every petty sessions. Every parish officer and pauper knows that a man with his wife and 3 children is entitled to have his wages 'made up' . . . to 12s.0d. a week and he is entitled to 1s.6d. per week for every child beyond three . . .[101]

Forty (85%) of 47 parishes in the *Answers* paid family allowances. Nineteen (65.5%) of 29 paid above the third child.[102]

Agricultural depression and inadequate wages created by unemployment and underemployment forced magistrates and parish officers to rescue those whose earnings were insufficient to support a family. The support was reluctant and parsimonious but unavoidable for those caught in a desperate poverty trap. While

95 Baugh, *op. cit.*, p. 67.
96 *Ibid.*, p. 61.
97 PP 1834 (44), XXVIII, p. 167.
98 Sir F. Eden, *The State of the Poor*, London 1797, p. 209. Board of Agriculture, *The Agricultural State of the Kingdom in 1816*, p. 126. PP 1834 (44), XXVIII, p. 878.
99 PP 1834 (44), XXXI, p. 237b.
100 PP 1834 (44), XXVIII, p. 218.
101 PP 1834, XXVII. Report from HM Commissioners for Inquiring into the State of the Poor Laws in England and Wales, pp. 103–4.
102 PP 1834, XXXI. Answers to Queries 24 and 25.

many labourers came to accept allowances as of right, any suggestion that they might be prohibited made many parish officers, mindful of the Swing Riots, draw back. Hartlip's overseer recognised that without a corresponding increase in wages labourers would 'be degraded to the condition of the Irish'. Others emphasised the distress which would arise and the renewed 'riots' and 'burnings' which would follow. 'It would cause general disturbance and rioting throughout the south of England', wrote a Tonbridge magistrate. '. . . Officers and occupiers', stated Joseph Exell of Tenterden, 'would for their own safety elude the law'.[103]

(5) Outdoor Relief in Kind

While the regular cash pension was a mainstay against poverty for the aged and infirm and the wage subsidy for the able bodied with large families, relief in kind, although burdensome to overseers, was also used extensively until implementation of the New Poor Law.

Housing was the basic need most frequently provided. 58.6% of Kent respondents to the *Answers* stated that 'very few' labourers owned their own cottages. In a further 30% of parishes no labourer owned a cottage. Twenty-six (60.4%) of the 43 respondents acknowledged payment of pauper rents. Goudhurst in 1830–32 paid an average of £175 per year for rents, approximately 5% of its total expenditure. Chilham, Hawkhurst and Westwell claimed the practice was discontinued, as did Brenchley which had formerly spent £250 a year. Ashford paid no cottage rents but many parishes paid not only for their own resident poor but also, like West Wickham, for their outlying poor to prevent their removal. Sevenoaks, Chiddingstone and Sundridge paid no rents directly but gave money for their payment.[104]

Almost 90% of respondents acknowledged that the rates of cottages were paid by the parish. 116 cottages were 'excused rates' at Gillingham. So, too, were all cottages at Tenterden inhabited by labourers and mechanics. Hartlip also paid the rates of outdwellers, as did Preston near Faversham 'rather than suffer a distress which might send them home.'[105]

Payment of cottage rents was regarded by the assistant commissioners as 'an evil of great magnitude' and the first step to permanent pauperism. It established an artificial rent and stifled all foresight by labourers who ultimately demanded it of right.[106] Nevertheless poor law records suggest that from at least the early eighteenth century it was practised upon a regular or occasional basis and in many parishes became a major item. 'They all pay cottage rents', stated Henry Boyce, overseer of Waldershare, to the Select Committee on the Employment or Relief of Able Bodied Persons.[107]

---

[103] PP 1834, XXXIII, pp. 248d, 263d, 264d.
[104] PP 1834, XXXI. Answers to Queries 17 and 21.
[105] PP 1834, XXXI. Answers to Query 21.
[106] PP 1834, XXVIII, p. 165.
[107] PP 1828, IV. Report of Select Committee on the Employment or Relief of Able Bodied Persons.

While many parishes paid rents others leased, bought or built dwellings for their poor which freed them from grasping landlords. Housing provision found a place in the 1598 Act which authorised building at parish expense upon the waste subject to manorial agreement. Chiddingstone was building in 1601. 'We have not got any new dwelling places erected for the poor but every one of them is well placed and provided', stated Allhallows in 1606.[108] Seal erected a cottage for a man with a wife and six children in 1632.[109] Such dwellings had to be repaired. West Wickham overseers 'Paid the glazier for the poor houses' 4s 0d in 1768. Ten years later a house undergoing major repair cost £2 13s 10d.[110] Meopham vestry borrowed £80 to build cottages for the poor in 1789 but while eighteenth century housing provision mainly took the form of paying rents for existing properties there seems to have been a movement in the early nineteenth century towards the building of new houses encouraged, perhaps, by the renewed pressures of population. Cranbrook decided in 1815 to build 'not exceeding six' cottages for the poor 'in consideration of the present high rents'. A decade later Meopham decided to build additional cottages 'in consequence of the great number of poor who are returning to the parish without the power of finding houses'.[111]

From the repair of parish cottages it was a short step to payment for property repairs generally. John Edwards of Cowden was paid £1 0s 0d in 1817 'for to repair his house', a year in which Sellindge vestry agreed 'to lead Thomas Ingleden's windows.'[112] Small items of furniture also constituted an occasional expense. Sellindge vestry in 1822 even agreed 'to give Johnstone a bed . . . if he gits lodgings but to return the bed . . . when he leaves it'.[113]

Free or cheap fuel was provided as well as housing. Ash overseers were responding to requests for 'burning' as early as 1708. In a county without coal such relief was usually given annually to the permanent outdoor poor. In October 1818 Sellindge vestry awarded half chaldrons of coals (12¼ cwt) to each of six parishioners. Another parishioner was granted a quarter of a chaldron.[114] Ash overseers fetched their coals from Sandwich and Elham overseers from Hythe. Sellindge also supplied faggots and half loads of wood as did Appledore.[115] In December 1829 Chartham vestry agreed to distribute 'roots' belonging to the parish free among 'the most deserving and industrious persons' and a month later bought and delivered 'to the deserving poor a quantity of faggots in proportion to the size of

108 CKS Q/SR2 m. 11d, no. 9. Michaelmas Sessions at Maidstone 1601. Cit. Melling, *op. cit.*, p. 33. F. J. Hammond, *The Story of an Outpost Parish*, 1914, p. 17.
109 CKS Q/SO W1. Easter Sessions at Maidstone, 1632. Cit. Melling, *op. cit.*, p. 34.
110 Knowlden and Walker, *op. cit.*, p. 130.
111 Golding-Bird, *op. cit.*, pp. 190–2. CKS P100/8/2 Cranbrook Vestry Minutes. Cit. Melling, *op. cit.*, p. 163.
112 Ewing, *op. cit.*, p. 200. CKS P329/8/3 Sellindge Vestry Minutes, 28.11.1817.
113 CKS P329/8/3 Sellindge Vestry Minutes, 12.4.1822.
114 *Ibid.*, 30.10.1818. Newman, *op. cit.*, p. 159.
115 CKS P329/12/3 Sellindge Overseers Accounts 1801–2. Newman, *op. cit.*, p. 159. Winnifrith, *op. cit.*, p. 62.

their familys . . .'.[116] Otford vestry, too, assigned free coal to 27 families in that year.[117]

Substantial sums were also spent on clothing and footwear for both the indoor and outdoor poor and for children going to apprenticeship or service. Often these were second hand or the property of deceased paupers. Until the mid-eighteenth century Ash overseers ran an extensive second hand and new clothes business. At Milton next Sittingbourne the parish paid £9 0s 9d for new shoes and shoe repairs and 14s 8d for the making and mending of clothes. £9 12s 0d was paid for the latter in 1808. In 1817 the vestry decided that all who applied for clothes should receive the same type according to their sex. It was, however, necessary to attend divine service to qualify.[118] Appledore's all male vestry also determined what clothing should be awarded. 'Scuffles' or scuffling aprons for work in the fields were usually granted but female 'frippery' like stays were almost always refused although 'stuff' for stays was allowed.[119] Sellindge overseers gave money for clothing to pauper parents or the worsted with which to make them. New shoes, well-nailed, were also often awarded. An annual bill was paid to a tailor and shoemaker.[120]

Because of the problems of distribution food relief was not normally given on a large scale. The earliest accounts at Ash mention provision from 1601 of corn and bread but these were only provided sporadically in East Kent until the late eighteenth century. Sellindge gave occasional sacks of 'taters' while Chartham, before the creation of its select vestry in 1823, gave annual gallons of flour. Elham bought wheat for sale to the poor at reduced prices from 1773 until 1802. In March 1822 Ash vestry embarked upon a scheme to supply the poor with 'good wheaten bread' relating relief to family size and bread requirements.[121] Scarcity and high prices, however, brought an expansion of food relief in the last decade of the eighteenth century. In December 1772 Goudhurst raised a subscription to sell subsidised wheat to 'such poor People who have three children or upwards in family'.[122] Waldershare in 1791 spent money on 'meat, yeast for the poor's bread and peas'. Only during the famines and high prices of 1795–6 and 1799–1801 did overseers become widely involved in the supply of free or subsidised food. At Beckenham in 1795 wheat was bought from a subscription, ground and sold to the poor at 9d a loaf.[123] Birchington overseers sold subsidised, rough meal, wheaten bread and wheat in 1795, 1801–2 and 1804 according to family size. Ightham vestry produced subsidised flour in November 1799. Meopham vestry also bought flour in bulk and retailed it at a cheap rate in 1795 to 53 families. Elham in that year spent

116 Weller, *op. cit.*, p. 10.
117 Clarke and Stoyel, *op. cit.*, p. 195.
118 Miller, *op. cit.*, p. 11. Newman, *op. cit.*, p. 157.
119 Winnifrith, *op. cit.*, p. 62.
120 CKS P329/12/3 Sellindge Overseers' Accounts 1801–2.
121 Newman, *op. cit.*, pp. 157, 161–3. Weller, *op. cit.*, p. 30. CKS P329/12/3 Sellindge Overseers' Accounts 1801–2. P329/8/3 Sellindge Vestry Minutes, 12.4.1822.
122 W. A. Raikes, *Records of Goudhurst*, Tunbridge Wells 1927, p. 33.
123 Newman, *op. cit.*, p. 163. Borrowman, *op. cit.*, p. 44.

a subscription on bread, meat, cheese and flour which was distributed in addition to money. Some schemes either continued until or were revived during the post-war depression. Meopham was still selling subsidised flour in 1822, a year when Chevening resolved that part of the poor rate should be paid in corn which could be distributed to those receiving parochial relief. Benenden, as late as 1832, allowed a gallon of flour for the fourth child.[124]

(6) Provision for the Sick

The 1601 Act made no provision for treatment of the sick but in 1601 payments were already being made to a doctor in Ash where the first reference to a medical contract for the poor appears in 1680. A further contract in 1725 covered workhouse inmates and regular recipients of relief.[125] By the mid-eighteenth century occasional payments were made to doctors even in the smallest parishes and, since the connection between sickness and pauperism was appreciated, many parishes had annual contracts with local medical men.[126] Cowden made a contract in 1732. Chislet, in 1742, paid a Herne doctor six guineas a year to care for the poor. At Meopham in 1776 Dr Rowley was paid two guineas less.[127] In 1783 Wateringbury agreed with the local doctor that he should supply the poor with 'proper medicines and attendance' for six guineas a year but receive extra for midwifery, fractures and inoculation.[128] Thomas Waring's agreement with Shoreham in that year was worth only £4 3s 9d but included 'all sickness, lameness, natural smallpox and all exidents of all kinds'. By 1815 the fee was £23 0s 0d a year but the responsibilities included 'venereal complaints'. An extra guinea was payable for midwifery. The fee of Appledore's parish doctor was 25 guineas in 1819 and had risen to £40 by 1823.[129]

By 1834 salaries and generosity of provision varied considerably. The medical salary at Ashford was £80 as was that at Faversham which also employed a midwife. Chatham paid a contract salary of £90 and Maidstone £100.[130] The Webbs condemned medical tendering as 'wholly bad' since they believed the lowest tenders were invariably accepted.[131] Per capita comparison of medical contracts in 1834 suggest, however, that while Ashford, conscious that low tenders would be self-defeating, was surprisingly generous, Chatham and Maidstone were

---

124 Barrett, *op. cit.*, pp. 154, 167. Melling, *op. cit.*, pp. 159–162. Golding-Bird, *op. cit.*, p. 185. Newman, *op. cit.*, p. 163. PP 1834, XXVIII, p. 210.

125 Newman, *op. cit.*, p. 159.

126 *Ibid.*, pp. 124, 161.

127 Ewing, *op. cit.*, p. 178. Newman, *op. cit.*, p. 160. Golding-Bird, *op. cit.*, p. 185.

128 CKS P385/12/2. Agreement between John Hosmer, surgeon and the parish of Wateringbury, 21.4.1783. Cit. Melling, *op. cit.*, p. 138.

129 Malcolm White and Joy Saynor, *Shoreham: a village in Kent*, Shoreham 1989, pp. 117–18. Winnifrith, *op. cit.*, p. 62.

130 PP 1834, XXVIII, pp. 212, 216, 220.

131 Sidney and Beatrice Webb, *English Poor Law History: The Old Poor Law*, London 1927, pp. 304–7.

niggardly although no more so than rural parishes like Appledore.[132] On the other hand the Rev. Henry Bishop found salaries in rural West Kent comparatively high:

> The population in the parishes of this neighbourhood is considerable and the extent of ground over which it is spread wide; the salaries of the medical men engaged for the poor are high compared with the sum usually paid in other parts of the country. From £50 to £70 is the usual salary, including every kind of medical attendance even on women during their confinements.[133]

Not all parishes made medical contracts. In 1832 Lenham paid no fixed salary to a surgeon, meeting medical costs as they arose.[134] Many parishes, particularly in East Kent, also took out subscriptions with the Kent and Canterbury Hospital after its opening in 1793. Dover St Mary's found that 'many . . . Parishioners have and do receive great benefit therefrom'. By 1829 145 parishes had become subscribers.[135] Other parishes patronised the London hospitals or subscribed to the urban dispensaries as they opened in the first half of the nineteenth century. In 1732 two Ash women were sent to London hospitals 'to be cured of the Itch and the Venereal disease'. Patients were sent from Meopham to Guys and from West Wickham to St Bartholomews and Guys. Ightham preferred the pest house of neighbouring Wrotham while Cranbrook erected its own.[136]

Surgeons and apothecaries were increasingly aided by ancillary workers such as nurses and midwives. Sellindge vestry granted John Potter a nurse for his wife in 1816 and paid Dame Kennet to nurse Simon Hubard's wife the following year.[137] Dame Ashby, a Boughton Monchelsea woman, acted as a form of home help 'doing for William Wenham'.[138] Surgical equipment was also provided. Folkestone overseers supplied an old Irishman with a pair of crutches while at Otford Jane Fullager, a permanent pauper, periodically received a new wooden leg.[139] Chartham select vestry in 1825 even gave John Blackham £5 0s 0d 'towards getting a false nose and upper lip made for him in London trusting that the benevolence of individuals would supply the remaining sum required . . .'[140] The same parish supported a pauper woman in lodgings at Whitstable 'to give her the

132 Per capita calculations made using 1831 census figures.
133 PP 1834, XXVIII, p. 876.
134 Ibid., p. 214.
135 Newman, op. cit., pp. 124–5.
136 Ibid., p. 160. Golding-Bird, op. cit., p. 185. Knowlden and Walker, op. cit., p. 129. Sir E. R. Harrison, History and Records of Ightham Church, Oxford 1832, p. 37. CKS P100/8/1 Cranbrook Vestry Minutes 23.5.1766, 14.10.1787. Cit. Melling, op. cit., p. 139.
137 CKS P329/8/1 Sellindge Vestry Minutes, 5.10.1816, 28.11.1817.
138 CKS P39/12/1 Boughton Monchelsea Overseers' Accounts 1786.
139 (F)olkestone (R)eference (L)ibrary. Folkestone Vestry Minutes, 24.2.1829. Clarke and Stoyel, op. cit., p. 194.
140 Weller, op. cit., p. 35.

benefit of Sea Air and Baths', a common treatment of the day.[141] If treatment was unsuccessful and the pauper patient died burial expenses were met by the parish.[142]

In contrast treatment of the mentally ill was often callous and distasteful. No special provision was made for the insane in 1601. In the absence of a county asylum some of the more acutely disturbed were placed in private 'mad houses'. John Woodhams, a Cowden lunatic, was sent to London's Bethlehem Hospital at considerable expense in 1735. A Cowden woman, who went mad in 1759, was attended by watchers 'Two every night and sometimes three', before she, too, was despatched to 'Bedlam'. After a time she was brought back and lodged with Dame Parsons who was paid 7s 0d 'for cleansing her from Vermine and for house room'.[143] Gillingham sent a pauper lunatic to Bedlam in 1769 and Phebe Bodkin of Chartham 'in a state of insanity' was sent there in 1817.[144] High costs, however, often tempted poor law authorities to keep lunatics and idiots in the poorhouse. Elizabeth Parker, Chartham's next lunatic, was treated by the purchase of a straight jacket although she, too, had to be removed to an asylum in 1827.[145] The inmates of River workhouse in 1829–30 included '7 insane' and '2 idiots'. In 1832 Ashurst Majendie found seven lunatics in St Mary's Workhouse, Dover. Two, including one who had recently almost murdered a fellow inmate, were kept chained to their beds. 'In many workhouses in this county', he reported, 'there are idiots and insane persons who are a great annoyance to the inmates in general . . .'[146]

Most poor law medical activity was concerned with cure rather than prevention. Some parishes paid weekly subscriptions to benefit clubs when members could not do so themselves. In 1826 Chartham paid for Thomas Homersham who was in hospital. Otford even agreed in 1831 to subsidise a sick club to the extent of £20 0s 0d spread over four years in an effort to encourage self-help.[147] The most crucial preventive medicine was smallpox inoculation which began in the eighteenth century and had become widespread by the nineteenth century. In 1769 Orpington agreed to inoculate all its poor who were willing 'to Undergo the opperation' at parish expense. There were pauper inoculations at Farnborough in 1773 and Meopham in 1776. Elham's workhouse children were inoculated in 1781. Cowden's parish doctor conducted inoculations in 1788 and inoculated 105 persons at 2s 6d each during the smallpox scare of 1807. All Eastry poor were inoculated in 1818 and next year the Appledore doctor was paid 3s 0d a head for inoculating the poor against 'the small or cow pox'.[148]

---

[141] *Ibid.*, p. 33.

[142] See Hammond, *op. cit.*, pp. 124–5. Knowlden and Walker, *op. cit.*, p. 129. James E. Bird, *The Story of Broadstairs and St Peter's*, Broadstairs 1974, p. 68.

[143] Ewing, *op. cit.*, pp. 180–1.

[144] CMS P153/8/1 Gillingham Vestry Minutes, 14.7.1769. Cit. Melling, *op. cit.*, p. 140. Weller, *op. cit.*, p. 32.

[145] *Loc. cit.*

[146] PP 1834, XXVIII, p. 218. Douglas Welby, *The Kentish Village of River*, Dover 1977, p. 109.

[147] Weller, *op. cit.*, p. 25. Clarke and Stoyel, *op. cit.*, p. 195. J. H. Blandford, *Farnborough and its Surroundings*, Bromley 1914, p. 59.

[148] Newman, *op. cit.*, pp. 160–1. Golding-Bird, *op. cit.*, p. 186. Ewing, *op. cit.*, p. 179. Winnifrith, *op. cit.*, p. 62. F. Chevenix Trench, *The Story of Orpington*, Bromley 1897, p. 40.

Inoculation was not always successful. Parish medical contracts were often awarded to those who accepted them on the lowest terms. Consequently there was always a temptation for a doctor to disregard his parish duties. 'If he receive a message from a rich patient in one and from a pauper patient in an opposite direction', wrote an embittered surgeon, 'it cannot happen otherwise than that the latter will be neglected'.[149] Nevertheless, by 1834, the occasional payment of doctors' bills had grown into an embryonic medical service for the poor which was a major achievement of the Old Poor Law.

(7) The Provision of Work

The Kent Poor Law authorities also continued to try to solve unemployment by setting the able-bodied poor to work or helping them to maintain themselves. If unemployment arose from lack of equipment or materials these were given, loaned or the purchase money provided. In 1781 Widow Conyers' spinning wheel was repaired by Ightham parish for 1s 0d. Folkestone overseers rented nets for their fishermen in the eighteenth century. John Mortley of New Romney was bought a boat and a Sellindge pauper a barrow. In 1801 Wye overseers provided Stephen Rains with a horse and cart to continue his trade.[150] Loans under the Sturges Bourne Act of 1819 were, for the most part, 'lost by the parish'.[151] Folkestone overseers sent two youths 'one month on Trial Onbord the Dover Fishing Smacks'.[152] In the absence of alternative employment in an agricultural county most parishes, however, fell back on their own public works schemes. Shorne poor were sent hop picking. Folkestone paupers were employed in street cleaning. John Cramp claimed that two mills at Garlinge and seventy acres of hired land provided full employment and reduced the poor rate by between 25% and 30%. Minster's able bodied pounded oyster shells for manure while Margate's flour mill, operated by human labour, gave work to the 'most refractory labourers'.[153] Staplehurst ran a subsidised small factory making sacks, bags and leather goods and other schemes were conducted within workhouses.[154]

Such schemes were largely an attempt to extract work in return for maintenance. In this respect parish farms were more successful. Appledore possessed a fifteen-acre parish farm. Chartham, in 1824, sent six unemployed to '. . . dig the land at the Hatch' at 40s 0d an acre. Three years later it was sending able bodied

---

[149] MG 9.10.1832.

[150] Harrison, op. cit., p. 36. Bryan Keith-Lucas, Parish Affairs, Maidstone 1986, p. 104. CKS P329/8/3 Sellindge Vestry Minutes, 2.4.1822. FRL K. Fol. 352. Folkestone Overseers' Accounts 1723–1787, pp. 10, 21, 204.

[151] PP 1834, XXXIII, Answers to Query 41.

[152] FRL K. Fol. 352. Folkestone Overseers' Accounts, 24.2.1829.

[153] Allen, op. cit., p. 103. PP 1833, V. Report from Select Committee on Agriculture, p. 269. PP 1828, IV HC 494. Report from Select Committee on that part of the Poor Laws relating to Employment or Relief of able bodied persons from Poor Rates. PP 1834 (44), XXVIII, p. 165. PP 1834 (44), XXXV. Appendix B2, Parts 1 and 2, p. 60g.

[154] Melling, op. cit., pp. 165–70.

unemployed to grub the '. . . piece of rough ground . . . which the parish has . . . rent free with all the profits thereon . . .'.[155] By 1832 Brenchley had a 26½ acre farm on which single men were employed at 1s 6d a day. Pembury's workhouse poor also cultivated a farm bought in 1819 and rented to the workhouse master. Less successful was the parish farm at Wye where farmers seized the chance to lay off their own labourers.[156] Ash vestry created a parish farm in 1819 so 'that the overseers may Employ the Paupers of the Parish rather than have them kept in idleness'. The outcome of wage reductions on this farm by its overseer, Thomas Becker, was the destruction of his barns and rickyard as described by Gleig.[157] Westerham, in contrast, claimed that its farm had brought reductions in poor law costs and wanted to preserve it after 1834.[158] The most successful of all Kent's parish farms was at Cranbrook. Here a farm had existed since 1774 keeping the rates lower than in adjacent parishes. In 1794 the parish leased the 499-acre Sissinghurst Castle Farm using the castle as a workhouse and employing a combination of unemployed paupers and regular labourers. At times the men employed exceeded a hundred. Workhouse boys, trained on the farm, were readily engaged by farmers who could also secure temporary adult labourers paying current wage rates. Between 1813 and 1818 the trustees handed the overseers £1,000 a year from the profits. After 1820, with the depression in agriculture, it was no longer profitable. It continued, however, until 1855 still helping to reduce the rates and funding families wishing to emigrate.[159]

The universal task of the hard-core unemployed and the unemployed in winter was road repair. 'The highways', stated John Cramp of Garlinge, 'have been the workhouse'. In 1828 Minster in Sheppey had been employing sixty pauper labourers on its roads for ten years.[160] Otford employed its able bodied in quarrying and road repair. When a roadstone quarry opened at Oldbury Hill in 1830 its road gang was despatched there, 'the overseer paying their lodging'. Beckenham in 1821 employed its able bodied sifting gravel at 8d a load. Preference was given to married men, single men working on the roads at 1s 0d a day. Bearsted, East Malling, Milton, Chartham and many other Kent parishes also resorted to stone picking, stone breaking and highway repair.[161] The poor of St Margaret's, Rochester broke granite stones 'by which, if they are inclined to work, they may earn their

---

155 Winnifrith, *op. cit.*, pp. 74–5. Weller, *op. cit.*, pp. 7, 9.

156 PP 1834 (44), XXVIII, pp. 213, 875, 877.

157 Newman, *op. cit.*, pp. 169–70. G. R. Gleig, *Chronicles of Waltham*, vol. 2, pp. 18–23.

158 PRO MH 12. Sevenoaks Union, 5315. Charles Thompson, Chairman of Westerham Parish Farm Committee to John Warde of Westerham, 4.9.1835.

159 PP 1834 (44), XXVIII, pp. 165, 210. C. C. R. Pile, *The Parish Farm at Sissinghurst*, Cranbrook 1952.

160 PP 1836, VIII–II. Third Report from the Select Committee on Agriculture, p. 9. PP 1828, IV HC 494. Report from Select Committee on that part of the Poor Laws relating to Employment or Relief of Able Bodied poor from Poor Rates. Evidence of Mr Lester of Minster, Sheppey.

161 F. R. J. Pateman, *Otford in Kent 1800–1850*, Otford 1957, p. 50. Borrowman, *op. cit.*, p. 169. McNay, *op. cit.*, p. 95. Miller, *op. cit.*, p. 14. Weller, *op. cit.*, p. 7. Carol Bowman, et al., *History of Bearsted and Thurnham*, p. 109.

subsistence'.[162] There were bitter complaints that men 'of idle character', particularly young, single men, preferred parish employment to any other and, if discharged, 'turned to the parish' if only for half a day. Otford vestry warned in 1826 that men not working from 6.00 am to 6.00 pm and observing the prescribed mealtimes would 'be stopt'. Three years later it was decided to pay 'young men who are paupers' 6d a day less than other labourers to encourage them to leave the parish.[163]

Supervision of highway work by overseers was difficult. In 1817 four Strood highway paupers '. . . being idle not working more than three hours in a day and frequently being intoxicated' were confined to the workhouse for a fortnight on broth and water gruel.[164] When attempts at stricter supervision were made at Hougham the men became 'menacing and refractory and complained of not being sufficiently well-paid'.[165] Elsewhere parish work was also ill-received. A Chartham girl was denied relief because her mother refused to tie hops while a Chartham man's allowance was reduced because he would not pick stones.[166] In 1832 seven labourers from Newington, where some of the early Swing rioting had taken place and the tricolour had been hoisted, seized control of a vestry meeting and refused to work in the neighbouring gravel pits at Rainham.[167] If their working conditions were similar to those described by Henry Boyce, a parish officer at Waldershare, their 'spirit of insubordination' is not surprising:

> . . . I have seen 30 or 40 young men in the prime of life degraded in their own estimation as well as in the estimation of their beholders, hooked onto carts and wheelbarrows dragging stone to the highways because they could not get employment elsewhere . . .[168]

On the other hand many contemporaries felt that 'the work done by parish workmen' was 'not a third what is paid them and no benefit to the parish' while at heavily-pauperised Lenham the greater part of the roadwork was believed to be unnecessary.[169]

The only other employment provided for the able bodied, apart from parochial work, was through the Roundsman and Labour Rate schemes. From about 1750 many English parishes began to send their unemployed around the farmers, particularly in winter, to do what work could be found. Roundsmen's wages were fixed by the parish and made up from poor relief to an income considered sufficient for subsistence according to family size. A ticket, signed by the overseer, was

---

162 PRO MH 12. Medway Union, 5249. St Margaret's, Rochester to PLC, 24.9.1834.
163 PRO MH 12. Dover Union, 4955. Hougham Parish to PLC, 20.9.1834. Pateman, *op. cit.*, pp. 40, 50.
164 Henry Smetham, *History of Strood*, Rochester 1899, pp. 293–4.
165 PRO MH 12. Dover Union, 4955. Hougham Parish to PLC, 20.9.1834.
166 Weller, *op. cit.*, p. 9.
167 PP 1834 (44), XXVIII, p. 216.
168 PP 1828, IV, HC 494. Report from Select Committee on the Poor Laws relating to employment or relief of able bodied. Evidence of Henry Boyce of Waldershare.
169 *Ibid.* Evidence of Mr Lester of Minster in Sheppey. Also PP 1834 (44), XXVIII, p. 214.

usually taken by the pauper to the farmer as a warrant for being employed and returned to the overseer signed by the farmer as proof that the conditions of relief had been fulfilled.[170]

The system, or local variations upon it, seems to have expanded during the immediate post-war depression. Milton Regis decided in 1817 that farmers should employ a certain number of men according to the rate they paid.[171] Ash met the 'great increase in paupers' in 1817 with a scheme to employ 68 men, a quarter of the parish's labourers, on the basis of teams of horses kept. The men to be employed were chosen by ballot. From 1817 to 1833 Ash vestry lurched from scheme to scheme in an effort to deal with the intractable problem of unemployment. Schemes introduced in 1822 and 1824 were a Roundsman system and a variation upon it, which included the notorious pauper auction described by Boyce.[172] In a bid to prevent abuse by farmers roundsmen were not employed on regular farm tasks.[173] A 'ticket' system based on rates was instituted at Goudhurst in 1821; and other schemes were devised at Elham and Penshurst in 1822 and at Charing in 1832. By 1825, however, the Roundsman system was in decline. Only six of fifteen districts acknowledged its existence and then only in a handful of parishes.[174] In 1832, only Nonington, of 54 respondents, acknowledged the existence of the system which was condemned as a 'bad system . . . found to answer no good purpose'. Only six of 53 parishes confessed that they had ever practised the system at all. These included Nonington and Preston near Faversham which were cited as examples in the 1834 report.[175]

The disappearance of the Roundsman system, even in those communities which had adopted it, was because by 1834 many Kent parishes had turned to the expedient of a Labour Rate whereby farmers employing a certain proportion of regular labourers according to their rating discharged a portion of their rates by taking some of the surplus hands. If they did not employ them, thus keeping them at agricultural work and avoiding the demoralising highway gangs, they paid a labour rate.[176] Labour rates were of doubtful legality before an Act of 1831. Thereafter they multiplied rapidly with the encouragement of some local magistrates.[177]

A system akin to a labour rate seems to have been introduced in Appledore in 1830. Others followed across the county during 1831–3.[178] In 1833 John Neve of

[170] Ed. S. G. and E. O. B. Checkland, *The Poor Law Report of 1834*, Middlesex 1974, p. 102.

[171] Miller, *op. cit.*, p. 23.

[172] Newman, *op. cit.*, pp. 165–71. PP 1828, IV, HC 494. Report from Select Committee relating to employment and relief of the Able Bodied. Evidence of Henry Boyce.

[173] Raikes, *op. cit.*, pp. 33–4.

[174] CKS P287/12/8 Scheme for the employment of the Poor of Penshurst, 21.11.1822. P78/8/7 Charing Vestry Minutes, 8.11.1823. Cit. Melling, *op. cit.*, p. 166. Newman, *op. cit.*, p. 173. PP 1825, XIX. Abstract of Returns respecting Labourers' Wages, pp. 24–5.

[175] PP 1834 (44), XXXI. Answer to query 27. Checkland, *op. cit.*, pp. 103–4.

[176] PP 1834, XXVIII, p. 207.

[177] Melling, *op. cit.*, p. 165. Winnifrith, *op. cit.*, p. 61. MG 9.11.1830. The *Maidstone Gazette*, 5.2.1833 provided a guide for parishes considering adopting a Labour Rate.

[178] Among those parishes who adopted a Labour Rate were Hever (1831), Charing, Chartham

Tenterden told the Select Committee on Agriculture that labour rates had 'generally failed' because 'the farmers . . . turned off their men'. William Taylor, a Gillingham farmer, was also critical. Tradesmen and small farmers at Lenham complained that the system was manipulated by large farmers who got most of their labour paid from the poor rates.[179] Sundridge found that 25 of their non-resident able bodied labourers were returned when other parishes adopted labour rates. In contrast Chevening, Westwell, Cowden, Sevenoaks and Brasted found the system worked well and 'took off the greater part of the men particularly those with the largest families'.[180] 'The labour rate is the best thing that was ever invented in this parish', re-iterated an Edenbridge ratepayer. The Rector of Staplehurst was not alone when he pleaded with the commissioners to retain the system which he claimed had saved the parish £328, improved its agriculture and reduced its unemployed by thirty labourers.[181] Resentment at the 1834 Act in some Kent parishes is, therefore, easy to understand.

(8) Workhouses

Knatchbull's Act of 1722 permitted parishes or groups of parishes to buy, build or rent workhouses so that they could receive 'the labour and services of their inmates'. Some Kent towns had already anticipated this legislation. Ashford vestry established a workhouse as early as 1705 and Maidstone created one in 1719. In 1720 the Reverend Caleb Parfect suggested a workhouse at Strood to employ children, widows and the elderly but not the able bodied. By 1723 the building was complete and fifteen parish orphans were spinning jersey for stockings.[182] The 1722 Act, however, provided a further impetus for the spread of workhouses. At least 25 parishes established them within a few years. Those at Canterbury (1727), Greenwich (1752), Deptford (1753), Chislehurst (1759) and Queenborough (1767) were created by local act.[183] At Canterbury, the Poor Priests' Hospital became a workhouse which included the bridewell and accommodation for sixteen Bluecoat boys which it still fed and maintained.[184]

(1832), Elham, Otford, Preston near Faversham, Knockholt. They had been joined by 1834 by Brasted, Bromley, Chevening, Cowden, Chiddingstone, Chislet, Edenbridge, Lenham, Sevenoaks, Staplehurst, Tenterden and Thurnham.

[179] PP 1833, V. Report of Select Committee on Agriculture. Evidence of John Neve, p. 251 and William Taylor, p. 251. PRO MH 12. Hollingbourne Union, T. Collins to PLC 7.2.1834.

[180] PP 1834 (44), XXVIII, pp. 207, 214. *Kentish Gazette*, 3.6.1834. PRO MH 12. Sevenoaks Union, 5315. Samuel Bly, assistant overseer, Sevenoaks, to PLC 4.10.1834. John Flavell, vestry clerk of Brasted to PLC 13.11.1834. Thomas Everest, vestry clerk,Cowden to PLC 2.10.1834.

[181] PP 1834 (44), XXXVIII, Appendix D, Labour Rate. PRO MH 12, Maidstone Union, 5195. Mr Hornbuckle, Rector of Staplehurst to PLC, 27.9.1834.

[182] Keith-Lucas, *op. cit.*, p. 111. Smetham, *op. cit.*, pp. 261–76.

[183] See Fig. 8.

[184] Tim Tatton Brown, Paul Bennett and Margaret Sparks, 'The Hospital of St Mary of the Poor Priests', in Alec Detsicas (ed.), *Collectanea Historica*, Maidstone 1981, p. 175. PP 1843, XXI. 9th Annual Report of the Poor Law Commissioners. E. C. Tufnell's Report on Canterbury, pp. 181–91. Robert A. Scott, 'The Administration of the poor law in Canterbury under a local act of

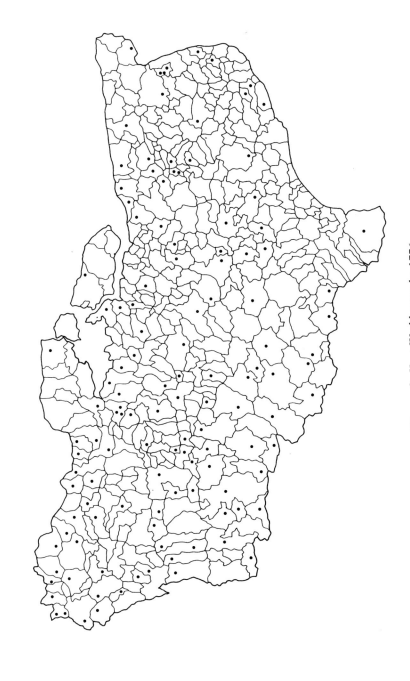

Figure 8. Kent Workhouses by 1776.
Parliamentary Papers 1776, iv, xxxiv. Abstract of Returns made by Overseers of the Poor.

Since Kent parishes were mostly small a number agreed to share workhouses. Farnborough workhouse, created in 1756, served nine other parishes. Lenham workhouse served six and Halling workhouse three.[185] By 1776 the basic pattern of a workhouse system had emerged and Kent had some 132 workhouses with accommodation for 5,819 inmates.[186] Only 29 of 391 parishes did not use workhouses, which were believed to be cheaper than outrelief, a deterrent and a means to employ the poor profitably. The 1722 Act also authorised a workhouse test whereby relief could be refused to those who would not enter the house. The large workhouses such as Greenwich (350), Chatham (250), Canterbury (250), Maidstone (150), St Nicholas, Deptford (130), St Paul's, Deptford (125) and Deal (115) were urban. Many were metropolitan. Sixty-six (50%), however, held thirty persons or less and were often only cottages.[187] Others were former stately mansions. Halling workhouse was an old palace. St Nicholas, Deptford, overseers rented Sayes Court, once the property of John Evelyn and occupied for a while by the Russian Tsar, Peter the Great.[188] A scheme of John Ward of Westerham for one large workhouse to serve West Kent came, however, to nothing.[189]

Gilbert's Act of 1782, which specified that workhouses should be used for children, the aged and infirm but not the able bodied, provided the next impetus for workhouse building. Parishes were encouraged to combine into unions with a central workhouse. Some twelve Gilbert unions were established, mostly in East Kent, while some large individual parishes also adopted the Act such as Dover St Mary's, Deal, Ramsgate and Margate. In all approximately a quarter of Kent parishes were affected.[190] By 1813 two thirds of Kent parishes, including the larger towns, were keeping the greater part of their poor in a workhouse of their own or of some other parish. Of 22,263 paupers, excluding children, 8,077 (36%) were receiving outdoor relief. This was a higher proportion than in any other English county save Middlesex and double the national average affording a clear indication of Kent's poor law problem.[191]

Kent's pre-1834 workhouses were satirised by Sir Francis Head. Few, however, fitted his description of River workhouse as 'a splendid mansion, a delightful retreat'. Most were 'old poorhouses more or less out of repair' and 'many really unsafe'.[192] During his tour of West Kent, Head found Chiddingstone workhouse

1727 with particular reference to the years 1834–c.1850', Kent Extended Essay, 0131, 1979. Melling, op. cit., pp. 79–84.

[185] Keith-Lucas, op. cit., pp. 115–16.

[186] PP 1776, IV, XXXIV. Abstract of Returns made by Overseers of the Poor. See Fig. 8.

[187] Loc. cit.

[188] Keith-Lucas, op. cit., p. 116. A. J. Dunkin, History of the County of Kent: Hundred of Blackheath, pp. 95, 242.

[189] Keith-Lucas. op. cit., p. 113.

[190] See Fig. 9. Keith-Lucas, op. cit., p. 117. PP 1834 (44), XXVIII, pp. 217–19. Melling, op. cit., p. 80.

[191] Keith-Lucas, op. cit., p. 117. Melling, op. cit., p. 78. Between 1792 and 1834 Appledore subscribed in turn to workhouses at Willesbrough, Brookland, Hamstreet and Tenterden. (See Winnifrith, op. cit., p. 60.)

[192] Head, op. cit., p. 474–5.

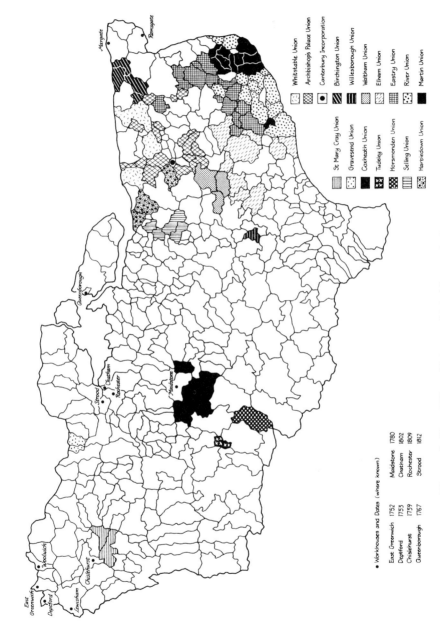

Figure 9. Kent Gilbert Unions and Workhouses built under Local Act.

Whitstable Union
Archbishop's Palace Union
Canterbury Incorporation
Birchington Union
Willesborough Union
Waltham Union
Elham Union
Eastry Union
River Union
Martin Union

St Mary Cray Union
Gravesend Union
Coxheath Union
Tudeley Union
Horsmonden Union
Selling Union
Harpiedown Union

• Workhouses and Dates (where known)

East Greenwich	1752	Maidstone	1780
Deptford	1755	Chatham	1802
Chislehurst	1759	Rochester	1809
Queenborough	1767	Strood	1812

'an old rattletrap house standing in a field'. Hever workhouse was 'a small, miserable mud-thatched cottage' and Edenbridge 'a tumbledown building with many holes in roof and walls'.[193] 'The poorhouses generally', he reported, 'are in the most wretched state . . . in many cases it seems a problem whether the aged pauper will survive the house that has sheltered him or it him'.[194]

While workhouses possessed some clothing and furnishings bought second-hand or acquired from deceased inmates it was customary for aged inmates to bring their furniture with them or sometimes it was bought by their parish. At Shorne the beginnings of workhouse furnishing were provided from the distrained goods of the first inmate bought second-hand.[195]

When possible workhouses were keen to implement work projects in order that the poor should maintain themselves. Most ventures were associated with textiles. The Gilbert workhouse at Martin had a manufactory for spinning and weaving linen, sacking and sheeting. River union workhouse had a manufactory and knit-ting house and Eastry union and Ash a manufactory for making hop bags and pockets, shirting, sheeting and clothes for the poor. Shoreham, Meopham and Tonbridge poor were employed at linen and woollen manufacture and those at Deal and Folkestone in spinning, weaving and making fishing nets. Sevenoaks' work-house shoe manufactory made all the parish shoes while Chatham inmates picked oakum. Given the nature of the inmates, with few able bodied and the majority consisting of children, 'motionless, worn out men', and 'old exhausted women', work schemes were far from profitable.[196] River manufactory made a profit of £135 in 1829–30 but in 1802–3, while Kent parishes spent £8,190 on materials for employing the poor, the money earned from their labour was £5,989 representing only 6.7% of the £88,267 spent on the relief and maintenance of the indoor poor.[197]

(9) The Administration of Indoor Relief

The most common form of eighteenth century workhouse management was to farm responsibility to an entrepreneur on a three-year contract, for a lump sum per annum or upon a per capita basis. The entrepreneur could then use the labour of the poor. The ten parishes in the Farnborough combination of 1756 contracted with James Brown, a city lacemaker, 'to try to keep 100 paupers in the workhouse, paying for them by the head and making additional payments if the number fell below 100'.[198] Cowden vestry farmed its workhouse inmates in 1769–76 and

[193] PRO MH 12. Sevenoaks Union, 5315. Head to PLC 29.11.1834.

[194] Loc. cit.

[195] Allen, op. cit., pp. 101–2. Keith-Lucas, op. cit., p. 117. White and Saynor, op. cit., p. 117.

[196] Golding-Bird, op. cit., p. 184. Head, op. cit., p. 476. CKS Q/CR 1706. Abstract of Accounts of River Union, 23.7.1795 – 23.7.1796. PRO MH 12, 5315, Sevenoaks Union. Samuel Bly to PLC 4.10.1834. PP 1803–4, XIII. Abstract of Answers and Returns relative to the Expense and Maintenance of the Poor 1802–3, pp. 219, 222–3, 233.

[197] PP 1802–3, XIII. Abstract of Answers . . .

[198] Knowlden and Walker, op. cit., p. 128.

RULES AND REGULATIONS,

FOR THE POOR-HOUSE OF

St. Margaret's Parish, Rochester.

THE Master and Mistress are to be up early in the morning, to arrange for Breakfast and other things necessary; and the House throughout to be carefully inspected and cleaned.

The times for each Meal are: Breakfast at 8 o'Clock, Dinner at half past 12 o'Clock, Supper at 7 o'Clock; and time allowed at each Meal, the same as usual with working or labouring people; and the Master and Mistress are to be present at each Meal, and to take care that the greatest decorum and regularity is observed; saying or ordering one of the Boys or Girls to say a Grace before and after each Meal.

The Master and Mistress are never to be absent at the same time, without particular leave from the Overseers, or the Select Vestry.

The Provisions are to be delivered to the People clean and wholesome, agreeable to the allowance ordered; and when they have any cause of Complaint, they are to make the same quietly known to the Master of the House, whose duty it will be to lay the same before the Select Vestry.

The Linen and Wearing Apparel of the Men, Women, and Children to be inspected every Wednesday in the Week; and those that want mending to be given out to such of the Women or Girls as are by the Mistress selected for that work.

The Clothes for washing, on the day appointed for that purpose, to be carefully inspected by the Mistress before they are given out; and the necessary quantity of Soap, &c. for the purpose to be given by her; she is also to inspect them after they are washed, and to take care that the Clothes are all properly aired before used.

When any of the men, women, boys, or girls want Shoes, Clothes want repairing, (or want replacing,) a report of the case to be delivered to the Select Vestry; but in cases where it is necessary to replace the Article immediately, application is to be made by the Master to the Overseers, for directions therein.

The People of all descriptions, in the House, are to be called over every morning before Breakfast, in time to send those to work that are employed out of the House; and the Master and Mistress are to take particular care that they go to their work with their Clothes as decent as possible.

The People in the House, of all descriptions, of an age to do so, are to say or sing regularly the Hymn and Prayer morning and evening, as hath been the custom in the House.

The young Children with out Parents, are to be put under the care of such of the Women as the Mistress may select, and they are to be answerable for the Cleanliness of the Children under their care, and to see that they have their Meals regular agreeable to the Established Hour, and the Children are to be learnt to say their Prayers morning and evening, that is, when they Arise and when they go to Bed.

The People of all descriptions, that are able to attend Divine Service on Sundays, are to be regularly called over for that purpose, and taken to the Parish Church by the Master or Mistress in the morning and afternoon.

The Morals and Conduct of all the People are to be particularly attended to; and when there is any cause of complaint against any of them, it is to be made known by the Master to the Select Vestry; and any occurrence take place that requires immediate remedy, it is to be reported to the Overseers, who will take such steps as may appear to them necessary and as the Acts, of Parliament direct.

The Provisions of all sorts, and necessaries received for the use of the Poor, are to be carefully inspected by the Master, in the presence of some person belonging to the House, if the Overseers are not present; and such Articles as are delivered by weight, are to be weighed, to see that they agree with the Account sent with them; and when the Master finds the Articles right, he is to charge himself therewith, and expend the same agreeably to the Books and Forms delivered to him for that purpose; and in the event of any deficiency appearing in the Goods or Articles sent, either as to quantity or quality, the Master is not to take upon himself to settle the business, but to report the same to the Overseers immediately who will take the necessary steps for rectifying it.

The Mistress to place weekly under the Cook, such of the Girls as may be of a proper age to learn the common methods of Cooking, Boiling, Roasting, &c. and when the Cook reports them to the Mistress as qualified in that way, the Select Vestry to be made acquainted therewith at their weekly Meeting. The Girls at all ages are to be learnt Sewing, (and such things as are proper for a female to learn intended to get her livelihood by industry, as far as the Mistress has in her power,) conformably to the Rules and Regulations of the House; and to keep an account of the Work done by each, and of their conduct, to be laid before the Overseers, in order to their rewarding such as deserve it.

The Master to keep the Men and Boys at work as much as possible, and when they work out, the money for their labour to be collected weekly by the Master, and paid into the hands of the Overseers, and he is to report to the Select Vestry, at their weekly Meeting, the names of people employed out, with their earnings and general conduct, to afford the Select Vestry an opportunity of rewarding those that appear industrious.

To the Master and Mistress of the Poor-House of Saint Margaret's Parish, Rochester.

ELVEY, PRINTER, ROCHESTER.

The Master of the Work-House to place a proper person at the Gate, who is not to let any pauper out of the Gate unless he or she has leave from the Master or Mistress. The Master to allow a boy to go on the errands of the House from Eleven to Twelve in the Morning, and from Three to Four in the Afternoon, and at no other time except in cases of urgent necessity; and in the event of any person belonging to the House being absent, or found to have been absent without regular leave, they will be punished for not conforming to the Rules and Regulations of the House. The House to be closed at Nine o'Clock in the Summer, and at Eight o'Clock in the Winter months.

The People of all descriptions in the House are to be treated with the greatest humanity and attention by the Master and Mistress. The children when behaving improperly to be temperately corrected, no improper language to be made use of towards them; and, when any person acts contrary to the Rules and Regulations of the House, the Master shall report the same to the Select Vestry.

The yeast, ashes, and grains made in the House, are to be regularly disposed of, and the money arising from the Sale thereof, to be paid into the Overseer's hands by the Master, who is to dispose of the Articles for the most he can get, when leave is given by the Overseers for that purpose.

The cultivation of the garden or ground appropriated for the use of the House, is to be regularly attended to by the Master, and the produce thereof expended for the use of the Poor in the Workhouse, or sold for the benefit of the Parish.

The soap, starch, and other articles wanted for the use of the Workhouse, are to be given out by the Mistress in such quantities as she may think necessary, taking care to use the utmost economy.

The Brewing is to be very particularly attended to by the Master, taking care that the proper quantity of Beer is made from the given quantity of malt and hops.

On Sundays, and when the work of the House will permit, the children are to be taught to Read.

The Master is to be answerable for all the provisions, necessaries, furniture, utensils, &c. committed to his charge; and should any deficiency or loss arise, unless satisfactory reasons for the loss or deficiency are given to the Select Vestry, the amount of such loss or deficiency will be stopped from the salary of the Master: and when any loss or deficiency arises, it is expected the Master will make the Select Vestry acquainted therewith as soon as possible.

The people in the House, of all descriptions, are to keep themselves as clean as the nature of their employ will admit; and the men are to be regularly shaved once a week, viz. on Saturdays.

When tea and sugar are given to the old men, women, and nurse, it is to be considered as an allowance solely for their use, and as an extra allowance owing to their age and infirmities; and whenever they act contrary to the Rules and Regulations of the House, or make use of any improper expressions, they will be liable to a stoppage of those Articles by the Master, the same being reported to the Select Vestry at their weekly meeting.

If any person maintained in the Workhouse shall embezzle or purloin any part of the wearing apparel, provided for or belonging to the said Work-house, or any materials for work, or make waste of any of the provisions, materials, or things provided in or for the said Work-house, or refuse to or neglect to perform the work or service which he or she shall be required to do, or shall otherwise misconduct himself, or herself, the Master to report the same to the Select Vestry, that they may be punished according to Law.

If any person in the House, or receiving relief out of the House, is found drinking, or known to have been drinking in any public house, or begging, they will in that case, have the sum allowed stopped, and not have any further relief; if belonging to the House, they will be punished in such a manner as the Select Vestry may think necessary.

If any person in the House has cause of complaint against the Master or Mistress, he is to make the same known in a becoming manner to the Select Vestry, at their weekly meeting, either personally, or in writing; if in writing, the party complaining to sign their name to the letter or complaint.

All misdemeanours not provided for in these Regulations, will be submitted to the Select Vestry at their weekly meeting, as before-mentioned, and such punishment inflicted on the party or parties offending as the Select Vestry may deem necessary; and that they may not plead ignorance thereof, such part of these Regulations as allude to the people in the House are to be read to them every Sunday morning before they go to church, or after it, as may best suit the convenience of the Master and Mistress.

These Articles and Regulations are to be strictly and rigidly attended too; but in case of absolute necessity where the Master or Mistress may find it necessary to deviate from these Rules and Orders, they are to make the same known, as soon after as possible to the Overseers, who will make the same known to the Select Vestry.

Figure 10. Rules and regulations for the poor house in St Margaret's parish, Rochester, c.1820.

returned to contracting again in 1781.[199] Cranbrook let its poor to a local farmer on a three-year contract in 1774.[200] Ightham workhouse master, employed under contract, received payments based on the number of inmates per week with free accommodation. He undertook to feed the paupers with 'good wholesome provisions', to provide and repair their clothing and to keep them employed. The money they earned passed to the parish but adults were allowed 2d in the shilling and children 1d in the shilling for themselves. Men and boys worked at husbandry and women and girls at spinning, weaving and sewing.[201]

Rapid inflation, however, could bring severe problems. Beckenham overseers in 1795 made an emergency allowance to the workhouse master 'in consequence of the dearness of provisions'.[202] Workhouse masters had also, as John Mockett of Broadstairs observed, the chance to enrich themselves 'by a cheap manner of feeding and clothing' the poor.[203] Farming was condemned anonymously in 1770 by John Toke of Godington, a kinsman and neighbour of Sir Edward Knatchbull, instigator of the 1722 legislation, and again in another anonymous letter to the overseers of Deal in 1778.[204] By 1802–3 only six Kent parishes farmed their poor although the system revived in the 1820s. Birchington farmed its paupers in 1822–5. William Nicholls secured a three-year contract for Greenwich workhouse in 1828. Edward Pilbrow, in 1834, held the contracts for workhouses at St Paul's, Deptford and Canterbury besides Maidstone and two others in London.[205]

Some protection was given to inmates by visiting committees of governors. Gravesend, Dartford, Ashford and Strood governors inspected weekly. Similar arrangements existed at many other workhouses.[206] Only a few parishes such as Sundridge and Westerham operated a workhouse test.[207] Workhouse life was not harsh although the rules of some larger workhouses appeared formidable and seemed to foreshadow post-1834 regulations. The Dartford inmates' day lasted from 6.00 am to 7.00 pm in summer and 7.00 am to 6.00 pm in winter. They retired at 8.00 pm in winter and 9.00 pm in summer. At Beckenham Workhouse lights were only allowed in the hall and in 1820 roll calls took place 3–4 times a day to prevent inmates entering and leaving as they pleased. Those working in the manufactory at Broadstairs workhouse forfeited breakfast if they were not up by 6.00 am. Rules were read frequently and fire, candles and provisions jealously guarded.

[199] Ewing, *op. cit.*, pp. 190–1.
[200] Pile, *op. cit.*, p. 6.
[201] E. V. Bowra, *Ightham*, Tunbridge Wells 1978, pp. 55–6.
[202] Borrowman, *op. cit.*, p. 46.
[203] Bird, *op. cit.*, p. 67.
[204] Keith-Lucas, *op. cit.*, pp. 112–13.
[205] PP 1803–4, XIII. Abstract of Answers . . ., p. 236. Barrett, *op. cit.*, p. 175. PRO MH 12, Greenwich Union, 5091. Abstract of contract dated 25 March 1828 between William Nicholls and Churchwardens, Overseers and Governors of the Poor of Greenwich. Letter from Edward Pilbrow to Edwin Chadwick, 14.10.1834.
[206] Keyes, *op. cit.*, p. 224. Ruderman, *op. cit.*, p. 22. White and Saynor, *op. cit.*, p. 117. A. J. Philip, *History of Gravesend and its Surroundings*, Wraysbury 1954, p. 142. Smetham, *op. cit.*, p. 269.
[207] PP 1834 (44), XXVIII, p. 208.

'Spirituous liquor' was forbidden. Offenders were confined for two months.[208] At Meopham cards, dice and other games were banned. Swearing, quarrelling, indecent behaviour or leaving the house without permission brought loss of meals.[209] Such rules, however, were often honoured more in the breach than the observance. Dartford Workhouse seems to have been conducted with some humanity despite the presence of difficult inmates. Every care was taken 'to keep the People and Children free from Lice and Filthiness and their Beds from Bugs'.[210] In fact the general mixed workhouse was characterised more by slackness and squalor than by deliberate cruelty. Many of the older buildings like St Paul's, Deptford, Maidstone and Chatham were impossible to classify. Maidstone had only one privy for all inmates. The youths destroyed work in the manufactory and by night committed depredations in the surrounding countryside. In the female ward prostitutes corrupted the young girls. Both sexes made assignations by climbing from their windows and passing over the roof. Chatham's overcrowded workhouse was 'injurious to health and morality' and a hotbed of fever. The children were exposed to the filthy language of criminals and prostitutes imprisoned in the town 'cage' within its gates.[211]

'It is impossible to conduct a workhouse properly without a good master and mistress', wrote an anonymous Kent author in 1778. Not all masters and mistresses were 'sober and orderly Persons'.[212] Untrained for their trying and low paid task some had to invoke their disciplinary powers. Strood workhouse master confined inmates to the 'cage' on water gruel for assault and for stealing and selling workhouse blankets and clothing. More serious offenders were brought before the magistrates. In 1830 Isaac Mears received 21 days hard labour for riotous and disorderly conduct in Harbledown Workhouse. Coxheath paupers neglecting their work were sent to the treadmill. Margate Workhouse had its own treadmill for the refractory.[213] Violence was never far away. In 1788 Abigail Hallam struck the master of Crayford Workhouse with a brick and 'pulled his hair off his head'. On the other hand Herne workhouse master was fined in 1830 for assaulting a female pauper.[214]

In 1832 Kent respondents were agreed that an able bodied labourer and family could subsist upon bread, cheese, bacon and potatoes with occasional fresh meat.[215] Workhouse diet followed this pattern. The striking feature of workhouse dietaries was the size of portions and the frequency of meat dinners. Strood

[208] Keyes, *op. cit.*, pp. 227–30. Borrowman, *op. cit.*, pp. 171–3. Bird, *op. cit.*, pp. 70–1.

[209] Golding-Bird, *op. cit.*, p. 183.

[210] Crispin Whiting, 'Attitudes towards the poor in the first half of the 18th century: the aims and actualities of the parish workhouse at Dartford', Kent Extended Essay, 0275, 1978. Keyes, *op. cit.*, p. 228. Melling, *op. cit.*, pp. 99–107.

[211] PRO MH 12. Greenwich Union, 5091. Edward Pilbrow to Edwin Chadwick, 14.10.1834. PP 1834 (44), XXVIII, pp. 215, 220.

[212] Anon., *A Letter to the Overseers of Deal*, 1778, p. 6.

[213] Keyes, *op. cit.*, p. 227. Smetham, *op. cit.*, pp. 296–7. *Kentish Gazette*, 26.3.1830. PP 1834 (44), XXVIII, pp. 216, 219.

[214] CKS QSB Bdl 217 Deposition 6.9.1788. *Kentish Gazette*, 8.6.1830.

[215] PP 1834 (44), XXXI. Answers to Query 14.

provided meat dinners on six days per week in 1722 and five days in 1817. River union provided meat dinners on four days including half a pound of cold beef on Sundays. Folkestone workhouse fare was more circumspect with only three meat dinners. In 1832 the select vestry of St Mary's, Dover complained that the work-house master allowed fifteen ounces of meat to every inmate and that the inmates consumed 164 gallons of strong beer during the month of March. At Chilham the paupers insisted upon having porter and gin rather than beer. An attempt to sub-stitute seconds bread almost provoked a mutiny.[216] 'The inmates of most work-houses especially in country parishes', reported Ashurst Majendie, 'live far better than labourers maintaining themselves . . . the diet is usually meat three to five days in the week with beer: the expense is great . . . even when no abuses exist . . .'.[217]

His case may have been overstated but Kent workhouse diet was comparatively good. Most workhouses provided little luxuries. Ightham in 1802 paid for work-house children to go to a fair and in 1806 provided 'ale and raisins' for the paupers.[218] In 1802–3 money spent on the indoor poor amounted to 41% of county relief expenditure. Often squalid, slackly administered and beset by problems of non-categorisation, Kent's mixed workhouses were open to criticism and did not reduce the rates. Nevertheless they cared tolerably well, like the workhouses of rural Cambridgeshire and the East and North Ridings, for their various inmates who were mostly beyond outdoor care.[219]

(10) Settlement

The 1601 Act made parishes responsible for relief of their own 'settled' poor. A child took its father's place of settlement if known; failing that its mother's or that failing its place of birth. If the child subsequently served an apprenticeship, was hired as a servant for a year or paid the rates of another parish this would change its settlement. So, too, did marriage in the case of a girl. The settlement legislation of 1662, 1691 and 1696 created a structure which facilitated removal of non-settled poor but not before they became chargeable provided they brought with them a settlement certificate guaranteeing maintenance by their own parish. Doubts re-garding settlement were resolved through examination by a magistrate who also issued the removal order. Population mobility was theoretically possible and in Kent was quite extensive.[220] There was, however, limited opportunity to gain a legal settlement elsewhere and much confusion, malpractice and expense.

Overseers were anxious to exercise control over population particularly in towns where strangers were less easily detected. In 1786 Dover St Mary's delivered

---

[216] Smetham, *op. cit.*, pp. 272, 293. Welby, *op. cit.*, p. 106. FRL Folkestone Vestry Minutes August 1824. PRO MH 12, Dover Union, 4955. St Mary's Select Vestry to PLC, October 1834. PP 1834 (44), XXVIII, p. 220.

[217] PP 1834 (44), XXVIII, p. 165.

[218] Harrison, *op. cit.*, p. 37.

[219] Hastings, 'Poverty and the Poor Law . . .', p. 26.

[220] Melling, *op. cit.*, pp. 55–8.

warning notices to inhabitants 'who make it a common practice of unlawfully taking into their Houses . . . Inmates and Lodgers who do not belong to this parish but frequently become chargeable hereto'.[221] Feelings in the rural parishes were equally strong. Headcorn residents 'warned off' a prospective newcomer in 1679 while Shoreham in 1708 brought ten inhabitants, who were in danger of becoming chargeable, before a magistrate to establish whether they had legal settlements.[222]

Fraudulent attempts to change a pauper's settlement were not unknown. In 1783 Meopham overseers paid the wedding expenses and £2 12s 6d to Timothy Lyons on marrying Sarah Cranhurst, a lame parishioner who would take her husband's settlement.[223] Otford vestry in 1829 offered rewards of £3 0s 0d to young men who went to service and spent a year out of the parish. Brighton overseers provided the rent and money to enable a baker to live for a year in a £15 0s 0d tenement at Rolvenden. At the end of the year he moved his family in and applied for relief. When he was removed another Brighton family was sent to the house 'with a similar design of gaining a settlement'. Only threat of an indictment for conspiracy caused the Brighton overseers to abandon their claim on Rolvenden.[224] Overseers elsewhere were more direct. In 1821 a widow who applied to Ightham Workhouse Committee for relief was refused 'on account that we think she don't belong to us'.[225] When two children were illegally and without warrant removed from Eastry to St Mary's, Dover in 1769 the St Mary's overseer, also without warrant, promptly returned them.[226]

The settlement laws undoubtedly produced much injustice and hardship with cases of repeated removal through disputed settlement, families divided and women moved on until the very moment of delivering a child. The child of Mary Blandford was 'born in 1806 on board a Gravesend boat – the mother then under order of removal'. In 1785 four starving children were left until parish responsibility could be established.[227] A poor widow who had lived twenty years at Sittingbourne, when ordered to be removed to Hythe, tried to drown herself.[228] Ten-year-old Edward Jackson, whose mother had re-married and taken the settlement of her second husband, kept the settlement of his dead father and in 1828 was returned from Milton Regis to Boughton under Blean.[229] George Moore, vicar of Wrotham, believed removal was 'cruelly oppressive on . . . the individual who having worked the best part of his life in a Parish and formed connections and friends . . . is, when old age or sickness have diminished his powers, removed to a

221 Newman, *op. cit.*, p. 131.
222 CKS P181/16/2, Letter from Churchwardens and Overseers of Headcorn to a prospective resident 1679. U442 O45, A Justice of the Peace in Shoreham considers the settlement of some of the inhabitants, 1708. Cit. Melling, *op. cit.*, pp. 58, 60–6.
223 Golding-Bird, *op. cit.*, p. 189.
224 Pateman, *op. cit.*, p. 40. PP 1834 (44), XXVIII, p. 211.
225 Harrison, *op. cit.*, p. 38.
226 Newman, *op. cit.*, p. 199.
227 *Loc. cit.*
228 *Maidstone Gazette*, 17.4.1832.
229 Miller, *op. cit.*, p. 6.

parish where he has lost all acquaintancies and friends . . . is unwillingly received
and relieved accordingly and . . . terminates his life in misery'.[230]

A high incidence of removals was associated with periods of economic difficulty. Of 171 removal orders at Ash 49 were issued in 1765–98 and 101 in
1799–1818. Ninety-five of the latter dated from 1807. Family groups, consisting of
men, wives and children, were the most vulnerable since they were potentially the
most expensive. Forty-two of the 101 orders fell into this category. Unaccompa-
nied women, who might become both chargeable and pregnant, were also highly
likely to be removed.[231] Since illegitimates took their birthplace as their settlement
Chartham overseers in 1827 hastily returned a pregnant Eliza Marsh to Petham and
rushed Elizabeth Allard, another pregnant singlewoman, to Ashford 'to swear her
child to William Banks'.[232] In such circumstances not all removals were effected by
means of an order. The Ash overseer in 1713 simply gave 2s 0d 'to a wench that
has a great belly to get her clear of the Parish'.[233]

Appeal against removal was unusual by those involved but parishes to which
they were removed could and did appeal. In 1817 there were 314 Kent appeals –
the largest county total apart from Leicestershire and Middlesex. Of these 105
were respited. 118 (56.4%) of the remaining 209 were quashed, 57 (27.2%) were
confirmed and 35 (16.4%) were dismissed.[234] Even without litigation removal
costs were high. Litigation was even more expensive. Ash seems to have retained a
lawyer to safeguard its interests.[235] Kent expenditure on litigation in 1776 was
£1,320. By 1813 it had risen to £17,210, the third highest total in the country.[236] In
the years 1829–31 Maidstone spent £626 on removals and £519 on litigation.
Chatham spent nearly £300 per year, Faversham £224 and Dover '£400 and upwards'.[237] Countywide the cost of lawsuits, removals and overseers' expenses
amounted to £3,961 or 3.7% of all poor law expenditure in 1785; £8,888 or 4.1%
of poor law expenditure in 1802–3; and £15,339 or 4.4% of poor law expenditure
in 1833–4.[238] In the 1816 Board of Agriculture Report a Thanet steward complained bitterly of the litigious disputes over settlement maintaining that the sum
paid in one year would build nationally all the factories which he believed could
keep the poor in work.[239]

[230] PP 1834 (44), XXXIV, p. 268e.
[231] A. E. Newman, 'Removal and Settlement in the Parish of Ash 1670–1834', in *Cantium*, vol. 2,
no. 3, July 1970, pp. 63, 71. This is corroborated by Melvyn Oxer, 'Operation of the Certificate
System as recorded by a study of the settlement papers of the Parish of Cranbrook 1697–1805',
Kent Extended Essay, 034, 1968, pp. 21–2.
[232] Weller, *op. cit.*, p. 16.
[233] Newman, 'Removal and Settlement . . .', p. 61.
[234] PP 1817, VI. Report from Select Committee on the Poor Laws. App. L, pp. 168–9.
[235] Newman, 'Removal and Settlement . . .', p. 67.
[236] Keith-Lucas, *op. cit.*, p. 110.
[237] PP 1834 (44), XXXVII, pp. 57–59k, 62k.
[238] PP 1774–1802, 1st Series, IX. Report of Select Committees on the Poor Laws 1775–7 and
1787. PP 1803–4, XIII. Abstract of Answers and Returns relative to the expense and Maintenance of the Poor 1802–3. PP 1835, XLVII. Returns on Poor Relief 1829–34.
[239] Board of Agriculture, *op. cit.*, p. 140.

While such spending was wasteful the sums at stake over a period of years were high and appeals, with all the legal complexities involved, had a good chance of success. The cost in human misery was higher. In 1791 Hester Noakes and her two young children were removed from Chatham to Milton Regis. On appeal Quarter Sessions decided that her settlement was Chatham to which the family was re-turned.[240] 'It often happens from the great difficulty in ascertaining a pauper's settlement', stated John Falera of Folkestone, 'that the overseers refuse relief to persons in the greatest distress'.[241] While some parishes were prepared to give non-resident relief to the temporarily unemployed, sick and aged, which was cheaper and more humane, many parishes by 1834 were hiring labourers for under a year 'to prevent parish settlement'.[242] Chiddingstone hired by the half year. 'In parishes purely agricultural', stated G. B. Chambers, churchwarden of Minster in Sheppey, 'servants are hired for 51 weeks to prevent a settlement; consequently they must obtain a fresh service every year; great injury is thus done to the poor'.[243] There were some pleas in 1832 for the abolition of the Law of Settlement 'as it now stands'.[244] Many respondents to the commissioners' questionnaire were, however, silent about the Settlement Laws. Behind the silence lay fear of a national or county rate which would strike at local self-government.

Respondents were less reticent about the bastardy laws. Nationally and locally there was a large increase in the illegitimacy rate from the 1770s which peaked in the first quarter of the nineteenth century.[245] 'The number of illegitimate children', reported Goudhurst, 'is frightfully large . . . 9 out of 10 of the wives of labourers are far advanced in pregnancy at the time of marriage. The mothers of bastards are less fortunate but scarcely less virtuous than the others'.[246]

Reasons for this problem are not clear. Women bearing more than one bastard were not unusual. Five West Wickham women delivered two illegitimates each between 1777 and 1802.[247] The majority of respondents, however, rejected the contemporary opinion that it was a profitable practice since the poor law child allowance 'did not repay the mother' or 'did not more than repay the woman for maintaining the child'.[248] Whatever its cause high illegitimacy meant loss to the parish where the children were born at a time of acutely rising costs. An affiliation order might be obtained upon the unsolicited testimony of the mother but ap-prehension and legal action were time-consuming and expensive. Many labourers could not pay and were prepared to suffer imprisonment. 'Not many more than half

[240] Miller, *op. cit.*, p. 7.
[241] PP 1834 (44), XXXVI, p. 60k.
[242] PP 1834 (44), XXXIII. See Answers to Rural Query 38 from Bapchild, Chiddingstone, Chilham, Farningham, Faversham, St Michael, Harbledown, Higham and Tonbridge.
[243] *Ibid.*, p. 255d.
[244] See Chislet and Chislehurst. *Ibid.*, pp. 241–2e.
[245] Newman, *op. cit.*, p. 315.
[246] PP 1834 (44), XXXIV, p. 246e.
[247] Knowlden and Walker, *op. cit.*, p. 128.
[248] PP 1834 (44), XXXIV. Answers to Rural Queries 47–9. Bapchild, Boughton Monchelsea, Chislehurst, Chislet, Cobham etc.

Plate 13a. Pupils at Rolvenden National School c.1900.

Plate 13b. Presentation of attendance certificates at Great Mongeham School c.1912.

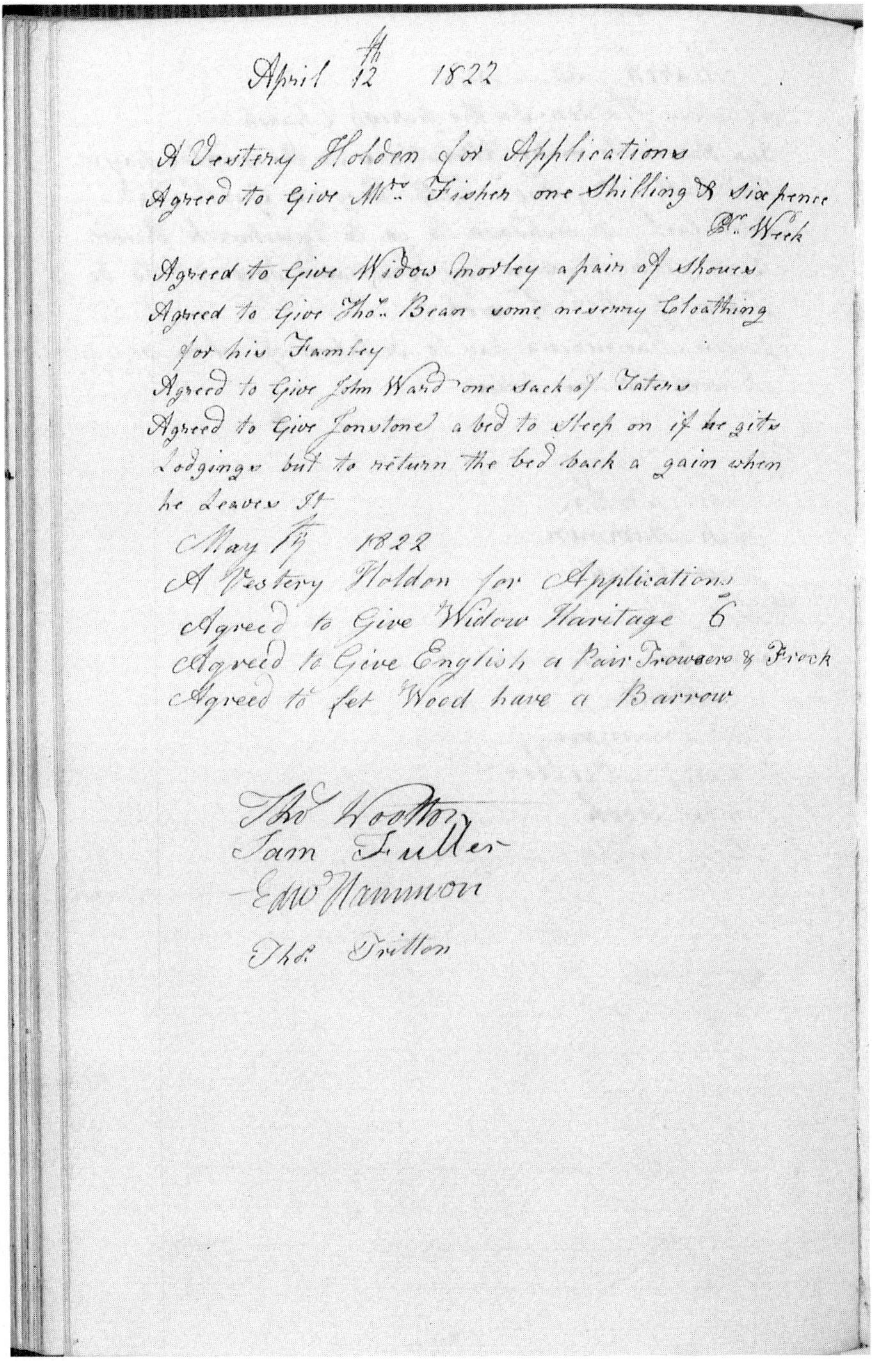

April 12th 1822

A Vestery Holden for Applications
Agreed to Give Mrs Fisher one Shilling & Sixpence
                                              Pr Week
Agreed to Give Widow Morley a pair of Shoues
Agreed to Give Thos Bean some neserry Cloathing
   for his Famley
Agreed to Give John Ward one Sack of Taters
Agreed to Give Jonstone a bed to Sleep on if he gits
Lodgings but to return the bed back a gain when
he Leaves it
   May 1th 1822
A Vestery Holden for Applications
   Agreed to Give Widow Haritage 6
Agreed to Give English a Pair Trowsers & Frock
Agreed to fet Wood have a Barrow

   Thos Wootton
   Sam Fuller
   Edw Hammon
   Thos Tritton

Plate 14. Applications for poor relief at Sellindge 1822.

Plate 15a. The Kent and Canterbury hospital 1810.

Plate 15b. Proposed Union Workhouse at Canterbury 1846.

Plate 16. Slum property in Rochester demolished in c.1910: (a) Cottages in Corporation Street and (b) Houses in Ironmonger Lane.

the fathers pay anything', stated the assistant overseer of Edenbridge. 'Some run away and some have a family to maintain'.[249] Gravesend and neighbouring Milton did well to recover all but 9% and 11% respectively of their bastardy expenditure in 1827–31. Maidstone incurred a loss of £3,762 (75%) on the massive 858 illegitimate children born during the same time which averaged 171 per year. Folkestone's 154 bastards brought a loss of £335 (62.6%) while Cranbrook's sixty illegitimates cost the parish a loss of £694 (64.6%).[250] Nor was the problem purely an urban one. In seventeen responding rural parishes 435 bastards were born over the five year period. Only ten parishes submitted their losses which amounted to £2,563.[251] Rev. Henry Bishop found the debt due at Brenchley to be £125, the vestry having recently struck off £500 as irrecoverable.[252]

Not all parish officers were as tolerant as William Lake of Bapchild who when asked what changes could be made in the bastardy laws replied 'None. Nature will prevail'. Others suffering from a combination of moral outrage and financial loss suggesting remedies ranging from changes in the Settlement Laws and the refusal of all monetary aid to the treadmill for women and heavier fines for men.[253] Barham's guardian of the poor saw allowances for bastards as 'an encouragement to the lowest and most depraved' while Ashurst Majendie and others were quick to emphasise that treatment was superior to that given to the mother of a legitimate child and to suggest that illegitimate children should be apprenticed in the colonies.[254] One can therefore understand the cruel treatment of pregnant singlewomen, one of the harshest aspects of the Old Poor Law, and why many parish officers urged that illegitimates should adopt the mother's settlement.

Closely related to the problem of settlement was that of vagrancy which still retained the criminal stigma given by sixteenth century legislation. The vagrant, a social nuisance, was liable to whipping or imprisonment before 'passing' from parish to parish to his original settlement. Because of the problem of obtaining a new settlement persons who had moved from their home and had undergone misfortune were unable to secure relief and often driven to vagrancy. Vagrants included a high proportion of widowed or deserted wives and wives of servicemen with their children. After 1699, when the cost of transporting vagrants fell not on individual parishes but county funds, they were increasingly joined by migrant workers and the unemployed taking advantage of free travel and subsistence.[255]

As early as 1739 Dover St Mary's appointed a beadle to help 'in taking up Beggars . . . and passing vagrants.'[256] By the 1790s small parish poorhouses like Meopham were finding it increasingly difficult to cope with vagrants and were

---

[249] PP 1834, XXXIV, p. 243e.

[250] PP 1834 (44), XXXVI, pp. 57k, 60–2k.

[251] PP 1834 (44), XXXIV. Answers to Rural Queries 47 and 48.

[252] PP 1834 (44), XXVIII, p. 877.

[253] PP 1834 (44), XXXIV, p. 236e. Answers to Rural Query 49.

[254] Ibid., p. 237e. PP 1834 (44), XXVIII, p. 165.

[255] Melling, op. cit., pp. 70–1.

[256] Newman, op. cit., p. 130.

obliged to lodge them out.[257] In the early nineteenth century the East Wickham overseer relieved 700 vagrants in a month. East Wickham was en route for the vagrant depot at Southwark.[258] After 1815 demobilisation, depression and an influx of Irish vagrants fleeing from famine augmented the annual hop picking and fruit picking migration. By 1834 Farningham with five miles of turnpike and a good stream was heavily burdened by vagrants since it had become a favourite resting place for the Irish on their way to the hop districts. Between 1,000 and 1,500 vagrants had passed through in one day occupying the outbuildings of roadside farms at night.[259] Gravesend and Milton, also en route to Southwark, had by this time abandoned monetary aid substituting tickets for the workhouse which entitled vagrants to a loaf and lodging in a newly-erected vagrant shelter which it was calculated would save £150 per year. Faversham also adopted the 'ticket system' which entitled vagrants to bread and a night's lodging in the workhouse and had reduced the number of applicants. So, too, did Canterbury, Sandwich and Dover. The last two also instituted a labour test. 2,611 vagrants were relieved in Canterbury workhouse in 1833 while the mayor of Sandwich, who found vagrants disorderly and unprepared to work, maintained that the evil of vagrancy existed to an alarming extent.[260] Vagrants were frequent victims of the brutality of frustrated overseers but the vagrant problem had come to stay.

(11) Pauper Children

Overseers were immediately concerned with keeping the adult poor alive and restoring them to independence. A different policy was required for children who, unless helped to self-sufficiency, would be pauperised for life. The 1601 Act stipulated that pauper children should be found work and,when old enough,apprenticed. Children of pauper parents had their keep included in the family pension and child allowances were paid to labourers in work with large families. Otherwise they were boarded out. Appledore in 1832 had 25 children out at board at 3s 6d per week. Most remained in the parish. The less fortunate were sent as far as Bethersden and Hythe.[261] Poor Law assistance in providing education was minimal. Meopham and West Wickham paid for the education of pauper children in the 1770s. Ightham overseers in 1797 paid 'Mrs. Parris for Schooling for the workhouse children and Books for one'.[262] The principal means of teaching skills to pauper children, however, was apprenticeship. Comment upon pauper apprenticeship has been mainly hostile since overseers in some regions frequently bound children to unskilled trades as cheap labour placing them with masters outside their

---

[257] Golding-Bird, *op. cit.*, p. 180.
[258] PP 1803–4, XIII. Abstract of Answers and Returns relating to the expense and maintenance of the poor 1802–3, p. 231.
[259] PP 1834 (44), XXVIII, p. 221.
[260] Newman, *op. cit.*, p. 130. PP 1834 (44), XXVIII, pp. 216–19. *Maidstone Gazette*, 16.10.1832.
[261] Winnifrith, *op. cit.*, p. 61.
[262] Knowlden and Walker, *op. cit.*, p. 129. Golding-Bird, *op. cit.*, p. 187. Harrison, *op. cit.*, p. 37.

parish to change their settlement or forcing unwilling parishioners to take them under the 1697 Act.

Poor girls were normally placed in service. Boys were apprenticed to various trades or failing that, to 'husbandry'. At Milton Regis between 1782 and 1832 surviving records for twenty male apprentices indicate that eleven were appointed to genuine trades such as cordwainer, carpenter, blacksmith and plumber. Nine were apprenticed to local dredgermen. Most apprentices were placed locally at Chatham, Milstead, Gillingham, Sittingbourne and Milton itself. The exception was a boy sent to Northiam, Sussex.[263] At Harrietsham in 1741–1832 and Speldhurst in 1776–1818 apprenticeship indentures indicate that in these two rural parishes the overseers were successfully attempting to provide poor boys with genuine craft apprenticeships throughout. Harrietsham sent all its apprentices to other Kent parishes. Speldhurst, because of its geographical situation, sent almost a third into Sussex and apprenticed the others at home or elsewhere in the county.[264]

Pauper children were often the least attractive apprentices and it would be unrealistic to expect overseers to place them in better situations than those given to ratepaying labourers. Only Chatham,however,seems to have considered sending pauper children to 'apprenticeships' with a Manchester cotton manufacturer.[265] Other children seem to have been bound to the best occupations available at the time.

(12) Conclusion

Compared with the northern counties the Kent poor law had reached crisis point by 1834.[266] In 1801 the Rev. John Andrews of Marden had predicted that 'the Poor Rates, if something is not done, will in a few years prove our ruin; they check the spirit of industry among the poor and we shall soon have no labourers to till our lands'.[267] The Victorian view that the Old Poor Law had 'depraved the labourer and almost ruined the farmer'[268] was, however, exaggerated as was Furley's view that 'the hardworking and honest mechanic' contributed 'towards the support of the fraudulent, idle and dissolute.'[269] Thomas Neve's description of able bodied young men, in receipt of relief, playing cricket on Benenden village green during hay-making was supported by Henry Boyce's statement to the Select Committee that 'singlemen often do not work'.[270] Yet welfare systems have always been abused and the fault here lay in the differentiation between single and married men.

[263] Golding-Bird, *op. cit.*, p. 189. Harrison, *op. cit.*, p. 34. Miller, *op. cit.*, pp. 27–8.

[264] CKS P173/14/1–2, Harrietsham Parish Poor Apprenticeship Indentures. P344/14/1–481, Speldhurst Apprenticeship Indentures.

[265] CKS P85/8/3 Chatham Vestry Minute, 11.4.1792. Cit. Melling, *op. cit.*, p. 135.

[266] See Hastings, *op. cit.*, vol. 2, pp. 309–12.

[267] Phyllis Highwood and Peggy Skelton, *A Wealden Village: Marden*, Chatham 1986, p. 30.

[266] Barrett, *op. cit.*, p. 175.

[269] Furley, *op. cit.*, p. 666.

[270] *Ibid.*, PP 1828, IV HC 494. Report from Select Committee on that part of the Poor Laws relating to Employment or Relief of Able Bodied persons. Evidence of Henry Boyce.

Ashurst Majendie was highly critical of poor law management. '. . . In the general sense (it) is no one's business; the overseer of one parish may take all advantages, fair or unfair, against adjoining parishes . . .'.[271] Yet there was some evidence of improvement. Before 1834 the child allowance system had already been discontinued at Sevenoaks, Cowden and elsewhere and pensions lists reduced. At Ash, Sittingbourne, Chevening, Dartford, and Cranbrook allowances were unknown. Brenchley, Faversham and Greenwich were seeking to put their house in order while M. J. Todd has shown that by 1834 the lavishness and laxity of outdoor relief in many parts of Kent had given way to much stricter administration.[272] Select vestries and assistant overseers were also claimed to be influential with Ashford vestry's Rules of 1786 anticipating the harshness of the New Poor Law.[273] Otford select vestry in 1826–30 granted just over 70% of relief applications so relief was by no means indiscriminate. In February 1830 work or relief were even denied to Otford paupers keeping dogs.[274] Not all workhouses were the 'small, tottering hovels' described by Head. Rev. Henry Bishop praised 'that powerful engine a workhouse' at Pembury while Majendie noted the well-regulated workhouses at Coxheath, Westerham and Eastry.[275] Head, himself, found that Garlinge had 'adopted so much the principles of 1834' that 'he could see no improvement to be made except in the bill of fare of the house' while Canterbury union, too, in many respects anticipated 1834.[276]

John Cramp, overseer of Garlinge, maintained that 'the old law was sufficient when it was well-carried into execution'. After 1815 it was not as Rev. A. J. Pearman maintained that 'a number of idle and dissolute men sought parochial relief' but the poor law had to operate in changed circumstances.[277] Its role as a wage supplement was longstanding but after the French Wars it had to meet a situation in which widespread unemployment and underemployment created by agricultural depression was compounded by large scale population growth. Much of the labour force was casual and highly vulnerable. As distress grew a variety of expedients were attempted to encourage farmers to employ men even if it meant subsidising wages. Such schemes were open to abuse by labourers caught in a hopeless poverty trap. They were also exploited to the maximum economic

271 PP 1834 (44), XXVIII, p. 169.
272 PRO MH 12. Sevenoaks Union, 5315. Thomas Everest, Cowden to PLC, 2.10.1834. Samuel Bly, assistant overseer, Sevenoaks to PLC, 4.10.1834. MH 12. Bromley Union, 4855. Officers of Bromley parish to PLC, September 1834. MH 12. Greenwich, 5091. William Stacey and William Grifffiths, overseers to Parishioners of Greenwich, n.d. M. J. Todd, 'The Operation of the New Poor Law of 1834 in Kent and Middlesex'. Kent Extended Essay, 1969, 041, p. 27. PP 1834 (44), XXVIII, p. 218. *Kentish Gazette*, 19.7.1831, 29.7.1831.
273 Ruderman, *op. cit.*, pp. 22–3. Furley, *op. cit.*, pp. 667–8.
274 Clarke and Stoyel, *op. cit.*, p. 194. Pateman, *op. cit.*, p. 57.
275 PP 1834 (44), XXVIII, pp. 165, 206, 218, 877. Head, *op. cit.*, p. 475.
276 PP 1836, VIII–II. Third Report from the Select Committee on Agriculture. Evidence of John Cramp of Garlinge, Thanet, p. 8. PP 1843, XXI. 9th Annual Report of Poor Law Commissioners, p. 109.
277 PP 1836, VIII–II. Third Report from the Select Committee on Agriculture. Evidence of John Cramp, p. 8. Rev. A. J. Pearman, *History of Ashford*, Ashford 1868, p. 140.

advantage by farmers who used the casual labour market to the full while keeping wages low.[278]

There were few overseers like the sadistic Michael Becker of Ash who made the unemployed dig and re-fill holes in the ground and forced an unemployed shepherd to walk daily the thirteen miles from Margate to Ash until he collapsed.[279] Overseers cannot be blamed for practising humane relief policies and many were desperately aware of the need to allay the deep-seated social discontent which had burst forth in the Swing Riots of 1830–1. Vestries were intimidated and wages maintained by the threat of arson. The property of farmers and overseers who reduced them were destroyed.[280] In highly pauperised parishes, like Lenham, where 54.6% of the population received relief,as poor rates increased farmers gave up their farms and agricultural capital diminished.[281] Goudhurst parish officers noted difficulty in collecting the rates in 1824. In 1832 37 of 42 respondents claimed that agricultural capital in their parishes was diminishing. Significantly 24 parishes did not attribute the diminution solely to the poor rates and some not to the poor rates at all. Among other causes listed were the low grain prices of agricultural depression, high taxation, rents, tithes and currency changes.[282] The contemporary view that the poor law itself was solely responsible for the condition of the labouring classes was untrue.[283] On the other hand many 'parish works' were so exhausted that agricultural capital could no longer bear 'the application of further funds to works yielding no profit'.[284]

Most would have agreed with the *Maidstone and Kent Advertiser* that 'there can be no doubt that the present state of the laws . . . is bad and capable of extensive improvement'.[285] Whether the grouping of parishes into unions supervised by elected guardians together with the abolition of outrelief and the rendering of the pauper's lot 'less eligible' than that of the lowest independent labourer was the solution remained to be seen. Rural Query 52 asked about the advisability of affording 'greater facilities for unions of parishes'. Of 57 respondent parishes three were in favour, twelve were against and forty-two did not reply. The majority, one suspects, thought, like Cobham, that 'small districts appear much better managed than large ones' or reiterated with Egerton 'we think it best as it is now'.[286]

[278] Newman, *op. cit.*, pp. 175–6, 365–6.

[279] *Ibid.*, p. 170.

[280] Head, *op. cit.*, p. 487. PP 1833, V. Report from Select Committee on Agriculture. Evidence of Richard Peyton, p. 340. PP 1834, XXVIII, p. 878.

[281] Frank W. Jessup, *Kent History Illustrated*, Maidstone 1973, p. 59.

[282] PP 1824, VI. Appendix to Report from Select Committee on Poor Rates. PP 1834 (44), XXXII. Answers to Rural Query 36.

[283] *Kent Herald*, 24.4.1834.

[284] PP 1834 (44), XXVIII, p. 166.

[285] *Maidstone and Kent Advertiser*, 3.3.1834.

[286] PP 1834, XXXIV. Answers to Rural Query 52.

The New Poor Law 1834–1914

(1) The Making of the Unions

Creation of the Kent unions was vested in Assistant Commissioner Sir Francis Bond Head, a member of a prominent North Kent family. A former army major and future Lieutenant Governor of Upper Canada, Head was a powerful advocate of the new system and a scathing critic of the old.[1] Forthright and impetuous he arrived in late 1834 in a county still heavily influenced by the Swing Riots and felt the urgent need to re-establish social control.

> ... The peasants ... have succeeded in intimidating the upper classes and ... the balance of social life being thus disordered the demands of the labourer are rising ... as the authority of the upper classes is sinking ... Most respectable people acknowledge they are afraid of the peasants ... the peasantry openly declare they are not afraid of those above them ...[2]

The message, which he delivered to all newly-elected boards of guardians at their initial meetings, was to elevate the character of the Kentish labourer by 'correcting the wretched system of our late Poor Laws which ... has depraved the labourer and almost ruined the farmer'.[3]

He began his task significantly in East Kent, where the Swing Riots had begun, although moving simultaneously into some western parts of the county. Everywhere he prepared his ground with military precision. Existing poorhouses were inspected. Meetings with parish officers and local magistrates emphasised the gains to be made from lower medical and administrative costs and a reduction in the rates.[4]

> To the parochial officers I particularly adopted myself ... and in the course of rather more than two hours succeeded in laying before them ... the immense advantages offered by the Act ... If these little tribunals do not disapprove of my proposition I believe the upper classes will be most readily concerned ...[5]

Care was nevertheless taken to consult local magnates whose support was crucial.

[1] Sydney W. Jackman, *Galloping Head*, London 1958, pp. 9–72. See also his scathing article on 'English Charity', *Quarterly Review*, liii, cvi (1835), pp. 473–539 which was 'a capable apologia for the new system'. (Jackman, *op. cit.*, p. 65.)

[2] (P)ublic (R)ecord (O)ffice, MH 12. Sevenoaks Union, 5315. Head to (P)oor (L)aw (C)ommissioners, 29.11.1834.

[3] (C)entre for (K)entish (S)tudies. G/Ea AM1 Eastry Board of Guardians Minutes, 30.4.1835.

[4] *(M)aidstone (G)azette*, 1.9.1835.

[5] PRO MH 12. Sevenoaks Union, 5315. Head to PLC, 29.11.1834.

Head's persuasive powers even converted Charles Warde, a Westerham magistrate and man of 'immense wealth', to whom the whole parish looked 'for everything'.[6] At the same time he was careful not to compromise his own impartiality.[7]

Despite his diplomacy there was considerable opposition in East Kent. Great Chart, which felt that its select vestry had already effected reform, was reluctant to join West Ashford Union. Smarden petitioned the commissioners to remain independent. Bethersden refused to elect a guardian or submit its parish books while in other parishes ratepayers stated they would not only not appoint guardians but would be driven from their farms rather than comply. In Ashford itself 'great exertions were made by interested individuals to oppose the formation of the union particularly among the small shopkeepers'.[8] Bridge Union ratepayers rejected Head's proposals and decided to petition Parliament.[9] Dover, Margate and Ramsgate, proud of their own relief systems and fearing rural domination, also initially sought a degree of independence.[10] Nevertheless by 13 July 1835 Head had created eleven East Kent Unions together with the Sevenoaks and short-lived Penshurst Unions in West Kent.[11] A conference of chairmen and vice-chairmen of the East Kent Unions in Canterbury agreed maximum scales for outdoor relief and a uniform diet for workhouses. It was also decided to buy a central consignment of iron bedsteads and that aged indoor paupers, who had been initially dispersed, should be gradually concentrated in one building per union.[12]

Head anticipated greater difficulties in West Kent.[13] At the North Aylesford meeting all but two parish officers present accepted his persuasive statement although many had previously been hostile. At Maidstone only fourteen out of 313 persons opposed the amalgamation of the town with the neighbouring rural Coxheath Incorporation although there was a serious reaction later.[14] Tonbridge, like some other Kent towns, preferred to form a union 'of itself' and a ratepayers' meeting, chaired by William Johnson, attacked the Act as 'injurious to the rights and interests of the poor' and protested against its adoption in Tonbridge.[15] When Head moved into Cranbrook in September 1835 he met further opposition which was championed, as at Tonbridge, by the Kent Liberal MP, T. L. Hodges.[16]

---

6 *Ibid.*, Head to PLC, 1.12.1834. Jackman, *op. cit.*, p. 62.

7 *Ibid.*, Head to PLC, 29.11.1834.

8 PRO MH 12. West Ashford Union, 4798. T. Manners Sutton, Rector of Great Chart, to PLC, 29.8.1834. Smarden to PLC, 26.5.1835. W. Toke of Goddington to PLC, 26.5.1835. Head to PLC, 7.6.1835, 28.7.1835.

9 MG 28.4.1835.

10 D. Hopker, 'The New Poor Law in Thanet; the first six years 1835–41', Kent Diploma in Local History, 1988, 2359, p. 4.

11 See Fig. 11. The East Kent unions were the Faversham, Milton, Sheppey, Blean, Bridge, Thanet, Eastry, River, East and West Ashford and Elham Unions. See (P)arliamentary (P)apers 1843, XLV. Name of each union in England and Wales. Also Guy Ewing, *History of Cowden*, Tunbridge Wells 1926, p. 207.

12 (F)olkestone (R)eference (L)ibrary G/EC AM1. Elham Board of Guardians Minutes, 13.7.1835.

13 PRO MH 12. Sevenoaks Union, 5315. Head to PLC, 19.8.1835.

14 MG 18.8.1835, 1.11.1835, 19.6.1838.

15 MG 10.11.1835.

16 MG 13.10.1835.

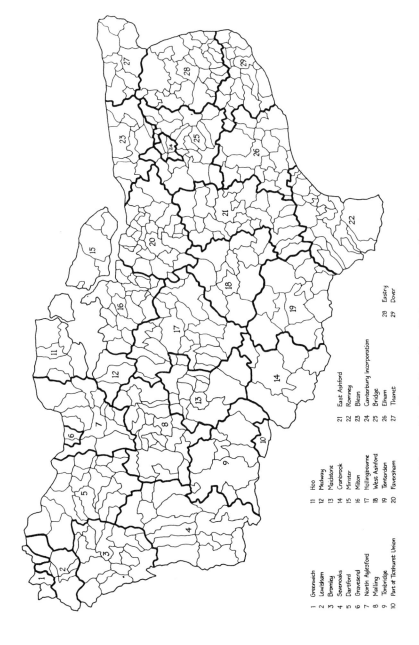

1 Greenwich
2 Lewisham
3 Bromley
4 Sevenoaks
5 Dartford
6 Gravesend
7 North Aylesford
8 Malling
9 Tonbridge
10 Part of Ticehurst Union
11 Hoo
12 Medway
13 Maidstone
14 Cranbrook
15 Minster
16 Milton
17 Hollingbourne
18 West Ashford
19 Tenterden
20 Faversham
21 East Ashford
22 Romney
23 Blean
24 Canterbury incorporation
25 Bridge
26 Elham
27 Thanet
28 Eastry
29 Dover

Figure 11. Kent Poor Law Unions created after the 1834 Act.

Nevertheless by the time of Head's departure for Upper Canada in December 1835 he had added a further ten unions to his impressive list.[17] He left expressing his satisfaction to the guardians in the last of many circulars couched in his habitual military tone:

> You are now sufficiently armed to protect the Poor Rates of your County, to repel every species of attack upon them, to detect every case of imposition, to crush every attempt of intimidation and force (into work) all those who would indolently hang on their Parishes for support . . .[18]

His successor, E. C. Tufnell, completed the changes by November 1836 with the formation of the Bromley, Dartford and Maidstone Unions and the metropolitan unions of Greenwich and Lewisham.[19] Calls by 1841 for the dissolution of Greenwich Union, which included Woolwich and Deptford and had a population of 80,811, passed unheeded although a Strood Union was formed from North Aylesford Union in 1854 and a Woolwich Union created in 1870.[20]

Union shape and choice of a centre for its guardians to meet was left to the assistant commissioners without specific instruction other than that unions should be centred round the market town to which guardians travelled on a market day. This, it was believed, would be convenient for paupers and guardians alike.[21] Head was adamant that large unions with big boards, which could not be terrorised like parish vestries, were the answer to the social unrest. '. . . Wherever I find the peasantry disposed to . . . act on the principle of intimidation I strongly recommend a large union . . .'.[22] Kent's 27 unions, with the exception of Hollingbourne, Sevenoaks and East Ashford, were smaller than the average poor law union of 49,900 acres and the unions dictated by geographical considerations in the rural North Riding. Despite the existence of such thinly-populated unions as Hoo and Romney Marsh, average population in Kent's unions was, however, above the national average population of 17,300.[23] In Northamptonshire rural union boundaries were 'often drawn by local magnates to delimit . . . areas of social and political deference . . .'. In Kent, Lord Templeman was 'architect' of the Sevenoaks Union. Bromley Union was run for nearly forty years by Lord Sydney and George Warde Norman, a director of the Bank of England. Milton Union was dominated by its chairman, Sir John Tylden, of Milstead.[24]

Head's anxiety to make his unions ones of equal population produced some

[17] These were Medway, Hoo, Malling, Cranbrook, Gravesend, North Aylesford, Hollingbourne, Romney Marsh, Tenterden and Tonbridge Unions (PP 1843, XLV).

[18] CKS G/Bl. ACa1, 30/11/1835. Cit. M. A. Crowther, *The Workhouse System 1834–1929*, London 1981, p. 45.

[19] PP 1843, XLV.

[20] MG 23.11.1841.

[21] R. P. Hastings, 'Poverty and the Treatment of Poverty in the North Riding of Yorkshire c.1780–1847', vol. 2, York D.Phil. 1977, pp. 172–3.

[22] PRO MH 12. Sevenoaks Union, 5315. Head to PLC, 29.11.1834.

[23] Hastings, *op. cit.*, p. 173. PP 1843, XLV.

[24] Crowther, *op. cit.*, p. 75. Roger Wells, 'Resistance to the New Poor Law in the Rural South', in

peculiar groupings of parishes. Molash was joined with Warehorne in the East Ashford Union. Westbere and Seasalter were both in Blean Union. Ridley, Bexley and Swanscombe were all in Dartford Union while Malling Union included villages as far apart as Wouldham, Stansted and East Peckham. Tufnell complained that his colleague had designed Maidstone Union 'like a comet with a tail of parishes ten miles long'.[25]

Rural union chairmen and vice chairmen were drawn from the ranks of the local gentry and principal landowners. Rural guardians, like select vestrymen before them, were largely farmers. The first Dartford, Sheppey and North Aylesford boards were dominated by farmers who still ruled Sevenoaks board in 1852. Three quarters of Thanet guardians were farmers and another 17% were men associated with agriculture.[26] Maidstone's four urban guardians could be consistently outvoted by guardians from the rural parishes. Only in the urban unions of Gravesend, Medway and metropolitan Kent was there substantial representation of urban interests. Medway guardians were mainly High Street tradesmen. Five of the eight guardians on Hoo board were allegedly from the same family. Women could undertake the office if they owned sufficient property but not until 1898 did Miss Randolph, a vicar's daughter, become Kent's first female guardian at Bridge Union. East Ashford followed in 1913 by co-opting two female guardians 'married or widowed . . . to deal sympathetically with women inmates'. Nor was continuity strong. Of the original Thanet board elected in 1835 only two were regular attenders six years later.[27]

With the exception of Lamberhurst in the Sussex Ticehurst Union no Kent unions ignored county boundaries but inevitably dissatisfaction arose from injured local loyalties and convenience. Country guardians of Dover Union strongly opposed their inclusion in the union because they feared an increased burden on rural ratepayers. Sittingbourne small traders petitioned the commissioners against their inclusion in Milton Union because they feared they would be subsidising the surrounding villages. Opposition was most resolute from Maidstone which had been added to the Coxheath Incorporation. Even the proposal to re-designate this amalgamation the Maidstone Union was insufficient to salve the pride of the town which argued that its pauper problems differed radically from those of the rural parishes. While Maidstone's paupers were drawn principally from the aged, the widowed and young children who could be given outrelief, the rural poor were

Ann Digby, Paul Hastings, Michael Rose and Roger Wells, *The New Poor Law*, University of Leeds Middlesbrough Centre Occasional Paper, I, 1985, pp. 30–1.

25 F. W. Jessup, *Kent History Illustrated*, Maidstone 1973, p. 59. PRO MH 32/70. E. C. Tufnell, 10.1.1839. Cit. Crowther, *op. cit.*, p. 37.

26 S. C. Keyes, *Dartford History Notes*, Dartford 1933, p. 236. MG 7.4.1835, 15.9.1835, 4.4.1837, 3.4.1838, 4.5.1832. Hopker, *op. cit.*, p. 43. Samuel Bagshaw, *History, Gazeteer and Directory of Kent*, vols 1 and 2, Sheffield 1847.

27 PRO MH 12. Maidstone Union, 5195. Tufnell to PLC 25.4.1836. C. T. Smythe to PLC April 1836. James Dufton, 'The Medway Union, 1835–1850', Kent Diploma in Local History, 1985, 1573, p. 4. Hopker, *op. cit.*, p. 46. MG 26.4.1836, 3.5.1836, 14.6.1836, 19.6.1838. *(K)entish (E)xpress*, 9.4.1898, 26.4.1913.

largely able-bodied unemployed. Coxheath workhouse was four miles from Maidstone. Its board day was Maidstone's market day. The commissioners dismissed the argument that there was no compatibility between urban and rural unions on the grounds that all paupers should be treated alike. Maidstone's bid to separate continued until finally denied by the Court of Queen's Bench in 1838. Even so it was resurrected in 1881.[28]

There was little difficulty with Kent's Gilbert Unions. Head noted that 'the guardians of nine extensive unions which we had no power to dissolve gave me their consent in writing'.[29] The exception was the Canterbury Incorporation of fourteen parishes created in 1727. The complaints levelled against other incorporated workhouses could not be directed at Canterbury Workhouse. Here the sexes were segregated and separate wards provided for the aged and deserted or orphaned children. The able bodied were set to work both within and without the workhouse.[30] In Canterbury public opinion was united in opposition to 'that sorry specimen of Whig legislation of 1834'. Tufnell, himself, was quick to perceive that the constitution and election of the Canterbury Court of Guardians did not materially differ from that of a board elected under the 1834 legislation. It was not, therefore, until March 1844 that the court eventually came under the direct control of the Poor Law Commissioners.[31]

(2) Opposition to the New Poor Law

The Poor Law Bill and its implementation met opposition in Kent. While Kent agriculturalists and Conservatives generally accepted the need for the New Poor Law, the Radicals and Liberal Whigs opposed it. Liberal groups in Maidstone and Gravesend petitioned against the Bill and the Kent Liberal MPs, T. L. Hodges and Thomas Rider, fought it in Parliament. So, too, did a few Kent ultra-Tory peers. The Earl of Stanhope became the strongest Kent spokesman against 'the grievous cruelties, the flagrant injustice and the intolerable oppression of the amended system and the dictatorship of the Commissioners'.[32] He declared himself 'the representative of the poor and the labouring classes for they had no representative in the other House'. Such was his enthusiasm that he felt obliged to explain that he was 'an old fashioned Tory' and not a spokesman from the Chartist National Convention.[33] While the Liberal *Maidstone Gazette* held back much of the Kent

---

28 Douglas Welby, *The Kentish Village of River*, Dover 1977, p. 108. KE 4.6.1881, 2.7.1881. *(S)outh (E)astern (G)azette*, 15.4.1862. MH 12. Milton Union, 5271, 6.4.1835.

29 PP 1835, XXXV. First Annual Report of the Poor Law Commission, Appendix B.

30 Robert A. Scott, 'The Administration of the poor law in Canterbury under a local act of 1727 with particular reference to the years 1834 to c.1850', Kent Extended Essay, 1979, 0131, pp. 9, 13.

31 *Ibid.*, pp. 8–9, 22.

32 J. H. Andrews, 'Political Issues in the County of Kent 1820–1846', London M.Phil., 1967, pp. 210–14.

33 *Ibid.*, pp. 213–14.

press severely criticised the 1834 Act. The *Kent Herald* loudly condemned this 'arbitrary attempt to drive the poor from misery to starvation'.[34] The *Kentish Gazette*, which had 'long since entered into protest against the measure', predicted within twelve months 'a scene bordering upon revolution of the most sanguinary description . . .'.[35] The Tory *Maidstone Journal* was equally explicit:

> . . . the fearful effects it must have in the agricultural districts . . . will create a moral pestilence in . . . our peasantry which cannot be contemplated without feelings of dismay . . . it will be physically impossible to carry it into operation . . . without plunging the country into the horrors of civil warfare . . .[36]

The Swing Riots had barely subsided and during the transitional period while workhouses were built many feared a repetition:

> . . . Unless subsistence be properly afforded [wrote the Rector of Staplehurst] they will assuredly join in predatory bands as they did three years ago to the manifest danger of life and property . . . We have no civil force to put them down . . .[37]

Such gloomy predictions were soon fulfilled. As the organisation of the first Kent unions began serious anti-Poor Law rioting swept through the Swale villages, a highly volatile area which had been seriously effected by Swing.[38] The Faversham and Milton unions, created in March 1835, were among the first in the country and the county. In the latter there was already widespread antagonism to the new system. The Rev. Dr John Poore, vicar of Rainham, and chairman of the local bench, was an influential critic. Head had hoped to overcome his hostility by making him chairman of the Milton board but he resigned almost immediately in favour of Sir John Tylden.[39] By the end of April granting of relief in both unions had been transferred to the newly-appointed relieving officers. It had been decided that child allowances should be reduced and that up to half of allowances should be given in bread tickets, redeemable at local shops, rather than in cash.

The first issue of bread tickets to the poor of Murston, Tong, Bapchild and Rodmersham on 30 April at Bapchild church produced a riot in which the relieving officer was mobbed and his books and papers destroyed. The Tong overseer was manhandled. Poore, who lived at Murston, was alarmed but did not request military aid. The Bapchild mob, encouraged by Sittingbourne traders who felt their livelihood threatened by union bread contracts, was so big that arrests were impossible.[40] When two ringleaders were arrested and brought before magistrates at

---

34 *(K)ent (H)erald*, 15.4.1834.
35 *(K)entish (G)azette*, 16.9.1834.
36 *(M)aidstone (J)ournal*, 8.7.1834.
37 PRO MH 12. Maidstone Union, 5195. Rector of Staplehurst to PLC, 13.10.1834.
38 See N. C. Edsall, *The Anti-Poor Law Movement*, Manchester 1971, pp. 27–32. D. Hopker, *Money or Blood*, Kent 1988. Wells, *op. cit.*, pp. 21–2.
39 Hopker, *Money or Blood*, p. 4. MH 12. Milton Union, 5279. Head to PLC, 6.5.1835.
40 PRO MH 12. Milton Union, 5279. Rev. Dr John Poore to PLC, 30.4.1835.

Sittingbourne next day their companions entered the court and threatened the bench. They were bound over, a sentence condemned as too lenient.[41] On 2 May only Poore and some special constables prevented serious trouble during distribution of relief at Bredgar. On 4 May a large demonstration, including Lenham and Newnham labourers, coincided with distribution of relief at Doddington poorhouse in Faversham union. A mob 250 strong, led by 'Major' Murton of Wichling and armed with bludgeons, forced paupers who took bread tickets to return them. Poore and another magistrate, General Gerselin, were besieged in the poorhouse for an hour and a half and then escorted by the crowd to Newnham. Here their resolve cracked. No tickets were issued. Only money payments were made and the mob triumphantly dispersed.[42] Similar demonstrations at Upchurch (4 May), where the relieving officer had already resigned, and at the notorious trouble spot of Hernhill (5 May) came to little. At the latter forty men, who set off to destroy the baker's cart carrying bread for relief, were thwarted by the Hernhill guardian who diverted it. At Lynsted and Teynham the same day the mob was also out in force. Nearly all the ringleaders were present and no tickets were issued. Next day relieving officer John Pringle underwent a five hour siege in Throwley poorhouse. Some men demanded and received much larger relief payments than they were entitled to. At a board meeting that day Milton guardians, unlike their Faversham counterparts, agreed to stand firm, to support the relieving officers when visiting their parishes, and continue plans for a new workhouse. As they left they were stoned until they turned their horses towards the demonstrators.[43]

Identification of rioters was difficult since some blacked their faces and many demonstrated in parishes to which they did not belong. By 5 May, however, Poore had requested and been granted military help together with assistance from senior officers of the Metropolitan police. Over 200 special constables were also enrolled at Faversham.[44] The first confrontation came at Rodmersham on 7 May when the relieving officer and overseers were interviewing relief applicants in the parish church. A crowd of 150, many from Bredgar and Doddington, urged on by Murton, William Robinson of Hollingbourne, who was wearing a red cap, and John Taylor of Bredgar, armed with a club, took relief tickets from paupers and ordered them back to demand cash. Female paupers were searched in a 'most indecent manner'.[45] When a Rodmersham overseer intervened he was attacked and forced back into the church with the local guardian where they were trapped for four hours. Chairman Sir John Tylden went in search of the military. Earliest to arrive were two Metropolitan police officers from Faversham who arrested the first threatening protester. The mob tried to overturn their chaise but was dispersed by the 28th Foot from Chatham who arrived at the same time as Poore and two other magistrates.

[41] MG 12.5.1835.

[42] Hopker, *Money or Blood*, pp. 7–10. MG 12.5.1835, 17.5.1835.

[43] Hopker, *Money or Blood*, pp. 9–13. PRO MH 12. Milton Union, 5279. Head to PLC, 6.5.1835. MG 9.6.1835.

[44] PRO MH 12. Milton Union, 5279. Poore to Lord John Russell, 8.5.1835. S. Phillipps to Poore, 6.5.1835.

[45] Wells, *op. cit.*, pp. 21–2.

Twenty arrests were made and the prisoners escorted in carts to Canterbury gaol by Yeomanry Cavalry who themselves were stoned en route. Four more were arrested at a small, defiant demonstration at Ospringe on 8 May. By 12 May more police had arrived from London heralding further arrests. In all 51 men were arrested. Twenty-eight were sentenced to three months hard labour or more. Murton and Robinson received two years. Compared with the treatment of the Swing rioters these sentences were light reflecting, perhaps, the feelings of Poore and other magistrates about the New Poor Law.[46]

The rioting did not end at Rodmersham. Fears of simultaneous disorder at Lydd did not materialise although a Metropolitan police sergeant and inspector were despatched there to organise a special constabulary and handbills were distributed warning the 'labouring classes' against 'violence or assembly'.[47] Trouble arose next in the short-lived Penshurst union. Henry Streatfield, the chairman and a local magistrate, had already warned the commissioners against '. . . building a work-house on such a scale so far from the protection and assistance of the town' where 200 paupers 'might for a time carry all before them'. He was, perhaps, influenced by the proximity of his own house at Chiddingstone to the new workhouse site but he also spoke of assembling and disturbances in the neighbourhood and of 'wide-spread reservation' with regard to aiding in the establishment of a union 'which is still generally deemed an injudicious and unnecessary measure'.[48] The workhouse, when complete, was the first of its type in West Kent. It attracted immediate hostility by its resemblance to a county gaol. After several weeks of threats from crowds of labourers the Tunbridge Wells Yeomanry was called out on two successive days in February 1836 to prevent the mob 'armed with fearful-looking bludgeons' from demolishing it. There were no injuries but the Penshurst guardians petitioned for the addition of their union to the Sevenoaks union on 13 September 1836. There was also violent feeling in St Nicholas, Deptford when it was merged into the Greenwich union.[49]

In March, twenty Bredhurst woodcutters, armed with bills and axes, prevented bailiffs from distraining for non-payment of poor rates. Eighteen months later the ringleaders of a mob of agricultural labourers were imprisoned for intimidating the relieving officer at Woodchurch in Tenterden union.[50] Popular protest ended, however, with the 'Last Rising of the Agricultural Labourers' on 31 May 1838 in which the self-styled Sir William Courtenay and nine of the labourers who followed him were killed by soldiers in a day-long battle in Bossenden Wood. Courtenay's small, rural following, drawn from Hernhill, Dunkirk and Boughton, was officially la-

[46] Hopker, *Money or Blood*, pp. 1, 17–21, 23. PRO MH 12. Milton Union, 5279. Rev. Dr John Poore to Lord John Russell, 8.5.1835. Sir John Tylden to Poore, 7.5.1835.

[47] PRO 110 41/12. Disturbance Book, vol. 12. Lord John Russell to David Denne, Lydd magistrate, 8.5.1835, 11.5.1835, 16.5.1835.

[48] PRO MH 12. Sevenoaks Union, 5315. H. Streatfield to PLC, 31.5.1835. Head to Sevenoaks Guardians, 12.6.1835.

[49] PRO MH 12. Sevenoaks Union, 5315. E. C. Tufnell to PLC, 8.2.1836, 9.2.1836. MH 12. Greenwich Union, 5091. PLC to Overseers of Deptford, 28.11.1836. MG 16.2.1836.

[50] MG 29.3.1836, 9.1.1838.

belled and has been long regarded as the victim of 'fanaticism, imposture and superstition'. Barry Reay, however, has recently shown that protest against the sudden changes wrought by the 1834 Act was of considerable significance in mobilising the labourers and that one of the intentions of Courtenay and his band was to blow up 'Hernhill Union (Blean Union) workhouse' erected in 1836.[51]

Not all Kent's anti-Poor Law protest was so open. The chairman of a meeting to petition against the Act at Sutton Valence hinted darkly that 'it would throw every village into . . . disorder . . . and be the cause of again sending firebrands through the land . . .' Incendiarism had not stopped since the Swing Riots. As the Act became law in November 1834 it was accompanied by renewed fire raising, the re-appearance of Swing letters and Associations for the Protection of Property.[52] 'If money payments are stopped before sufficient workhouses are built', wrote Robert Jaynes JP of Frindsbury, 'I apprehend excitement among the poor . . . November is the month of our trial in this quarter in respect to the management of the poor . . .'.[53] His worst fears were confirmed four days later when eight corn stacks and a number of farm buildings belonging to John Smith, a farmer and overseer near Frindsbury, were destroyed.[54] Other fires followed as incendiarism in 1835 returned to the level of 1831.[55] Most spectacular was the destruction on 5 September 1835 of fifteen stacks in the extensive rickyard near Sevenoaks belonging to Lord Templeman, prime mover in the Sevenoaks union. This fire was celebrated on its anniversary in 1836 by the firing of his clover stacks. His losses totalled over £2,600.[56]

Nor was opposition to the Act limited to the labourers. A meeting of East Ashford Union ratepayers in June 1835 passed by 400 votes to three a resolution to petition for its repeal. The comment of the *Maidstone Gazette* that 'The New Poor Law . . . is certainly anything but popular here' was a masterpiece of understatement.[57] Yet by 1837 the incidence of arson had almost disappeared and did not recommence until the 'hungry forties'. In 1839, however, it was still rumoured that Kent workhouse children were killed to make pies and that the bodies of the elderly were used to manure the guardians' fields to save the cost of coffins.[58]

---

[51] See *A Canterbury Tale of Fifty Years Ago being the story of The Extraordinary Career of Sir William Courtenay alias John Nichols Thom*, Canterbury 1896. Also Barry Reay, *The Last Rising of the Agricultural Labourers*, Oxford 1990, and review article by R. P. Hastings in *Journal of Kent History*, 33 (September 1991), pp. 13–14.

[52] MJ 15.7.1834, 18.11.1834, 25.11.1834, 2.12.1834. MG 20.10.1834, 18.11.1834, 25.11.1834. KG 11.11.1834.

[53] PRO MH 12. Medway Union, 5249. R. Jaynes JP to PLC, 31.10.1834.

[54] *Ibid.*, MG 4.11.1834.

[55] See Swing Riots statistics taken from local press 1831. MG 4.11.1834, 18.11.1834, 25.11.1834.

[56] MG 8.9.1835. Wells, *op. cit.*, p. 30.

[57] MG 17.5.1835, 9.6.1835.

[58] Crowther, *op. cit.*, p. 31.

(3) The Union Officers

The first task of each board after appointment of its chairman and vice-chairman was the selection of a treasurer and its salaried officials – a clerk, auditor, relieving and medical officers.[59] Salaries were low to save the ratepayers. The clerk, usually a solicitor or accountant, was the commissioners' direct representative among the guardians through whom all correspondence passed. As a part-time officer he usually possessed a supplementary income. Clerks' salaries in Kent were normally around £80. The majority were tolerably efficient. Honesty was encouraged by the fate of Joseph Exhall, clerk to Tenterden union, who embezzled over £500 and was transported for fourteen years.[60] The number of relieving officers depended on the size of the union. Salaries were often similar to those of clerks. They were, however, full-time officials whose task of investigating applications and distributing relief was arduous and difficult. In rural unions a horse had to be kept from the officer's own pocket. Relieving officers were frequently abused and sometimes assaulted. The anti-Poor Law riots were a particularly difficult time for them but violence was never far away. In January 1845 a Ramsgate pauper was imprisoned for seizing the Thanet relieving officer by the throat and kicking him in the abdomen.[61] Cranbrook Union wisely selected an ex-police sergeant as relieving officer in 1878. In 1855 the Canterbury Incorporation relieving officer did not even live in the district.[62] There were monetary temptations, too, and George Bailey, Hollingbourne relieving officer committed suicide in 1845 owing the union £30.[63] Not all relieving officers were dishonest or had bad relationships with paupers. John Topfield, relieving officer for East Farleigh who died in 1851, was praised for his work during the 1849 cholera epidemic and was 'kind and considerate to the poor who lost in him a . . . compassionate friend'.[64]

Good workhouse officers were as important for successful administration of indoor relief as were good relieving officers for the efficient provision of outdoor relief. Head felt that the workhouse master 'should be a person accustomed to the habits of your peasantry, acquainted with their character, of irreproachable moral conduct, with great firmness and mild temper'.[65] Given the salaries paid by most boards such virtues were often hard to find. Initially the assistant commissioners tried to unify Kent officers' salaries. Tufnell was particularly keen to press for the lowest acceptable wages and unsuccessfully tried to stop unions paying more than their neighbours. For him £80 a year plus board jointly for master and matron was ample recompense.[66] The first master and matron of Hoo union were appointed at a joint salary of £25 per annum plus 'soap, candles and provisions of same quality as

[59] PP 1837, XXXI, HC 546–1. Appendix A. Documents issued by the Poor Law Commission, No. 1. Instructions issued to Boards of Guardians on their formation, pp. 47–57.
[60] MG 2.3.1847, 22.3.1847.
[61] MG 24.1.1845.
[62] MG 8.5.1855. SEG 4.5.1878.
[63] MG 28.1.1845.
[64] MG 28.1.1851.
[65] CKS G/Bl. ACa1. 27.9.1835. Cit. Crowther, *op. cit.*, p. 116.
[66] Crowther, *op. cit.*, pp. 123–4.

the paupers'.[67] The commissioners did not insist that the matron should be the master's wife but propriety and economy made this the preferred situation. When Bromley guardians appointed an unmarried master in 1888 because they wished to keep their recently widowed matron he realised promotion would be impossible without a wife and so immediately secured the guardians' permission to marry, his wife remaining for the time being outside the workhouse.[68]

The presence of a matron did not always protect the inmates against inadequate masters. A Blean union master fathered the bastard of an inmate. A second Blean master locked a five year old girl in the mortuary with a corpse for several nights.[69] James Miles, sadistic master of Hoo workhouse, was dismissed in 1841 and imprisoned for indecently flogging a woman of weak mind and children 'particularly the girls of the age of 13–14'.[70] Mr Atherley, a former Fusilier sergeant who was elevated from schoolmaster to governor of Cranbrook workhouse, had a wife and four children. Nevertheless this 'highly competent person for the office' left chargeable to the union in 1851 a pregnant inmate and a pregnant woman in Goudhurst. He was ultimately convicted of inducing one of these ladies to procure a miscarriage.[71] In 1862 Hollingbourne workhouse master was dismissed for drunkenness but by this time a more professional class of workhouse master was beginning to emerge.[72] The master and matron appointed to Tenterden workhouse in 1858 had already held similar positions in Nuneaton union for eight years. In 1869 superannuation payments were made to the outgoing master and matron at Canterbury.[73] In the same year Kent workhouse masters met in an early attempt to establish a professional association similar to one in London. Its object was 'to discuss poor law legislation, promotion of mutual interests and other matters affecting the social position of poor law officers'.[74] There was to be an annual subscription of 10s 6d and two meetings a year. By 1893 a Kent branch of the National Association of Poor Law Officers existed and a superannuation scheme was under discussion. Yet another separate workhouse masters' association was established in 1896.[75]

Not all masters and matrons were sadists. The scandals created by some low-paid, inadequate officials naturally gained more prominence than work about which there was no complaint. The master and matron of Faversham workhouse resigned in 1868 after 33 relatively uncontroversial years. Mr and Mrs Church, appointed at Tenterden in 1858 were hailed for 'their uniform kindness . . . and the

[67] P. MacDougall, *The Hoo Peninsula*, Rochester 1980, p. 104.
[68] Crowther, *op. cit.*, pp. 116–17.
[69] MG 2.4.1844, 23.6.1846. Crowther, *op. cit.*, p. 32.
[70] Crowther, *op. cit.*, p. 32. MacDougall, *op. cit.*, p. 106. MG 5.1.1841, 12.1.1841, 26.1.1841, 22.3.1842.
[71] MG 22.7.1851.
[72] SEG 25.11.1862.
[73] SEG 31.8.1868, 12.4.1869.
[74] SEG 14.6.1869.
[75] KE 2.9.1893, 3.10.1896.

order, cleanliness and health which prevailed' in their previous house.[76] From mid-century annual treats for workhouse children were augmented by occasional outings led by workhouse masters. Parties from Dartford, Gravesend, Medway and Sheppey unions went to the Great Exhibition in 1851. The latter were taken free by the Medway Steamboat Company to Chatham and thence by train to London. Faversham workhouse children went in 1865 for a day's holiday at Whitstable. Canterbury children, who were less fortunate, went to a temperance demonstration at Crystal Palace.[77] While increased professionalism helped to create more suitable officers than many initially appointed after 1834, guardians also became more punctilious over selection demanding previous poor law experience. In the latter part of the century Bromley guardians even sent a selection committee to enquire into the performance of applicants in their existing posts.[78]

The only officials with comparable standing to the master were the chaplain and medical officers. In the early years the doctor was less secure than other officials because of an annual contract. Initially, too, appointments were often subject to patronage. A Bromley appointment in 1836 was alleged to have been 'a hole and corner job' and similar allegations were made at Maidstone in 1840.[79] The size of salaries and union medical districts is an indication of the low priority given to medical relief by most boards. Head, himself, 'saw no reason why the parish doctor should meet with . . . more consideration than the parish tradesman'.[80] Blean union was initially divided into two medical districts whose surgeons received £35 and £24 per annum respectively.[81] The former had additional responsibility for work-house inmates. In West Ashford a similar division was made. Doctors contracted to 'furnish medicine, medical and surgical attendance and leeches together with vaccination for all paupers in the union. Midwifery and trusses were excepted'.[82] By 1848 Blean union districts had increased to three whose medical officers received £90, £40 and £20 respectively.[83] Even so it remained essential for most medical officers to remain in private practice. Francis Young, a Hawkhurst surgeon who was medical officer to the Hawkhurst district of Cranbrook union, covered an area of 2,650 acres and in 1843 attended 320 paupers for a payment of £47 10s 0d including the extras allowed by the 1842 General Medical Order. The pre-1834 value of the medical contract for the district had been £81 10s 0d. A horse was essential to cover the 35 miles of parish roads.[84]

---

[76] SEG 31.8.1858, 24.6.1868.

[77] MG 29.7.1851, 19.8.1851, 16.9.1851. SEG 29.6.1865, 6.9.69.

[78] Crowther, *op. cit.*, pp. 125–6.

[79] *Ibid.*, p. 127. MG 22.12.1840. PRO MH 12. Bromley Union, 4855. Thomas Pritchard to PLC, 7.6.1836.

[80] PRO MH 12. Sevenoaks Union, 5315. Head to Sevenoaks Guardians, 18.5.1835.

[81] Sharon Neate, 'Blean Union; the study of a Victorian Workhouse 1835–1850', Dundee M.A. 1986, p. 40.

[82] MG 7.6.1836.

[83] Neate, *op. cit.*, p. 40.

[84] PP 1844, IX. Accounts and Papers. Third Report from the Select Committee on Medical Poor Relief, pp. 300–1.

In the early 1840s Kent's 103 medical officers each served an average medical district of 9,200 acres with an average population of over 5,000. This was superior to the other most populous counties such as Lancashire and Middlesex. Kent expenditure on medical relief, which fluctuated between 3.5% and 4% of total poor law costs in 1843–5, was also greater than that of these counties or the rural North Riding which all remained below 3%. In 1843 half the English counties paid below Kent's rate of 3d. per head on medical expenditure. Nevertheless 'the impossibility of one medical man, without horse or assistant, properly attending the wants of 6,000 poor spread over 25 parishes' was highlighted by a case of neglect in Faversham union.[85] Although the medical provision of the New Poor Law represented the beginnings of a National Health Service contemporary attitudes died hard and as late as 1878 the *British Medical Journal* denounced Hollingbourne union for failing to supply the expensive medicines to paupers recommended by the Select Committee on Poor Relief in 1844.[86] Within the workhouse the conscientious doctor remained frustrated by the workhouse master's control over the infirmary. In 1856 the Blean union doctor complained that sixty patients occupied an infirmary designed for thirty and that the sick were bedded throughout the workhouse lacking care and spreading infection. The previous year he had been overridden by guardians when he objected to the bulk purchase of trusses since they would not fit patients.[87]

Chaplains, in contrast, commanded respect because of their calling and ratification of their appointment by the bishop. Kent, an Anglican stronghold, soon appointed Anglican chaplains in most unions although protests from Tenterden dissenters were still echoing on in 1867.[88] Since chaplaincies were part-time some, as in Thanet union, were undertaken by local curates.[89] Pay, despite local protest, was comparatively high for conducting Sunday service, catechising the children monthly, visiting the sick and ministering to the dying. Coxheath union chaplaincy was advertised at £100 a year. Bridge, a small rural union, paid its chaplain £50 while its master and matron received only £70. Good remuneration did not guarantee good service. Bromley union had seven chaplains between 1864 and 1876. Most were unsatisfactory. One used vulgar language and misused the sacramental wine. A second was dismissed after falling heavily into debt.[90]

The master dominated all other workhouse officers. His complaint could cost them their job. Tied to the workhouse without holidays, pension or family life and on wages little above a domestic servant, porters and schoolteachers led an unenviable existence. In 1836 Blean union's porter and his wife, who was

---

[85] *Ibid.*, PP 1846, XXXVI. Amount spent on Medical Relief. PP 1852–3, LXXXIV. Returns relating to Medical Officers. PP 1844, XL. Accounts and Papers. Returns relative to the Poor Law Unions of England and Wales.

[86] SEG 1.7.1878.

[87] Crowther, *op. cit.*, pp. 160, 163.

[88] *Ibid.*, pp. 127–9. SEG 1.1.1867.

[89] Hopker, 'New Poor Law in Thanet . . .', p. 21.

[90] Crowther, *op. cit.*, pp. 128, 130.

schoolmistress, received 14s 0d a week jointly.[91] A second Blean porter refused to cut inmates' hair in case he lost face, and resigned in 1844 'being . . . quite tired of this secluded way of living'.[92] The first Sevenoaks porter, in contrast, was dismissed for drunkenness and violence in 1837.[93] In 1836 Hollingbourne union advertised for a schoolmaster who was a member of the established church 'to instruct the workhouse boys and girls in reading, writing and the principles of the Christian religion . . . and to train them to . . . usefulness, industry and virtue'.[94] Many workhouse teachers fell below these high standards. Thanet union's first schoolmaster was a pauper paid 1s 0d a week. His successor's brief term was ended for 'continued unpunctuality, openly doubting the scriptures and flogging a boy'. The next master, who used stinging nettles as a rod, survived somewhat longer.[95] Bromley guardians in 1862 pressed their mistress to resign after fighting with other officers and when the children's heads were found to be verminous.[96] In 1837 the Eastry schoolmistress was imprisoned 'for nauseating treatment of a child'.[97] In the same year the Blean chaplain suggested that the master's son was eligible to be schoolmaster since he had been initiated into the methods of teaching and discipline for a month at Canterbury National School. The chaplain's sister-in-law was simultaneously proposed as schoolmistress.[98]

After 1848 conditions became marginally more favourable for teachers when the treasury began to make direct grants to unions to subsidise their pay. Grants were related to qualifications and competence. In this way it was hoped guardians would employ qualified teachers. Thus encouraged the schoolmaster and schoolmistress in Blean union sat the examination in 1849 but qualified status did not free teachers from the master's control nor the constant imprisonment with pauper children and other workhouse officials.[99] Guardians, too, inflicted their petty humiliations. In 1837 Milton's schoolmaster and schoolmistress were each allowed the 'coal, candles and rations' of an able bodied pauper.[100] In some other unions rations were twice those of the paupers. Since the staple diet of Kent paupers was bread and cheese teachers received huge, inedible portions of these. Blean's schoolmaster pleaded for £10 per year to buy his own rations but it was some time before the guardians agreed.[101] When meals were eaten together, as at Blean, the less affluent officers had to watch the master and matron consume their superior

91 Neate, *op. cit.*, p. 40.
92 Crowther, *op. cit.*, p. 133.
93 F. R. J. Pateman, *Otford in Kent 1800–1850*, Otford 1957, p. 69.
94 MG 7.6.1836.
95 Hopker, *op. cit.*, pp. 23, 26.
96 Crowther, *op. cit.*, p. 131.
97 MG 24.1.1837.
98 Neate, *op. cit.*, p. 14.
99 *Ibid.*, pp. 9–10.
100 PRO Milton Union, 5279. Clerk to PLC, 30.3.1837.
101 Crowther, *op. cit.*, p. 131.

diet. It was, perhaps, small wonder that the schoolmaster and schoolmistress of Canterbury union were accused of drinking 182 gallons of porter during 1871.[102]

(4) Indoor Relief

Head was emphatic about the role of an efficient, central workhouse in 'elevating the character of the Kentish labourer'. 'The principal object we should keep in view', he told Blean guardians, 'is the erection of the workhouse without which our trouble will be in vain'.[103] He was equally emphatic that workhouses should be new. The commissioners had not originally intended that the poor should be under a single roof but that guardians should retain some existing poorhouses for economy and classification.[104] Soon, however, the idea of the general mixed workhouse had prevailed and in Kent Head was pressing guardians to adopt the 'same, low, cheap, homely building' as a model rural workhouse. Conscious of the turbulence of Kentish society and the weakness of Kent landowners in the face of intimidation he believed that not only would a single workhouse be more economical but it would also be a more impressive symbol of the New Poor Law strengthening the resolve of guardians.[105]

> The very sight of a well-built, efficient establishment would give confidence to the . . . guardians; the . . . weekly assemblage of all servants of their union would make them proud of their office; the appointment of a chaplain would give dignity to the whole arrangement while the paupers would feel it was . . . impossible to contend against it.[106]

Furthermore, Head argued, it would be easier for the handful of assistant commissioners to inspect one central workhouse rather than a number of scattered ones. Tufnell, his successor, also believed the poor were less likely to riot if families were under the same roof albeit separated.[107]

While the northern rural counties prevaricated for years over new workhouse buildings Head had, by August 1835, persuaded all eleven East Kent unions to erect new buildings which were already mostly roofed in.[108] In Thanet there was no debate about using existing poorhouses. A site was chosen at Minster within twelve days. St Lawrence poorhouse closed on 4 July 1835 and its inmates were transferred to St Peter's poorhouse.[109] St Peter's closed on 15 March 1836 and 'the poor of this parish were removed to the Union at Minster much against the general wish

---

[102] *Ibid.*, p. 132. SEG 25.2.1871.
[103] CKS G/H6 ACc1. Head to Hollingbourne Guardians 1835. CKS G/BC AM1 Head to Blean Union guardians, 12.5.1835.
[104] Crowther, *op. cit.*, p. 37.
[105] PRO MH 12. Sevenoaks Union 5315. Head to PLC, 29.11.1834.
[106] Jackman, *op. cit.*, p. 63.
[107] Crowther, *op. cit.*, pp. 38–9.
[108] PRO MH 12. Sevenoaks Union, 5315. Head to PLC, 19.8.1835.
[109] Hopker, 'New Poor Law in Thanet . . .', pp. 8–12.

GENERAL DIETARY.

		Breakfast.		Dinner.				Supper.	
		Bread. oz.	Cheese or Butter. oz.	Meat Pudding (with Vegetables.) oz.	Suet Pudding (with Vegetables.) oz.	Bread. oz.	Cheese. oz.	Bread. oz.	Butter or Cheese. oz.
SUNDAY	Men	6	1	16	....	....		6	1
	Women	5	- $\frac{1}{2}$	10	....	....		5	- $\frac{1}{2}$
MONDAY	Men	6	1	....	....	7 -	1	6	1
	Women	5	- $\frac{1}{2}$	....	....	7 -	1	5	- $\frac{1}{2}$
TUESDAY	Men	6	1	....	16	....		6	1
	Women	5	- $\frac{1}{3}$	....	10	....		5	- $\frac{1}{2}$
WEDNESDAY	Men	6	1	....	....	7 -	1	6	1
	Women	5	- $\frac{1}{2}$	....	....	7 -	1	5	- $\frac{1}{2}$
THURSDAY	Men	6	1	....	....	7 -	1	6	1
	Women	5	- $\frac{1}{2}$	....	....	7 -	1	5	- $\frac{1}{2}$
FRIDAY	Men	6	1	... .	16	...	....	6	1
	Women	5	- $\frac{1}{2}$	....	10	....	....	5	- $\frac{1}{2}$
SATURDAY	Men	6	1	....	....	7 -	1	6	1
	Women	5	- $\frac{1}{2}$	....	....	7 -	1	5	- $\frac{1}{2}$

OLD PEOPLE being all 60 yrs. of age & upwards { The Weekly addition of 1 oz. of Tea and Milk, also an additional Meat Pudding Dinner on Thursday in each Week, in lieu of Bread and Cheese, for those whose age and infirmities it may be deemed proper and requisite.

CHILDREN- - { Bread and Milk for their Breakfast and Supper, or Gruel, when Milk cannot be obtained, also such proportions of the Dinner diet as may be requisite for their respective ages.

SICK - - - - - Whatever is ordered for them by the Medical Officer.

Figure 12. General dietary of Hollingbourne Union Workhouse 1835.

of the inhabitants and to the sorrow of the paupers'.[110] Erection of the new Dover union workhouse took nine months. Transfer was effected on 22 April during which an old man died.[111] In West Kent the two assistant commissioners were, as they predicted, less quick in obtaining new buildings. Hoo workhouse was built in thirteen months but Dartford union only extended its existing building in 1837. Sevenoaks union erected a new workhouse at Sundridge in 1845 after an unsavoury scandal. Gravesend and Tenterden followed two years later. A new Canterbury workhouse was constructed in 1849.[112] Medway union made more prolonged use of its former parish poorhouses. Chatham workhouse was extended in 1837–8 with the intention of housing all union paupers but separate workhouses still remained at Chatham and in the parishes of St Margaret and St Nicholas, Rochester. Although the subject of highly critical reports in the 1840s the workhouse at Chatham was not replaced by a new union building at Luton until 1855. The new building was partially financed by the sale of the old Chatham and St Nicholas poorhouses.[113] Nevertheless by 1841 at least 19 of Kent's 27 unions had new workhouses. As befitted a model poor law county the capacities of these buildings were large. In 1847 the total number of workhouse places, excluding Canterbury, amounted to nearly 11,000. Greenwich workhouse, 'a spacious brick building built in 1840 at a cost of £241,000 . . . in the Elizabethan style . . .' held over a thousand inmates. Twelve other Kent workhouses held 400 paupers or more each.[114]

With new workhouses in hand the question of diet came next. Here Head was at pains to emphasise that the proper diet should equal the subsistence which any outdoor pauper could procure for his family.[115] Most Kent unions ultimately opted for a dietary which provided daily breakfasts and suppers and dinners four days a week of bread and butter or cheese for able bodied adults with dinners of suet pudding and vegetables on two days and meat pudding with vegetables on one day. The elderly were additionally allowed an ounce of tea with milk for breakfast and supper and an optional meat pudding dinner. Children received bread and milk or gruel for breakfast and supper.[116] Indoor paupers undoubtedly remained adequately if unattractively fed. Nevertheless the assistant commissioners met considerable difficulty in persuading guardians to accept the dietary. West Ashford guardians were 'hostile beyond measure' until they had tried it for a month and found it 'to be more than they could possibly eat and ample for the enjoyment of perfect

---

[110] J. Mockett, *Mockett's Journal*, Canterbury 1836, p. 297. Cit. Hopker, *op. cit.*, p. 12.

[111] Douglas Welby, *The Kentish Village of River*, Dover 1977, p. 108.

[112] Keyes, *op. cit.*, p. 236. Bagshaw, *op. cit.*. CMS G/Ho AM1. Hoo Guardians' Minutes Sept. 1835. Scott, *op. cit.*, pp. 26–7.

[113] Dufton, *op. cit.*, pp. 7–10. Perry and Company, Rochester Directory 1871–73, p. 30. Philip MacDougall, 'Parish Workhouses of the Medway Towns', *Bygone Kent*, vol. 8, No. 8, p. 445.

[114] Bagshaw, *op. cit.* See vol. 2, pp. 18–21 and place entries. See also CKS/0351K/1.

[115] CKS G/DO. River (later Dover) Guardians' Minutes, 4.8.1835.

[116] FRL G/El AM1. Elham Guardians' Minutes. Head to Guardians, 14.7.1835. Public Poster printed by Hollingbourne Union, 6.11.1835, fig. 12.

health'.[117] When Eastry guardians wished to add to the dietary each week 'a pint of strong, nourishing beef soup mixed with rice and vegetables', Head responded that 'it would instantly make your poorhouse attractive and break the spirit of your independent labourers . . . no country in the world can afford to feed its paupers on such a diet . . .'.[118] Similarly when Bromley guardians wanted to substitute a pint of warm soup for bread and cheese on three days, since most inmates were infirm and over sixty-five, a note on the correspondence reads 'in any other than a Kentish union we should consent'.[119] In 1837 inquest jurors on a pauper who died in Chislehurst poorhouse declared the workhouse diet 'altogether insufficient for the support and nourishment of able bodied persons . . .' and requested more frequent allowances of 'meat, potatoes, pudding and porridge'.[120] Tufnell had already banned beer from Kent workhouses when, in 1855, the Poor Law Board withdrew table beer from the workhouse of Canterbury Incorporation except for the aged and infirm and meat puddings were replaced by bread and cheese for children, the sick and the elderly.[121] There was a possibility of more meat with the arrival of cheaper Australian tinned mutton in 1871. Canterbury and Malling guardians decided to use it but its introduction into Medway workhouse produced a strike of inmates.[122] While workhouse diet was ample but unattractive, claims of anti-poor law campaigners that workhouse diets were worse than prison diets was true in Kent. Ashford prisoners on the treadmill had more food than workhouse inmates.[123] John Day, a Southwark anti-poor law protester, complained that North Aylesford workhouse inmates not only got 18 of 21 meals of bread and cheese but that it was 'even a less allowance of food than they would procure in prison'.[124]

David Roberts has alleged that the worst workhouse conditions were found in unions where opponents of the new system were influential. These guardians neglected their workhouses and failed to build new, large, clean institutions with separate wards which were orderly and disciplined partly because they did not believe in them and partly because they were indifferent to the poor. This was true in the North Riding and seems to have been so in the Sevenoaks and Medway unions.[125] Sevenoaks union was overshadowed by Lord Stanhope, inveterate anti-poor law campaigner and founder of the short-lived National Anti-Poor Law Association.[126] In 1835 Head bemoaned that after seventeen guardians' meetings preparations for a new workhouse had not progressed. In 1836 Stanhope publicly

---

117 CKS G/Ea. AM1. Eastry Guardians' Minutes, 22.9.1835.
118 *Loc. cit.*
119 PRO MH 12. Bromley Union, 4855. Bromley Union to PLC, 3.11.1836.
120 *Ibid.* Bromley Union to PLC, 12.6.1837.
121 Crowther, *op. cit.*, p. 218. SEG 15.5.1835.
122 SEG 21.11.1871, 2.12.1871, 9.3.1872.
123 Crowther, *op. cit.*, p. 214.
124 MG 12.2.1850.
125 David Roberts, 'How Cruel was the Victorian Poor Law?', *Historical Journal*, vi (1963), pp. 97–107. Paul Hastings, 'The New Poor Law in the North Riding: the first ten years 1837–47', in Digby and Hastings, *op. cit.*, pp. 65–7.
126 N. C. Edsall, *The Anti-Poor Law Movement 1834–1844*, Manchester 1971, pp. 126, 135, 137, 139.

expressed regret that two of his tenants had become guardians and trusted that no more would do so. Lord Amherst, too, was opposed to the New Poor Law.[127] A board was elected but the old workhouse remained. There were soon indications that all was not well. In March 1837 the clerk reported that:

> ... Management of the house has been very sadly neglected. The Itch prevails amongst all classes to a lamentable extent and many of the inmates are in a state of great uncleanliness ... The presence of vermin ... is remarkable.[128]

In 1837, with prohibition of outdoor relief to the able bodied and introduction of the workhouse test, pauper numbers began to outstrip the workhouse capacity of 300 and in the winters of 1838–9 and 1840–1 disease among the children was aggravated by overcrowding. Women lying-in were badly accommodated and imperfectly attended. Stanhope and his supporters in the union seized their opportunity. In November 1841 *The Times* reported that between May and November 1840 the children had not been properly washed and that in April 1841 75 boys had been sleeping in sixteen beds and 86 girls in nineteen beds. A week later it was reported that 57 men shared 31 beds and forty women twenty beds. 78 boys and 91 girls were reported suffering from goitre and glandular fever. In the lying-in ward five women were alleged to be confined in two beds 'beastly beyond description'. Three had been delivered simultaneously in one bed.[129] A ratepayers' meeting chaired by Stanhope produced a week-long, bad-tempered local enquiry by E. C. Tufnell. The commissioners' report blamed the master, matron and medical officer. The anti-poor law activists blamed the new system, the commissioners and the guardians maintaining that what had become a national scandal of Andover proportions could have been avoided by paying outdoor relief.[130] 'No union house in the county or in England has been conducted with so little attention to the interests and comfort of the inmates and the poor generally', commented the *Kentish Gazette*.[131] The outcome was 'a handsome new edifice three storeys in height' built to house 500 inmates on Ide Hill above Sundridge at a cost of £12,000 in 1845.[132]

Contemporaneously came a number of critical reports of Chatham workhouse. An adverse report by the medical officer in 1841 was followed by a report from the guardians' visiting committee in 1842 which condemned the condition of the vagrant ward where the straw was changed monthly and blankets swarmed with lice. Further criticism produced an enquiry at which these allegations were refuted but in the 1850s Assistant Commissioner Sir John Walsham found the children at Chatham workhouse 'much too closely packed'. The able bodied, before the new

127 PRO MH 12. Sevenoaks Union, 5315. Head to PLC, 19.8.1835.
128 D. Clarke and A. Stoyel, *Otford in Kent: a History*, Battle 1975, p. 196.
129 MG 16.11.1841. *The Times*, 6.11.1841, 4.12.1841, 9.12.1841, 12.1.1842. Report printed by D. Booth, Vestry Clerk of Sundridge, 8.1.1842. *Morning Herald*, 8.11.1841, 1.12.1841.
130 *The Times*, 4.12.1841.
131 *Kentish Gazette*, 8.12.1841.
132 Bagshaw, *op. cit.* MG 2.9.1845.

workhouse was built at Luton, exercised in an underground room seven feet long and an outdoor yard eighteen feet in length. Ten men were accommodated in a room nine feet by six and eighteen females 'hopelessly insane' exercised in a yard 32 feet by eighteen.[133]

It was not only the unions with old workhouses which showed a callous disregard for paupers. In Kent's new workhouses cruelty tended to be psychological and insensitive rather than physical. No window in Dover workhouse provided an outside view.[134] In 1836 of 241 paupers who left Tonbridge workhouse eighty ran away. In 1837 the guardians raised the walls to prevent escape. Dartford workhouse was described in 1870 as '. . . a few low buildings enclosed within high walls with nothing but a few ventilation gratings to be seen from the road'.[135] Paupers were often not allowed to leave the house. Tufnell believed they should only attend church under strict supervision and in the obnoxious workhouse uniform which became mandatory.[136] Tobacco and other gifts were denied. Canterbury workhouse children were refused visitors and the cakes and sweets they brought. 'I find', wrote John Day, 'the aged and deserving poor transported 10 miles . . . from their friends, locked up within the gates of this building like so many criminals . . .'.[137] Workhouse discipline was much stricter than in northern England but occasionally inmates managed to temporarily escape like the two women 'one with two bastards and the other a widow with five children' who left Bridge workhouse via a bedroom window 'to go to a cheap ball in a pub'. A pauper in Malling workhouse was denied access to her children in the infant ward. Another was refused the right to follow her dead husband to the grave. When she did so she was expelled from the house. Maidstone guardians in 1877 refused Christmas dinner to able bodied inmates since 'they should be out at work' although this resolution was rescinded.[138] In 1853 an orphan in Greenwich workhouse died from cruelty inflicted by a pauper nurse. In 1865 a widower in Canterbury workhouse was denied medicine and clothing.[139] While the workhouse was undoubtedly to some extent 'a sealed sepulchre' there were, however, comparatively few reported cases of deliberate cruelty.

Kent paupers who had lived through the Swing Riots and the anti-Poor Law riots were also prone to fight back. Between 1835 and 1842 841 offences were committed in Kent workhouses – more than in any other county save Middlesex. 592 of these offences involved misbehaviour, drunken and disorderly conduct, wilful damage and refusal to work. Forty-five were for assault and breach of the peace.[140]

[133] Dufton, op. cit., pp. 7–10. SEG 18.8.1857.
[134] J. B. Jones, Annals of Dover, Dover 1916, p. 429.
[135] Keyes, op. cit., p. 237. M. J. Todd, 'The operation of the New Poor Law of 1834 in Kent and Middlesex', Kent Extended Essay, 1969, 041, pp. 71, 73.
[136] Crowther, op. cit., p. 129.
[137] MG 12.2.1850. SEG 22.7.1871.
[138] See Hastings, op. cit., pp. 253–6. MG 18.1.1870, 10.1.1871, 10.12.1877, 1.3.1886.
[139] SEG 1.2.1853, 22.8.1865.
[140] PP 1843, XLV. Accounts and Papers, 63. Return of Persons committed to prison for workhouse offences, 1835–42.

BLEAN UNION.

REGULATIONS relating to the VISITING OF INMATES.

WHEREAS by Articles 47 and 51 of the Poor Law Institutions Order, 1913, the Guardians are empowered to make Regulations as to visits which may be paid by relatives and friends to inmates of the Institution.

IT IS HEREBY ORDERED that :—

1. AN inmate of the Sick Ward, who is on the danger list, may be visited at any time, subject to any directions which may be given by the Medical Officer in any individual case.

2. THE time appointed for the visitation of inmates in the Sick Wards is Wednesday in each week between the hours of 2 and 5 in the afternoon, and Sunday in each week between the hours of 2 and 3 and 4 and 5 in the afternoon, the maximum number of persons allowed to visit any one inmate during the appointed period shall be in the discretion of the Master.

3. THE time appointed for the visitation of inmates other than those in the Sick Wards shall be the same as specified in Paragraph No. 2, and the maximum number of persons allowed to visit any one inmate during the appointed period shall be in the discretion of the Master.

4. THE father and mother of an infant or child who is an inmate of the same Institution, unless the Medical Officer otherwise directs, shall be allowed to have access at least daily to the infant or child.

5. A married couple resident in the Institution in wards other than the married couples' quarters, shall be allowed to see each other once in each week.

6. INMATES shall be allowed to see their children resident in homes provided by the Guardians within the Union area once in each month.

7. THE following general rules shall be observed :—

(a) Order and quietness shall be observed whilst in the Institution.

(b) Visitors are prohibited from bringing anything whatever to a patient, except flowers, sound oranges, good grapes and acid drops.

(c) All parcels are to be left at the gate.

(d) Visitors may not pass from one Ward to another, nor from one bed to another.

(e) They may not stay more than one hour with their friends.

(f) No smoking is allowed.

(g) No gratuity is on any account whatsoever allowed to be given to anyone in the Institution.

(h) Anyone introducing spirituous or other liquors into the Institution is liable to a fine of £10 or two months imprisonment.

(i) All changes of address should at once be notified to the Master.

By Order,

W. T. BROOKS,

12th day of May, 1914.

Clerk to the Guardians.

Figure 13. Regulations relating to the visiting of inmates at Blean Union Workhouse 1914.

Some of these offences were attributed to vagrants but the problem of vagrancy had not yet intensified. All inmates were supposed to work ten hours a day if fit and over seven years of age. Work was hard and monotonous. The only employment for men in Medway workhouse in 1835–50 was the picking of 8lbs of oakum a day for Chatham Dockyard. Cranbrook inmates broke stones while those at Pembury picked junk and oakum and crushed bones for fertiliser.[141] Sevenoaks guardians installed a hand corn mill. Not surprisingly violence and frustration was directed towards workhouse officers. In Thanet workhouse there were 41 minuted incidents over a 63-month period involving forty named paupers. In January 1841 the master was attacked by five inmates and a constable called to the scene was assaulted by a sixth. Some thirty men were involved in the disturbance and subsequently all five workhouse officers were made special constables.[142] A pauper who attacked the matron of Goudhurst workhouse got eight months imprisonment. Two years later two paupers tried to set the workhouse on fire.

Charges of refusing to obey orders, refusing to work or of breaking windows were commonplace in the late 1840s. Many of the incidents were in the Thanet, Faversham or Tenterden unions. A woman was sentenced to 21 days hard labour for breaking 23 panes of glass in Thanet workhouse in April 1849. A second inmate, who tried to lead a mutiny in 1861, was given the same sentence.[143] Most masters awarded their own punishments for minor offences such as leaving the house without permission. Thanet and Chatham had their own 'cage' or 'black hole' for solitary confinement on bread and water but for insubordination or violence boards sought custodial sentences from the magistrates. The value of such sentences on hardened paupers is hard to determine. Susan Jackson, a Thanet pauper given a month's hard labour for refusing to work, responded '. . . It is only sending me from one prison to another'.[144]

(5) Outdoor Relief

The terror of a well-regulated workhouse featured prominently in the commissioners' thinking and in the folklore of anti-Poor Law propagandists. Yet the hope that indoor relief could be substituted for outdoor relief, with the workhouse acting as a testing place for the able bodied, was never realised. Adequate supervision by the assistant commissioners, who were supposed to visit each union for two days at six monthly intervals, was impossible. Tufnell had twenty-five Kent unions and twenty in Sussex. By 30 March 1840 he had been employed for 1,280 working days during which he had made 725 visits taking an average of 1.4 days for each.[145]

---

[141] Dufton, *op. cit.*, p. 16. Todd, *op. cit.*, p. 65. MH 12. Sevenoaks Union, 5316. Clerk to PLC, 25.5.1838.

[142] Hopker, *op. cit.*, pp. 31–2.

[143] Todd, *op. cit.*, p. 71. MG 7.1.1845, 21.1.1845, 3.4.1849, 10.4.1849, 14.1.1851. SEG 1.2.1853, 26.2.1861.

[144] Hopker, *op. cit.*, pp. 29–30. Dufton, *op. cit.*, p. 18. MG 4.4.1848, 12.6.1849, 11.12.1849, 7.1.1845.

[145] PP 1840, XXXIX. Accounts and Papers. Assistant Poor Law Commissioners districts and visits made to unions by 30 April 1840.

BLEAN UNION.

REGULATIONS

relating to the Hours and Places of Meals and Work, and the Hours of Rising and going to Bed.

WHEREAS the Guardians of the above named Union are required by Article 47 of the Poor Law Institutions Order, 1913, to make regulations relating to the hours and places of meals and work and the hours of rising and going to bed for the Inmates of the Institution.

It is Hereby Ordered :--

1. THAT the hours of meals shall be as follows :—

	Time.	Except for the following classes.	When the time shall be.
Breakfast	6.30 a.m., 25th Mar. to 29th Sep. 7. 0 a.m., 29th Sep. to 25th Mar.		
Dinner	12 noon to 1 p.m.		
Supper	6 p.m.	Inmates of the Sick Wards	4.30 p.m.

2. MEALS shall be served in the general dining hall except for the following classes of inmates for whom meals shall be served in the appropriate wards :—
INMATES of the Receiving Wards.
INMATES of the Sick Wards.

3. THE following shall be the hours and places of work :—

Class.	Period.	Hours for Work.	Place of Work.
Able-bodied Men	25th March 29th Septr.	7 a.m. to 12 noon 1 p.m. to 5.30 p.m.	As directed by the Master.
Ditto	29th Septr. 25th March	7.30 a.m. to 12 noon 1 p.m. to 5.30 p.m.	Ditto
Able-bodied Women	25th March 29th Septr.	7 a.m. to 12 noon 1 p.m. to 5.30 p.m.	As directed by the Matron.
Ditto	29th Septr. 25th March	7.30 a.m. to 12 noon 1 p.m. to 5.30 p.m.	Ditto

ONLY the necessary work shall be performed by the inmates on Sunday, Good Friday and Christmas Day. An inmate who is pregnant or recently confined ; or suckling an infant, shall only be employed at such work and for such hours as the Medical Officer may approve.

AN Inmate shall not, unless approved for the particular employment by the Medical Officer and acting under the immediate supervision of a paid Officer, be employed in any capacity in the sick wards, lunatic wards, or nurseries, and shall not in any circumstances be employed in nursing a sick inmate.

ANY Inmate who shall refuse or neglect to work after being required to do so, shall be deemed disorderly, and may be punished accordingly.

AN Inmate shall not be employed on any work which in the opinion of the Medical Officer would be injurious to his health.

4. THE following shall be the hours of rising and going to bed :—

DURING THE SUMMER MONTHS.			DURING THE WINTER MONTHS.		
Class.	Time of Rising.	Time of going to Bed.	Class.	Time of Rising.	Time of going to Bed.
Able-bodied	5.45 a.m.	8 p.m.	Able-bodied	6.15 a.m.	8 p.m.
Infirm	5.45 a.m.	8 p.m.	Infirm	6.15 a.m.	8 p.m.
Children	6 a.m.	7.30 p.m.	Children	6.30 a.m.	7.30 p.m.

THE hours for rising and going to bed for inmates of the sick, maternity, and lunatic wards, and for infants, and their sleeping arrangements generally, are subject to the directions of the Medical Officer.

5. A printed copy of these Regulations shall be exhibited by the Master in the dining hall of the Institution.

By Order,

W. T. BROOKS,

12th day of May, 1914. *Clerk to the Guardians.*

Figure 14. Regulations relating to the hours and places of work, and the hours of rising and going to bed, at Blean Union workhouse 1914.

In the first quarters of 1840–5 only 14%–16% of paupers in England and Wales received relief in workhouses. Kent, a model county with its new workhouses, managed to reduce outdoor relief to the able bodied more than most. While the more blatant abuses of the Old Poor Law such as payment of rents vanished, total prohibition of outdoor relief proved impossible as guardians adopted the relief system which they considered most appropriate to meet local problems of surplus labour and seasonal unemployment. Outdoor relief was considered fairer to the pauper and cheaper to the ratepayer. Consequently temporary outrelief paid before workhouses were complete continued afterwards and there was considerable continuity with the old system.[146] Hoo union made extra relief payments to paupers outside the workhouse. Cranbrook union consistently used the 'urgent necessity' clause to a greater extent than the commissioners intended when the workhouse was overcrowded and when there was widespread sickness or harsh weather.[147] 'For a short period', wrote Tufnell of the severe winter of 1837–8, 'the principle of relief established was completely overthrown. Severity of the weather forbade the application of the labour test to those who sought relief which was consequently given on the old, injurious system of taking nothing in return for it'.[148] To avoid taking large families into the workhouse, Cranbrook gave outrelief to fathers even when its new workhouse was not full. Sheppey also gave outrelief and a labour test of wheeling ballast from the sea shore when it had workhouse places available. When Faversham workhouse was full outrelief was given to 253 heads of families.[149] Sevenoaks made bread allowances to able bodied labourers with large families and Tonbridge guardians gave allowances when the winter price of flour increased.[150]

Head, upon his departure, had warned Kent guardians to resolutely stop all outrelief.[151] In 1840–2, however, only 24.1% of Kent paupers were relieved indoors. An average of 29.3% of Kent's able bodied paupers had to enter the workhouse in the quarters ending Lady Day 1842 and 1843. Only 31% of total county poor law expenditure was spent on indoor relief in 1858–9 while 49.9% of Kent poor were relieved indoors in the first week of January 1900. These figures were lower nationally but clearly indicate that while Kent outdoor relief was severely curtailed it was certainly not abolished.[152]

Parish officers, local landowners and guardians also organised schemes to

[146] Figures based upon statistics in J. R. McCulloch, *A Descriptive and Statistical Account of the British Empire*, 1847, p. 664. MH 12. Sevenoaks Union, 5316. PLC to Sevenoaks Guardians, 25.5.1835. Crowther, *op. cit.*, pp. 45–6.

[147] MacDougall, *op. cit.*, p. 105. Todd, *op. cit.*, pp. 87–9.

[148] PP 1837–38, XXVIII. 4th Report of Poor Law Commission.

[149] Todd, *op. cit.*, pp. 87–91.

[150] *Ibid.*, pp. 92–3. Sevenoaks Union, 5316. Guardians to PLC, 25.5.1838.

[151] Neate, *op. cit.*, p. 37.

[152] PP 1843, XLV. Sums expended in poor law unions in England and Wales in indoor and outdoor relief for years ending 25 March 1841 and 25 March 1842. PP 1844, XL. Accounts and Papers, 42. Number of indoor and outdoor paupers relieved in each county in England and Wales during quarters ending Lady Day 1842 and 1843. SEG 31.1.1860. Report of J. S. Davy, Local Government Board Inspector, on Poor Law in Kent and Sussex, January 1899 – January 1900.

provide work, particularly in winter, to keep able bodied labourers from the work-house. Thanet guardians continued to employ men on road work. Bearsted used the 1832 Allotment Act to aid 'industrious labourers who are likely to be effected by the New Poor Law Bill'. Brabourne illegally continued a labour rate. Charles Milner of Preston Hall offered Aylesford parish a three-year contract to grub his woodland while Chart Sutton parish officers planned to cultivate five acres of parish hop ground for poor parishioners with large families 'to prevent the necessity of coming into the union workhouse by which their establishment would be broken up and their chances of work lessened.'[153] At Lenham T. Pemberton Leigh, Chancellor of the Duchy of Lancaster, employed nearly all surplus labour on his 3,000-acre estate while those attending East Kent Quarter Sessions in 1844 were reminded of the importance of providing winter work 'since no one would wish to see the poor and their families driven to the unions however well-managed they might be'.[154] Thanet union even developed an eleven acre industrial farm adjacent to Minster workhouse which kept able bodied paupers at work and trained boys for work at home or 'in a new colony'.[155]

While guardians and ratepayers were prepared to circumvent poor law regula-tions on behalf of their own poor, treatment of non-settled poor remained callous, producing some of the harshest incidents of the New Poor Law, although often these were no crueller than under the Old Poor Law. In 1839 Lewisham's relieving officer removed a pauper with pneumonia in an open cart to Bromley. Bromley returned him and he died on the journey at St Mary Cray. Another destitute pauper collapsed lame in Northfleet having been previously removed from Sheerness to Northfleet to Strood. A woman with four children, chargeable to Bridge union, was sent from Herne to walk ten miles to Bridge in biting cold with an infant at her breast. She fainted in Canterbury but survived. She was more fortunate than the pregnant woman refused medical relief at Edenbridge in 1862 who died as a result, or the girl who gave birth in a Stelling hop garden and was denied admission to Elham workhouse and sent on to Canterbury.[156]

Between 1860 and 1870 outrelief increased nationally by £770,000 a year. The Poor Law Board, therefore, decided to try to cut back. Kent paupers had risen from 26,999 in 1860 to 30,389 in 1870. Kent indoor relief had correspondingly grown from 19.8% of all paupers to 22.5%. This figure was comparatively high. Never-theless in 1872 Canterbury guardians were censured for the amount of outrelief they paid.[157] A meeting of Kent unions which followed decided outrelief should be refused to single able bodied paupers suffering from temporary sickness, and

[153] Hopker, op. cit., p. 39. Carol Bowman et al., History of Bearsted and Thurnham, Bearsted 1988, pp. 108–9. CKS P41/8/2 Brabourne Vestry Minutes, 1844. P12/8/1, Aylesford Vestry Minutes, 1834. P18/8/1, Bearsted Vestry Minutes, 1834. G/Hb/Acb1, Hollingbourne Guardians to Poor Law Commissioners, November 1837.
[154] MG 14.11.1843, 29.10.1844.
[155] SEG 28.2.1854.
[156] MG 2.4.1839, 28.1.1851. SEG 19.2.1861, 15.4.1862, 26.9.1870.
[157] SEG 20.1.1872, 27.2.1872, 23.3.1872.

wives living apart from their husbands except those of soldiers, sailors or lunatics. Moreover, outrelief was not to exceed three months and was only to be granted after a visit from the relieving officer who was to continue to visit at least fortnightly. Medical extras to outdoor paupers were to be granted only until the next guardians' meeting. No outrelief was to be given non-residents except widows in the first six months of widowhood.[158] Four years later Tonbridge guardians ruled that recipients must prove their destitution was not caused by their own improvidence and that while working they had done all possible to provide against sickness or unemployment. Outrelief was refused to strikers; the temporarily unemployed; able bodied widows with one child or less; deserted wives or wives with husbands in prison; and persons living with relatives where the combined family income would support all members. Even those unemployed through harsh weather were excluded to force persons 'by thrift to make provision for themselves'.[159]

Between 1881 and 1885 the cost of Kent's in-maintenance increased from 50.2% of total poor law expenditure to 55.2% for the half years ending 25 March.[160] Nevertheless in 1888 Medway guardians resolved to refuse outrelief to all but destitute women and children and those suffering from sickness, accident or old age. Elham guardians refused outrelief to paupers living outside the district and at a London Poor Law Conference urged refusal of outrelief to the improvident and argued that refusal to widows with families often meant the children were taken in by friends or relatives.[161] These arguments were used by the board's inspector in 1890 who urged a workhouse test and reduction of outrelief to a minimum. His model was Milton union where, he argued, rigid refusal of outrelief had driven paupers to seek help from their friends and created 'such prudence' that during the brickmakers' lock-out of 1890 few had applied for poor relief.[162] The central drive to reduce outrelief did not, however, meet with universal approval. A proposal in 1891 by G. F. Deedes, Vice-Chairman of Elham union, to abolish outrelief was emphatically rejected by his fellow guardians. Four years later, in a move diametrically opposed to central policy, Elham guardians decided to double their weekly outrelief to the aged and infirm. The prime movers were the newly-elected Folkestone guardians who commentators claimed 'were introducing old age pensions in disguise'.[163] The board was also influenced by the evidence of John Ladd of Sellindge to the Royal Commission on the Aged Poor in 1894 which highlighted the desperate poverty of the elderly and the inadequacy of outrelief given even by more humane unions like Elham.[164] 49% of Kent paupers were relieved in

---

[158] SEG 23.3.1872.
[159] SEG 27.11.1876.
[160] SEG 4.1.1886.
[161] KE 19.5.1888, 23.6.1888, 15.12.1888.
[162] KE 28.4.1890, 10.5.1890.
[163] KE 14.2.1891, 2.2.1895.
[164] PP 1894, XVI (1) Report of the Royal Commission on the Aged Poor, vol. 1, Minutes of Evidence. John F. Ladd, Q.14344–14502, pp. 786–92.

workhouses in the first weeks of January 1899 and January 1900 but only Milton, Faversham and Eastry unions relieved more paupers within the workhouse than outside.[165]

(6) Vagrancy

Below the able bodied settled poor remained the vagrant poor entitled only to a night's lodging of the most primitive kind in the workhouse. The commissioners ordered boards to provide casual wards for their reception but often only outhouses and sheds, sometimes without straw or beds, sufficed. At Elham the casual ward was a stable containing a horse and through which ran a stable drain. Here, after a bread and water supper, men and women huddled together on coarse rags. Latecomers lay on other sleepers or on the brick floor. 'Travellers often complain about the room', commented a judge on Faversham's vagrant ward. 'They lie on straw, have no light or fire and are allowed a little bread and some water . . .'.[166] A work task waited the following morning.

Kent's vagrant numbers were swollen by the annual influx of hop pickers. In 1876 36,000 pickers, described by Maidstone's relieving officer as 'mostly the scum of London', travelled by train to Kent.[167] Irish reapers and refugees from famine were joined by the large migrant labour force created by Kent railway building and the many unemployed who took to the road in search of work during the recurrent economic crises of the 1840s and the great depressions in industry and agriculture in the last decades of the century. Certain unions bore the brunt of these migrants. Bromley union was in a harvest area where casual labour was badly needed. Mid and East Kent unions received most of the hop pickers. Ashford was en route for Folkestone and the work available from Dover harbour board.[168] The Poor Law, however, did not separate the shiftless and sometimes diseased vagrant from the genuinely unemployed. Consequently the treatment of all vagrants remained harsh. In 1843 Elham guardians admitted 450 railway navvies in four months. East Ashford union rejected further railroad labourers after many succumbed to fever.

> The importation of so large a number of men . . . is a heavy tax on parishes through which the line runs . . . The men are an abandoned and reckless set and falling ill they become chargeable to the parish. With such a class of men more liable to infectious disease than our labouring population their indiscriminate admission to a workhouse must be wrong.[169]

---

[165] Annual Report of J. S. Davy, Local Government Board Inspector, January 1899–January 1900, Kent and Sussex.

[166] MG 26.3.1850. KE 26.8.1893.

[167] Alan Bignall, *Hopping Down in Kent*, London 1977, p. 118. PP 1868–9, XIII. Report of Royal Commission on Employment of Children, Young Persons and Women in Agriculture, 1867, p. 62.

[168] Crowther, *op. cit.*, p. 248.

[169] MG 18.4.1843.

In winter elderly vagrants had to walk from East Ashford union across Romney Marsh 'through snow storms only comparable to the blizzards of America'. Elham workhouse, nearly six miles from Folkestone, was also difficult to reach. Vagrants easily got lost and in 1892 a party almost perished in the snow. In 1893, after questions in the Commons, the guardians ordered that the aged and infirm should be sent by train and the very ill by covered conveyance. Even so the workhouse was still a mile from Lyminge station. When an Irish hop picker was dying at Bromley he was immediately driven to Paddock Wood on a dung cart and tipped onto the grass. He expired before the train arrived.[170]

This inhumanity was not without some reason since the more violent vagrants often terrorised rural workhouses. An influx of vagrants in the late 1840s brought an unprecedented outbreak of violence.[171] In 1847 a Dartford overseer sought police protection from an influx of Irish 'casuals' en route for Gravesend claiming relief from parish overseers as they went and nightly stripping the gardens on the Crayford road.[172] At Tonbridge female vagrants burned their oakum and tore up workhouse clothes while at Faversham five young Irishmen fired the straw in the vagrant ward 'to keep warm'.[173] In 1848 special constables were needed to quell rioting Irish at Hollingbourne workhouse on two successive nights and serious riots were suppressed by police at Tenterden and Tonbridge in 1848 and 1852. At the latter 326 panes of glass were broken and it was feared the house would be burned to the ground.[174] 254 panes were smashed at North Aylesford in 1851 when female casuals barricaded themselves in the ward. Nine vagrants at Maidstone workhouse, who refused to work after their overnight stay, began a wholesale destruction of property and were arrested in 1863.[175] Canterbury workhouse, which had not implemented a labour test, found itself inundated by vagrants.[176]

From the close of the 1860s vagrant numbers again began to climb. 3,550 'casuals' passed through Canterbury workhouse in the last six months of 1869. This was an increase of 1,660 on the previous six months. During 1867–70 vagrant numbers rose countywide by 78,000. Numbers in the metropolitan unions declined but in the hop-growing mid-Kent unions the increase was massive. The only deterrents suggested were uniform diet, work and hot baths upon admission but this the Poor Law Board inspectors failed to achieve.[177] By 1881 vagrancy was still on the increase. Kent vagrants again outnumbered the average for the previous decade. The general trade depression was held 'mostly accountable' and there were again cries for uniform treatment in diet, sleeping and bathing arrangements which varied wildly.[178] A conference of guardians in 1883 again agreed that uniformity of

---

170 MG 16.9.1856. KE 12.8.1893, 26.8.1893, 9.2.1895.
171 MG 15.2.1848, 29.8.1848.
172 MG 18.5.1847, 11.3.1851.
173 MG 29.12.1846, 14.1.1851.
174 MG 26.9.1848, 19.12.1848, 27.1.1852.
175 MG 7.1.1851. SEG 26.1.1858, 3.2.1863.
176 SEG 24.4.1866.
177 SEG 1.11.1869, 20.12.1870. Crowther, *op. cit.*, p. 250.
178 KE 1.1.1881. SEG 16.1.1882.

treatment was desirable and a sub committee was appointed to consider details. It was agreed that a full labour task should be exacted when physically possible but by mid-1884, with vagrants still increasing, it was felt a more stringent deterrent was required.[179] In 1885 there were 143,467 admissions to casual wards, an increase of 34,775 compared with 1884. 214,420 nights' lodgings were provided – 39,126 more than the previous year. In 1875 nights' lodgings had stood at only 46,732 but there had been a 40% increase since the Casual Poor Act of 1882.[180]

> The penal system applied to the wayfaring poor evidently does not answer in Kent [wrote the *Kentish Express*] . . . There is more casual labour about in the country parishes than has been known for many years. The union houses are filled every night.[181]

In 1890 West Ashford union closed its vagrant ward which was attracting 4,000 casuals a year.[182] In contrast, influenced by the criticism of Folkestone Municipal Reform League, Elham guardians abolished labour for casual paupers. They were obliged, however, to restore three hours digging, pumping, or the breaking of 4 cwts of stones for men and two hours washing or needlework for women. New buildings at East Ashford workhouse significantly included ten stone cells in which casuals could pound their 1½ cwts of flints until they passed through a quarter inch mesh sieve.[183]

Yet another conference of Kent unions in 1894 debated vagrancy which 'was assuming the dimensions of a chronic national calamity'. All the problems were laid bare. Uniformity was completely lacking. Twenty unions had attempted to adopt the Casual Poor Act of 1882 whereby professional vagrants were detained for two nights and the genuinely unemployed, upon production of a ticket showing where they were last employed, were discharged and told where they might find work. Many unions had spent substantial sums on expanding their vagrant accommodation accordingly. In only five unions, however, had there been any decrease in vagrancy. Many unions did not have the accommodation to enforce two nights' detention and casual labour was still essential for hop picking. The conference, too, was dogged by the crucial problem of whether the unemployed in search of work should be deterred in the same way as the professional tramp.[184]

> The casuals are not all . . . habitual tramps. Sturdy mechanics from the North flock towards Dover in search of a job at the new harbour works. Men come in quest of employment at Shorncliffe camp . . . all the year round there is a stream of work seekers flowing towards Folkestone and its neighbourhood.[185]

179 SEG 5.3.1883, 14.5.1883, 24.5.1884.
180 SEG 25.1.1886.
181 KE 24.1.1885, 23.5.1885.
182 KE 28.6.1890.
183 KE 26.8.1893, 24.12.1898.
184 KE 17.3.1888, 3.11.1894, 2.2.1895, 10.8.1895.
185 KE 26.8.1893.

At Cranbrook vagrants had to be housed in tents in a field behind the workhouse. There were claims from Milton and Canterbury unions that stone pounding and detention had produced a fall in vagrant numbers in 1898 but by 1913 the poor law in Kent, as elsewhere, had still to find a suitable means to cope with large scale unemployment.[186]

(7) Conclusion

The immediate effect of the 1834 Act was to produce a dramatic fall in able bodied paupers and poor law expenditure. In the second report of the Poor Law Commissioners Tufnell eulogised over a reduction of 50%–94% of able bodied male paupers and their dependents in the Blean, Faversham, Milton, Sheppey and Bridge unions claiming a general financial saving of 50% countywide. On 20 August 1836 there were reported to be only five able bodied male paupers in the twelve East Kent unions. A succession of chairmen and officers of Kent unions, identified by Tufnell as likely to provide favourable reports, testified to the overnight regeneration of the Kentish labourer. Most, formerly receiving relief, had found work. Poaching and sheep stealing had diminished; beer shops were less frequented; savings on the poor rate had enabled farmers to employ more men; incendiarism had ceased; some labourers had migrated and the rest 'now go cap in hand asking for work as a favour'.[187] J. M. Cramp, chairman of Thanet union and a convert to the new system, described the Act as 'the kindest and best measure for the relief of the poor ever passed by the British legislature' while Tufnell optimistically questioned the need for 'those 500-pauper workhouses with which East Kent is studded . . . built for the able bodied'.[188]

Total county poor law expenditure plummeted from £345,878 in 1834 to £185,309 in 1837 and never approached the 1834 level again. In 1899–1900 it stood at £148,289.[189] The years 1831–5 were years of falling wheat prices and good harvests. Initial savings were undoubtedly made by the closure and sale of parish workhouses and cottages and concentration of paupers within fewer specialist institutions. There were savings, too, on salaries, legal expenses and purchase of supplies by open contract. Margate's poorhouse governor alone was paid £84 before reform. The Thanet union workhouse master received only £80. Assistant overseers disappeared. Sir John Tylden boasted that medical expenses paid by eighteen parishes under the old system were nearly as large as 'the whole of the present union expenditure'.[190] The new system also brought an end to many of the abuses of the Old Poor Law which might have been practised by surplus labourers,

---

[186] KE 31.8.1895, 5.11.1898.
[187] PP 1836, XXIX. 2nd Annual Report of the Poor Law Commission. Report of E. C. Tufnell on the County of Kent, pp. 195–214. Crowther, *op. cit.*, p. 34.
[188] *Loc. cit.*
[189] PP 1843, XXI. 9th Annual Report of the Poor Law Commission, Apppendix D, pp. 494–5. Annual Report of J. S. Davy, Local Government Board Inspector, January 1899–January 1900.
[190] Hopker, *op. cit.*, p. 53. CKS G/Mi AM1 Milton Guardians' Minutes, Address by Chairman, Sir John Tylden.

farmers or ratepayers. Application of the workhouse test, reduction of indoor and outdoor relief and the end of indiscriminate monetary relief produced a rapid fall in pauper numbers while railway building and the Dover Harbour Works offered alternative employment. In the parishes of Milton union a pauper population of 'near 2,000' fell to below 1,000. Men with families who depended on the parish for work dropped from 761 to 148.[191]

This apparent success, however, was short-lived. In most Kent unions expenditure began to rise again from 1839. County expenditure increased to £208,786 in the harsh winter of 1840–1 and remained at £206,715 in 1841–2.[192] This increase was reflected in the unions. In Cranbrook union, whose average expenditure in 1833–7 fell by 42%, total expenditure stood at £6,100 in 1839. In Tonbridge union outdoor relief costs increased from £4,769 in 1837 to £6,453 in 1839. Thanet union expenditure, which was 53% below the 1834 level in 1836–7, and 38% below in 1837–8, also began to climb again in 1839.[193] When severe weather and harvest problems presented their challenge in the hungry forties the New Poor Law was found wanting. In December 1837 Cranbrook guardians stated that the number of able bodied receiving relief had fallen substantially since formation of the union but denied that 'the circumstances of these paupers had as yet materially, if at all, improved.'[194] While the Old Poor Law reduced wage rates the New Poor Law did not lead to any substantial increase. Many contemporaries would have agreed with Samuel Bagshaw that if the cost of building new workhouses was taken into account 'the ratepayer has not been much benefited nor yet the condition of the poor at all ameliorated'.[195]

The new bastardy legislation, which placed the onus upon the woman, and, if destitute, forced her to enter the workhouse, was again greeted by Kent union chairmen with claims which were premature. 'The reduction in the number of illegitimate children is sufficiently remarkable to deserve especial notice', stated the chairman of Faversham union. 'The bastardy regulations have proved a very important check to the birth of illegitimate children as the new laws have been to improvident marriages . . .', re-iterated the East Ashford chairman.[196] Nationally, however, illegitimacy increased in the period 1830–42. In Kent there was initially a slight decrease with 1,428 illegitimate children registered in 1832–4 as opposed to 1,360 in 1835–7 – an average of 476 as opposed to 453 per annum. Numbers rose, however, to 904 in 1842, 982 in 1851 and in 1859 1,082 or 6.1% of the population of extra-metropolitan Kent.[197]

[191] *Ibid.* PP 1836, XXIX. 2nd Annual Report of Poor Law Commission, pp. 198–200.
[192] PP 1843, XXI. 9th Annual Report of Poor Law Commission, Comparative Statement of expenditure for relieving the Poor. PP 1840, XXXIX, pp. 425–31. Accounts and Papers, Abstract of Returns of Workhouses and expenditure of unions 1836–9.
[193] Todd, *op. cit.*, pp. 101–2. PP 1840, XXXIX. Hopker, *op. cit.*, p. 53.
[194] Todd, *op. cit.*, p. 113.
[195] Bagshaw, *op. cit.*, vol. 2, p. 18.
[196] PP 1836, XXIX, p. 207.
[197] W. G. Lumley, 'Observations upon the Statistics of Illegitimacy', *Journal of Statistical Society*, 25 (1862), pp. 222–3, 227.

Despite the increased central emphasis on indoor relief and the continued harsh treatment of the casual poor, a gradual improvement in the treatment of Kent's deserving poor is perceptible from the 1860s, reflecting a change of spirit nationally. In November 1866 a conference presided over by the Bishop of Rochester advocated improved classification in workhouses, removal of workhouse children to proper educational institutions and better treatment of the sick poor. 'Poverty seeking relief', stated one delegate, 'should no longer be treated as a crime'.[198] Greenwich guardians in 1861 had already resolved to erect a range of apartments for married inmates over sixty who had previously been separated. Ten years later the Poor Law Inspector ordered Canterbury guardians to provide looking glasses for the aged, children and sick and emphasised that workhouse married quarters should be used solely for that purpose.[199] Canterbury workhouse medical officer in 1867 proposed the installation of a few pictures 'to break the monotony of the dead walls'. West Ashford union established a small library in 1869.[200] The new Thanet union hospital, opened in 1862, had lavatories, baths and numerous rooms for its four infirmary wards. Canterbury workhouse infirmary was heated in 1876 'for the greater comfort of the inmates'. By 1879 Malling guardians had decided to employ professional as opposed to pauper nurses.[201] Sevenoaks union in 1892 modified the workhouse dress of the deserving poor so that they were not identifiable outside the house. Faversham's tea and sugar allowance to women was doubled in 1894. Tonbridge guardians substituted a Sunday meat dinner for bread and cheese in 1896 while Thanet union awarded tea, sugar and milk to its old women in accordance with a Local Government Board order in 1897. Maidstone's elderly male inmates were awarded a weekly ounce of tobacco in 1900 – a year in which the Board again pressed unions to provide better accommodation and greater liberty for the aged and deserving poor.[202] In response East Ashford union provided separate cubicles, lockers and an increased tobacco allowance for men together with four armchairs for the men's day room. While Canterbury workhouse library in 1858 was 'far more calculated for theological students about to take orders', New Romney union in 1900 asked the South Eastern Railway and the Chatham Railway to place boxes on their stations 'for the receipt of books, periodicals and papers for workhouse inmates'.[203] A sign of improving personal relationships was provided at Elham union where, in 1896, inmates collected for a wreath for the matron's dead father.[204]

Specialist care also increased slowly. The 1834 Act prohibited detention of dangerous lunatics and idiots in workhouses for over fourteen days. In 1836 of 468 Kent lunatics and idiots, 144 were confined in the county asylum and only 31 in

[198] SEG 20.11.1866.
[199] SEG 12.11.1861, 20.5.1871.
[200] SEG 3.12.1867, 3.5.1869.
[201] SEG 2.12.1862, 7.2.1876, 24.3.1879.
[202] KE 31.12.1892, 17.3.1894, 29.2.1896, 10.4.1897, 24.2.1900, 11.8.1900.
[203] KE 4.8.1900, 17.11.1900. MG 26.1.1858.
[204] KE 4.1.1896.

more expensive private asylums. A further 223 remained illegally in workhouses or were boarded out.[205] By 1840 'there had been . . . a great increase in this disease among the paupers of Kent' doubtless arising from the stresses of the age. In 1843, of 522 lunatics and idiots, 225 were in the county asylum and 54 were in licensed houses. 143 remained in union workhouses while 100 were still 'with friends'. The Act had therefore brought little progress. In 1879, however, guardians were authorised to subscribe to any asylum or institution for the deaf, dumb, blind or those suffering from any permanent disability and gradually the lot of lunatics and others improved.[206]

The final group to benefit from improved attitudes to the poor were Kent's numerous orphaned and deserted children. In 1839 Kent workhouses contained over 2,000 children, mostly orphaned or deserted. Five years later they held 1,033 orphaned and a further 330 deserted children. 3,246 widows receiving outrelief were responsible for a further 4,093 dependent children.[207] Early thinking on pauper children held that to give them education provided them with an unfair advantage over the children of independent labourers. For guardians, therefore, workhouse schools and their teachers had a low priority. Tufnell, however, quickly came to believe from Kent evidence that pauperism could only be eradicated if pauper children were sufficiently well-educated to be taken from the workhouse into employment and become independent adults. When Eastry and Tenterden guardians complained to him that they could not dispose of pauper children he severely criticised the teaching standards of workhouse schools and came out in favour of district schools common to several unions, staffed by superior teachers and free from the influence of masters, matrons and adult paupers.[208] Despite his championship of district schools they found little favour in Kent. Some Elham guardians supported them in 1853 on the grounds that the education of pauper children prepared them neither for service or agricultural labour but even here a bid to petition for their general establishment was defeated.[209] Instead some Kent unions, such as Hoo and later Sheppey, sent their pauper children to local National schools or maintained their own workhouse schools.[210] Tufnell, himself, who visited the union schools of Medway, Canterbury, Sheppey and Tenterden as Government Inspector of Workhouse Schools in the 1850s found them satisfactory or above.[211]

In a further attempt to make pauper children more marketable some Kent unions

---

[205] PP 1837, XLIV. Return relating to Lunatic Paupers and Idiots, pp. 2–5.
[206] MG 28.7.1840. PP 1844, XL. Pauper lunatics and idiots chargeable to each of the unions in England and Wales in August 1842 and 1843, pp. 24–5.
[207] Report of E. C. Tufnell on the Education of Pauper Children published in MG 5.11.1839. PP 1844, XL. Accounts and Papers (534). Return of Orphan Children and Children deserted by parents in workhouses, p. 2.
[208] Report of E. C. Tufnell on the Education of Pauper Children published in MG 5.11.1839, 12.11.1839.
[209] MG 27.12.1853.
[210] CMS G/Ho, Hoo Guardians' Minutes, 4.2.1841. KE 27.6.1896.
[211] SEG 24.5.1853, 13.12.1853, 3.10.1854, 19.12.1854, 11.8.1859.

turned also to industrial training and boarding out. In 1882 Thanet guardians, discussing the rapid return of workhouse girls sent to service, concluded that this was because they received no domestic training except scrubbing floors. In 1888 Milton guardians appointed an industrial trainer at £25 per year.[212] Boarding out was intended to rescue children from the debilitating environment of the workhouse. West Ashford guardians began boarding out in 1881 despite doubts as to whether farmers could provide adequate training. Maidstone and Elham followed in 1887 and Tenterden in the 1890s. Hoo commenced in 1912. Children were placed with cottagers for a weekly sum. Their welfare was cared for by a committee of ladies besides the guardians.[213] The next step was the establishment of cottage homes where children could be separated from regular inmates and properly educated. Elham union was the pioneer largely owing to the indefatigable efforts of Colonel Symes, an ex officio guardian. Elham's cottage homes opened at Cheriton in December 1888 and an appeal was launched for toys and pictures. Thanet followed in 1899 and a year later the Local Government Board inspector recommended Sevenoaks union to do the same.[214]

By 1900 only 2.4% of Kent's population was in receipt of indoor or outdoor relief as opposed to 11% in 1801. The nature of poverty, too, had changed. In most South Kent workhouses by 1895 able bodied men were conspicuous by their absence and able bodied women so few that 'they hardly suffice for the necessary domestic work of the house'. It was, instead, the sick, aged and infirm who 'greatly preponderated' and for whom the Local Government Board was recommending 'milder treatment'. Kent unions were largely prepared to comply with this recommendation although many boards still adamantly refused to countenance any change in outdoor relief. In 1900 the chairman of West Ashford union bluntly stated that he did not believe in outdoor relief at all.[215]

By the Edwardian Age the new or adapted workhouses of the 1830s and 1840s were also growing old and unsusceptible to the changes in organisation and classification proposed by the Board. The view of Mr Terry, an Elham rural guardian who saw no need for 'pauper palaces', was still not uncommon but Old Age Pensions, which some Kent boards had already tentatively discussed, were not far away.[216]

---

[212] SEG 27.3.1882. KE 29.9.1888.
[213] KE 8.1.1881, 31.12.1887, 2.9.1899, 14.10.1899. CMS G/Ho WRM, Hoo Workhouse Master's Journal, February 1912.
[214] KE 17.3.1888, 22.12.1888, 2.9.1899.
[215] Davy, op. cit. KE 8.2.1895, 6.10.1900, 17.11.1900.
[216] SEG 1.6.1868, 26.3.1883. KE 5.3.1887, 11.10.1890, 25.7.1891, 11.5.1895, 22.5.1897, 14.1.1899, 6.10.1900.

Epidemics and Public Health 1640–1914

(1) Smallpox and Early Medical Provision

From the second half of the seventeenth century bubonic plague was superseded by smallpox as the most dreaded epidemic disease. An outbreak at Folkestone in 1720 brought 145 deaths.[1] Sixty-one of 503 smallpox cases died at Dover and 33 of 362 cases at Deal in 1725–6. 1,385 Canterbury residents were attacked in 1729 and 140 died.[2] At Dartford, visited in 1741, 'the country people became so alarmed that the market was nearly deserted and did not recover for some years.'[3] Inoculation throughout Kent, however, was virtually unknown in 1724. Seventy more smallpox victims died in Maidstone in 1753 and over a hundred in 1760.[4] During the two decades 1740–63 'the speckled monster' accounted for 28% of all deaths in the county town.[5] Five years later 158 more victims were carried off at Folkestone.[6]

In July 1766 Maidstone vestry invited the controversial inoculator, Daniel Sutton, to conduct a general inoculation and several hundred Maidstone residents were inoculated in one session. During the autumn Sutton transferred his Kent business to his partner, a surgeon named Peale. By October Peale had over 600 patients in his care including some of the county aristocracy. By early 1767 he had inoculated some 2,000 persons in Kent as part of the general revival of the practice in the southern counties.[7] Other inoculators were also at work such as Watson in Romney and Charles Kite in Gravesend.[8] John Howlett, a contemporary clergyman, was convinced that inoculation brought a reduction in smallpox mortality in Kent and elsewhere:

> In the 30 years before that date (1766) smallpox deprived the town (Maidstone) of between five and six hundred of its inhabitants whereas in the 15 or 16 years that have elapsed since that general inoculation it has occasioned the deaths of only about 60 . . .[9]

---

[1] C. H. Bishop, *Folkestone*, London 1973, p. 71.

[2] Charles Creighton, *A History of Epidemics in Britain*, vol. 2, Cambridge 1894, p. 519. Duncan Harrington, 'An outbreak of smallpox in Canterbury', *Kent Family History Society Journal*, 1 (December 1974), pp. 10–15.

[3] J. Dunkin, *History of Dartford*, 1844, p. 397. Cit. J. Smith, *The Speckled Monster*, Chelmsford 1987, pp. 21–2.

[4] Creighton, *op. cit.*, p. 470. J. M. Russell, *The History of Maidstone*, re-printed Rochester 1978, p. 236.

[5] Smith, *op. cit.*, p. 61. Russell, *op. cit.*, p. 236.

[6] Bishop, *op. cit.*, p. 71.

[7] Creighton, *op. cit.*, pp. 495–509. Smith, *op. cit.*, pp. 79–80.

[8] Smith, *op. cit.*, p. 83. Creighton, *op. cit.*, p. 515.

[9] J. Howlett, *Observations on the Increased Population . . . of Maidstone*, 1782, p. 8. Cit. Peter Razzell, *The Conquest of Smallpox*, 1977, p. 152.

Not all inoculations were successful. The death of William Marten, aged twenty-five, at Meopham in 1761 was 'unhappily procured by inoculation'. Two Headcorn infants also succumbed in 1784. Maidstone statistics on smallpox mortality 1740–99, compiled by Peter Razzell, certainly suggest, however, a dramatic reduction in the three decades after 1764.[10] Other evidence comes from the Kent countryside where smallpox was equally endemic but more intermittent. John Haysgarth cites three Kent parishes with only ten smallpox deaths in twenty years. At Cowden there were recurring outbreaks in 1730, 1739, 1747, 1750, 1756 and 1761. In these circumstances vestries authorised parish doctors to inoculate the poor. In 1769 the Orpington overseers paid 'an Apothecary or Docktor to inoculate all the poor inhabitants . . . at the expense of the parish'. In 1807, Cowden's parish doctor received £13 2s 6d for inoculating 105 parishioners at 2s 6d each.[11]

Howlett again claimed beneficial results. At Great Chart, where 'almost 100' of the 192 burials in 1683–1707 resulted from smallpox, in the twenty years beginning in 1760 there appears to have been only four or five who died.[12] Creighton, on the other hand, claimed that smallpox in Britain was little touched by inoculation.[13] While the expansion of inoculation after 1766 may have contributed to Kent's population growth even when joined and, in 1840, superseded by Jenner's safer cowpox vaccination, administered free by union medical officers, it did not eradicate smallpox which continued to spread death and disfigurement throughout the nineteenth century. In June 1814 a surgeon was paid to vaccinate 35 Dymchurch parishioners.[14] In 1819 Snave vestry 'thought it right to have Poor children . . . Enoculated with the Cow Pox as the Doctor recommended Eacelly (equally) Safe . . .'[15] Nevertheless Kent, and particularly Canterbury, suffered severely during the national epidemic of 1817–19 and, despite large scale vaccination by the Kent and Canterbury Hospital, smallpox recurred in the city in 1823–5.[16] The great epidemic of 1837–40 produced 817 deaths in extra-metropolitan Kent.[17] Four hundred people of all ages were vaccinated at Goudhurst in May 1849 when smallpox became prevalent there.[18] Thereafter, while the disease remained omnipresent, there was no further major outbreak until the final great epidemic of 1871–2 when the extra-metropolitan Kent death roll was 537.[19]

---

[10] C. H. Golding-Bird, *The History of Meopham*, London 1934, p. 186. Duncan Harrington, 'Smallpox Inoculation Deaths', *Local Population Studies*, 18 (Spring 1977), p. 58. Razzell, *op. cit.*, p. 143.

[11] Creighton, *op. cit.*, p. 527. Guy Ewing, *The History of Cowden*, Tunbridge Wells 1926, pp. 178–9. F. Chevenix Trench, *The Story of Orpington*, Bromley 1897, p. 40.

[12] J. Howlett, *An Examination of Dr. Price's Essay on the Population of England and Wales*, 1781, p. 83. Cit. Smith, *op. cit.*, p. 60.

[13] Creighton, *op. cit.*, p. 517.

[14] *William Harvey and 400 Years of Medicine in Kent*, Maidstone 1978, p. 11. (C)entre for (K)entish (S)tudies. P125/8/1 Dymchurch Vestry Minutes 1814.

[15] CKS P341/12/1 Snave Vestry Minute Book 1819.

[16] Creighton, *op. cit.*, pp. 577–8, 581. Smith, *op. cit.*, pp. 110–11.

[17] Creighton, *op. cit.*, p. 615.

[18] *(M)aidstone (G)azette*, 22.5.1849.

[19] Creighton, *op. cit.*, p. 615.

While smallpox produced high mortality in epidemic years more regular if less spectacular mortality arose from tuberculosis, typhus, typhoid, influenza, scarlatina and diphtheria. These, although often more widespread, tended to be eclipsed in the popular mind by smallpox as they had been subordinated to plague in the seventeenth century.[20] The forces ranged against these 'men of death' were slender. The connection between sickness and pauperism was already appreciated. Parishes were legally responsible for supporting the sick and their families so the sooner they could be cured the better. While small townships preferred to pay doctors separately per patient larger parishes often appointed a doctor who would submit an annual account. In March 1783 Shoreham vestry agreed that Thomas Waring should '. . . Attend the poor . . . as Apothecary and Surgeon . . . for a year at £4.3s.9d. To supply . . . with attendance and medisens all the poor . . . including all sickness and lameness, natural smalpox and all exidents . . .'.[21]

By 1815 the fee had increased over fivefold with an additional guinea for midwifery.[22] When hospital treatment was needed the poor were sent to the nearest hospital. West Kent parishes sent largely to the London hospitals. Dartford patients were sent to St Thomas's or Guy's and Farningham parishioners to St Bartholomew's. There was no general hospital for Kent poor until the opening of the Kent and Canterbury Hospital in 1793 which served the needs of both in and out patients.[23] Financed initially by a legacy it remained dependent upon donations, legacies and annual subscriptions. Donors and subscribers could recommend poor patients for treatment.

Patients, drawn largely from agricultural labourers and domestic servants, came from well beyond Canterbury since parishes were prepared to subscribe for its use by their poor. After the 1834 Poor Law Amendment Act some Kent unions became subscribers for twenty guineas a year. In-patients were rejected who were '. . . disordered in their senses or suspected to have the Smallpox, Itch, Venereal Disease or any other infectious disorder, who are not clean in Person or apparel or have inveterate Ulcers . . .'.[24] From 1804 it offered free vaccination against smallpox and by 1831 16,175 out-patients had been vaccinated. Dr Alfred Lochée, Honorary Physician to the hospital and President of the British Medical

[20] See C. W. Chalkin, *Seventeenth Century Kent*, London 1965, pp. 38–41. Creighton, *op. cit.*, p. 614. George Rigden, *The Sanatory Condition of Canterbury*, Canterbury 1847, lists in Canterbury in the period 1837–67, 9 epidemics of measles and whooping cough, 7 epidemics of scarlet fever and 6 of typhus/typhoid as opposed to 4 of smallpox. Mortality from typhus/typhoid (631 deaths) and scarlatina (322 deaths) was far greater than from smallpox (216). Rigden was surgeon to Canterbury Dispensary. A measles epidemic at Maidstone caused 47 deaths in 1832. (MG 31.1.1832.)

[21] Malcolm White and Joy Saynor, *Shoreham: a village in Kent*, Shoreham 1989, p. 117.

[22] *Ibid.*, p. 118.

[23] G. Porteus, *The Book of Dartford*, Dartford 1979, p. 79. Golding-Bird, *op. cit.*, p. 185. *William Harvey and 400 Years of Medicine in Kent*, pp. 16–17.

[24] *William Harvey . . .*, pp. 15–16. For fuller accounts of the hospital and its work see John Whyman, 'Medical Care at the Kent and Canterbury Hospital 1836–76', *Archaeologia Cantiana*, cv (1988), pp. 1–38 and F. M. Hall, Richard S. Stevens and John Whyman, *The Kent and Canterbury Hospital 1790–1987*, Canterbury 1987.

Association in 1861, claimed that its cures indicated 'a tolerable degree of success' while its records for 1836–76 reveal 'evidence of positive and beneficial care'.[25]

Hard on the heels of the Kent and Canterbury came the Margate Seabathing Infirmary opened in 1796 and also financed by subscription.[26] The first half of the nineteenth century saw also the appearance of dispensaries for the poor modelled on the London dispensaries. Ramsgate and St Lawrence Dispensary was founded in 1820. Tunbridge Wells 'Dispensary for Poor People' opened in 1829 and was followed in 1830 by the Maidstone Dispensary which subsequently developed into the West Kent hospital. A dispensary was mooted at Sheerness in 1834 and by 1850 there were others at Folkestone, Canterbury, Greenwich, Hawkhurst, Sandgate and Gravesend. All were based upon subscription with the right to recommend. A full-time dispenser or apothecary was paid a salary. Local doctors gave their services free.[27]

At Sittingbourne a medical club was established in 1836 with the support of Sir John Tylden, Chairman of the Milton Union. Covering the town and seventeen adjacent parishes it was 'to enable the labouring classes to ensure themselves medical and surgical attendance . . . independent of parochial aid'.[28] A third hospital, the Kent Ophthalmic, was founded in 1846. These apart, it was left to local overseers to create isolation hospitals in cottages or barns to reduce the rapid spread of epidemics. Like the Kent and Canterbury, the dispensaries also offered free vaccination.[29] Tunbridge Wells dispensary vaccinated 54 patients in its first year and Maidstone dispensary 3,483 in 1830–8.[30]

(2) The Cholera Epidemics

Smallpox was driven from the public mind by the dramatic onset of four epidemics of Asiatic Cholera which attacked Kent and the British Isles in the period 1831–66. Until 1817 cholera had been restricted to the swamps of Bengal and the Ganges Delta where it claimed thousands of victims. In 1817 it began to travel slowly eastward and westward along the trade routes of the world. By May 1831 it was at the Baltic coast and in October crossed to Sunderland. The cholera bacillus enters the intestine through food or drinking water contaminated by cholera excreta. Poor sanitation and water supply and the activities of flies are important contributory factors. Cholera spread rapidly, struck without warning and was highly virulent. In its early stages it was not always possible to separate from the more benign English cholera or summer diarrhoea. Essentially an urban disease it also found its way into the countryside.

---

[25] Whyman, *op. cit.*, pp. 37–8. *William Harvey . . .*, p. 16. MG 1.11.1836.

[26] *William Harvey . . .*, pp. 16–17.

[27] *(K)entish (G)azette*, 26.2.1830. MG 13.2.1834, 1.11.1836, 8.5.1838, 28.8.1838, 5.7.1848, 15.1.1850. *(S)outh (E)astern (G)azette*, 28.7.1857. Bishop, *op. cit.*, pp. 144–5.

[28] MG 19.7.1836.

[29] MG 9.11.1847, 13.8.1850.

[30] MG 5.2.1839.

Kent was particularly vulnerable as a maritime county with major ports and because of its proximity to London. It was also subject to an annual influx of seasonal migrant labour from the capital for hop picking. The presence of convict hulks and military barracks were additional concerns. In 1831 the government was pre-occupied with parliamentary reform and with the pacification of southern England after the Swing Riots and was, therefore, slow to react to the approach of a disease whose cause and cure were unknown. In the summer of 1831 'choleraic disorders' were already 'uncommonly rife' aboard the Medway warships.[31] In the autumn, in response to government instructions, the Kent ports imposed a strict quarantine on continental vessels.[32] Shots were fired at ships which did not comply and by 29 November Stangate Creek, the Medway quarantine station, was 'a forest of masts' with 200–300 sail under quarantine restrictions.[33] Quarantine was also imposed at Dover, Faversham, Whitstable, Milton and Ramsgate.[34]

Meanwhile a Central Board of Health, temporarily established in London, issued instructions for the creation of local boards of health consisting of magistrates, clergy and medical men in every town and village. A board was quickly established at Chatham which applied to the Admiralty for a hospital ship and to the Board of Ordnance to flush the drains. The Vagrant Act was enforced and the town divided into districts with a surgeon attached to each.[35] Gravesend, Maidstone, Tunbridge Wells, Sheerness, Faversham, Tonbridge, Dover and Ashford followed.[36] At Canterbury, a magistrate's meeting to discuss prevention proved abortive since 'several medical men made light of the matter' but a fortnight later a committee of parishes was established.[37]

Each board began the task of raising subscriptions to feed and clothe the poor; fumigate and limewash their homes; cleanse the streets and the drains; remove nuisances; and earmark buildings as hospitals.[38] Sandgate secured use of the military hospital at Shorncliffe Camp. Deal poor law officials were refused the North Infantry Barracks. Sheerness dockyard offered free medical care and full pay to employees suffering from cholera during their absence. Workers were denied entry to the yard if their families were attacked.[39]

During the winter cholera's progress was slow. London's first cases were not reported until February 1832.[40] The first Kent victim was a female vagrant from London who died in Rochester which had no board of health. A month elapsed before a Chatham seaman working on the London hoys also succumbed together

---

[31] Creighton, *op. cit.*, p. 795.

[32] MG 1.11.1831. KG 22.11.1831.

[33] MG 16.11.1831, 29.11.1831.

[34] MG 16.11.1831, 28.2.1832.

[35] MG 1.11.1831.

[36] CKS GR/AC 62. Minutes of Gravesend Cholera Morbus Committee, 22 October 1831. MG 8.11.1831, 16.11.1831, 22.11.1831.

[37] KG 4.11.1831, 18.11.1831.

[38] MG 8.11.1831, 16.11.1831, 22.11.1831. KG 6.12.1831.

[39] MG 16.11.1831, 21.2.1832. CKS De/A214. Letter from General Bryham to James Leeth of Deal, 9 November 1831.

[40] MG 14.2.1832.

with another victim in Rochester.[41] In April deaths increased with the warmer weather. The Mayor of Queenborough died followed by two young Milton children and the woman employed to clean the filthy hovel in which they had lived. Milton established a board of health but more cases followed at Dartford in May and aboard the convict ship *Cumberland* in June. Thirty-two of 198 victims ultimately died including the surgeon, two nurses and a guard. At Mile Town, Sheerness, twelve died within a few days. Most were 'persons in low circumstances'. Of more concern were three cases 'among the middle classes of society'.[42] The first Maidstone victim, a waterman, was struck down in June. Other outbreaks occurred at Dover, Upnor, Minster and Faversham. At the latter, where a dozen died, 'veget-able refuse and other filth were collected daily and pumps used to purify the town drains'.[43]

'We are happy to learn that this frightful disease has somewhat abated in the last two days . . .' reported the *Maidstone Journal* at the close of August.[44] In Minster, including Sheerness, which with 47 deaths from 103 cases had suffered most, the epidemic gradually subsided.[45] A handful of harvest labourers died at Eastchurch and Borden in the summer but compared with a London death roll of 5,275 and mortality in most other counties, Kent with 135 deaths and only eleven outbreaks, had escaped lightly.[46] Yet as the fatalities fell to a trickle, Mid-Kent received a foretaste of horrors to come.[47]

In early September, an acrimonious debate had ensued over whether hop pickers from places with cholera should be employed in Kent.[48] There was no way of stopping them and by late September cholera had claimed three 'strangers' hopping in the Farleighs and nine at Barming. By early October Barming had nineteen cases and a government cholera hospital on Barming Heath. A major epidemic was avoided by the rector who obtained the services of a doctor from a London cholera hospital. By mid-October the danger had passed but the lesson went unheeded.[49] Local boards were quickly disbanded and their work abandoned. A Chatham correspondent bemoaned the disappearance of the local board 'caused by the cruel notion that this awful visitation will confine itself . . . to the lower orders.'[50] The death of Lady Blane at Broadstairs at the height of the epidemic seemingly passed unnoticed.

In the seventeen years which followed cholera lingered on. Individual cases

[41] MG 27.3.1832.

[42] MG 17.4.1832, 29.5.1832, 12.6.1832, 19.6.1832, 3.7.1832.

[43] MG 26.6.1832, 10.7.1832, 17.7.1832, 31.7.1832.

[44] *(M)aidstone (J)ournal*, 28.8.1832.

[45] MG 14.8.1832, 21.8.1832, 2.10.1832.

[46] CKS P35 1/7 1832, Borden Burials Register. P127/1/6 Eastchurch Burials Register, 2 July 1832, 4 August 1832. Creighton, *op. cit.*, pp. 821–2.

[47] MG 21.8.1832, 18.9.1832, 20.9.1832, 23.10.1832.

[48] MG 11.9.1832.

[49] MG 18.9.1832, 27.9.1832, 9.10.1832, 16.10.1832.

[50] MG 23.10.1832.

periodically erupted into minor epidemics.[51] In 1834 there was an outbreak at Whitstable and, to the great embarrassment of the authorities, 28 cholera deaths at Herne Bay, a developing seaside resort, which made desperate efforts to suppress the adverse publicity.[52] In the same year cholera was again rife among Barming hop pickers. At East Farleigh thirteen were buried in a week 'and many at other places'.[53] In 1844 an outbreak in Blean union affected inmates of the workhouse. Seven of fourteen cases died at Gillingham in 48 hours in December 1848 and six months later Kent fell victim to the second major national epidemic.[54]

This time cholera was more widespread. Few Kent towns save Deal, Folkestone and Tunbridge Wells remained untouched. The outbreak began in Upper Rainham, in cottages to the rear of which lay a black ditch 'containing all sorts of abominable things'. Nine persons died as the parish authorities began whitewashing and fumi-gating and appropriated a large house as a hospital.[55] By July cholera was in Maidstone, Lewisham, Deptford, Greenwich, Gravesend, Dartford, Tonbridge, Canterbury, Chatham, Milton Regis workhouse and the convict ships at Woolwich.[56] Every possible remedy was attempted ranging from caramel and opium; purging; bleeding; mustard poultices; galvinisation in Maidstone; and burning tar barrels at Milton. Between July and November the Kent and Canter-bury Hospital treated some 675 patients with premonitory cholera symptoms. Local boards were hastily resurrected and a belated clean-up began.[57]

At Milton, where cholera spread rapidly from the workhouse to the inhabitants, 'the passing bell was discontinued'. At Chatham soldiers were confined to bar-racks and armed sentries posted at the gates.[58] In Gravesend, despite the provision of chloride of lime by the guardians, it was significant that the epidemic was '. . . almost exclusively confined . . . to the neighbourhoods where . . . poverty, hunger and dirt are the ruling tyrants . . . neighbourhoods that cause the Registrar's lists to show such a fearful mortality . . .'[59]

Margate and Ramsgate were hard hit but tried to conceal the severity of the attacks as Herne Bay had done in 1834. At the former it penetrated the Sea Bathing Infirmary where the resident surgeon was left to carry the dead from the wards. The marshy district of St Giles was again visited in 1849 when twelve persons in Blean union, mostly agricultural labourers and members of their families, died.[60] The most fatal outbreak, however, occurred at East Farleigh among some 2,000

[51] See MG 25.6.1833, 16.7.1833, 30.7.1833, 5.11.1833, 26.11.1839.
[52] MG 2.9.1834, 9.9.1834. Canterbury Archives U3/65. Herne St Martin Burials Register, 1834.
[53] MG 15.9.1835.
[54] Sharon Neate, 'Blean Union: the study of a Victorian Workhouse 1835–50', Dundee M.A. 1986, pp. 28–9. MG 12.12.1848.
[55] MG 19.6.1849, 25.9.1849, 2.10.1849, 16.10.1849. MJ 9.6.1849.
[56] MG 3.7.1849, 10.7.1849, 17.7.1849, 24.7.1849, 31.7.1849, 28.8.1849.
[57] MG 10.7.1849, 17.7.1849, 24.7.1849, 31.7.1849, 18.9.1849, 25.9.1849. Whyman, op. cit., pp. 34–5.
[58] MG 24.7.1849, 21.8.1849.
[59] MG 21.8.1849, 28.8.1849.
[60] MG 18.9.1849. Neate, op. cit., p. 53. Royal Sea Bathing Infirmary, Court of Directors' Minute Book 1826–51. Reports of Mr Field to Committee of Management, 4 September 1849, 11

hoppers, two thirds of whom were Irish, employed by Mr Ellis of Court Lodge Farm, the largest grower in Kent.[61] The epidemic broke out on 12 September. Dr Plomley of Maidstone, who arrived four days later, found an indescribable scene:

> . . . Sixty-two persons were suffering more or less from the disease. Four were in the agonies of death and eight more in the most profound collapse all of whom died before the following morning . . . The melancholy was much heightened by the almost incessant wailings of the Irish in 'waking' their lost friends.[62]

The local school was hastily converted into a hospital and a cholera ward prepared at the union workhouse. Plomley was joined by the union surgeon and other doctors including some from Guy's Hospital. A nursing team was created from the ladies of the district including the wives of the vicar and Thomas Rider, owner of Boughton Monchelsea Place. Roman Catholic priests from Tunbridge Wells and Sisters of Charity from London also helped. Nevertheless, of nearly 300 cases Rev. Henry Wilberforce buried 43 in a mass grave in East Farleigh churchyard. Over 30 more died among hop pickers at nearby Yalding and Loose.[63]

Cholera had killed 34 pickers at the same farm in 1834 but no lesson had been learned. Its basic cause was unknown and still hotly debated by miasmatists and contagionists. Its link with insanitary living conditions was already recognised and Plomley, who was quick to appreciate that local pickers who slept at home avoided infection, castigated the accommodation with which 'strangers' were provided.

> . . . the disease . . . arose entirely from causes which are remediable and removable; namely impure air arising from overcrowded and ill-ventilated apartments; impure water derived from wells containing the soakage of cow yards and human filth and impure food sold at a cheap rate by unprincipled itinerant vendors of putrid fish and adulterated bread.[64]

In one room of 700 cubic feet he found fourteen persons including a child suffering from cholera. The 'effluvium' was so powerful that he could not enter. Mortality for extra-metropolitan Kent in 1849 was 1,208 which was much below that of London and ten other counties in England and Wales.[65] Such precautions as had been taken again quickly lapsed. Only a bitter controversy as to whether medical responsibility for 'strangers' lay with the hop farmers or the Poor Law guardians lingered on.

A minor outbreak at Headcorn was transferred to Chart Sutton by Irish hop

---

September 1849. I am indebted to Dr John Whyman for kindly lending me his notes on this source.

[61] (P)arliamentary (P)apers, 1850, XXI. Appendix B to Report of the General Board of Health on the Epidemic Cholera of 1848 and 1849, pp. 26–7. MJ 18.9.1849.

[62] MG 18.9.1849, 16.10.1849.

[63] MG 18.9.1849, 25.9.1849, 16.10,1849.

[64] PP 1850, XXI.

[65] Creighton, *op. cit.*, pp. 843–4.

pickers in 1850.[66] The national outbreak of 1853 was small, sporadic and limited to North Kent.[67] Next year, however, 'the terrifying visitor' reappeared in all his fury sweeping through Canterbury, Greenwich, Sheerness, Maidstone, Sevenoaks, Milton and Tunbridge Wells. Ramsgate also suffered from the prevailing epidemic which penetrated into the countryside to High Halden, Sturry and Staplehurst. There were 1,186 cases in the 30 parishes of Eastry union.[68] At Deptford, where 'large accumulations of filth lay in the vicinity of the dwellings of the poor', 75 died. 2,914 diarrhoea cases were treated by Chatham dispensary in August and September. At Canterbury free medicines were provided by the hospital and dispensary. Handbills at Folkestone offered free treatment to the poor from a local chemist or the dispensary at any hour.[69] Nine hundred dysentery cases coincided at Tonbridge with 170 cases of cholera. Thirty-nine of the latter died and the medical services were overwhelmed.[70]

The most telling outbreak of 1854, however, occurred at the coastal watering place of Sandgate. Before 1848 Sandgate's sewage was discharged on the beach. There was no main sewer and nearly all wells were polluted.[71] In 1848 some ratepayers, alarmed at the high death rate, petitioned the General Board of Health to set up a local board. This was achieved, despite opposition, and considerable improvement was made in drainage and water supply.[72] On 24 August 1854, however, to the consternation of its inhabitants, a cholera outbreak caused 48 deaths. The enquiry which followed, while unable to attribute the epidemic to any specific cause, highlighted the nightmare of sanitary reformers throughout the century. Despite a large capital outlay the new drainage system was defective. The drains were blocked and leaking. The old cesspools were imperfectly closed. Private water supplies remained polluted while the public water supply was 'short in quantity and not unexceptionable in quality.'[73]

A total mortality of 1,056 in extra-metropolitan Kent was exceeded only in London and Lancashire.[74] Thirty-four men and seven local washerwomen died

---

[66] MJ 23.10.1849, 30.10.1849. CKS G/Hb Acb. Letter from Hollingbourne Union to General Board of Health, 21 October 1850.

[67] MJ 26.7.1853. SEG 25.10.1853, 1.11.1853, 15.11.1853.

[68] SEG 1.8.1854, 8.8.1854, 22.8.1854, 29.8.1854, 12.9.1854, 26.9.1854. MJ 9.9.1854, 14.10.1854. CKS G/Ea Aca. Eastry Union Correspondence. Clerk to Poor Law Board, 17 January 1855.

[69] SEG 12.9.1854, 19.9.1854, 14.11.1854. MJ 26.7.1854, 26.8.1854.

[70] M. Barker-Read, 'The Public Health Question in the Nineteenth Century: Public Health and Sanitation in a Kentish Market Town, Tonbridge 1850–1875', *Southern History*, iv (1982), pp. 179–80.

[71] Thomas Webster Rammell, *Report to the Board of Health on a preliminary enquiry into the sewerage, drainage and supply of water and the sanitary condition of the inhabitants of the Town of Sandgate*, 1849, pp. 12–15.

[72] *Ibid.* Also Thomas Webster Rammell, *Report to the General Board of Health on a further inquiry held in the town of Sandgate and the parishes of Cheriton and Folkestone in the County of Kent*, 1850.

[73] Ed. R. P. Hastings, *Cholera in Sandgate 1854*, Kent County Council 1982. Also Thomas E. Blackwell, *Report to President of General Board of Health on the Drainage and Water Supply of Sandgate in connection with the late outbreak of cholera in that town*, 1855.

[74] Creighton, *op. cit.*, pp. 852–3.

when cholera re-appeared in August 1855 among foreign legionnaires at Shorncliffe camp. Eleven years then elapsed before Kent's final major outbreak. In July 1866 the 'black illness' was again reported in London and aboard the *Queen of the Colonials* at Gravesend. From London it was carried by barge to Faversham, Sittingbourne, Maidstone, Sheerness and Aylesford. By late October it was in Chatham where three dispensaries were opened and the roads watered with diluted carbolic acid.[75] The Maidstone guardians persuaded the South Eastern Railway to take as many hop pickers as possible directly to the hop gardens to protect the town. Work was slow starting because of heavy rains. 'Hovels . . . into which the rain readily enters or old Crimean tents' were the only shelter. Inspectors were appointed to seize bad food from itinerant vendors but cholera appeared again at Yalding, Hunton, Nettlestead, Teston, Marden, Staplehurst, Otham, Bearsted and Barming. The awful mortality of 1849 was, however, avoided in the hop gardens and only 284 deaths ensued throughout extra-metropolitan Kent.[76] There was a frenzied clean-up as cholera again reached the Baltic provinces in 1871. Gravesend applied to use a naval vessel as a cholera hospital. Chatham obtained Gibraltar Tower, a Medway fort, for the same purpose.[77] Precautions, including quarantine, were again taken by Kent sanitary authorities in 1892 and 1893 but cholera did not materialise. The cholera visitations had been spectacular but nevertheless the overall effect of cholera mortality on Kent's population growth remained minimal.[78]

(3) Public Health Reform 1830–1871

Between 1801 and 1911 Kent's population more than quadrupled increasing from 308,667 to 1,511,806. Much of this increase was in metropolitan Kent or the ports and market towns. Urban density expanded with population. Housing increased from 98,320 dwellings in 1841 to 153,687 in 1891 but there was, for much of the century, no corresponding increase in drainage or water supply.[79]

The chaos of local administration hindered rapid improvement. Responsibility for water and sanitation rested at Sittingbourne with eighteenth century improvement commissioners. At Sandwich, Dover, Folkestone, Canterbury, Faversham, Rochester and Ramsgate it was with pavement commissioners whose powers were insufficient to cope with rapid urbanisation. Where a borough corporation existed power was often divided and relations strained.[80] Elsewhere authority rested with

---

[75] SEG 20.11.1855, 24.7.1866, 31.7.1866, 14.8.1866, 28.8.1866, 4.9.1866, 30.10.1866, 6.11.1866, 13.11.1866, 5.2.1867. KE 18.8.1866.

[76] KE 22.9.1866, 29.9.1866. SEG 25.9.1866, 2.10.1866. Creighton, *op. cit.*, p. 852.

[77] SEG 8.8.1871, 22.8.1871, 5.9.1871.

[78] KE 3.9.1892. J. D. Murray, *The Martial, Medical and Social History of the Port of Rochester, Kent* 1952, p. 15. See Alan Armstrong, 'The Population of Kent 1801–1914' in the forthcoming volume in this series *The Economy of Kent 1640–1914* and the same author's article on 'The Population of Victorian and Edwardian Kent' to be published in *Archaeologia Cantiana* (1995). I am indebted to Professor Armstrong for early sight of his work.

[79] Census 1801–1911.

[80] SEG 17.5.1864, 6.11.1866.

parish vestries. All such local authorities jealously guarded their rights from central interference and were terrified of the costs of improvement. When Walmer vestry enquired into sewerage to the sea it concluded it would be 'too expensive'. In 1849, when cholera ended, Maidstone Council reduced the salary of its nuisance inspector since '. . . the duties of an officer would not be so great . . .' Canterbury and Maidstone rejected adoption of the Local Government Act in 1865 because the ratepayers 'feared increased taxation'.[81] Sanitary progress was also impeded by ratepayers. In 1849 the *Maidstone Gazette* accused opponents of sanitary reform of '. . . opposing principally on mercenary grounds the sewerage and draining of the town'.[82] Drainage improvements at St Mary Cray were defeated by property owners whose properties required better drains. In 1871 a frustrated Canterbury local board member accused cottage owners of securing election 'to take care of themselves'. 'Had there been fewer', he stated, 'there would have been less obstruction to sanitary measures'.[83] In many towns powerful ratepayers' associations emerged to fight major improvement.[84]

Even if local authority sanction was obtained difficulties remained. Civil, and particularly sanitary engineering was a new and inexact science.[85] In 1858, Folkestone Waterworks Company was criticised for its lack of constant pressure and limited supply. The Dover Water Company's supply quickly became insufficient because of an enormous leakage which remained unsealed thirteen years later. Dartford waterworks, erected in 1853, was 'useless' while the 'fine new tower' of Sheerness waterworks collapsed before use in 1862.[86]

The laying of sewerage and water pipes in winter to give work to the unemployed did not ensure a service which was trouble-free. When Canterbury's new drainage system was completed in 1868 it was found that there was no water to flush it, the pipes were not watertight and the system flooded after only 20 houses had been connected.[87]

Most towns drained into rivers which meant further conflict. A proposal in 1856 to bring the outfall from London's sewerage into the Thames produced angry protest from Stone and Erith that the river would become '. . . a floating surface of pestilential matter . . . passing and re-passing the most thickly inhabited part of our parish . . .'[88] Eight years later Woolwich local board attributed the district's high mortality to the discharge of metropolitan sewage into the Thames near Barling creek.[89] When it was proposed that Maidstone's new drainage scheme should fall

81 MG 12.12.1848, 3.7.1849. SEG 29.11.1853, 21.3.1865, 18,8.1865.
82 MG 3.7.1849, SEG 10.1.1860.
83 SEG 30.11.1868, 5.12.1871.
84 SEG 15.2.1869, 24.1.1865, 8.7.1870.
85 See letter from J. C. Pilbrow to SEG 14.9.1871 in which he speaks of 'these experimental days'. Pilbrow was the controversial engineer to the Canterbury Sewerage works.
86 SEG 20.5.1856, 23.2.1858, 31.1.1860, 6.5.1862, 3.6.1863, 16.8.1864, 16.1.1866, 6.9.1869.
87 Audrey Bateman, 'Public Health in mid-nineteenth century Canterbury', Kent Diploma in Local History, 1988, 2350, p. 55. SEG 26.2.1861.
88 Bexley Local Studies Centre P137/8/2 Erith Vestry Minutes, 19 June 1856. CKS P352/8/2 Stone Vestry Minutes, 17 July 1856.
89 SEG 22.11.1865.

into the Medway, Aylesford complained to the Secretary of State. Ashford's entire outfall was discharged into the Stour making the river 'a stagnant cesspool'. Until 1883 Canterbury also discharged 1½ million gallons of sewage a day into the Stour near Fordwich bringing clashes with the River Commissioners.[90]

In view of these difficulties it is not surprising that sanitary reform was slow. The principal catalyst was cholera but even that did not bring immediate change.[91] In the aftermath of the first epidemic there was some minor improvement in water supply and paving at Maidstone. A waterworks company was established at Folkestone. Tonbridge and Tunbridge Wells began drainage schemes. The last was abandoned because of opposition from farmers. Elsewhere the lessons of 1832 were quickly forgotten.[92]

Evidence in Chadwick's *Report on The Sanitary Condition of the Labouring Population of Great Britain* in 1842 emphasised the fact that Kent's sanitary condition was unchanged.[93] A doctor on a vestry committee which examined the state of West Malling's Back Lane in 1843 found that 'the most abandoned rookery in St Giles does not contain so much of the elements of mischief to health as does the Back street'.[94] At Gillingham the road from the drawbridge was still saturated by the soil of leaky nightcarts and 'the stench during the hot weather was pestilential'.[95]

In 1846 the *Maidstone Gazette* violently criticised the insanitary condition of the River Len and the grossly overcrowded state of adjacent All Saints churchyard. '. . . Every south-west wind,' it stated 'must, . . . waft into the centre of the town the offensive exhalations of these two sources of malaria . . .'[96] Yet two years later a highly critical report of the sanitary condition of the town written by two local doctors in support of the Health of Towns Bill provoked a fierce reaction.[97] Similarly, despite the renewed threat of cholera, public meetings in 1848 at Rochester and Deal opposed the Bill 'in consequence of the great increase in taxation'.[98]

There was a spate of prosecutions in Kent towns under the Nuisance Removal and Diseases Prevention Act of 1846 before and during the 1849 outbreak particularly regarding yards storing manure.[99] Many prosecutions were instituted by local boards of health created by the Public Health Act of 1848 which not only established a General Board of Health for a trial period of five years but created the possibility of local boards or single health authorities. The Act was only mandatory

[90] SEG 10.1.1865, 15.2.1869, 19.7.1869, 15.8.1870. Audrey Bateman, *Victorian Canterbury*, Canterbury 1991, pp. 91, 122.

[91] SEG 4.9.1866.

[92] MG 30.7.1839, 23.4.1844, 8.9.1846, 7.12.1847, 11.9.1849, 31.10.1849.

[93] Ed. M. W. Flinn, Edwin Chadwick, *Report on the Sanitary Condition of the Labouring Population of Great Britain*, 1842, re-printed Edinburgh University Press, 1965, pp. 76–7, 88–9.

[94] CKS P 243/8/1 West Malling Parish Vestry Book, 13 December 1843.

[95] MG 26.9.1843.

[96] MG 29.12.1846.

[97] See Report on the Sanitary Condition of Maidstone by Drs F. Plomley and D. Walker in MG 2.2.1848, 29.2.1848, 7.3.1848, 10.3.1848, 4.4.1848, 25,4.1848. Also MG 27.2.1849.

[98] MG 11.4.1848, 12.12.1848.

[99] MG 9.1.1849, 30.1.1849, 28.8.1849, 4.9.1849.

where the death rate exceeded 22 per 1000 or if a tenth of the ratepayers petitioned. In this event an enquiry was held by a superintending inspector and a report produced. The General Board, however, could not insist that the local board carried out suggested reforms. Consequently much potential improvement was impeded by ratepayers or local improvement commissioners.

Sheerness, Dover and Chatham petitioned for local enquiries. At Sheerness, where 'the offal of a population of eight thousand lay upon the streets,' the only drain was the town ditch overflowing with black and stagnant matter.[100] Water supply was inadequate and drainage plans drawn up by W. Ranger, the General Board inspector, remained unimplemented in 1854 because of cost.[101] At Dover when Dr Soulby, a local improvement commissioner and reformer, warned that cholera would return a counter petition of ratepayers claimed that the town was healthy and did not require implementation of the Public Health Act. Ranger also visited Chatham and Dartford. At the latter, where the only sewer spread liquid over the principal thoroughfare, a strong 'dirty party' also emerged and implementation of legislation proved difficult.[102] A petition from Whitstable was not even pursued since local opposition was considered too powerful.[103]

At Margate, where 'the capabilities of the sewers were totally inadequate', 400 ratepayers petitioned the General Board over the town's sewerage in September 1849. When the government inspector recommended sweeping changes in drainage, sanitation and water supply at a cost of £18,000 opposition soon crystallised.[104] Neighbouring Ramsgate improved its sewers somewhat in 1852. A new Tonbridge waterworks also opened in July 1852. The ceremony was marred by a cesspool from the town drain producing an 'intolerable stench'.[105] At Canterbury reformers claimed that 'a well-directed effort of sanitary reform would save an immense amount of money' but even the economic argument made no headway and inhabitants of the cathedral city remained obliged to keep their windows closed to exclude the smells from the slaughter houses and ninety uncapped drains. Deal's nightsoil remained deposited within two minutes walk from the town centre while Sevenoaks also boasted 'a square, open dunghill in its midst'.[106]

The renewed approach of cholera re-emphasised the inactivity of boards of health. At Sheerness, where a board had existed for four years, not one of the original nuisances had been removed.[107] Chatham Board circulated handbills warning of cholera's approach but this was scant comfort to the occupants of houses

[100] *The Times*, 28.10.1848.
[101] CKS UD/Sh/Am 1/1 Minutes of Sheerness Local Board of Health, 19 September 1850, 25 November 1852, 31 August 1854. MG 2.10.1849.
[102] Robert Rawlinson, *Report to the General Board of Health on the Sanitary Condition of Dover*, 1849. MG 6.3.1849, 23.7.1850, 20.4.1852, 2.11.1852, 15.3.1853, 19.4.1853, 10.5.1853, 31.5.1853, 4.6.1853, 12.7.1853, 19.7.1853.
[103] R. A. Lewis, *Edwin Chadwick and the Public Health Movement 1832–54*, London 1952, p. 286.
[104] MG 3.7.1849, 25.9.1849, 16.10.1849, 4.2.1850, 21.5.1850, 28.2.1851, 21.10.1851, 17.2.1852.
[105] MG 21.11.1850, 6.4.1852, 18.5.1852. SEG 27.7.1852.
[106] MG 4.5.1852. SEG 18.8.1852, 31.8.1852, 12.7.1853, 27.9.1853.
[107] SEG 27.9.1853.

abutting the High Street 'where should the cholera visit us its victims would be . . . most numerous'.[108] Local boards and boards of guardians again began the panic-stricken flushing of sewers and a spate of prosecutions for nuisances.[109] Despite the clearance of 170 nuisances at Margate, the board, in the wake of the epidemic, postponed implementation of sewerage improvements on cost grounds. When the bed and banks of the Stour were cleaned at Canterbury for £150 an alderman from the 'Dirty Party' claimed he could have done what was needed for £10.[110]

The General Board of Health ended in 1854 but was renewed annually until 1858 when the Public Health Act replaced it by the Medical Office of the Privy Council from which John Simon's inspectors instituted enquiries into every aspect of health. Local activity was also accelerated by the Nuisances Removal Act of 1855 which empowered parishes to establish committees to remove nuisances and appoint sanitary inspectors, although often unpaid. A number of Kent parishes appointed such committees like Sevenoaks and Rainham, where an unpaid sanitary inspector was entitled to charge for the removal of manure. At Preston near Faver-sham a nuisance inspector, with a salary of £5 a year, was expected to remove all nuisances and to inspect the parish twice yearly.[111] Finally the Sanitary Act of 1866 made authorities liable for prosecution for failure to provide drainage,water supply or remove nuisances. Assisted by this legislation and two further epidemics a slow and often almost imperceptible improvement began.

As awareness of the inter-relationship between water supply, cleansing and sewerage increased there was an expansion of water provision after mid century. '. . . It is water which is needed to make the town pure', wrote a Sevenoaks correspondent in 1862. Folkestone Water Company was founded in 1848 although its open reservoir had become a potential health hazard by 1870. A Dover reservoir and waterworks began in June 1854. The reservoir held 500,000 gallons and was built with 2 million bricks. Other private water companies were established at Chatham in 1855 and Margate next year. The latter supplied 1,500 households and was extended in 1866. The Chatham and Rochester waterworks did not have mains throughout the district until 1862. A year later it supplied water to 1,970 houses in Old and New Brompton, Chatham and Rochester.[112]

Before 1800 the town, fort and dockyard at Sheerness had received fresh water from Chatham in barrels. In 1856 the only supply came from three wells. A loan of £7,000 was obtained in 1858 and by 1865 a waterworks was approaching comple-tion and 1,780 of 2,200 houses were connected to its mains.[113] Sandgate and Margate began work on waterworks in 1859 and a works was finished at

[108] SEG 27.9.1853.
[109] SEG 18.10.1853, 15.11.1853, 13.12.1853, 8.8.1854, 29.8.1854.
[110] SEG 4.10.1853, 21.2.1854, 5.12.1854.
[111] CMS P296/8/3 Rainham Vestry Book, 12 September 1857. CKS P294/8/1 Preston Vestry Book, 25 March 1856.
[112] SEG 27.6.1854, 28.11.1854, 17.7.1855, 29.4.1856, 28.7.1857, 2.9.1862, 1.9.1863, 19.9.1865, 23.10.1866, 28.2.1871. Bishop, op. cit., p. 107.
[113] SEG 18.11.1856, 21.12.1858, 3.1.1865.

Broadstairs in 1860.[114] An Act for a North-West Kent Waterworks Company to supply Erith, Bexley, Bexley Heath, Eltham, Crayford and Dartford was passed in 1861. Previously Dartford's sole supply had been from private wells often polluted by cesspools. Dover determined to upgrade its existing waterworks in 1860 and Ashford in 1868. A company to supply pure water to Faversham was mooted in 1863. Tunbridge Wells, in an early example of municipal socialism, bought up the Calverley Water Company in 1867.[115] Other communities also began to investigate improved water supplies. Cranbrook consulted an engineer in 1858. Headcorn investigated the possibility in 1859 and Herne Bay decided to establish a water-works in 1866. A new works opened at Wincheap, Canterbury, in 1870 and at Sittingbourne Keycol Hill Waterworks opened in 1871.[116]

At Maidstone, where authority still lay with the Pavement Commissioners, the battle was hard fought. The principal supply was piped to conduits from Rocky Hill across the Medway. Water also came from pumps, wells and springs. By late 1859, after ten years of prevarication, only 12,000 gallons of good water per day were supplied to the town's 24,000 inhabitants and people waited for hours to procure water from the conduits. Of six plans proposed each had its protagonists on the town council. Ultimately, however, despite a petition signed by 1,000 of the town's 'largest ratepayers and most influential inhabitants', a company was estab-lished to pipe water from wells near Farleigh Lock to Maidstone. By March 1861 over 200 navvies were constructing the boiler house at Barming Heath and laying pipes for the works of the Maidstone Water Company which formally opened in October 1861.[117] The Sevenoaks Water Company, established in 1863, had laid mains through nearly every street by 1865.[118]

Hand in hand with better water went some progress in administrative reform and sanitary provision. Margate Town Council took the powers of a Local Board in 1857. Milton applied the Public Health Act in 1858. Tunbridge Wells applied to adopt the Local Government Act in 1864 and Sevenoaks in 1871.[119] Administrative reform coupled with publication of the Registrar General's annual statistics of mortality often led in turn to sanitary enquiries sometimes resulting from local initiative and sometimes conducted by the Privy Council who then produced loans for improvement.

In 1864, stunned by the Registrar General's revelation of a death rate of 22 per 1000, a mortality above that of all England which placed it last in the country's 27 principal watering places, Margate conducted a local continuation of the 1849 inquiry.[120] Next year a government enquiry, arising from an application to adopt

---

114 SEG 12.4.1859, 23.8.1859, 14.2.1860.
115 SEG 24.12.1861, 1.9.1863, 9.4.1867, 19.10.1868.
116 SEG 18.5.1858, 16.8.1859, 18.12.1866, 11.4.1870, 2.5.1870, 29.8.1871, 5.9.1871.
117 SEG 17.7.1855, 16.10.1855, 17.7.1856, 5.10.1858, 19.10.1858, 14.12.1858, 16.8.1859, 22.11.1859, 6.12.1859, 13.3.1860, 20.3.1860, 27.3.1860, 17.4.1860, 15.5.1860, 9.8.1860, 29.10.1861.
118 SEG 3.3.1863, 14.3.1865.
119 SEG 1.12.1857, 4.5.1858, 11.10.1864, 3.6.1871.
120 SEG 25.5.1864.

the Local Government Act, revealed that many densely populated parts of Canterbury had no drainage whatsoever; that the Pavement Commissioners, whom the 'Dirty Party' supported, had no powers for reform and that sewage from a number of cottages passed through an open dyke into the Stour which supplied many residents with domestic water.[121] A similar enquiry in 1867 at Ramsgate, where 'sewage from 600 dwellings poured into a gully under the West Cliff and from thence into the harbour,' revealed that two thirds of the town required sewerage and recommended that all cesspools should be removed. Plans, however, were not adopted until 1871.[122] There were other Privy Council enquiries at New Town, Speldhurst, whose drainage was 'a crying evil' and at Chatham and Rochester. Rochester in 1867 had no main drainage but a proposal that the corporation should become a board of health was accepted in principle only. During the Chatham enquiry Holborne Lane was described by a local board member as 'the dirtiest place in the world'.[123]

After the Privy Council report, Speldhurst was pressed to submit drainage plans within six weeks. At Ashford and Milton the Privy Council also attempted to exert pressure. At Ashford, where the main drains had been built by a succession of parish surveyors, increasing pollution of the Stour and high mortality from scarlatina and typhoid resulted in plans from the engineer, Baldwin Latham. His proposals were attacked by the local vicar on grounds of expense and that extensive opening of drains would damage trade. No progress was made.[124] The Milton enquiry showed that not only was the local sanitary inspector illiterate but the township's death rate from fever was the highest in the kingdom. The Milton Improvement Commissioners were not only terrified of expense but also afraid that they would be forced into a joint water scheme with neighbouring Sittingbourne.[125] Since the Privy Council lacked teeth progress was difficult. Sewerage improvement was also discussed at Staplehurst, Cranbrook, Lenham and Edenbridge but nothing was done.[126] In the larger towns the availability of a good water supply did not mean that good drainage automatically followed.

At Maidstone, the powers of the Pavement Commissioners, created for a town of 7,000, were inadequate for an expanding community of 30,000. The streets were only half sewered and the town 'filled with cesspools'. On the growing estates to the west not 'one in fifty of the new houses had cesspools connected to the town drain' thus creating a principal source of mortality. Only 532 houses out of 4,200 were connected to the public sewers. Rows of cottages had 30–40 people to one privy. The Local Government Act was adopted in 1866. An attempt to reverse the decision failed and the council agreed in 1867 to introduce a system of drainage. Here unanimity ended. Almost ten years had elapsed since a scheme 'which would

121 SEG 25.7.1865, 1.8.1865.
122 SEG 12.3.1867, 19.10.1867, 10.2.1868, 30.3.1868, 23.9.1871, 7.10.1871.
123 SEG 20.1.1868, 17.5.1869, 16.5.1870, 11.7.1870, 27.6.1871.
124 SEG 15.8.1870, 8.11.1870, 15.11.1870, 29.11.1870, 15.8.1871.
125 SEG 25.7.1870.
126 SEG 9.6.1863, 15.3.1869, 16.5.1870, 14.1.1871.

be thoroughly efficient but not necessarily costly,' had been proposed by Mr Wickstead, a Westminster civil engineer. This was now replaced by a scheme from Baldwin Latham to drain into the Medway which immediately met serious opposition from Aylesford. Councillors were divided over the best system to install and it was twelve years before Maidstone obtained a proper sewerage system.[127]

At Canterbury, where opposition to adopting the Local Government Act was even more vigorous, James Pilbrow's drainage scheme, undertaken in 1867, was a failure compounded by a lack of water from unconnected water closets in poorer dwellings and by 1871 only 1,200 of 4,000 houses were connected to the sewer.[128] Folkestone adopted a drainage scheme proposed by Joseph Bazalgette in 1866. There was some improvement but the drains had a bad reputation and in 1875 Lord Robert Montagu criticised them in the Commons.[129] Margate secured its local board in 1866. The local surveyor described the town as 'perfectly riddled with cesspools'. Bazalgette was consulted and in 1871 the council adopted by a majority of one a proposal for sea drainage which was felt to be cheaper and healthier. The waterworks was purchased to provide a water supply for sewerage improvement but it was not until 1890 that Margate's sewerage was properly completed.[130] Local politics, economy and imperfect knowledge of sanitary engineering held back sanitary reform until after the setting up of the Local Government Board in 1871. In the meantime the '. . . lanes and alleys in Sevenoaks were as bad as any in the back streets of London' and the township's sewage flowed into Knole House paddock and the railway cutting despite the threat of legal action by the South Eastern Railway.[131]

During nineteenth century urban expansion little notice was taken of building standards or the housing conditions of the urban or rural poor. The Public Health Act permitted creation of by-laws for sanitation. Ashford Board rejected them since they would increase housing costs and because other Kent towns did not have them. By the late 1860s, however, Maidstone Board was prosecuting for contravention of local by-laws. So, too, were boards at Bromley and Chatham. Such scrutiny, however, could not reduce chronic overcrowding which was blamed by the Privy Council doctor for the Woolwich typhoid epidemic of 1864.[132] The Folkestone Improvement Act of 1855 produced demolition of some slum property.[133] In contrast, 'something like 135 persons living in Margate High Street property disseminating fever and pauperism' were town council tenants. Rural conditions differed little. Three hundred villagers occupied 39 houses in Teynham and the *Report of the Royal Commission on the Employment of Children, Young Persons*

---

127 SEG 13.11.1860, 4.6.1861, 12.11.1861, 10.11.1863, 12.11.1863, 17.5.1864, 14.11.1865, 12.12.1865, 2.1.1866, 23.1.1866, 1.5.1866, 22.5.1866, 16.7.1867, 8.6.1868, 26.4.1869, 25.10.1870, 28.7.1870.
128 SEG 19.9.1865, 22.1.1867, 4.5.1867, 5.4.1869, 18.4.1871, 5.12.1871.
129 Bishop, *op. cit.*, p. 107.
130 SEG 11.12.1866, 11.10.1870, 17.10.1871, 7.12.1871.
131 SEG 3.6.1862, 3.6.1871.
132 SEG 27.10.1863, 24.1.1865, 20.4.1868, 11.5.1868, 27.7.1868, 19.9.1870.
133 Bishop, *op. cit.*, pp. 102–3.

and Women in Agriculture 1867 was a timely reminder that the only difference between rural and urban slums was a matter of scale.[134]

(4) Epidemic Disease 1871–1914

Cholera remained influential after 1871, but there was no further Kent outbreak.[135] Instead there was a resurgence of smallpox accompanied by scarlatina, typhoid, measles and influenza.

Compulsory vaccination had become lax. Between 1865 and 1868 there were smallpox outbreaks at Maidstone, Sheerness, Woolwich and Greenwich. 'No class . . . seemed exempt' and nearly all deaths were 'from want of timely vaccination'.[136] These outbreaks culminated in the great epidemic of 1871–2 in which smallpox spread from London to Canterbury, Dartford and Sittingbourne and thence to Milton, Iwade, Dover, Rochester, Chatham and New Brompton where the anti-vaccination movement was strong. Prosecution of Canterbury parents for failure to vaccinate did not stop its progress into East Kent and mortality remained high among the unvaccinated.[137] It lingered in the Medway towns until 1874 and erupted into a second major epidemic at Chatham, Rochester, Maidstone, Loose, Thanet, Tonbridge, West Malling, Gravesend, Sittingbourne, Deptford and Bromley in 1877–8. At Chatham there was no hospital. Seventy-three of 176 cases were treated at Medway Workhouse and nineteen died. Only two had been vaccinated. Rochester Sanitary Committee, which also had no hospital, was denied use of Strood Workhouse. At St Peter's, Thanet, where there had been a campaign against vaccination five years before, the community isolated itself and the labourers did not go to work. None of the 46 cases had been re-vaccinated and many had never been vaccinated at all.[138] At Maidstone, where five per cent of children avoided vaccination, the guardians also refused use of the workhouse hospital and the town was forced to establish a temporary hospital of its own.[139]

Smallpox was receding throughout the 1880s. A minor Maidstone outbreak in 1880 originated from a rag cutter at a paper mill. Next year 68 cases were reported at Dartford and seventeen at Greenwich. In Maidstone, 57 cases and five deaths again stemmed from Springfield paper mill where eleven girls were infected by sorting and cutting rags and the outbreak spread to adjacent barracks. When a further case occurred at Lower Tovil Mill in 1882 the Maidstone medical officer persuaded nearly all its workforce to be re-vaccinated. Nevertheless the Kent

134 SEG 8.10.1867, 19.4.1869. PP 1868–69, XIII. Report of the Royal Commission on Employment of Children, Young Persons and Women in Agriculture 1867, pp. 43–4, 55–7.
135 SEG 6.8.1872, 19.4.1886. KE 9.5.1873, 3.9.1892.
136 SEG 12.12.1865, 14.5.1867, 27.1.1868, 24.2.1868.
137 SEG 2.5.1871, 30.5.1871, 13.6.1871, 7.10.1871, 19.12.1871, 13.1.1872, 16.1.1872, 25.6.1872, 16.7.1872, 6.8.1872. *The Times*, 10.1.1872.
138 SEG 18.5.1874, 11.12.1876, 1.1.1877, 8.1.1877, 13.1.1877, 5.2.1877, 19.2.1877, 12.3.1877, 19.3.1877, 23.4.1877, 23.4.1877, 14.5.1877, 26.8.1878. KE 21.4.1877, 4.5.1878, 3.8.1878.
139 SEG 4.5.1878, 6.5.1878, 18.5.1878.

Anti-Vaccination League remained active despite prosecution of many members.[140] Thereafter incidence of smallpox was slighter. A Whitstable outbreak in 1884 was begun by a seaman from Sunderland. There were also cases at Milton, Maidstone, Bearsted, Wouldham, Larkfield and West Malling in 1885–6. Ashford's disinfecting chamber was in constant use in September 1891 and food was passed through the windows of infected houses which victims were not allowed to leave. At Pluckley, where smallpox was again spread by infected rags from Little Chart paper mills, West Ashford guardians bought an isolated cottage for patients. Refuse from London hospitals, brought to Sittingbourne by barge as manure, reintroduced smallpox to Kent in 1893 and by 1894 it was again in Maidstone. In 1900 9%–11% of children born in Faversham and East Ashford unions were still unvaccinated but smallpox was markedly on the decline.[141]

Diphtheria had re-appeared in Kent in 1858. Scarlatina was widespread in 1864. Both remained endemic for the next eighty years and a particular threat to children: '. . . In some villages, especially in Mid Kent . . . upon the resumption of scholastic duties after the hopping holidays, the gaps in the classes . . . caused by the ravages of diphtheria and kindred diseases were a very painful illustration of the high mortality among children . . .'[142] There were 25 diphtheria deaths at Bromley in 1876 and eleven of 37 cases at Biddenden were fatal in 1878. Four children from Bredgar National School, where a polluted well was situated near the churchyard, also died from diphtheria in that year. In the event of an outbreak the only answer was to close the school where often the seat of infection lay. At Ashford in 1883 '. . . nearly all cases were traceable to the British schools, the closet arrangements of which were believed to be defective' while a government inspector threatened to terminate the grant to Seabrook National School 'unless sanitary arrangements were improved'.[143] Diphtheria was at Harrietsham, Tovil, Loose and Maidstone in 1889. Next year it recurred at Loose and visited Romney Marsh. Two months of diphtheria at Warehorne brought many deaths and 1890 closed with outbreaks at Kennington and Boughton Aluph. Marden schools were closed in December 1893 by diphtheria and scarlatina. Strood suffered two years later while on the eve of World War One there was a diphtheria epidemic at Ashford.[144]

Scarlatina brought forty deaths in Romney Marsh at Christmas 1870, one of the great scarlatina years nationally. North-east Maidstone, despite extensive disinfecting, Sittingbourne, Sevenoaks, Chatham and West Malling suffered in a major, urban epidemic in 1875–6. Eighteen persons died at Maidstone in May–June 1875 and nineteen at Chatham.[145] 1879–80 saw outbreaks at Maidstone and Barming

[140] *Report of Borough of Maidstone Medical Officer of Health*, 1880, pp. 2–3. M. A. Adams, *Report to the Local Board on the Outbreaks of Smallpox in Maidstone*, 1881, pp. 2–8. KE 23.4.1881, 30.4.1881, 18.6.1881, 6.5.1881, 14.5.1881, 3.4.1882, 31.12.1887.
[141] SEG 28.4.1884. KE 5.9.1891, 12.9.1891, 22.4.1893, 24.2.1894, 3.2.1900, 10.2.1900
[142] SEG 11.10.1864. KE 11.11.1893. Creighton, *op. cit.*, pp. 739, 741
[143] SEG 5.8.1878, 2.9.1878, 26.11.1883. KE 2.9.1893.
[144] KE 2.2.1889, 30.3.1889, 13.7,1889, 21.12.1889, 7.6.1890, 5.7.1890, 6.9.1890, 9.12.1893, 9.11.1895, 13.12.1913.
[145] SEG 8.5.1875, 6.6.1875, 2.8.1875, 4.10.1875, 17.1.1876, 13.3.1876, 27.3.1876.

and in North Kent at Bredgar, Key Street, Murston and Lower Halstow where 33 cases closed the school for a fortnight. To the horror of medical officers infected children were often allowed to play in the streets thus defeating the aim of numerous school closures.[146] While isolation was the customary method for preventing scarlatina's spread, the crowding of large families into small cottages often made this impossible.[147]

Diphtheria and scarlatina were not the only epidemic diseases to close schools as log books testify. Measles closed Eastry school in 1879 and Ashford and Headcorn schools in 1887. At the latter 150 pupils were absent when the school shut. In a Canterbury epidemic which raged from November 1887 to mid-January 1888, 56 of 1,000 measles cases died. Small communities suffered as well as large ones. Ulcombe school closed for a month in 1889 and East Farleigh School, where 120 children were absent, shut in 1896.[148]

The final decade of the century also saw the re-emergence of influenza which attacked adults and children alike. Influenza had hit Mid and West Kent hard in the severe winter of 1836–7.[149] It re-appeared in Kent early in 1890 as part of the great national and European epidemic of 1889–94.[150] Erupting initially at Walmer marine depot and among the Dover garrison it spread rapidly to Maidstone, Sittingbourne and the South Eastern Railway works at Ashford. River school board closed its schools and influenza cost the Kent and Sussex Agricultural Labourers' Union £600 a week in sick pay. It also produced widespread absence from work at Rochester, Strood and Chatham.[151] While the influenza of 1890 was debilitating but not fatal, another epidemic the following year was more dangerous. Many fell victim in April and May. By early December it was spreading across East Kent. Of sixty victims sent to Elham workhouse, eight died in a fortnight. Whole families were decimated at Canterbury and Lyminge. Dover Corporation, Elham Sanitary Authority, and Ashford and Walmer local boards fined sufferers who appeared in public places under the Public Health Act. Nevertheless influenza 'quite unknown except to History by the present generation of doctors', continued its progress through Cranbrook, Hollingbourne, Chartham, Ulcombe, Hunton, Milton and Sittingbourne and into the Weald and Romney Marsh. Bromley schools closed. A thousand cases were reported at Maidstone and half the porters at large railway stations were absent.[152]

In 1893–4 influenza was less widespread but again virulent, erupting severely in Gillingham in March and spreading across East Kent to Ashford. It was again rampant in 1898 at Tonbridge, Cranbrook, Romney Marsh and Hythe. There were

[146] SEG 14.6.1879, 29.9.1879, 1.12.1879, 29.1.1881, 12.3.1883. KE 9.7.1881, 20.12.1890, 5.12.1891, 5.10.1892, 20.8.1898.
[147] KE 19.11.1892.
[148] KE 2.1.1887, 26.2.1887, 14.1.1888, 15.9.1888, 29.6.1889, 25.1.1896. SEG 4.10.1879.
[149] MG 10.1.1837, 31.1.1837, 7.2.1837, 14.2.1837.
[150] Creighton, op. cit., pp. 393–8.
[151] KE 11.1.1890, 18.1.1890, 25.1.1890, 1.2.1890, 8.3.1890, 22.3.1890.
[152] KE 27.12.1890, 5.12.1891, 12.12.1891, 26.12.1891, 2.1.1892, 9.1.1892, 16.1.1892, 23.1.1892, 30.1.1892, 6.2.1892.

300 cases at Benenden from a population of 1,600.[153] Yet another epidemic in 1900 affected Woodchurch and adjacent parishes. The isolation wards of Milton work-house were filled. Children suffered particularly in the epidemic at Dover. There were a number of fatal cases at Whitstable and 33 deaths at Canterbury.[154]

Finally typhoid continued to act as an indicator of inadequate water supply and sewerage. In the first half of 1886 67 cases of bad well water were detected in East Kent Sanitary Authority alone.[155] During the last three months of 1887 poor law expenditure on typhoid cases in Faversham Urban District was £59 prompting a reminder from the medical officer that 'the presence of typhoid meant the inhabi-tants were drinking diluted sewage'.[156] Brenzett's well water was 'a subterranean solution of sand and filth' while drainage and water supply at Sandwich were described as 'a disgrace to nineteenth century civilisation'. Polluted water was increased by the practice of using disused wells as cesspools.[157]

In such circumstances typhoid flourished. In 1874 it was in High Street and Church Street, Gillingham 'owing to the disgraceful sanitary state of these localities'. In 1880 it appeared in Milton where the privies of the houses were 'full, offensive and void of ventilation'.[158] A Maidstone outbreak the same year was attributed to the water which was 'poor and insufficient for so large a town'.[159] Faversham and adjacent parishes suffered in 1884, in 1887 and again in 1888. There were many cases in the brickmaking village of Murston in 1890 where brickyard labourers were drinking water from a contaminated well.[160]

The Maidstone typhoid epidemic of 1897, however, completely shattered Victorian complacency over sanitary progress, locally and nationally, with an outbreak 'unique for its magnitude in the annals of British medicine'. Before 1896, Maidstone water supplies had undergone monthly analysis for a fee of a guinea. Since some members of the council considered this extravagant a quarterly exam-ination was substituted. The source of infection was Farleigh springs which had been polluted by hoppers. Since the last analysis had been conducted the previous June pollution passed undetected. Other sources of contamination were faulty drains and sewers in the town where almost half the houses still had water closets without mechanical flushing and two thirds of dwellings had closets attached to imperfectly flushed drains.

The Water Company's supply from Farleigh was cut off on 29 September 1897, but by then there were 1,172 typhoid victims. Emergency hospitals were opened in schools and missions but most cases were nursed in their homes by 139 nurses from London hospitals including probationer Edith Cavell. Infected clothing and bedding were washed and disinfected free in a special laundry in the grounds of

153 KE 30.12.1893, 9.12.1893, 6.1.1894, 20.1.1894, 29.1.1898, 16.2.1898.
154 KE 6.1.1900, 13.1.1900, 20.1.1900.
155 SEG 29.11.1886.
156 KE 18.2.1888.
157 SEG 30.3.1868. KE 27.4.1889, 5.10.1892.
158 SEG 4.4.1874, 4.10.1880.
159 SEG 27.11.1880.
160 SEG 12.5.1884. KE 17.9.1887, 18.2.1888, 16.8.1890, 23.8.1890, 30.8.1890.

Fant Lane Hospital and all houses of victims disinfected and fumigated. Three relief stations were established to help 'the poorer classes' from which many sufferers came. A Charitable Relief Fund received contributions from all over England and abroad and a Mansion House Relief Fund was also established. The County Assizes and the County Fruit Show were diverted. The railway companies did little business; outsiders shunned the town and trade suffered. Only a handful of cases materialised in the surrounding villages among people who had visited Maidstone. Nevertheless by the time the epidemic subsided at the end of June 1898 there had been 1,847 cases of whom 132 had died. The total cost of fighting the epidemic was £17,753. The local government enquiry which followed was virtually a trial of the water company and the town council from which neither emerged with credit. A second epidemic which had begun earlier at Willesborough, where some of the polluted wells were 'mud holes', was overshadowed by events at Maidstone.[161] Both epidemics highlighted that there remained much sanitary progress to be made and precipitated considerable activity.

(5) Public Health Reform 1871–1914

Not only epidemics were influential. The 1870s also saw important legislative and administrative changes. Following hard upon the Report of the Royal Commission on Sanitation in 1871, came the creation of the Local Government Board, an amalgamation of the Privy Council Medical Department and the Poor Law Board which took over the administration of public health. The 1872 Sanitary Act divided England and Wales into urban and rural sanitary authorities, the former being town councils and local boards of health and the latter boards of guardians. Appointment of inspectors of nuisances and medical officers of health became compulsory although the latter could be, and usually were, poor law medical officers. Moreover, the Act for the first time placed a definite obligation on local authorities to provide a proper water supply. The great Public Health Act of 1875 consolidated previous legislation and enabled districts to amalgamate and share medical officers. It also permitted local authorities to build sewage farms and forbade pollution of watercourses. The Artisans' Dwellings Act of the same year empowered the compulsory purchase of property condemned as insanitary by medical officers of health and authorised its improvement or demolition. The Public Health (Water) Act of 1878 provided an easier legislative path for municipal purchase of private waterworks.[162] Finally the Local Government Acts of 1888 and 1894 created county councils and urban and rural district councils which had fuller powers than

---

[161] Irene Hales, 'Maidstone's Typhoid Epidemic September 11, 1897–January 29, 1898', *Bygone Kent*, vol. 5, No. 4, pp. 217–23. Graham's *Maidstone Almanack*, 1898, p. 15. SEG 28.9.1897, 5.10.1897, 12.10.1897, 19.10.1897. KE 25.9.1897, 2.10.1897, 9.10.1897, 16.10.1897, 23.10.1897, 30.10.1897, 6.11.1897, 20.11.1897, 18.12.1897, 1.1.1898, 29.1.1898, 12.2.1898, 3.9.1898.

[162] K. Dawson and P. Wall, *Society and Industry in the Nineteenth Century: Public Health and Housing, Oxford, 1970*, pp. 28–34. Anthony S. Wohl, *Endangered Lives: Public Health in Victorian Britain*, London 1983, pp. 111, 247.

the local boards and boards of guardians, which they replaced, as sanitary authorities.

The remainder of the century was devoted to implementing and applying the machinery thus created. This was no easy task. Local authorities remained slow to adopt much of the legislation. Sittingbourne local board was created in 1875 following the Public Health Act and Broadstairs local board in 1879. Milton's improvement commissioners were not replaced by an urban sanitary authority until 1891.[163] Local authorities were also divided over implementation of the 1872 Act. Dover and Ashford local boards feared large districts would produce extensive and costly drainage schemes created by officials lacking local interests. Other boards favoured large areas on grounds of economy.[164] When larger districts were created they often posed enormous difficulties for the officers concerned. Tonbridge Rural Sanitary Authority covered 40,767 acres and had 2,834 houses with a population of 14,681 but only one inspector of nuisances.[165] In 1898 only 22 of the 61 sanitary authorities in the county had appointed joint medical officers and there were only two joint medical districts. The remainder had local men whose independence 'was not what it should be' and who also had to conduct local practices as well. Twenty-seven authorities were not enforcing the Public Health Act of 1875. Not surprisingly most were not prepared to accept the creation of a county medical officer of health nor participate in further amalgamations.[166] Instead each continued to jealously guard its own rights.

Nuisance inspectors varied in quality. The New Romney medical officer described his colleague as 'an ornamental nonentity'. Nuisance abatement figures were impressive. 505 nuisances were swept away in Sevenoaks Rural Sanitary Authority in 1879–80 and 475 in Tonbridge Rural Sanitary Authority in 1876–7, but while the 1872 Act helped in the removal of small nuisances the major problems of drainage and water took much longer to resolve.[167] Opposition remained firmly rooted in 'economy'. When a local board was proposed at Bexley Heath local shop windows were plastered with notices stating 'No local board. No more taxes'. Tunbridge Wells water users preferred an intermittent supply to increased cost. Bromley and West Malling drainage schemes and a Whitstable water project were opposed for the same reason.[168] Influential ratepayers opposed a Ramsgate drainage scheme in 1885 while next year members of Gillingham local board all but mobbed a Local Government Board inspector trying to enforce compulsory emptying of cesspools. Rochester corporation, castigated by *The Lancet* in 1887 for the town's unsanitary condition, also refused to empty cesspools because it would add 2d to the rates.[169] During the Margate drainage controversy a proclamation

163 KE 14.2.1891, 2.2.1895.
164 SEG 4.2.1873, 8.2.1873.
165 SEG 26.8.1878.
166 KE 9.7.1898, 20.8.1898.
167 KE 28.3.1874, 30.6.1877, 10.5.1880, 30.5.1885, 11.1.1890.
168 SEG 13.12.1872, 18.5.1874, 15.5.1875, 2.7.1877, 21.4.1879.
169 SEG 11.10.1886, 15.10.1887. KE 4.4.1885. *Chatham and Rochester Observer*, 22.1.1887, 12.2.1887. I am indebted for this reference to Bruce Aubrey.

issued by Councillor Simmonds whipped its opponents into a frenzy: 'Arouse, Arouse! Fellow ratepayers and come to the rescue of your town. The tubular drainage is about to be forced upon us . . . Your town will be ruined and the hospitals, workhouse and gaols full of destitute and debtors unable to pay their rates . . .'[170]

When Sturry's wells were condemned its ratepayers rejected a connection with Canterbury waterworks because it meant a higher rate. When Chartham turned down a similar proposal on grounds of economy a local doctor added the more original concern that he 'did not believe in water which had to travel so long a distance'. Lydd town council dismissed the Local Government Board's recommendations for pure water, sewerage and an isolation hospital as 'Boardism'. Bethersden, where there had been an annual outbreak of fever since 1892, rebuffed a rural district council drainage plan in 1897, again because of cost. When Tonbridge Rural District Council proposed a drainage scheme for Hildenbrough costing £7,000, the ratepayers countered with a scheme costing £3,000.[171]

Owners and occupiers in rural parishes not directly benefiting from improvements often refused to pay. Cottage property owners remained implacable opponents. Romney Marsh Sanitary Authority was obliged to prosecute the Dean and Chapter of Canterbury for refusing to sink a well for £10 at cottages whose only water came from a drainage ditch.[172] When the Mid-Kent Water Company proposed in 1899–1900 to seek parliamentary sanction to supply 46 parishes opposition quickly resulted because cottagers would ask for connections at landlords' expense.[173]

Sewerage and water were not the only innovations opposed on economic grounds. Isolation hospitals were obstructed too. Hythe even refused to adopt the Notification of Infectious Diseases Act believing that it would lead to the provision and staffing of a 'sanitorium'.[174] Nevertheless Tonbridge laid the foundation stone for its isolation hospital in 1879.[175] Thereafter provision quickened as a result of epidemics and relentless pressure from the Local Government Board. Faversham Rural Sanitary Authority replaced its old isolation hospital behind the workhouse in 1888. By 1893 the Dover Urban, Dover Rural, East Ashford, West Ashford, Thanet, Broadstairs and Blean authorities had also established hospitals for infectious diseases while Elham, Hythe, Bridge and Eastry were negotiating to create them. Canterbury, after a long rearguard action, opened the City Isolation Hospital in 1897. The Local Government Board was still, however, pressing Sheerness Urban District Council to build a hospital in August 1900.[176]

Economy was not the only problem. Rapid urbanisation still outstripped even improved facilities. The population of Strood doubled between 1846 and 1896 with

170 KE 4.2.1888.
171 KE 17.11.1888, 20.10.1894, 10.9.1898, 20.5.1899, 5.8.1899, 22.7.1899.
172 KE 8.6.1889, 27.12.1890.
173 KE 2.12.1899, 9.12.1899, 23.12.1899, 27.1.1900.
174 KE 11.1.1890.
175 SEG 28.6.1879.
176 KE 28.7.1888, 10.6.1893, 4.8.1900.

the advent of cement works. So, too, did that of Gillingham. Two hundred and fifty houses were built in Tonbridge in 1894–7. By 1894 Pembury reservoir, built twelve years before with a capacity of 40,000 gallons, was no longer sufficient for Tunbridge Wells. Nicholas Mansergh recommended development of a fresh source of supply costing £100,000 to allow for growth over the next twenty years but ratepayers were tempted by the short-term expedient of an identical reservoir costing only £40,000.[177] Sheerness in 1894 was obliged to renew its main sewerage 'the town having outgrown the capacity of the old system thirty years before it was anticipated'.[178]

Sanitary engineering still remained in its infancy and the scope for error was still great. Each district had its own peculiar problems associated with terrain, soil and property rights. A member of Maidstone local board described sewerage, with good reason, as 'one of the most difficult problems of the present age'.[179] The size of major sewers made them feats of Victorian engineering in their own right. Bromley's system, laid in 1879, was 23 miles long. Margate's new sewer was 22 miles and Maidstone's 20 miles in length. The Darenth Valley scheme, laid at a rate of 1½ miles a month, extended for 19½ miles.[180] Tenders were frequently made at prices which could only result in loss.

Contractors calculated that they could evade terms to which they had agreed. Mr Angell's original estimate for Maidstone's drainage scheme was £32,000 but 'with part of the works reported stopped', he increased it to £46,000.[181] Lucas and Bird, the Hythe sewerage contractors, demanded an additional £3,000 to cover 'a vast amount of pumping and excavation beyond their calculations'.[182] Even Sir Joseph Bazalgette, who took the West Kent sewerage contract for £81,000, subsequently raised it to £108,000. Broadstairs local board, which received tenders for its sewage outfall ranging from £5,000 to £26,000, enthusiastically accepted the former. The work was unsatisfactory leaving the board to spend much more in rectifying the errors. Patching up the Canterbury sewer was alleged to have cost as much as the system itself. Rising costs of materials could also play havoc with estimates but when the contractor for Cheriton sewer claimed the cost of pipes had increased by 15% and demanded a corresponding increase new tenders were invited.[183]

Underestimates led in turn to poor workmanship. When part of the Canterbury sewage works, built by the ill-fated Mr Pilbrow, collapsed after five years the engineer claimed that it was not a permanent structure and therefore was not built in a 'needlessly costly manner'.[184] When Dartford local board opened its new low level sewer in 1880 it immediately flooded. A month later forty yards of it caved in. The joints of the West Kent main sewer were 'inefficiently and negligently made'.

[177] KE 20.1.1894, 10.3.1894, 5.1.1895, 14.11.1896, 26.6.1897.
[178] KE 10.3.1894, 8.4.1897.
[179] SEG 20.12.1879.
[180] SEG 6.12.1879, 17.5.1880, 19.7.1880, 27.11.1882. KE 28.1.1893.
[181] SEG 29.7.1878.
[182] SEG 28.9.1878.
[183] SEG 14.12.1878, 31.5.1880. KE 1.11.1890, 9.7.1892.
[184] SEG 3.12.1872, 24.12.1872.

It was not watertight and the defective parts had to be replaced for 4,660 feet across Dartford Marsh and a further 1,785 feet over the Cray valley.[185] Broadstairs local board sacked the engineers to its drainage scheme and required them to relay the pipes at their own expense 'since they were quite useless for . . . for draining the basements of houses in Albion and Harborne streets'.[186] Not only sewers were subject to leakage. In 1888 Margate reservoir lost 203,000 gallons of water in five days while Hythe, in 1899, was losing 6,000 gallons a day.[187]

Whenever sewers were constructed the roads sustained serious damage. Resorts in particular were concerned at 'the damage to the town' if roadways were blocked and the air polluted. If old works were opened in summer there was a serious risk of disease.[188]

> Apprehensions are entertained of a serious outbreak of disease in the town (Dartford) similar to that which occurred during the progress of the former sewage works. [reported the *Daily Chronicle*, 20 August 1880] The well supply has entirely failed . . . and there is a very general prevalence of diarrhoea . . . The opening of old drains and the cartage of their contents is much complained of . . .

On the other hand, although winter work still alleviated local unemployment and discomfort to visitors, it had serious perils. Mr Marshall, a Brighton contractor, who boldly stated in December 1880 that 'it would have been madness . . . to attempt to open up the streets of Milton at this time of the year . . .' was unusually honest and his outburst cost him the contract. That he was correct was illustrated at Ashford in December 1887 when sewerage work was suspended by flooding and navvies experienced 'some of the heaviest work they are likely to encounter' in the black, slippery, Wealden clay.[189]

Mindful of 'the unlimited demand for nightsoil for hops' many authorities believed they could make money from sewage.[190] 'It seems as if every enterprising chemist has some scheme for turning sewage . . . into gold', wrote the *Kentish Express*.[191] In 1874 alone some 32 patents were taken out for sewage treatment and although municipal delegations constantly visited rival sewerage systems few had any real idea of which to choose.[192] 'There is no perfect system of sewage disposal in the Kingdom' lamented a disillusioned Canterbury alderman,[193] a view re-iterated by the Maidstone Board after a grand tour of sewerage systems at West Ham, Tottenham and Coventry.[194]

[185] SEG 13.10.1879, 17.1.1880, 10.5.1880, 14.5.1880.
[186] SEG 5.2.1883.
[187] KE 25.8.1888, 14.1.1899.
[188] SEG 22.11.1880. KE 5.6.1897.
[189] SEG 11.12.1880. KE 3.12.1887, 19.3.1888.
[190] SEG 27.5.1873, 19.1.1874.
[191] KE 24.1.1885.
[192] Wohl, *op. cit.*, p. 104.
[193] SEG 23.3.1878.
[194] SEG 28.4.1879.

New sewer ventilators fitted at Maidstone and Ashford emitted 'abominable stinks' and were blamed for the spread of typhoid. Sinks and closets connected directly to sewers drew back the smell into houses.[195] Authorities often, however, had only themselves to blame for their problems. When Ashford Board found that its new system was working imperfectly and blamed the engineer, it emerged that the fault lay with the board which was pumping the tanks every five weeks instead of weekly and providing no treatment for sewage at night or on Sundays in order to cut labour costs. Moreover, only half an acre of the nine acre plot bought for filtration was in use. The rest was used for growing mangel wurzels. 'The secret of the whole matter', reported the engineer, 'is . . . a determination on the part of some to study economy without reference to efficiency . . . An unwise economy is the most expensive mistake a local board can make . . .'[196]

Apart from stupidity of this kind one must sympathise with authorities which hesitated before plunging into 'the financial abyss of sanitary engineering'.[197] When the river commissioners alleged that Canterbury was polluting the Stour in 1889 the board responded bitterly that since 1868 it had abortively spent £45–50,000 on sewerage.[198] A similar complaint to Maidstone, which had spent nearly £80,000, about polluting the Medway, produced the reply that the town was '. . . waiting for the development of sanitary science before embarking on additional expenditure . . . River Commissioners are apt to forget the difficulties in the way of satisfactory sewage disposal and how little scientists have as yet groped their way to the truth about it'.[199] 'The only difficulty', commented Hythe's medical officer, 'is the inevitable outlay of money which every step in sanitary improvement involves'.[200] Despite this, the period 1871–1914 saw considerable improvement in the drainage, water supply and housing of some Kent communities.

Progress was least in housing. Housing in urban Kent was no better than elsewhere. 'Many of the existing cottages are of such a wretched sort', wrote John Hooker of Sevenoaks to the *South Eastern Gazette* on 20 August 1872, 'that the new local board must take action against them . . .' '. . . A more scandalous neglect of the most ordinary rules of sanitation I have seldom witnessed' re-iterated a medical officer's report on the coastguard houses in Faith Street, Sittingbourne in 1876.[201]

Insanitary property was often in the hands of local notables. When Lord Montagu alleged in Parliament that 'there were more evils and fever dens . . . in small towns than large', he also indicated that in Folkestone one such 'den' belonged to a local councillor.[202] Cottages at Hythe, whose occupants had to throw

[195] SEG 18.8.1879, 20.12.1879.
[196] KE 10.12.1892.
[197] Wohl, *op. cit.*, p. 105.
[198] KE 28.12.1889.
[199] KE 29.12.1888.
[200] KE 12.2.1881.
[201] SEG 4.12.1876.
[202] SEG 10.4.1875.

their sewage into the street, were the property of a member of Hythe Corporation.[203]

Consequently housing improvement was slow. Dover and Folkestone led the way in a bid to improve their status as resorts. In 1876 Dover proposed to demolish 79 houses under the Artisans' Dwellings Act and rehouse their 250 inhabitants.[204] Two years later the proposal was revived for Barwick's Alley and other streets containing '. . . all those radical evils inimical to healthy existence . . . damp and filthy foundations, decaying walls and roofs, inadequate size of rooms wanting thorough ventilation and insufficiency of office accommodation . . . natural results where two or three houses have been erected on . . . ground which should have been dedicated to only one . . .'[205] A Dover Artisans' and Labourers' Dwellings Company followed 'to build, rebuild or improve the dwellings of the working class' but the corporation's principal concern was to relieve overcrowded traffic by creating new streets and widening the old.[206] Folkestone Corporation ordered some improvements under the 1875 Public Health Act in 1880. The Grace Hill improvement scheme, involving the demolition of old and unsightly houses in the town centre, was concluded despite opposition and by 1885 'the gloomy and dirty looking fishing town of half a century ago had been transformed . . . into one of the leading seaside resorts'.[207] The Folkestone Municipal Reform League, however, continued to press for 'cheap and comfortable dwellings for the working classes'.[208] 'We shall never clear dilapidated property', stated a Folkestone councillor, 'unless the occupants have somewhere to go'.[209] Ultimately fifty artisans' dwellings were erected on the East Cliff at low rents.[210]

Other resorts which undertook improvements were Ramsgate and Deal. The former began discussions on street widening as early as 1878 and by 1894 there were 'magnificent roads' to the east and west cliffs and the Chatham and Dover station.[211] Deal, more dependent on visitors with the coming of steamships, by 1895 was contemplating improvements in Broad Street and the town centre.[212] Maidstone's medical officer suggested the building of houses for the labouring classes in 1875. Four tenements were demolished in Thomas's Yard, Upper Stone Street, under the Artisans' Dwellings Act in 1880 but thereafter Maidstone's improvements were limited to town centre road widening. In 1899 the Maidstone sanitary inspector reported that only 447 of a total of 2,204 houses were in a satisfactory condition.[213]

---

203 KE 10.10.1885.
204 SEG 11.9.1876.
205 SEG 18.11.1878.
206 SEG 8.1.1881, 27.2.1882. KE 31.10.1891, 27.2.1892.
207 SEG 10.7.1880. KE 18.4.1885, 25.4.1885, 26.9.1885.
208 KE 17.12.1892, 14.1.1893, 27.10.1894, 10.11.1894.
209 KE 23.11.1895.
210 KE 23.11.1895, 7.8.1897.
211 SEG 16.11.1878, 25.11.1878, 31.3.1879, 29.12.1894.
212 KE 5.1.1895.
213 SEG 20.11.1875, 12.4.1880, 25.12.1880. KE 1.4.1899.

The Local Government Act of 1858 had empowered sanitary authorities to make by-laws enforceable under the Public Health Act of 1848. The Local Government Board produced model building by-laws but local authorities like Hythe were reluctant to accept them. While some Kent authorities took builders to court builders elsewhere continued to ignore building regulations.[214] When the Canterbury medical officer suggested in 1895 that the council should proceed against the owners of 35 overcrowded and insanitary cottages in Stour Street the matter was referred to a committee. A year later, when it was agreed that the site should be acquired and used for new working class housing, the 'Dirty Party' rallied and the motion was rescinded.[215] In 1896 George Leavey, Mayor of Chatham, reluctantly acknowledged the need for 'brighter and more open streets . . . and creation of proper sanitary dwelling houses for workers . . .' Nevertheless families were still housed in cellars in 1901.[216] Working class housing was an issue in the Ashford UDC elections of 1899 but in 1913 Ashford still had parts where back-to-back houses lacked air and light and where valuable space was occupied by stables and attendant manure heaps. Ashford differed little from other Kent towns which still contained 'very many objectionable and insanitary dwellings for the poor'. 'Local authorities in Kent', stated the *Kentish Express*, 'do not seem to care about putting the Artisans' Dwellings Act into operation'.[217]

If Kent's housing improvement was slow, improvement in water supply and sewerage progressed more rapidly due to the constant pressure of the Local Government Board. The Local Government Act of 1858 had sanctioned loans for sanitary purposes. Before the Local Government Board would recommend a loan to the Public Works Loan Commissioners it conducted a local enquiry through its own inspectors drawn largely from retired members of the Royal Engineers. This not only highlighted defects but encouraged local improvement. The board also had responsibility for ensuring that work for which a loan was granted was satisfactorily completed. Between 1872 and 1899 the board conducted over 58 public enquiries in Kent concerning water supply and drainage. The former was usually less controversial particularly in the towns where the principal movement was towards the enlargement of supply to keep pace with population growth and assist sewerage.

A waterworks was completed at Whitstable in 1879. Dover, where intermittent supply was still a serious disadvantage, sought to extend and improve its supply in 1881, although a year later an irate ratepayer still condemned the water as a 'dangerous disgrace'.[218] Tonbridge decided to acquire a new reservoir and a more powerful pumping engine in 1885. Neighbouring Tunbridge Wells opened a new reservoir the same year. In 1891 the town applied for a £10,600 loan to install a

214 SEG 3.1.1874, 20.2.1882. KE 9.7.1881, 10.5.1890.
215 KE 16.11.1895, 5.9.1896, 7.11.1896.
216 KE 25.1.1896. *Chatham and Rochester News*, 3.8.1901. I am indebted to Bruce Aubrey for this reference.
217 KE 29.12.1894, 18.3.1899, 9.8.1913.
218 SEG 10.6.1873, 26.8.1873, 8.2.1879. KE 5.11.1881.

larger pumping engine and new rising mains and three years later was again debating increasing storage or finding a new source of supply.[219]

Minster, whose previous supply came from shallow wells liable to pollution, was connected with Ramsgate in 1888 although the new supply was not entirely satisfactory.[220] A new waterworks for Hythe and Seabrook opened in 1890, a year in which Ramsgate Town Council applied to borrow £130,000 for its municipal water undertaking. Sandwich, previously supplied by the Delf stream 'liable to contamination in passing through the streets', laid the first pipes of a municipal waterworks in 1894.[221] In 1877 only half Sittingbourne's 1,447 houses were supplied with water. By 1894 Keycol Hill waterworks was unable to meet demand. The reservoir held only sufficient water for twelve hours' consumption and during a frost emptied in a single night leaving homes waterless for hours. Therefore in 1898 new pumping machinery was installed and a reservoir created with a capacity of 300,000 gallons.[222]

Margate Council, which had bought the local water company in 1879 for £59,000, needed more water by 1896 particularly during the holiday season. In 1897 it requested a loan to extend its mains and search for a supplementary supply. Sheerness had enlarged and improved its supply by 1894 and Folkestone was considering a loan for a new works by 1897.[223] Ashford Council, in common with the prevailing trend for municipal ownership, bought its waterworks in 1881 and opened a new 300,000 gallon reservoir in 1898. In 1900, with a population which had increased by 5,000 in twenty years, it was still trying to obtain a 'full and effective' supply and Durham and Devon miners were working night and day digging storage adits. Faversham water company hoped it had solved its water problem with a reservoir holding a million gallons. Deal, on the other hand, in 1896 only received water between 6.00 am and 1.00 pm and in the evenings only in summer. Gravesend still lacked piped-in-water in 1909.[224]

Demands for pure water in greater quantities also multiplied with the coming of public analysts in the 1870s. Their work highlighted the great number of polluted wells which were gradually removed from use. Of 59 samples of well water examined at Canterbury in March 1884 44 were polluted by sewage. In another Canterbury sample in 1898 only water from the waterworks was pure. In 1893 26 samples of Ashford well water supplying 124 houses were all contaminated save one.[225] After the Maidstone typhoid epidemic in 1897 demands for regular analysis intensified in town and countryside particularly after typhoid survivors decided to sue the water company.[226]

Where possible small groups of rural communities connected up with nearby

[219] KE 11.4.1885, 12.12.1885, 21.3.1891, 20.1.1894.
[220] KE 4.4.1885, 10.3.1888, 9.6.1888.
[221] KE 11.10.1890, 1.11.1890, 4.3.1893, 17.3.1894.
[222] SEG 8.9.1877. KE 13.1.1894, 15.1.1895, 22.1.1898.
[223] SEG 1.3.1879. KE 10.3.1894, 15.2.1896, 27.11.1897.
[224] KE 6.8.1881, 1.2.1896, 5.3.1898, 20.1.1900, 27.1.1900. Wohl, *op. cit.*, p. 63.
[225] SEG 17.4.1884, 4.2.1893, 26.6.1898.
[226] KE 2.10.1897, 30.10.1897, 5.3.1898, 28.4.1898, 30.4.1898.

urban water companies. Ospringe was supplied by Faversham Water Company from 1877 and Newington, Murston and Lower Halstow from the Sittingbourne works after 1880.[227] Elsewhere, however, when proposals for supply were made, as at Marden, responsibility was thrown back on property owners.[228] Villages surrounding Dover were notoriously short of water but when the medical officer proposed that a water cart be sent round them rural sanitary authority members objected on grounds of expense.

At Challock, water was fetched from Wye or Charing over five miles away. On the Hastings branch line of the South Eastern Railway water was carried in tubs to railwaymen in isolated signal houses. The medical officer to the Local Government Board in a startling report on Eastry Rural District in 1889 criticised Ash, Wingham and Eastry for their 'impure and ineffective water supplies' citing 40 recent typhoid outbreaks at Ash alone.[229]

The decade after 1890, however, saw a dramatic improvement in water provision for Kent villages which accelerated after 'the fearful results of using polluted water at Maidstone'.[230] During these years Biddenden, Wingham, Boughton-under-Blean, Fordwich, Willesbrough, Eastry, Sutton Valence, Lyminge, Grafty Green and Platt obtained fresh supplies while acquisition of pure water was under consideration at Littlebourne, Woodnesbrough, Patrixbourne, Bridge, Bekesbourne, Bishopsbourne and Trottiscliffe.[231] An attempt to establish a South Kent Water Company failed in 1889 but a Cranbrook and District Water Company was formed in 1894 to carry water from a central 2½ million gallon reservoir at Hawkhurst to Cranbrook, Goudhurst, Tenterden, Sittingbourne, Benenden and Rolvenden, previously much dependent on rainfall.[232] By 1898 the mains of the Mid Kent Water Company were also laid through Staplehurst to Hawkenbury and Headcorn.[233] Blean RDC borrowed £1500 to supply water to Chislet, Sturry and Westbere in 1900.[234] Nevertheless in 1898 ponds supplied the only drinking water in a substantial part of West Ashford Rural District and in 1913 the President of the Local Government Board was asked in the Commons whether he knew of the inadequate supplies in rural Kent and the number of Kent parishes still dependent upon ponds.[235]

While many water projects met little opposition sewerage schemes remained more contentious until the 1890s owing to cost and uncertainty of success. Of the smaller towns, West Malling had completed a sewage works by 1878 although

[227] SEG 28.7.1877, 13.11.1880.
[228] KE 5.9.1885.
[229] KE 1.8.1885, 27.8.1885, 20.4.1889.
[230] KE 30.10.1897.
[231] KE 13.9.1890, 28.2.1891, 7.3.1891, 28.1.1893, 6.3.1897, 12.2.1898, 27.8.1898, 15.10.1898, 10.12.1898, 6.5.1899, 16.9.1899, 11.11.1899.
[232] KE 27.10.1894, 16.5.1896.
[233] KE 22.10.1898.
[234] KE 20.10.1900.
[235] KE 20.8.1898, 1.2.1913.

treatment of the sewage remained uncertain. Dartford opened a new low level sewer in 1880 but flooding problems occurred almost immediately. At Sheerness, where the state of the drains was bad in many parts of the town in 1884, main sewerage was renewed ten years later.[236] Faversham, whose old sewer was too small, flooding the lower part of the town, laid a new sewer with 36-inch pipes in 1893. Tonbridge and Tunbridge Wells also dealt with their sewerage problems without major controversy. The latter instituted a proper system of drainage for the west of the town in 1886. The former, despite ratepayers' opposition, opened a new sewage farm in 1892 and introduced a new system in the late 1890s.[237] Sevenoaks, which had a piecemeal drainage system, began works in 1880 but a petition signed by over 500 residents ten years later suggested drainage was still poor.[238] At Gillingham, where sewerage was based on cesspools and the local board had stated that it would not be 'prepared to establish any scheme for some years to come', a system was sanctioned by the Local Government Board in 1895.[239]

At Hythe, where the old sewerage system was faulty in construction, extent and outfall, a new system was built by 1884. The main outfall was located 1½ miles from the town keeping the bathing ground and promenade free from pollution.[240] Broadstairs, in installing new drainage in 1884, also carried its sewage out to sea, a point emphasised in the holiday edition of the *London Medical Record*.[241] Folkestone, after delaying the inevitable by casing its main sewer in cement, adopted a plan devised by Nicholas Mansergh in 1892. Ramsgate, conscious that holidaymakers tended to consult the Registrar General's mortality returns before selecting a resort, made sewerage improvements in the 1870s and 1880s although not without opposition.[242]

While, prompted by Local Government Board pressure, inquiries and loans, many Kent towns made sanitary progress the problems of the larger towns were reflected in the experience of Canterbury, Maidstone, Margate and Ashford. Canterbury's controversial sewerage works had been completed in 1868. By 1872 only 2,100 of 4,500 houses were connected to the sewer and the Commissioners of Sewers were still urging the local board to prevent fouling the Stour from which 1,900 cubic yards of black town sewage had been removed the previous year. Having failed to let the sewage works to a private contractor and spent £36,000 to £40,000 of ratepayers' money to little avail Canterbury was again accused by the commissioners of polluting the river in 1877. After a Local Government Board inquiry in 1879 a new sewage works was opened in 1881 on 22½ acres east of the Sturry Road but the commissioners again alleged pollution in 1889. The sewage

---

[236] SEG 10.5.1880, 15.1.1883, 28.1.1884. KE 10.3.1894.
[237] KE 20.12.1890, 24.12.1892, 31.12.1892, 9.12.1893, 26.6.1897, 26.3.1898, 4.6.1898. SEG 8.11.1886.
[238] SEG 26.7.1875, 10.7.1880, 25.1.1890.
[239] SEG 11.6.1883. KE 5.1.1895.
[240] SEG 21.7.1884.
[241] SEG 16.6.1884.
[242] SEG 1.2.1875, 11.12.1875, 28.8.1876, 12.11.1883, 4.4.1885, 23.7.1887.

farm was extended in 1890 by 56 acres but Canterbury was still wrestling with the need for further improvement in 1898.[243]

Maidstone's sewerage had been almost entirely carried out before 1849 although the local board, formed in 1866, had extended some old sewers and developed others. The town, however, remained 'imperfectly sewered' and cesspools above the springs endangered water supplied at public taps. Water closets existed in 'the better class of houses only' while the privy and ash pit system prevailed elsewhere. Of 22 streets built since 1855 only 14 were drained. Fant, Kingsley and Tovil were 'innocent of any drainage'.[244] John Thornhill Harrison, Local Government Board inspector, who conducted an inquiry in 1873 found that 'it was not easy to conceive anything more disgusting than the bed of the Medway' into which Maidstone's sewage was discharged. He stipulated that before any loan could be made the council should not only extend the sewerage system but construct an outfall sewage works for the clarification of sewage which should be discharged into the river below Allington Lock. Since this was a re-iteration of an 1867 recommendation, Lewis Angell of London was consulted and his plans, costing £30,000, adopted in 1875. Drainage was a borough election issue in 1875 but the scheme was inaugurated and Angell cut the first sod at Allington in 1877.[245] By October 1878 it was necessary to apply for an additional loan of £26,454 which was duly granted. Six months later with town cesspools overflowing because householders would not pay to empty them with the coming of the sewerage, the local board was chafing at the delay. When it emerged that the council had no legal access to Allington Lock except by river, and that Angell was undecided how to treat and dispose of the sewage, there was uproar.[246] The sewer was completed in November 1879 but since the system would not work without water flushed closets the board now attempted to enforce their installation which quickly became another election issue. 'The wealthier inhabitants', argued John Potter, the working class Liberal candidate for Westborough Ward, 'possess the means . . . to protect themselves against the evils of an imperfect system of drainage. The poor . . . are in the hands of speculative builders who are not too careful in their attention to the drainage of the houses.'[247] By this time councillors were describing Angell's system as 'incomplete' and 'ineffective'. There were calls for an investigation by an independent expert and complaints of 'a river of sewage on the London Road'. Smells from sewer ventilators were explained by the surreptitious emptying of cesspools into the new sewer and 'hundreds of closets connected without a drop of water'. By 1882 1,392 connections had been made but there were many outstanding. Moreover there was no register of connections and much confusion between

[243] SEG 13.1.1872, 28.5.1872, 13.7.1872, 14.9.1872, 27.4.1874, 28.12.1874, 29.9.1877, 28.6.1879. KE 27.8.1881, 28.12.1889, 27.12.1890, 7.5.1898.
[244] SEG 19.1.1874, 27.2.1875.
[245] SEG 19.1.1874, 2.11.1874, 29.7.1875, 30.10.1875, 19.3.1877.
[246] SEG 12.10.1878, 26.10.1878, 17.3.1878, 28.7.1879, 11.10.1879.
[247] SEG 8.11.1879, 2.2.1880, 23.10.1880.

the old and the new sewers and the cesspools which had not been completely closed.[248] As the furore subsided there were renewed complaints of river pollution by the Malling and Hollingbourne unions in 1888 and 1890 and of defective drainage in the town.[249] One of the complainants was the Local Government Board and by 1896 Maidstone was again investigating an improved system.[250]

At Margate, where an imperfect sewer discharged into the sea at a low level, improvement was recommended from 1872. At high tide in the lower town sewage found its way into the basements of houses and a committee of sixty formed to promote a 'thorough and efficient drainage' warned that 'unless Margate would lose her high position among watering places . . . she must follow the example of her sister town, Ramsgate . . .'[251] A new system was rejected, however, in 1872. Next year a Local Government Board inquiry highlighted that 'in only seven English towns was death from preventible disease higher than at Margate'.[252] Two years later an article in the *Morning Advertiser* again castigated Margate's insanitary state: '. . . The state of the town . . . is most dangerous to the visitors who flock thither in search of health . . . It has outgrown the primitive arrangements for draining it and . . . some fearful epidemic . . . may visit it at any time . . .'[253]

A drainage scheme was agreed in 1877 but after further delay the 'Dirty Party' again attacked plans approved by the Local Government Board and council and the subject remained in abeyance until publication of yet another report forced the council to agree to a completely new system of drainage. This precipitated violent opposition which argued that drainage was unnecessary and would ruin the sea bathing. A petition from 'some hundreds of influential ratepayers' urged the council to re-consider, launching a controversy which was joined by civil engineers and national journals.[254] *The Times* designated Margate 'a cesspool town' and the municipal election of 1888 was fought on the drainage question. In January 1889 Baldwin Latham was appointed engineer. The result was an entirely new system 22 miles long embracing every Margate street with an outfall at Foreness Point two miles away and described by Margate's mayor as 'second to none in the world'.[255]

If Margate's tribulations ended in comparative success this did not apply to Ashford. Here six outfalls seriously polluted the Stour. Nevertheless a succession of proposals to review the drainage were defeated on grounds of cost. Even a writ issued against the local board by the Commissioners of Sewers did not produce immediate action in a matter already under discussion for twelve years. Messrs. Jones and Ballard were, however, invited to prepare plans for a system on the gravitating principle. These were adopted in August 1885 since 'the volume of

---

248 SEG 13.12.1880, 25.12.1880. KE 19.2.1881, 20.2.1882.

249 KE 29.12.1888, 30.8.1890, 29.12.1894.

250 KE 7.11.1896.

251 SEG 2.4.1872, 15.10.1872.

252 SEG 17.12.1872, 8.4.1873.

253 *Morning Advertiser*, 4.11.1875.

254 SEG 26.5.1877. KE 10.12.1881, 26.11.1887, 3.12.1887, 7.1.1888, 4.2.1888, 10.3.1888, 26.5.1888.

255 KE 29.9.1888, 12.1.1889, 7.9.1889, 23.12.1893, 15.2.1896.

sewage sent into the river would be greatly augmented by the continued addition of new houses in the district'. Ballard was the son-in-law of the board's chairman.[256] A report from a correspondent of *The Medical Press* who visited Ashford in 1886 underlined the urgency of positive action:

> ... The river near the town is simply an open sewer. Close to the parish church ... the drains smell dreadfully. South Ashford, mainly occupied by working men, is improperly drained and in case of an epidemic they would suffer terribly. The summer is not the best time to visit imperfectly drained towns![257]

Despite the sanction of the Local Government Board, opposition, led by a shop-keeper, Councillor Spain, secured further postponement of the scheme until finally after twenty years of discussion a tender was accepted in September 1887 and the sewage works formally opened in 1889.[258] By 1892, however, defects were re-ported in the system and the river commissioners were again threatening High Court action under the Rivers Pollution Act.[259] False economy by the board was found to be partially responsible. In 1894, W. G. Hancock, chairman of the local board, forecast that with a few improvements Ashford's drainage would become 'thoroughly satisfactory' but in 1913 the town was still polluting the Stour as Maidstone was the Medway. The close of the century also saw Chatham, Rochester, Sittingbourne, Tenterden and Cranbrook still without main drainage.[260]

Until the late 1880s attention was largely focused on Kent's towns. Sanitary improvement in the countryside remained slight. The exceptions, which served both town and country well, were the West Kent and Darenth Valley drainage schemes upon which work began in 1877. The West Kent scheme, created largely by Colonel Lennard, Chairman of Bromley Sanitary Authority and his colleagues, consisted of a line of sewers extending from Beckenham to the Thames at Long Reach, near Dartford, and embracing the parishes of Bromley union and part of Lewisham. The Darenth Valley scheme, sanctioned in 1878, authorised a sewer to run from Westerham along the Darenth Valley to link with the West Kent sewer at Dartford and serve the Sevenoaks Rural and Urban Sanitary Authorities.[261]

In the late 1880s there was a noticeable increase in Local Government Board drainage inquiries at smaller communities like Woodchurch, Penshurst, Thanning-ton and Ash.[262] In the 1890s the pace quickened with local opposition decreasing as it had over water supply. During the decade 1890–1900 drainage works and inquiries took place at Cheriton, Kennington, Walmer, St Peter's, Broadstairs,

256 SEG 5.9.1874, 8.1.1877, 7.7.1877, 28.5.1881, 5.2.1883, 29.10.1883. KE 25.4.1885, 16.5.1885, 22.8.1885, 27.8.1885.
257 SEG 26.7.1886.
258 KE 19.3.1887, 23.4.1887, 21.5.1887, 10.9.1887, 16.2.1889.
259 KE 10.9.1892, 5.11.1892.
260 KE 17.2.1894, 4.1.1913, 9.8.1913. John Ballard, 'Sewage Disposal by Steam Engine', *Bygone Kent*, vol. 4, No. 1, January 1983, pp. 14–16.
261 SEG 5.11.1877, 13.5.1878.
262 SEG 5.7.1886. KE 17.3.1888, 21.7.1888, 22.11.1890.

Seabrook, Borstal, Newington, Aylesford, Eccles, Saltwood and Willesbrough.[263] Deal, largely undrained, introduced a new system without opposition in 1898. Herne Bay had adopted a system prepared by Baldwin Latham the previous year. Murston, Birchington, Orleston, Benenden, Smarden and Great Chart were among the many communities considering drainage by the new century.[264]

An Act of 1900 ended pollution of the notorious Milton Creek preparing the way for Milton and Sittingbourne to create further drainage.[265] Sewerage schemes were pending at Whitstable and Tenterden in 1913 but communities like Staplehurst, Loose, Bearsted and Hollingbourne still lacked main drains. At Rainham, whose sanitary organisation the Milton RDC medical officer described as 'futile, uneconomical and a danger to the neighbouring districts', there was still no sanitary inspector and disinfection and sanitary investigation were in the hands of a Sittingbourne road scavenger.[266]

Sanitary progress was reflected in mortality rates. Nineteenth century Kent, like other south-eastern counties, enjoyed a comparatively low level of mortality by contemporary standards. Nevertheless infant mortality rates remained high. In 1874 27% of all deaths in Thanet Rural Sanitary Authority were of children under five. 40% of deaths at Chatham in 1876 were of children under two years old. At Maidstone in 1878 one in three children died before they were five. In Faversham Rural Sanitary Authority 24.7% of deaths in 1899 were still of children under one and 14.9% of children under five. Infant mortality at Ashford in 1892 still accounted for 148 per 1000 deaths as opposed to 140 per 1000 for all England while at New Romney in 1900, although the average death rate was 13.2 per 1000, half the deceased were still children.[267]

On the other hand overall mortality rates fell. An Ashford death rate of 16 per 1000 in 1874–6 had dropped to 14.4 per 1,000 by 1890. Maidstone's mortality rate of 24 per 1,000 in 1855 was down to 13.57 per 1,000 by 1887–90. Folkestone's death rate of 18 per 1,000 in 1876 had been reduced to 13.3 per 1,000 by 1891. A Sittingbourne mortality of 18 per 1,000 in 1875 was 13.8 per 1,000 in 1890.[268] This improvement was reflected in statistics county-wide. Some of the reduction was undoubtedly due to preventive medicine and to nineteenth century medical discovery and to better diet arising from improved living standards. On the other hand the fall in mortality undoubtedly also owed something to seventy years of tortuous improvement in public health.

[263] KE 8.11.1890, 7.3.1891, 28.3.1891, 30.5.1891, 21.11.1891, 25.11.1893, 13.7.1894, 5.12.1896, 9.1.1897, 17.7.1897, 18.9.1897, 30.10.1897.
[264] KE 1.2.1896, 11.9.1897, 27.11.1897, 5.3.1898, 7.5.1898, 14.5.1898, 30.7.1898, 5.8.1898, 7.4.1900.
[265] KE 22.7.1899, 26.5.1900, 9.6.1900.
[266] KE 4.1.1913, 12.4.1913, 23.8.1913, 25.10.1913.
[267] SEG 15.2.1875, 31.7.1876, 24.2.1879. KE 1.3.1890, 4.2.1893, 10.3.1900. See Armstrong, loc. cit.
[268] SEG 15.10.1855, 8.1.1877, 22.1.1877, 26.2.1877. KE 14.2.1891, 23.1.1892, 5.3.1892. Report of Maidstone Borough Medical Officer of Health, 1890, p. 3.

Guide to Further Reading

This guide is designed to refer the general reader to recent and useful background material to the subjects covered in this volume. It should be supplemented by the more detailed references provided in the footnotes to each chapter.

(1) Religious History
There is no modern study covering the whole religious history of England in the period 1640–1914. The best introductory monographs are, in chronological order, J. Spurr, *The Restoration Church of England 1646–1689*, New Haven and London 1991; E. G. Rupp, *Religion in England 1688–1791*, Oxford 1986; W. R. Ward, *Religion and Society in England 1790–1850*, London 1972; and W. O. Chadwick, *The Victorian Church*, 2 vols, London 1966–70. The best coverage of dissent before the end of the eighteenth century is M. R. Watts, *The Dissenters*, Oxford 1978. For a rather idiosyncratic overview of the last two centuries see E. R. Norman, *Church and Society in England 1770–1970*, Oxford 1976; it is very well written but betrays too many of the author's prejudices and needs to be treated with caution. The history of Roman Catholicism in England has been well served by J. Bossy, *The English Catholic Community 1570–1850*, London 1975, and E. R. Norman, *The English Catholic Church in the Nineteenth Century*, Oxford 1984.

Regional studies of the impact of religion on English society are still too few but a guide to the main issues is provided by J. H. Bettey, *Church and Parish*, London 1987; C. Binfield, *So Down to Prayers*, London 1977, provides several delightful vignettes of nonconformity in the provinces between 1780 and 1920. Changes in church buildings are chronicled in W. N. Yates, *Buildings, Faith and Worship*, Oxford 1991; there are good studies of non-Anglican buildings by B. Little, *Catholic Churches since 1623*, London 1966, and K. Lindley, *Chapels and Meeting Houses*, London 1969.

The sociological aspects of religion in England have been well surveyed in A. D. Gilbert, *Religion and Society in Industrial England*, London 1976; R. Currie, A. D. Gilbert and L. Horsley, *Churches and Churchgoers*, Oxford 1977; and R. Gill, *The Myth of the Empty Church*, London 1993. Two specialist studies that can be strongly recommended are D. W. Bebbington, *Evangelicalism in Modern Britain*, London 1989 and the excellent survey of Victorian revivalism by J. H. S. Kent, *Holding the Fort*, London 1978.

(2) History of Education
The most useful introduction is the lucid and well-illustrated J. Lawson and H. Silver, *Social History of Education in England*, London 1973; V. E. Newburg, *Popular Education in Eighteenth Century England*, London 1971, contains a helpful chapter on literacy and an excellent bibliography. A highly readable and well-illustrated anthology covering the period 1800–1950 is P. H. J. H. Gosden, *How They Were Taught*, Oxford 1969. A wide selection of sources on the history of education is to be found in D. W. Sylvester, *Educational Documents 800–1816*, London 1970, and its companion

volume, J. S. Maclure, *Educational Documents, England and Wales 1816–1967*, London 1968. Among specialist local studies A. F. Munden, *Eight Centuries of Education in Faversham*, Faversham 1972, is an exemplar of thoroughness and careful documentation.

(3) The Poor Law

G. Oxley, *Poor Relief in England and Wales 1601–1834*, Newton Abbot 1974, and J. D. Marshall, *The Old Poor Law 1795–1834*, London 1968, provide an excellent introduction to the problems and workings of the Old Poor Law. A. Digby, *The Poor Law in Nineteenth Century England and Wales*, Historical Association, London 1982, analyses events from the last years of the Old Poor Law to the end of the New Poor Law in 1929. Opposition to the New Poor Law is considered by N. Edsell, *The Anti-Poor Law Movement 1834–44*, Manchester 1971, and M. Rose, 'The Anti-Poor Law Agitation', in *Popular Movements c. 1830–1850*, ed. J. T. Ward, London 1970. *The New Poor Law in the Nineteenth Century*, ed. D. Fraser, London 1976, contains a series of essays on different aspects of the New Poor Law. Victorian workhouses are examined in M. A. Crowther, *The Workhouse System 1834–1929*, London 1981, and P. Wood, *Poverty and the Workhouse in Victorian Britain*, Stroud 1991. There are two important articles on the theme 'How Cruel was the Victorian Poor Law?' in the *Historical Journal* by D. Roberts (iv, 1963, pp. 97–107) and U. Henriques (ix, 1968, pp. 365–71).

(4) Epidemics and Public Health

The best book on nineteenth century medicine and disease is F. B. Smith, *The People's Health*, London 1979. There are many urban investigations of nineteenth century public health but few county studies. A. Wohl, *Endangered Lives*, London 1983, is both eminently readable and, at the same time, a penetrating and comprehensive analysis of the general issues and problems in Victorian Britain. J. Burnett, *A Social History of Housing 1815–1985*, London 1978, examines both urban and rural housing and housing conditions.

Index

Abbot, Robert, 4
Act of Uniformity (1662), 9, 10, 93
adult education, 106
aged *see* elderly
agriculture
    agricultural labourers, poverty, *1640–1834*,
        112, 113–17
    needs of, effects on school attendance, 103,
        107, 108–9
    provision of work for paupers, 133–4, 135–7
Aldington, 73
Alexander, Edward, 10
Alford, Henry, dean of Canterbury, 60
Allard, Elizabeth, 147
Allhallows, 34, 128
Allington, 221
Allotment Act (1832), 179
allotments, 117
America, emigration to, 117–18
Amherst, Jeffery, 7
Amherst, William Pitt, Earl, 173
Anabaptists, 13, 15
Andrews, John, 151
Angell, Lewis, 213, 221
Anglican church *see* Church of England
Anglo-Catholics, 74–5, 85
Appledore
    poor relief, 116, 121, 136, 139n, 150
        emigration, 118
        medical treatment, 130, 131, 132
        outdoor relief in kind, 128, 129
        parish farm, 133
    religion, 25
apprenticeship, of pauper children, 150–1
Archbold, Edward, 5
Arianism, 41
Arminian Baptists, 15
Artisans' Dwellings Act (1875), 210, 216, 217
Ash-next-Sandwich
    poor relief, 130, 131, 136, 147, 152, 153
        outdoor relief, 123–4, 125, 126, 128, 129
        parish farm, 134
        workhouse, 141
    poverty, 113, 114
    public health, 219, 223
    religion, 14, 15, 84
Ashby, Dame, 131

Ashford
    epidemics and public health, 193, 200, 203,
        204, 205, 207, 208
        public health reform, *1871–1900*, 211,
            214, 215, 217, 218, 220, 222–3, 224
    grammar school, 91, 109
    poor relief (*see also* Ashford, East, Union;
        Ashford, West, Union), 120, 127, 130,
        147, 152, 155
        workhouse, 137, 143
    religion, 8, 25, 26, 28
        nonconformity, 16, 17, 43, 46, 81, 85
    schools (*see also* grammar school), 92, 94,
        99, 104, 110, 208
Ashford, East (rural area), 61, 62, 212
Ashford, East, Union, 120, 157, 158, 163,
    181–2, 185, 207
    workhouse, 183, 186
Ashford, West (rural area), 62, 212, 219
Ashford, West, Union, 120, 155, 166, 188, 207
    workhouse, 171–2, 183, 186
Ashow (Warwickshire), 25
Atherley, ____, 165
Atterbury, Francis, bishop of Rochester, 21,
    Plate 2
Austen family, 40
Australia, emigration to, 118
Aylesford
    epidemics and public health, 198, 200, 205, 224
    nonconformity, 62
    poor relief (*see also* Aylesford, North,
        Union), 155, 179
Aylesford, North, Union, 157, 158
    workhouse, 172, 182

Badlesmere, 25, 44
Bagot, Richard, dean of Canterbury, 56
Bagshaw, Samuel, 185
Bailey, George, 164
Ballard, ____, 222–3
Banks, William, 147
Bapchild, 115, 119n, 148n, 149, 160–1
Baptists (*see also* General Baptists; Particular
    and Strict Baptists)
    1640–1714, 8, 9, 15, 16, 18, 21
    1714–1830, 40, 42, 44, 45, 101n
    1830–1914, 61, 63, 64, 65, 66, 75, 77, 86

Barfrestone, 13
Barham, 10, 126, 149
Barming
    epidemics and public health, 194, 195, 198,
        207
    religion, 30–1, 32, 34–5, 86
Barming Heath, 194, 203
Barnes, David, 50
Barns, Rebecca, 34
Barton, John, 10
bastardy see illegitimacy
Bates, _____, 39
Bazalgette, Sir Joseph, 205, 213
Bearsted, 134, 179, 198, 207, 224
Beckenham, 109, 223
    poor relief, 129, 134, 143
    religion, 34, 66, 74
Becker, Michael, 153
Becker, Thomas, 134
Beeman, Isaac, 63–4
Beeman, Thomas Oyler, 64
Bekesbourne, 219
benefit clubs see friendly societies
Benenden
    epidemics and public health, 209, 219, 224
    poverty and poor relief, 117, 123n, 130, 151
    religion, 15–16
    schools, 97, 102
Bentley, Thomas, 119
Beresford-Hope, Alexander, 71, 78
Bessels Green, 45
Bethersden, 150, 155, 212
Betteshanger, 14, 121
Bexley, 36, 42, 119n, 158, 203
Bexley Heath, 106, 203, 211
Bible Christians, 43–4, 61, 64, 77, 88–9
Bicknor, 28, 81
Biddenden, 14, 91, 207, 219
Bilsington, 25
Birchington, 96, 129, 143, 224
Birling, 119
Bishop, Henry, 116, 131, 149, 152
Bishopsbourne, 219
Black Book, 55
Blackham, John, 131
Blackheath, 105
Blandford, Mary, 146
Blane, Lady, 194
Blean, 62, 212
Blean Rural District Council, 219
Blean Union, 158, 166, 184, 195
    workhouse, 163, 165, 167–8, 169, 175 (Fig.
        13), 177 (Fig. 14), 195
Blew, W.J., 70
Bligh family, Earls of Darnley, 54, 115
board schools see School Boards
boarding out, of workhouse children, 188

boards of guardians see guardians
boards of health (see also Central Board of
    Health; General Board of Health)
    creation of, 193, 195, 197, 200–1, 211
Bodkin, Phebe, 132
Bodley, G.F., 81
Bonnington, 24
Book of Common Prayer, 3, 4, 5, 7, 9
Borden, 27, 194
Borough Green, 75
Borstal, 224
Bossenden Wood, battle of (1838), 42, 162
Boughton Aluph, 24, 207
Boughton Malherbe, 15, 63
Boughton Monchelsea, 131, 148n
    Boughton Monchelsea Place, 196
Boughton-under-Blean, 18, 38, 99, 104, 146,
    162, 219
Bowtell, John, 19
Boxley, 10, 25, 27, 28
Boyce, Henry, 118, 127, 135, 136, 151
Boys, John, 113, 114, 121
Brabourne, 179
Brasted, 69, 70, 137, 137n
Bredgar, 161, 207, 208
Bredhurst, 24, 162
Brenchley, 7, 116, 127, 134, 149, 152
    church, 10, Plate 1
    school, 107
Brenzett, 209
Brethren, 61, 77
Brett, Thomas, 17–18
Bridge, 61, 62, 212, 219
Bridge Union, 155, 158, 167, 179, 184
    workhouse, 174
Bridgland, William, 34
Brighton (East Sussex), 146, 214
British and Foreign Schools Society, 97, 104,
    105
    British Schools, 104, 105, 108, 109, 207
Broadstairs, 143
    epidemics and public health, 194, 203
        public health reform, 1871–1900, 211,
            212, 213, 214, 220, 223
    Holy Trinity chapel, 50
    workhouse, 143–4
Bromley, 182
    epidemics and public health, 205, 206, 207,
        208, 211, 213, 223
    poor relief (see also Bromley Union), 137n
    religion, 34, 62, 66
    schools, 110
Bromley Union, 157, 166, 167, 179, 181, 223
    workhouse, 165, 166, 168, 172
Brompton, 43, 64, 202, 206
Brook, William and James, 34
Brookland, 44, 139n

Broomfield, 28
Brown, James, 141
Brownists, 14
Buckland, 104
Burmarsh, 24
Burton, Decimus, 49–50
Butterfield, William, 60

Calverley Water Company, 203
Calvinists, 3, 7, 42, 43, 63, 77, 93
Cambridge
    Christ's College, 92
    St John's College, 23
Camden, Earls see Pratt
Canada, emigration to, 118
Canterbury
    archbishops of (see also Howley; Laud;
        Manners-Sutton; Moore; Sancroft;
        Secker; Sheldon; Sumner; Tait; Tenison;
        Wake)
        patronage of Kent benefices, 23, 24
    archdeaconry of, 23, 24–8, 58
    cathedral, 6–7, 12–13, 58–9
        clergy (see also deans): 1640–1714, 6,
            14, 15, 20, 94; 1714–1830, 23, 24, 25;
            1830–1914, 58–9, 212
        fabric, 6–7, 11, 12, 20, 60
        library, 58
        sermon on French Revolution (1789), 36
        services, 6–7, 12, 19–20, 58, 60
        Six Preachers, 6, 14, 20, 25, 58
    City Isolation Hospital, 212
    deanery of, 14
    deans of (see also Alford; Bagot; Horne;
        Lyall; Smith; Tillotson; Turner), 6, 13,
        23, 58, 94, 212
    diocese of
        1640–1714, 7, 10
        1714–1830, 23–4, 49
        1830–1914, 55, 56, 72, 104–5
    dispensary, 192, 197
    Eastbridge Hospital, 24
    epidemic disease, 191n, 208, 209
        cholera, 193, 195, 197
        smallpox, 189, 190, 206
    gaol, 162
    grammar school (King's School), 58, 91,
        93–4
    hospitals see City Isolation Hospital;
        Eastbridge Hospital; Jesus Hospital;
        Kent and Canterbury Hospital; Poor
        Priests' Hospital
    Jesus Hospital, 91
    Kent and Canterbury Hospital, 131, 190,
        191, 195, 197, Plate 15
    King's School see grammar school
    Poor Priests' Hospital, 137

poverty and poor relief
    1640–1834, 113, 120, 159; workhouse,
        101, 137, 139, 143, 150, 152
    1834–1914 (see also Canterbury
        Incorporation), 179
public health reform
    1830–71, 198, 199, 200, 201, 202,
        203–4, 205
    1871–1900, 212, 213, 214, 215, 217,
        218, 220–1
religion (see also cathedral)
    1640–1714, 13, 19–20; nonconformity,
        6–7, 9, 10, 15, 16, 17
    1714–1830, 23, 26, 28, 36, 37, 38;
        nonconformity, 43, 45–6
    1830–1914, 54, 72, 74, 75, 78;
        nonconformity, 62
St Alphege's church, 37
St Gregory's church, 78
St Margaret's church, 20
St Mary Northgate, church, 13
schools (see also grammar school), 91, 101,
    104, 105, 107–8, 110, 168
silk weaving, 112
Canterbury Incorporation (later Union), 159,
    164, 179, 184
    school, 187
    workhouse, 159, 166, 171, 172, 174, 186,
        Plate 15
    officers, 165, 169
    vagrants, 182
Carpenter, R.C., 79
Carr, George, 35
Carr, James, 46–7
Casual Poor Act (1882), 183
cathedrals see Canterbury; Rochester
Catholic Apostolic Church, 77
Catholic Emancipation (1829), 53–4
Catholics see Roman Catholics
Caton, William, 8–9
Cavell, Edith, 209
censuses, religious, 60–7
Central Board of Health, 193
Chadwick, Edwin, 200
Chalk, 119n
Challock, 219
Chambers, G.B., 148
chapels see church and chapel buildings;
    nonconformity
Charing, 26, 27, 136, 136n, 219
    deanery of, 14
charities, parochial, 35–6
Charity Commissioners, 102
charity schools, 97, 98, 99, 100 (Fig. 3), 101
Charles I, King, 3, 5, 12
Chart, Great, 120, 126, 155, 190, 224
Chart, Little, 207

Chart Sutton, 45, 179, 196
Chartham
  epidemics and public health, 208, 212
  poor relief, 119, 121, 131–2, 133–4, 135,
    136n, 147
  outdoor relief, 124, 128–9
Chatham, 161, 176, 202
  epidemic disease, 206, 207, 208
    cholera, 193, 194, 195, 197, 198
  poverty and poor relief, 113, 118, 130–1,
    147, 148, 151
    workhouse, 139, 141, 144, 171, 173–4,
      176
  public health reform
    1830–71, 201–2, 204, 205
    1871–1900, 217, 223, 224
  religion
    1640–1714, 7, 16
    1714–1830, 43, 46, 48
    1830–1914, 61, 62, 74
  St John's church, 48
  schools, 104, 105, 110
Cheriton, 188, 213, 223
Chevening, 130, 137, 137n, 152
Chichester (West Sussex), 24, 42
Chiddingstone, 73, 162
  church, Plate 1
  poor relief, 119n, 127, 128, 137n, 148
    workhouse, 139–41
children (see also education; illegitimacy)
  poverty and poor relief
    1640–1834, 117, 150–1
    1834–1914, 166, 171, 172, 173, 174,
      187–8
Chilham, 127, 145, 148n
Chislehurst, 69, 137, 148n, 172
Chislet, 113, 124, 130, 137n, 148n, 219
cholera, 164, 192–8, 200, 201–2, 206
Church, Mr and Mrs, 165–6
Church Army, 87
Church Building Commission, 48, 50
church and chapel buildings
  1640–1714, 10, 11–12, 16, 20
    gifts to, 18, 20
    iconoclasm during Civil War and
      Interregnum, 6–7
  1714–1830
    building and extension, 20, 44–52
    condition of fabric and fittings, 32–4
  1830–1914, building and restoration, 67,
    75–83, 88, 89
Church of England
  1640–1714, 3–21, 102
  1714–1830, 22–52, 98, 102–3
  1830–1914, 53–90, 104–5, 108, 109, 167
  and education (see also National Society for
    Education; Society for Promoting

Christian Knowledge), 98, 102–3, 104–5,
  108, 109
church magazines see parish magazines
church rates, 57–8, 80
church services, pattern of
  1640–1714, 11, 12
  1714–1830, 19–20, 26–9
  1830–1914, 58, 59–60, 69, 72–5, 88, 89
'Church Whigs', 21
Civil War and Interregnum
  education, 92–3
  religion, 5–9, 11–12
Clarendon Code, 93
Clark, Erskine, 88
Clark, William, 64
clergymen (see also Church of England)
  income, 29–32, 55
  non-residence, 25–6, 38–9, 55, 56, 60
  pluralism, 10, 11, 14, 24–6, 55, 56
  role in local community, 83–90
  workhouse chaplains, 166, 167, 168, 169
Clerical Guide, 55
Cliffe, 56
Close, Francis, 76
cloth industry, Wealden, 95, 112, 121
clothing, provided for paupers, 129
clothing clubs, 84, 88
coal, provided for paupers, 128–9
coal clubs, 84
Cobbett, William, 113
Cobham, 148n, 153
Cockerell, S.P., 47
Colfe, Abraham, 93
Collard, Richard, 50
Collier Street, 76, 78
Comenius, John, 92–3
communion see Holy Communion
Compton Census (1676), 15
confirmation, in Church of England, 39
Congregationalists see Independents and
  Congregationalists
convict ships, cholera, 193, 194, 195
Conyers, Widow, 133
Cooke, Ralph, prebendary of Rochester, 11
Cooling, 34
Corn Law (1815), 114
cottage homes, 188
Countess of Huntingdon's Connexion, 43, 44,
  61, 66, 77
Courtenay, Sir William see Tom
Cowden, 7, 190
  poor relief, 123, 128, 129–30, 131, 132,
    137, 152
    workhouse, 141–3
Coxheath, workhouse, 144, 152, 159
Coxheath Incorporation, 155, 158–9, 167
Cramp, John, 133, 134, 152, 184

Cranbrook
  epidemics and public health, 203, 204, 208, 219, 223
  poor relief (*see also* Cranbrook Union), 128, 131, 134, 149, 152, 155
    workhouse, 134, 143
  religion
    1640–1714, 4, 8, 18; church, 18; nonconformity, 15, 16, 17, 18
    1714–1830, 25, 26, 28; nonconformity, 40, 42
    1830–1914, nonconformity, 62, 63–4
  schools, 91, 101, 109–10
Cranbrook Union, 164, 166, 178, 185
  workhouse, 165, 176, 184
Cranhurst, Sarah, 146
Crayford, 54–5, 144, 203
Creed, Henry, 120
Crockenhill, 87
Crouch, John, 7
Crump, John, 10
Crundale, 19, 20
Culmer, Richard, 6, 7
Curteis, Thomas Sackville, 31, 47

dame schools, 96
Dance, George, the elder, 45
Darenth Valley sewerage scheme, 213, 223
Darnley, Earls of *see* Bligh
Dartford
  epidemic disease, 189, 194, 195, 206
  poor relief (*see also* Dartford Union), 152, 191
    workhouse, 143, 144
  public health reform, 199, 201, 203, 213, 214, 219–20, 223
  religion, 9, 36, 62, 74
  rural deanery, 32–4
  schools, 91, 94, 110
Dartford Union, 157, 158, 182
  workhouse, 166, 171, 174
Day, John, 172, 174
Deal
  epidemic disease, 189, 193, 195
  poverty and poor relief, 112
    workhouses, 112, 139, 141, 143
  public health reform, 200, 201, 216, 218, 224
  religion
    1640–1714, 13, 14, 20; nonconformity, 15, 16, 17
    1714–1830, 27, 28
    1830–1914, 74, 76, 78
  St Andrew's church, 76, 78
  St George's chapel, 20, 27, 28
  St Leonard's church, 20, 28
  schools, 94, 99, Plate 8

Deedes, G.F., 180
Defoe, Daniel, 112
Denne, John, archdeacon of Rochester, 32
Denton, 25
Deptford
  adult education, 106
  epidemic disease, 195, 197, 206
  nonconformity, 15, 43
  poor relief, 157, 162
    workhouses, 137, 139, 143, 144
  St Nicholas' parish, poor relief, 139, 162
  St Paul's parish, workhouse, 139, 143, 144
  schools, 97, 99, 105–6, Plate 8
Dering family, 40
Dering, Sir Edward, 4–5
Dering, Henry, 19
Detling, 19, 20
Diggers, 8
diphtheria, 191, 207
disabled *see* sick and disabled
Disciples of Christ, 77
disease *see* epidemic disease
dispensaries, 131, 192, 197, 198
Dissent *see* nonconformity
Ditton, 87, 109
doctors *see* medicine
Doddington, 19, 161
Dogood, Henry, 11
Dorset, Dukes of *see* Sackville
Dover
  castle, 16–17
  epidemic disease, 189, 193, 194, 206, 208, 209
  harbour works, 181, 183, 185
  poverty and poor relief (*see also* Dover Union; St Mary's parish), 113, 116, 133, 147, 150, 155
  public health reform
    1830–71, 198, 199, 201, 202, 203
    1871–1900, 211, 212, 216, 217, 219
  religion
    1640–1714, 8; nonconformity, 8, 10, 15, 16, 17
    1714–1830, 23, 28; charities, 36; nonconformity, 40, 43, 46
    1830–1914, 54, 74–5; nonconformity, 62
  St Mary's parish
    church, 28
    poor relief, 131, 145–6, 149; workhouse, 132, 139, 145
  schools, 93, 94, 101, 103, 105, 109, 110
Dover Union, 158
  workhouse, 171, 174
Downe, 24
Dunkirk, 42, 162
Dutch community, at Sandwich, 9
Dymchurch, 25, 52, 86, 190

East, place names beginning with, *see under second element*
East Kent Sanitary Authority, 209
Eastchurch, 25, 72, 194
Eastry
  epidemics and public health, 208, 212, 219
  poor relief (*see also* Eastry Union), 123, 128, 129–30, 131, 132, 146
    workhouse, 141, 152
  religion, 14, 25, 62
Eastry Union, 154n, 181, 197
  workhouse, 168, 172, 181, 187
Ebony, 25
Eccles, 224
Ecclesiastical Commission, 55–6
ecclesiastical reform, *1830–1914*, 53–60
ecclesiological movement, 76, 78, 79–80, 81
Edenbridge, 137, 137n, 141, 149, 179, 204
education (*see also* grammar schools; Sunday schools)
  1640–60, 91–3
  1660–1811, 10, 93–103, 150
  1811–1914, 103–11
    epidemic disease in schools, 207–8
    of workhouse children, 167–9, 186, 187
Education Act (1870), 107–8, 109
Education Act (1902), 110
Edwards, John (fl. 1661), 16–17
Edwards, John (fl. 1817), 128
Egerton, 72, 153
elderly, poverty and poor relief
  1640–1834, 117, 121, 124, 139, 141
  1834–1914, 155, 171, 172, 174, 180, 186, 188
Elham
  epidemics and public health, 208, 212
  poor relief (*see also* Elham Union), 128, 129–30, 131, 132, 136, 137n
  religion, 62
Elham Union, 155n, 171n, 180, 187, 188
  workhouse, 179, 181, 182, 183, 186, 208
Ellis, ____, 196
Elmley, 72
Eltham, 203
Elwil, Lady, 34
emigration overseas, 117–18, 134
enclosure, 113
endowed schools *see* charity schools
epidemic disease (*see also* cholera; smallpox), 191–2, 206–10
Erith, 66, 106, 199, 203
Evangelical movement (*see also* Countess of Huntingdon's Connexion; Methodists)
  1714–1830, 22, 42–3
  1830–1914, 68, 69–70, 72, 74–5, 76, 83, 85, 86
evangelists, lay, Congregational, 85–6

Evelyn, John, 139
Exhall, Joseph, 127, 164
Eythorne, 14, 15, 24

Fairfield, 44
Falera, John, 148
Fane family, Earls of Westmorland, 7
Farleigh, East and West
  epidemics and public health, 194, 195–6, 208, 209
  poor relief, 164
    workhouse, 196
  religion, 69, 70, 87n
farming *see* agriculture
Farnborough, 87, 132, 139, 141
Farningham, 119n, 148n, 150, 191
Faversham
  epidemic disease, 193, 194, 198, 209
  grammar school, 91
  poverty and poor relief (*see also* Faversham Union), 113, 119, 120, 130, 147, 148n, 152
    workhouse, 150
  public health reform, 198, 203, 212, 218, 219, 220, 224
  religion
    1640–1714, 10; nonconformity, 15, 16
    1714–1830, 25, 27, 28; charities, 36; church, 45; nonconformity, 43
    1830–1914, 74, 79n; nonconformity, 61, 62
  schools, 91, 94
Faversham Rural Sanitary Authority, 212, 224
Faversham Union, 160, 167, 178, 181, 184, 185, 207
  opposition to, 161
  workhouse, 165, 166, 176, 178, 181, 182, 186
Fawkham, 116
Fifth Monarchy Men, 8
Finch-Hatton, George William, 9th Earl of Winchilsea, 53
Five Mile Act (1665), 93
Folkestone, 181, 182, 183
  dispensary, 192, 197
  epidemic disease, 189, 195, 197, 205
  poverty and poor relief
    1640–1834, 113, 121, 131, 133, 148, 149; workhouse, 141, 145
    1834–1914, 180, 183
  public health reform
    1830–71, 198, 199, 200, 202, 205
    1871–1900, 215, 216, 218, 220, 224
  religion
    1640–1714, 8, 17
    1714–1830, 26, 28
    1830–1914, 71, 72, 74, 75
  schools, 101, 110

Footscray, 7
Fordcombe, 76, 78
Fordwich, 200, 219
Forster, Richard, 19
France
    French Revolution, 23, 36
    religion, 14, 22–3, 61
Free Church of England, 77
free sittings, increase in, 49, 52, 69, 80–1
French Revolution, 23, 36
friendly societies and benefit clubs, 117, 132
Friends, Society of *see* Quakers
Frindsbury, 32, 163
Frittenden, 15, 87
Froude, J.A., 68
fruit pickers, missions to, 87
fuel, provided for paupers, 128–9
Fullager, Jane, 131

Gambier, J.E., 31
Garlinge, 134, 152
gathered church, concept of, 85
General Baptists, 40, 41–2, 77
General Board of Health, 197, 200–1, 202
Gerselin, General, 161
Gibbon family, 40
Gibbons, Grinling, 20
Gibraltar Tower, 198
Gilbert's Act (1782), 139
    Gilbert unions, 120, 139, 159
Gillingham
    epidemics and public health, 195, 200, 208,
        209, 211, 213, 220
    poor relief, 127, 132, 137, 151
    religion, 66, 76
girls, education for
    1640–1811, 91, 96
    1811–1914, 104, 105, 106, 108, 110–11
Gladstone, William, 71
glebe, 29, 30
Gleig, G.R., 114, 134
Glorious Revolution, impact on religion, 17–21
Glynne, Sir Stephen, 80
Goddington, 143, 155n
Goodnestone-next-Wingham, 20
Goudhurst, 31, 165
    epidemics and public health, 190, 219
    poor relief, 119n, 126, 127, 129, 136, 148,
        153
    workhouse, 176
    religion, 26, 28
    schools, 92, 96, 101
Grafty Green, 219
Grain, Isle of, schools, 94
grammar schools
    1640–1811, 91, 93–4, 97, 102
    1811–1914, 58, 59, 105–6, 109–11

Grant, Thomas, bishop of Southwark, 65
Gravesend, 182
    dispensary, 192
    epidemics and public health, 189, 193, 195,
        198, 206, 218
    poverty and poor relief (*see also* Gravesend
        Union), 113, 146, 149, 150, 159
    workhouse, 143, 150
    religion, 45, 70, 74
        nonconformity, 62, 81; Roman Catholics,
        65, 70
    St George's church, 45
    schools, 94, 110
Gravesend Union, 158
    workhouse, 166, 171
Great, place names beginning with, *see under
    second element*
Great Exhibition (1851), 166
Greenwich
    adult education, 106
    epidemics and public health, 192, 195, 197,
        206
    poor relief (*see also* Greenwich Union),
        120, 152
    workhouse, 137, 139, 143
    religion, 24, 34, 42
    schools, 93, 96, 99, 101, 108
Greenwich Union, 157, 162
    workhouse, 171, 174, 186
Griffiths, W.P., 80
guardians, in poor law unions, 158, 164
Guilford, Earls of *see* North
Gunning, George, 32
Guston, 13–14
Gyles, Richard, 10

Hadlow, 57n, 75, 82
Halden, High, 93, 101, 197
Hall, J.R., 83
Hallam, Abigail, 144
Halling, 139
Halstead, 87
Halstow, Lower, 208, 219
Ham, 14, 21
Hamstreet, 139n
Hancock, W.G., 223
Harbledown, 144, 148n
Harrietsham, 25, 151, 207
Harrison, Benjamin, archdeacon of Maidstone,
    56, 57, 70, 82–3, 86, Plate 3
Harrison, John Thornhill, 221
Hart, Percivall, 45
Hartlip, 64, 106, 109, 127
Harty, 72
harvest, celebration of, 87, 88
Hassell, John, 101

Hastings, Selina, Countess of Huntingdon (see also Countess of Huntingdon's Connexion), 43
Hawkenbury, 219
Hawkhurst, 31, 101, 105, 127, 166, 192, 219
Hawksmoor, Nicholas, 20
Hayes, 24
Head, Sir Francis Bond, 120, 154–7, 159, 160, 166, 178
  on workhouses, 139–41, 152, 164, 169–72
Headcorn
  epidemics and public health, 190, 196, 203, 208, 219
  poverty and poor relief, 117, 146
Hearth Tax (1664), 120
Herne, 130, 144, 179
Herne Bay, 195, 203, 224
Hernehill, 161, 162–3
Hever, 136n, 141
High, place names beginning with, see under second element
Higham, 119, 148n
higher education, 109
highway repair see road repair
Hildenborough, 212
  church, 76, 78, Plate 4
Hillborough, 48
Hills, Robert, 6
Hoare, Edward, 75
Hodges, Thomas Law, 117, 155, 159
Hollingbourne, 24, 62, 99, 161, 208, 224
Hollingbourne Union, 157, 164, 167, 169n, 222
  workhouse, 165, 168, 170 (Fig. 12), 182
Holy Communion, frequency of
  1714–1830, 26, 27–8
  1830–1914, 58, 59–60, 69, 72–5, 88, 89
Homersham, Thomas, 132
Honywood family, 40
Hoo (see also individual places by name)
  nonconformity, 61, 62
Hoo Union, 157, 158, 178, 187, 188
  workhouse, 164–5, 171
Hooker, John, 215
hop growing
  cause of absenteeism from schools, 103, 107, 109
  epidemic disease among hop pickers, 193, 194, 195–7, 198, 209
  missions to hop pickers, 86–7
  sewage as fertiliser, 214
  and vagrancy, 150, 181, 182, 183
  work for paupers, 101, 179
Horne, George, dean of Canterbury, 37–8, 41, Plate 2
Horsley, Samuel, bishop of Rochester, 38–9, Plate 2
Horsmonden, 7, 116
Horton Kirby, 7

hospitals (see also Kent and Canterbury Hospital), 191–2, 209–10, 212
  for cholera, 193, 194, 195, 196, 197, 198
  isolation hospitals, 192, 212
  in London, 131, 132, 191, 196, 207, 209
  for smallpox, 206
  for typhoid, 209–10
Hothfield, 28
Hougham, 135
housing improvement, 1871–1900, 215–17
housing provision, as type of poor relief, 127–8
Howlett, John, 189, 190
Howley, William, archbishop of Canterbury, 54, 55, 56, 59, 60, 69–70, 78
Hubard, Simon, 131
Huguenots, French, 14
Huntingdon, Countess of see Countess of Huntingdon's Connexion
Huntington, William, 42, 63
Huntingtonians, 42, 63
Hunton, 20, 198, 208
hymns, 29
Hythe, 128, 150
  influenza epidemic, 208
  poor relief, 146
  public health reform, 212, 213, 214, 215–16, 217, 218, 220
  religion, 8, 20, 81
Hythe, West, 20

Ickham, 10
iconoclasm, Civil War and Interregnum, 6–7
Ightham, poor relief, 129, 131, 133, 146
  workhouse, 143, 145, 150
illegitimacy, 117, 148–9, 185
Incorporated Church Building Society
  1818–30, 48–9, 50, 51–2, 57, 78
  1830–1914, 78, 79
Independent Calvinists, 63
Independents and Congregationalists
  1640–1714, 7, 8, 9, 15, 16, 21
  1714–1830, 40, 41, 42, 44, 101n
  1830–1914, 61, 63, 64, 65, 66, 77, 81, 84, 85–6
indoor relief see workhouses
industrial schools and 'schools of industry', 96, 97, 108
industrial training, for workhouse children, 188
influenza, 191, 206, 208–9
Ingleden, Thomas, 128
inoculation see smallpox
insane see mentally ill
Interregnum see Civil War and Interregnum
Irish immigrants, 127, 196–7
  Roman Catholics, 53, 89
  vagrancy, 150, 181, 182
iron industry, Wealden, 95, 112

Irvingites, 61
isolation hospitals *see* hospitals
Iwade, 206

Jackson, Edward, 146
Jackson, Susan, 176
James II, King, 17
Jaynes, Robert, 163
Jenkins, William, 46
Jenner, Edward, 190
Jews, 61, 77
Jezreelites, 76, 77
Johnson, ____, 92
Johnson, John, 17, 18
Johnson, Peter, 10
Johnson, William, 155
Johnstone, ____, 128
Jones, William, 36
Jones and Ballard, Messrs., 222–3

Keble, John, 67, 68
Kemsing, 28
Kenardington, 24, 28–9
Kennet, Dame, 131
Kennington, 207, 223
Kent and Canterbury Hospital, 131, 190, 191, 195, 197, Plate 15
Kent County Industrial School for Girls, 108
Kent Education Committee, 110–11
Kent Ophthalmic Institution, 88, 192
Keston, 97
Key Street, 208
Kilndown, 78
King, Walker, archdeacon of Rochester, 57, 81, 82
King, Walker, bishop of Rochester, 39
Kingham, Thomas, 17
Kingsnorth, 95, 108
Kite, Charles, 189
Knatchbull family, 40
Knatchbull, Sir Edward (fl. 1722), 143
Knatchbull, Sir Edward (fl. 1828), 53–4, 115
Knatchbull's Act (1722), 137, 139, 143
Knockholt, 137n
Knole House, 205

Labour Rates, 135, 136–7, 179
Ladd, John, 180
Lake, John, 115
Lake, William, 149
Lamberhurst, 15–16, 158
Langdon, East, 13, 14
Langdon, West, 13, 14
Langley, 29–30, 31, 102–3
Larkfield, 207
Latham, Baldwin, 204, 205, 222, 224
Latter, Thomas, 34

Latter Day Saints, 61, 77
Laud, William, archbishop of Canterbury, 4
Lauderdale, Earls of *see* Maitland
Laurence, Richard, archbishop of Cashel, 41
Leathersellers' Company, 93
Leaveland, 25
Leavey, George, 217
Lee, 105
Leeds, 10, 28
Leigh, T. Pemberton, 179
Lenham
    epidemics and public health, 204
    poverty and poor relief
        1640–1834, 117, 119–20, 125, 131, 135, 137, 137n, 153; workhouse, 139
        1834–1914, 161, 179
    religion, 10, 15, 23, 26
Lennard, Colonel, 223
Levellers, 8
Lewes (East Sussex), 42
Lewis, John, 19–20
Lewisham, 93, 102, 195, 223
    Granville Park, 110
Lewisham Union, 157, 179
Leybourne, 96, 97
Leysdown, 25, 72
libraries, 106
    parochial, 18–19
Linton, 28, 81
literary and scientific institutions, 106
Little, place names beginning with, *see under second element*
Littlebourne, 107, 219
Local Government Act (1858), 199, 203, 204, 205, 217
Local Government Act (1888), 210
Local Government Act (1894), 210
Local Government Board
    creation of, 210
    and hospitals, 212
    and housing, 217
    and sanitation, 211, 212, 217, 220, 221, 222, 223
    and water supply, 212, 217, 219
Lochee, Dr Alfred, 191–2
London
    Bethlehem Hospital, 132
    Crystal Palace, 166
    epidemic disease
        cholera, 193, 194, 198
        smallpox, 206
    Goldsmith's College, 110
    hop pickers from, 181, 193
    hospitals, 131, 191, 196, 207, 209
    Merchant Taylors' School, 14
    Metropolitan Police, 161, 162
    Quakers, 8–9

London (*continued*)
    St Mary-le-Strand, 25
    sewerage, 199
    Sisters of Charity, 196
    University, 110
    Westminster Abbey, 24, 45
Longfield, 7
Loose, 27, 28, 196, 206, 207, 224
Lower, place names beginning with, *see under second element*
Lownes, Henry, 17
Lucas and Bird, sewerage contractors, 213
Luddenham, 25
Lullingstone, 44–5
lunatics *see* mentally ill
Luton, 171, 174
Lyall, W.R., dean of Canterbury, 56
Lydd
    poor relief, 162
    public health, 212
    religion, 8, 14, 16, 17, 27
Lyminge, 182, 208, 219
Lynsted, 25, 161
Lyons, Timothy, 146

magazines *see* parish magazines
magistrates, and poor relief, *1640–1834*, 119, 124–5
Maidstone, 196
    All Saints church, 79–80
        churchyard, 200
    archdeaconry of, 58
    archdeacons of *see* Harrison
    dispensary (later West Kent Hospital), 192
    epidemic disease, 191n, 207, 208
        cholera, 193, 194, 195, 197, 198
        smallpox, 189, 190, 206, 207
        typhoid, 209–10, 218
    grammar school, 79, 91
    Holy Trinity church, 48, 73
    linen thread industry, 112
    Maidstone Bank, 120
    poverty and poor relief
        1640–1834, 113, 114, 117, 120, 130–1, 147, 149; workhouse, 137, 139, 143, 144
        1834–1914 (*see also* Maidstone Union), 155, 159
    public health reform
        1830–71, 199–200, 203, 204–5
        1871–1900: housing, 216; sanitation, 213, 214, 215, 220, 221–2, 223, 224; water supply, 218
    religion
        1640–1714, 8–9, 10; nonconformity, 8, 16, 17; parochial library, 19
        1714–1830, 26, 28, 48; nonconformity, 40, 41, 43, 45, 101n

1830–1914, 54, 60, 65–6, 72, 73, 74, 75, 79–80; nonconformity, 62, 63, 65–6, 75, 81; Roman Catholics, 64
    schools (*see also* grammar school), 94, 96, 100 (Fig. 3), 101, 104, 105, 108, 110
    West Kent Hospital, 192
Maidstone Union, 157, 158–9, 166, 181, 188
    workhouse, 174, 182, 186, 196, 206
Maitland, James, 7th Earl of Lauderdale, 24
Majendie, Ashurst
    on administration of poor relief, 118, 119, 120, 149, 152
    on poverty, 112, 116
    on workhouses, 132, 145, 152
Malling, rural deanery, 32–4
Malling, East
    poverty and poor relief (*see also* Malling Union), 118, 134
    religion, 7, 62, 86
Malling, West
    epidemics and public health, 200, 206, 207, 211, 219
    poor relief (*see also* Malling Union), 124–5
    religion, 15, 39, 62
Malling Union, 158, 222
    workhouse, 172, 174, 186
Manchester
    Kent pauper children apprenticed in, 151
    migration to, 118
Mann, Horace, 66
Manners-Sutton, Charles, archbishop of Canterbury, 24, 52, Plate 2
Manning, Henry, Cardinal, 69
Mansergh, Nicholas, 213, 220
March, Thomas, 92
Marden, 31, 117, 119, 151, 198, 207, 219
Margate
    adult education, 106
    epidemic disease, 195
    Holy Trinity church, 48, 50–1
    poor relief, 133, 155
        workhouse, 139, 144, 184
    public health reform
        1830–71, 201, 202, 203, 205
        1871–1900, 211–12, 213, 214, 218, 220, 222
    religion (*see also* St John-in-Thanet)
        1714–1830, 28, 48, 50–1; nonconformity, 43, 46
        1830–1914, 54, 66, 74; nonconformity, 61, 62
St John-in-Thanet, parish
    church, 50
    religion, 18, 19, 27, 28, 50
    school, 92
schools, 92, 99, 104, 105, Plate 9
Seabathing Infirmary, 192, 195

market gardening, 95, 101, 114
Marsh, Eliza, 147
Marshall, ____, 214
Marshall, Catherine and John, 34
Marsham, Charles, 3rd Earl of Romney, 79
Marten, William, 190
Martin, 141
Masters, Richard, 16
Matthew, Thomas, 34
Mears, Isaac, 144
measles, 191n, 206, 208
mechanics' institutes, 106
medicine (see also dispensaries; epidemic
   disease; hospitals; public health)
   medical treatment as part of poor relief
      1640–1834, 130–3, 191
      1834–1914, 166–7, 173, 180, 184, 186–7
Medway, river, sewage pollution, 200, 205,
   215, 221, 223
Medway Union, 158, 172, 180
   school, 187
   workhouse, 166, 171, 172, 176, 206
mentally ill, treatment under poor law, 132,
   186–7
Meopham
   epidemics and public health, 190
   poor relief, 128, 129, 130, 131, 132, 146,
      150
      workhouse, 141, 144, 149
   religion, 75
Mereworth, 15–16, 45
Mersham, 17, 41
Methodists (see also Bible Christians;
   Primitive Methodists; Wesleyan Methodists)
      1714–1830, 22, 43–4, 45–6, 67, 83
      1830–1914, 61, 65, 66, 77, 109
Mid Kent Water Company, 212, 219
migration, to northern industrial districts, 117,
   118
Miles, James, 165
Mill, William Hodge, 69, 70
millenarianism, 42, 76
Milner, Charles, 179
Milstead, 97, 151, 157
Milton (Gravesend), 113, 149
Milton Regis
   epidemic disease, 206, 207, 208, 209
      cholera, 193, 194, 195, 197
   grammar school, 91
   nonconformity, 62
   poor relief (see also Milton Union), 121,
      129, 134, 136, 146, 148, 150, 151
   public health reform, 203, 204, 211, 214,
      224
Milton Union, 157, 180, 181, 184, 185, 188,
   192
   and education, 109

opposition to, 158, 160, 161
   workhouse, 168, 181, 184, 195, 209
Minster (Sheppey)
   epidemics and public health, 194
   poor relief, 134, 148
   religion, 72
Minster (Thanet)
   epidemics and public health, 218
   poor relief, 133
      workhouse see Thanet Union
   religion, 7, 28
missions to hoppers and fruit-pickers, 86–7
Mockett, John, 143
Molash, 158
Mongeham, Great, 13, 14
   school, Plate 13
Mongeham, Little, 14, 20
Monkton, 10
Montagu, Lord Robert, 205, 215
Moore, George, 146–7
Moore, John, archbishop of Canterbury, 24, 41
Mortley, John, 133
Mothers' Union, 87
Muggletonians, 8
Mundella's Act (1880), 108
Municipal Corporations Act (1835), 55
Murray, Francis, 69
Murray, Lord George, bishop of Rochester, 54,
   56
Murston, 160, 208, 209, 219, 224
Murton, 'Major', 161, 162
music in churches, 28–9, 37, 58, 59, 88

Nailor, C.B., 48
National Society for Education, 57, 97, 104–5
   National Schools, 104–5, 109, 187, 207,
      Plates 10–11, Plate 13
Nayland (Suffolk), 36
Nettlestead, 86, 87n, 198
Neve, John, 136–7
Neve, Thomas, 151
New, place names beginning with, see under
   second element
New Poor Law (1834) see Poor Law
   Amendment Act; poor relief
New York, emigration to, 117
Newcastle Commission (1858), 106
Newenden, 25
Newington, 135, 219, 224
Newman, John Henry, Cardinal, 67, 69
Newnham, 85, 161
newspapers, 19th cent., 106n
Nicholls, William, 143
night schools, 107
Noakes, Hester, 148
Noble, Mark, 30–1, 32, 34–5
non-juring schism, 17–18, 21

non-residence of clergymen (*see also* pluralism), 25–6, 38–9, 55, 56, 60
nonconformity (*see also* Baptists; Bible Christians; Calvinists; Independents and Congregationalists; Methodists; Presbyterians; Puritans; Quakers; Roman Catholics)
  1640–1714, 8, 10, 14–17, 21
  1714–1830, 40–4, 101
  1830–1914, 53, 57, 61–7, 75, 76, 77, 81
  and education, 104, 105, 109
  role in local community, 83–6
  and workhouse chaplaincies, 167
Nonington, 17, 136
Norman, George Warde, 157
North, Francis, 1st Earl of Guilford, 24
North, place names beginning with, *see under second element*
North-West Kent Waterworks Company, 203
Northbourne, 14, 15
Northfleet, 24, 179
Northiam (East Sussex), 151
Nuisance Removal and Diseases Prevention Act (1846), 200
Nuisances Removal Act (1855), 202
Nuneaton (Warwickshire), 165

O'Bryan, William, 64
Old, place names beginning with, *see under second element*
Oldbury Hill, 134
one-parent families *see* illegitimacy
Orleston, 224
Orpington, 24, 87, 99, 132, 190
Ospringe, 27, 162, 219
  deanery of, 14
Otford, poverty and poor relief, 113, 116, 129, 137n, 146, 152
  medical treatment, 131, 132
  provision of work, 134, 135
Otham, 32, 37, 198
Otterden, 45
outdoor relief *see* poor relief
overseers and assistant overseers, and
  administration of poor relief, 118–19, 120, 123, 153, 184
  settlement, 145–50
Oxford
  All Souls College, 23
  Assize Sermon (1833), 67
  Christ Church, 24
  Oriel College, 59
Oxford Movement (*see also* ritualists; Tractarians), 67–75
Oxinden family, 40

Paddock Wood, 182

Papillon, David, 24
Papillon, Philip (fl. 1703), 16
Papillon, Philip (fl. 1784–5), 24
Paramore, Thomas, 13
parish farms, 133–4
parish halls, 85
parish magazines, 84, 88
Parker, Elizabeth, 132
parochial libraries *see* libraries
Parris, Mrs, 150
Parsons, Dame, 132
Particular and Strict Baptists, 40, 63, 75, 77, 104
Patrixbourne, 19, 219
patronage of Kent benefices, 23–4, 55
Payment by Results, 106
Peale, ____, 189
Pearman, A.J., 152
Peckham, East, 7, 15–16, 76, 78, 158
Peckham, West, 34
Peculiar People, 77
Pembury, 15, 213
  church, 76, 78
  poor relief, 118, 134
  workhouse, 134, 152, 176
Penenden Heath, 32, 53–4
Penshurst, 78, 136, 223
Penshurst Union, 155, 162
  workhouse, 162
Perfect, Caleb, 137
Perronet, Vincent, 42, 43
Peter the Great, Tsar of Russia, 139
Petham, 147
Petty, William, 93
petty schools, 91–2
pew rents, 29, 49, 81
Piers, Henry, 42, 43
Pietist movement, 22, 42
Pilbrow, Edward, 143
Pilbrow, James, 205, 213
Platt, 76–8, 219
Plaxtol, 11, 24
Pleydell-Bouverie, William, 3rd Earl of Radnor, 54
Plomley, Dr, 196
Pluckley, 36, 99, 103, 207
Plumstead, 34
pluralism, 10, 11, 14, 24–6, 55, 56
Polhill family, 40
poor, educational provision for
  1640–1811 (*see also* charity schools), 91, 93, 94, 95, 97, 98–9, 150
  1811–1914, 103–4, 105, 108
Poor Law Amendment Act (1834), 116, 184, 191
  making of unions, 154–9
  opposition to, 159–63

poor rates
  1640–1834, 118, 121, 125, 126, 151, 153
  1834–1914, 157, 184
poor relief (*see also* workhouses)
  1640–1834, 112–53
    administration, 118–20, 141–5
    children, 117, 150–1
    cost, 120–3
    indoor relief *see* workhouses
    medical treatment, 130–3, 191
    outdoor relief, 123–30
    settlement, 145–50
    vagrancy, 149–50
    work, provision of, 133–7, 141
  1834–1914, 154–88
    children, 166, 171, 172, 173, 174, 187–8
    guardians, 158, 164
    indoor relief *see* workhouses
    medical treatment, 166–7, 173, 180, 184,
      186–7
    officers, 164–9
    opposition to New Poor Law, 159–63
    outdoor relief, 176–81
    settlement, 179
    unions, setting up, 154–9
    vagrancy, 176, 181–4
    work, provision of, 176, 179, 183
Poore, Dr John, 160, 161–2
poorhouses *see* workhouses
population, rises in
  and poor relief, *1640–1834*, 114, 118
  and public health reform, 198, 212–13
Potter, John (fl. 1816), 131
Potter, John (fl. 1879), 221
Poyntel, Daniel, 10, 16
Pratt, John Jeffreys, 2nd Earl Camden, 53, 115
Presbyterians
  1640–1714, 5, 8, 13, 14, 15, 16, 20, 21
  1714–1830, 40, 41, 44, 45
  1830–1914, 61, 66, 77
Preston Hall, 179
Preston near Faversham, 127, 136, 137n, 202
Preston near Wingham, 19, 95
Primitive Methodists, 43–4, 61, 64, 66, 77
Pringle, John, 161
Protestant Association, 54
public health (*see also* epidemic disease)
  1640–1830, 189–92
  1830–71, 191–2, 198–206
  1871–1900, 210–24
Public Health Act (1848), 200, 201, 217
Public Health Act (1858), 202, 203
Public Health Act (1875), 210, 211, 216
Public Health (Water) Act (1878), 210
Public Worship Regulation Act (1874), 71
Pugin, A.W.N., 76
pupil-teacher system, 106

Puritans, 3–8, 9–10, 20
  and education, 92–3, 98
Puttin, Robert, 17

Quakers (Society of Friends)
  1640–1714, 8–9, 13, 15, 16–17
  1714–1830, 40
  1830–1914, 61, 66, 77
Queen Anne's Bounty, 55
Queenborough, 20, 24, 27, 72, 137, 194

Radnor, Earls of *see* Pleydell-Bouverie
railways (*see also* South Eastern Railway)
  building, 181, 185
Rainham, 135, 160, 195, 202, 224
Rains, Stephen, 133
Ramsay, James, 42–3
Ramsgate
  dispensary, 192
  epidemic disease, cholera, 193, 195, 197
  poverty and poor relief, 113, 155, 164
    workhouse, 139
  public health reform
    1830–71, 198, 201, 204
    1871–1900, 211, 216, 218, 220
  religion
    1640–1714, 20; nonconformity, 16, 20
    1714–1830, 25, 28, 48
    1830–1914, 54, 74; nonconformity, 62,
      81; Roman Catholics, 64–5, 78n
  St George's church, 48
  schools, 104, 105, 110, Plate 12
Randolph, Miss, 158
Ranger, W., 201
Ranters, 8
Rawson, Edward, 7
Reculver, 48
recusancy *see* Roman Catholics
Reformation Society, 54
Reigate (Surrey), 89
Religious Census of 1851, 60–7
rents, payment of *see* housing provision
Revised Code, 106
Rider, Thomas, 159, 196
Ridley, 158
Ridsdale, C.J., 71
Ripple, 15, 25
ritualists, 68–72, 75, 76
River, 208
  workhouse, 132, 139, 141, 145
River Union, 171n
Riverhead, 73
road repair, by paupers, 134–5, 179
Roberts family, 40
Roberts, William, 17
Robinson, William, 161, 162
Robynson, _____, 92

Rochester
  archdeaconry of, 26, 32–4, 58
  archdeacons of *see* Denne; King; Warner
  bishops of (*see also* Atterbury; Horsley;
    King; Murray; Warner), 70, 186
  patronage of Kent benefices, 23
  cathedral, 6, 11–12, 59–60
    clergy (*see also* deans), 6, 14, 24, 59;
      patronage of benefices, 23, 51, 59
  deans of, 6, 14, 25, 59
  diocese of, 31–2
    1640–1714, 7
    1714–1830, 23–4, 38–9, 49
    1830–1914, 55–7, 72
  epidemic disease, 193, 194, 206, 208
  grammar school, 59, 91
  poverty and poor relief (*see also* St
    Margaret's; St Nicholas'), 118
  public health reform
    1830–71, 198, 200, 202, 204
    1871–1900, 211, Plate 16
  religion (*see also* cathedral), 32, 51, 74, 79
    nonconformity, 10, 15, 16, 17, 46, 62
  rural deanery, 32–4
  St Margaret's parish
    church, 51
    poor relief, 134–5; workhouse, 142 (Fig.
      10), 171
  St Nicholas' parish
    church, 79, Plates 6–7
    workhouse, 171
  schools, 59, 91, 94, 96, 102
Rodmersham, 160, 161–2
Rogers, Lewis, 92
Rolvenden
  poor relief, 126, 146
  public health reform, 219
  religion, 25, 72–4, 87, 88
    church, 20
    nonconformity, 10, 15
  school, 96, 101, Plate 13
Roman Catholics
  1640–1714, 3, 4, 6, 7, 15–16
  1830–1914, 53–4, 61, 64–5, 76, 77, 88–9
    Anglican converts, 69
    fear and censure of, 54, 65, 69
    restoration of hierarchy, 54, 65, 70
    schools, 109
Romney, Earls of *see* Marsham
Romney, New, 20, 26, 133, 189, 211, 224
Romney, New, Union, workhouse, 186
Romney, Old, 44
Romney Marsh
  epidemics and public health, 207, 208, 212
  poor relief, 157
  religion, 61, 62, 86
  schools, 93, 94, 95

Romney Marsh Sanitary Authority, 212
Root and Branch Petition (1640), 4
Rose, George, 8
Rose, Henry, 47
Roundsman schemes, 135–6
Rowley, Dr, 130
Ruckinge, 18
Rumsey, John, 87, 88
rural dean, revival of office, 14
Rusthall, 78

Sackville family, Dukes of Dorset, 31, 47
St John-in-Thanet *see* Margate
St Lawrence-in-Thanet, 10, 14, 15, 27, 28, 92,
  169, 192
St Margaret's-at-Cliffe, 25
St Mary Cray, 87, 96, 99, 179, 199
St Mary-in-the-Marsh, 25
St Paul's Cray, 87
St Peter-in-Thanet, 28, 96, 169, 206, 223
Saltwood, 224
Salvation Army, 64, 77
Sancroft, William, archbishop of Canterbury,
  13, 14, 17
Sandgate, 192, 193, 197, 202
Sandhurst, 15
Sandwich, 128
  deanery of, 14
  epidemics and public health, 198, 209, 218
  grammar school, 91, 102
  poverty and poor relief, 112, 150
  religion
    1640–1714, 7, 9, 13, 14, 20;
      nonconformity, 10, 14–15, 16, 17
    1714–1830, 27, 28; nonconformity, 41,
      43
    1830–1914, 79; nonconformity, 64, 84
  St Clement's church, 14, 79, Plate 3
  St Mary's parish, 13, 14–15
  St Peter's parish, 13, 14, 20, 27
    church, 7
  schools, 91, 102, 103
Sanitary Act (1866), 202
Sanitary Act (1872), 210, 211
sanitation
  1830–71, 197, 198–206
  1871–1900, 209–15, 217, 219–24
Sayes Court, workhouse, 139
Scandinavia, religion, 58
scarlatina, 191, 204, 206, 207–8
School Boards, 107–8, 109
schools *see* education; grammar schools;
  Sunday schools
'schools of industry' *see* industrial schools and
  'schools of industry'
Scott, Sir G.G., 60
Seabrook, 207, 218, 224

Seal, 81, 128
Seasalter, 158
Secker, Thomas, archbishop of Canterbury,
    103
Selby, John, 34–5
select vestries, 119–20, 123
Sellindge
    church, 81, Plate 5
    poor relief, 119n, 124, 128, 129, 131, 133,
        180, Plate 14
services *see* church services
settlement, poor law and, 145–50, 179
Sevenoaks
    epidemic disease, 197, 207
    grammar school, 91
    poverty and poor relief (*see also* Sevenoaks
        Union), 116, 119, 127, 137, 137n, 152
    workhouse, 141
    public health reform
        1830–71, 201, 202, 203, 205
        1871–1900, 211, 215, 220, 223
    religion, 31, 46–8, 74
        nonconformity, 43, 62, 81
    schools, 91, 97, Plates 10–11
Sevenoaks Rural Sanitary Authority, 211, 223
Sevenoaks Union, 154n, 162, 163, 169n, 178,
    188
    guardians, 158, 172–3
    setting up, 155, 157
    workhouse, 168, 171, 172–3, 176, 186
sewerage *see* sanitation
Sheerness
    epidemic disease, 206
        cholera, 192, 193, 194, 197, 198
    poor relief, 179
    public health reform
        1830–71, 199, 201, 202
        1871–1900, 212, 213, 218, 220
    religion, 43, 61, 62, 64, 72
Sheldon, Gilbert, archbishop of Canterbury, 12
Sheppey, Isle of (*see also* individual places by
    name)
    religion, 61, 62, 72
    schools, 94
Sheppey Union, 158, 178, 184, 187
    school, 187
    workhouse, 166
Shewell, Thomas, 10
Sholden, 14
Shoreham
    poor relief, 130, 146, 191
        workhouse, 141
    religion, 23, 42, 43, 56, 87
Shorncliffe Camp, 183, 193, 198
Shorne, 34, 121, 133, 141
sick and disabled, poor relief (*see also*
    medicine), 117, 121, 130–3

Simmonds, ____, 212
Simon, John, 202
Sissinghurst Castle Farm, 134
Sittingbourne
    epidemic disease, 192, 198, 206, 207, 208
    poor relief, 146, 151, 152, 158, 160–1
    public health reform
        1830–71, 198, 203, 204
        1871–1900, 211, 215, 218, 219, 223, 224
    religion, 27, 43
    schools, 104, 110
Sloane, Charles, 45
Slowman, John, 17
Smallhythe, 25
smallpox, 189–92, 206–7
    inoculation and vaccination, 132–3, 189–90,
        191, 192, 206–7
Smarden, 15, 93, 101, 104, 155, 224
Smirke, Sir Robert, 45
Smith, Henry, 34
Smith, John (fl. 1656), 93
Smith, John (fl. 1834), 163
Smith, Robert Payne, dean of Canterbury, 60
Snargate, church, 81, Plate 5
Snave, 190
Snodland, 15
social role of the churches, *1830–1914*, 83–90
Society of Friends *see* Quakers
Society for Promoting Christian Knowledge
    (SPCK), 18–19, 98, 99
Socinianism, 41
Soman, John, 34
Somerscales, Daniel, 19
Somner, William, 6
Soulby, Dr, 201
soup kitchens, run by churches, 84
South, place names beginning with, *see under
    second element*
South Eastern Railway, 186, 198, 205, 208, 219
Southwark, 172
    bishops of, 65
    diocese of, 55
    vagrant depot, 150
Spain, ____, 223
SPCK *see* Society for Promoting Christian
    Knowledge
Speenhamland system, 124–5
Speldhurst, 41–2, 151, 204
Stangate Creek, 193
Stanhope, Philip, 4th Earl, 159, 172–3
Stansted, 158
Staplehurst
    epidemics and public health, 197, 198, 204,
        219, 224
    poor relief, 133, 137, 137n, 160
    religion, 8, 10, 15, 16, 26
    school, 93

Stelling, 44, 179
Stevens, Edmund, 106
Stockbury, 79, 80
Stoke, 88-9
Stonar, 14
Stone-next-Dartford, 9, 199
Stour, river, sewage pollution, 200, 202, 204,
    215, 220, 222-3
Stratton, J.Y., 87
Streatfeild family, 40
Streatfield, Henry, 162
Streeter, Ann, 34
Strict Baptists see Particular and Strict Baptists
Strood
    epidemics and public health, 207, 208,
        212-13
    poor relief (see also Strood Union), 135, 179
        workhouse, 135, 137, 143, 144-5
    religion, 45, 72
Strood Union, 157
    workhouse, 206
Stubs, John, 8-9
Sturges Bourne Act (1819), 118, 119, 133
Sturry, 197, 212, 219
Sumner, John Bird, archbishop of Canterbury,
    56, 70, 88, Plate 3
Sunday schools
    1714-1830, 37-8, 39, 102-3
    1830-1914, 61, 63, 84, 88, 104
Sundridge, poverty and poor relief, 116, 117,
    119, 123n, 127, 137
    workhouse, 143, 171, 173
surplice fees, 29
Sutton, Daniel, 189
Sutton, deanery of, 14
Sutton-next-Dover, 14
Sutton Valence, 27, 51, 91, 102, 118, 163, 219
Swan, John, 10
Swanley, 87, 110
Swanscombe, 158
Swedenborgians, 61, 77
Swing Riots (1830-1), 31, 116, 123, 135, 153,
    154, 160, 163
Swingfield, 17
Sydney, Viscounts see Townshend
Symes, Colonel, 188

Tadman, Lena, 31
Tait, Archibald Campbell, archbishop of
    Canterbury, 71
Tanner, Mary, 34
Taunton Commission (1868), 105-6
Taylor, John, 161
Taylor, William, 137
teachers see education
technical schools, 109
Templeman, Lord, 157, 163

Tenison, Thomas, archbishop of Canterbury,
    20, 60
Tenterden
    grammar school, 91, 102
    poverty and poor relief (see also Tenterden
        Union), 114, 118, 123n, 127, 137, 137n
        workhouse, 139n
    public health reform, 219, 223, 224
    religion
        1640-1714, 8; nonconformity, 15, 16, 17
        1714-1830, 26, 28; nonconformity, 40,
            45, 167
        1830-1914, nonconformity, 62
    schools, 91, 102, 105
Tenterden Union, 162, 164, 167, 188
    school, 187
    workhouse, 165, 171, 176, 182, 187
Terry, ____, 188
Test and Corporation Acts, repeal of (1828), 53
Teston, 42, 45, 198
Teynham, 161, 205
Teynham, Lord, 53
Thames, river, sewage pollution, 199
Thanet (see also individual places by name)
    epidemics and public health, 206, 212, 224
    poverty and poor relief (see also Thanet
        Union), 113, 116, 147
    religion, 7, 62, 76, 77
    schools, 95, 96
Thanet Rural Sanitary Authority, 224
Thanet Union, 158, 164, 167, 179, 184, 185,
    188
    workhouse, 105, 168, 169-71, 176, 179,
        184, 186
Thannington, 223
Thomason, D.R., 64
Thoroughgood, Nicholas, 10
Throwley, 161
Thurnham, 19, 137n
Ticehurst (East Sussex) Union, 158
Tilden, Freegift, 93
Tillotson, John, dean of Canterbury, 12
Tilmanstone, 14
Tithe Commutation Act (1836), 32
tithes, 10-11, 29, 30-2
Toke family, 40
Toke, John, 143
Tom, John Nichols, alias Sir William
    Courtenay, 42, 162-3
Tonbridge
    epidemic disease, 193, 195, 197, 206, 208
    nonconformity, 43, 62, 63
    poor relief (see also Tonbridge Union), 127,
        148n, 155
        workhouse, 141
    public health reform
        1830-71, 200, 201

1871–1900, 211, 212, 213, 217, 220
    schools, 91, 110
Tonbridge Rural Sanitary Authority, 211
Tonbridge Union, 178, 180, 185
    workhouse, 174, 182, 186
Tong, 160
Topfield, John, 164
Tovil, 207
Townshend, John Robert, Viscount Sydney, 70, 157
Tractarians, 68–72, 76, 78, 83, 88
Trottiscliffe, 5–6, 28, 45, 219
tuberculosis, 191
Tudeley, 34, 45
Tufnell, E.C., 164, 176–8
    and formation of unions, 157, 158, 159
    and workhouses, 169, 172, 173, 174, 184, 187
Tunbridge Wells, 42, 162
    dispensary, 192
    epidemic disease, cholera, 193, 195, 197
    Holy Trinity church, 48, 49–50, 75
    King Charles the Martyr, church of, 11, 79
    public health reform, 200, 203, 211, 213, 217–18, 220
    religion
        1640–1714, 11; nonconformity, 16
        1714–1830, 23, 48, 49–50;
            nonconformity, 44
        1830–1914, 54, 66, 74, 75, 79;
            nonconformity, 62, 75, 196
    schools, 99, 104, 105, 110
Turner, Thomas, dean of Canterbury, 12
Twopeny, David, 80
Twysden family, 40
Tylden, Sir John, 157, 160, 161, 184, 192
typhoid
    before 1830, 191
    1830–71, 204, 205
    1871–1900, 206, 209–10, 215, 218, 219
typhus, 191

Ulcombe, 208
Ullock, Henry, 14
unemployment (*see also* vagrancy)
    and poor relief
        1640–1834, 114–17, 124–6, 133–7
        1834–1914, 178–9, 180, 181, 183
Unitarian Baptists, 63
Unitarians
    1714–1830, 41, 42, 44, 45
    1830–1914, 61, 63, 66, 77
United States, emigration to, 118
Upchurch, 54, 87, 88, 161
Upnor, 194

vaccination *see* smallpox

vagrancy, 149–50, 176, 181–4
vestries *see* select vestries

Wake, William, archbishop of Canterbury, 19
Waldershare, 14, 118, 127, 129, 135
Walmer, 15, 76, 78, 199, 208, 223
Walsham, Sir John, 173
Walter, Thomas, 92
Walters Green, 78
Waltham, 17
Ward, John, 139
Warde, Charles, 155
Warehorne, 158, 207
Waring, Thomas, 130, 191
Warne, Cleave, 87, 88–9
Warner, John, archdeacon of Rochester, 10
Warner, John, bishop of Rochester, 5, 6, 9
water supply
    1830–71, 198, 199, 200, 201, 202–3, 205
    1871–1900, 209–15, 217–19
Wateringbury, 29, 39, 57n, 82–3, 86, 107, 130
Watson, _____, 189
Webb, Sidney and Beatrice, 130
Wenham, William, 131
Wesley, John and Charles, 43, 45–6
Wesleyan Methodists
    1714–1830, 42, 43–4, 45
    1830–1914, 61, 63, 66, 77, 86, 104
West, Charles, 19
West, place names beginning with, *see under second element*
West Kent Hospital, 192
West Kent sewerage scheme, 213–14, 223
Westbere, 158, 219
    deanery of, 14
Westcliffe, 49
Westerham
    epidemics and public health, 223
    poor relief, 134, 139, 155
        workhouse, 143, 152
    religion, 19, 81
    school, 92
Westgate, Holy Cross, 120
Westminster Abbey, 24, 45
Westmorland, Earls of *see* Fane
Westwell, 127, 137
Whitfield, 14
Whitstable, 131–2, 166
    epidemic disease, 193, 195, 207, 209
    poverty and poor relief, 113
    public health reform, 201, 211, 217, 224
Wichling, 161
Wickham, East, 150
Wickham, West, 121, 125, 127, 128, 131, 148, 150
Wickhambreux, 10, 93
Wickstead, _____, 20

Wilberforce, Henry, 69, 70, 196
Willesborough, 15, 139n, 210, 219, 224
Williamson, Sir Joseph, 102
Wilmot, Nathaniel, 10
Winchilsea, Earls of see Finch-Hatton
Wingham, 17, 107, 115, 125, 219
Wiseman, Nicholas, Cardinal, 65, 70
women
    education for (see also girls), 110
    as poor law guardians, 158
    poverty and poor relief (see also
        illegitimacy), 117, 147, 149, 180
    as preachers, 64
Woodchurch, 162, 209, 223
Woodhams, John, 132
Woodnesbrough, 219
Woodruff, John, 54, 87, 88
Woodward, Matthew, 71
Woolwich
    epidemics and public health, 195, 199, 205,
        206
    poor relief (see also Woolwich Union), 157
    religion, 15, 34
Woolwich Union, 157
Wootton, 25
workhouses
    1640–1834, 137–41, 152
        administration of indoor relief, 141–5

    diet, 144–5
    masters and mistresses, 141–3, 144, 145
    medical treatment, 130, 132
    schools, 95
    work, provision of, 133, 141
    1834–1914, 169–76, 184–8
        chaplains, 166, 167, 168, 169
        diet, 170 (Fig. 12), 171–2
        masters and matrons, 164–6, 167–9, 184
        medical treatment, 166–7, 173, 186–7
        porters, 167–8
        schools, 105, 167–9, 187
        vagrants housed in, 181–4
        work, provision of, 176, 183
worship see church services
Worth, 14, 25
Wouldham, 158, 207
Wrotham (see also Plaxtol), 16, 24, 117, 131,
    146
Wye, 219
    agricultural college, 110
    grammar school, 91
    poor relief, 133, 134
    religion, 15, 28, 38

Yalding, 9, 196, 198
Young, Francis, 166

value livings 38
Sunday schools 38, 102-3, 61
1851 Religious Census 60
The Weald & dissent 63
Pew rents 29, 49 80-3
Seating plans. 84.-5.
qu. dissenters as intruders for C of E. 86.
cooperation among dissenters 86

37, Horne & caths.